D0911975

Sound Fragments

Noel Lobley

SOUND FRAGMENTS

From Field Recording
to African Electronic Stories

Wesleyan University Press   Middletown, Connecticut

Wesleyan University Press
Middletown CT 06459
www.wesleyan.edu/wespress
Text and photographs unless otherwise noted © 2022 Noel Lobley
All rights reserved
Manufactured in the United States of America
Designed by Mindy Basinger Hill
Typeset in Minion Pro

Library of Congress Cataloging-in-Publication Data
available at https://catalog.loc.gov/
cloth ISBN 978-0-8195-8076-4
paper ISBN 978-0-8195-8077-1
e-book ISBN 978-0-8195-8078-8

5   4   3   2   1

FOR NOMI, ZAKIR, AND KIERAN

MUM AND BOB

DAD, NAN, AND GRANDAD

whose love, energy, and laughter

always sound so warm, strong, and bright

CONTENTS

PROLOGUE

Masimameleni sisonke izandi zezinyanya
Masiqondeni ubuntu yintoni

"I've got a space now, *mfowethu*, you must come and see it. You cannot walk there, I'll come and pick you up." It took some time for X to return from the industrial area of Grahamstown and arrive back in the center of town. He always drives slowly, anticipates where each pothole collapses, and he knows and greets almost everyone he sees. A mobile headset and multiple active apps allow him to manage bookings for his arts space, plan his festivals, communicate, and coordinate. Driving slowly creates time to notice the environment, dry and scrolling through the car windows, and time to pay attention to a revolving cast of passengers; time to attend to a relentless web of messaged requests; and time to pull over by the side of the road and see how people are.

Much had changed for Xolile "X" Madinda in the last decade plus. Married and living in town rather than township, he was now father to a powerful young daughter. And X had changed much in this decade-plus as well, as he quietly, gracefully, and sometimes disruptively pursued his relentless communal vision to increase well-being for his amaXhosa brothers and sisters and mothers and fathers in the townships of Grahamstown-Makhanda. "My brother," he says, "I will always be willing to work for a community that is willing to build itself." I had known X for more than a decade at this point, and we had shared lots of time, music, and ideas in many different spaces in the Eastern Cape, the United Kingdom, and the United States, tracked inside hundreds of hours of WhatsApp and FaceTime conversations at all points of the day and night. I am convinced that our online data trails prove that X never sleeps. Back in 2008 he was living in DefKamp, a small bedroom studio in Fingo Village township, from where he

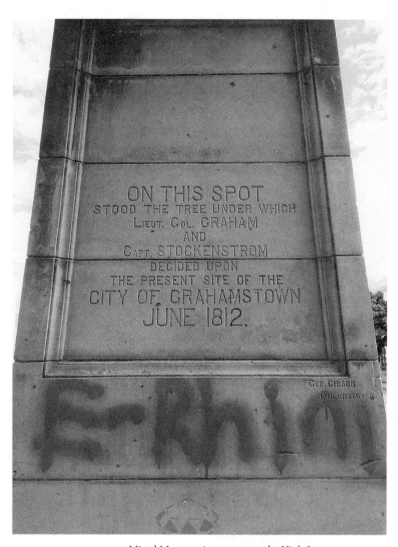

ON THIS SPOT
STOOD THE TREE UNDER WHICH
LIEUT. COL. GRAHAM
AND
CAPT. STOCKENSTROM
DECIDED UPON
THE PRESENT SITE OF THE
CITY OF GRAHAMSTOWN
JUNE 1812.

GEO. GIBSON
Queenstown

FIGURE FM.1 Mixed Messages in a statue on the High Street of Grahamstown-Makhanda. August 5, 2018. *Photo by the author.*

ran a constantly evolving series of activist art community projects for youth. A leading hip-hop artist and founding member—along with beatmaker Mxolisi "Biz" Bodla—of DefBoyz, one of the most influential groups in the Eastern Cape, X had long been working hip hop as a public tool to share and teach language, ethics, posture, and poise. He then abruptly decided to retire from stage performance to bring about the changes he came to feel he was, until then, only rapping about.

Together for a year across 2007 and 2008 we had walked the streets of Grahamstown and Grahamstown East—the other side of the tracks—where town clearly becomes township. We were meeting many people and navigating improvised public listening sessions sparked with small sonic fragments taped from an archive of African sounds collected by a colonial Englishman half a century earlier. Now X was physically building his own grassroots community arts space to house, frame, produce, amplify, and archive the isiXhosa poetry, cyphers, sound art, political debates, Book'ona reading sessions and other performances that sprung from the fiercely independent artistry nurtured in the street atmosphere of his community festivals.[1] The arc of this artistry—from taped Xhosa sound fragments shared on township street corners to the creation of an independent Xhosa arts space, The Black Power Station—is the subject of this book. It traces the path from a colonial recording project settled in South Africa's Eastern Cape to the contemporary pioneers and artists such as X who have another story to tell of their history, their past, present, and the future.

NOTES

1. Book'ona is a curated library and reading corner in The Black Power Station, a blend of "book" and "ikhona" (it is there/is available in isiXhosa). See www.youtube.com /watch?v=sQi3GTZNbqk (accessed February 28, 2021).

NOTES ON LANGUAGE, NAMES, TERMINOLOGY, AND ABBREVIATIONS

The focus of this book is the Eastern Cape of South Africa, which is a predominantly Xhosa-speaking province, established in 1994. The correct term for Xhosa people is amaXhosa, and the language spoken is isiXhosa. I use the term "Xhosa" mostly as an adjective when it is not referring directly to the group of people or their language. In November 2018 the city of Grahamstown was renamed "Makhanda." I mostly refer to the place as "Grahamstown-Makhanda," but also use "Grahamstown" and "Makhanda" when it is appropriate to the period and to people's own preferences. When referring to Hugh Tracey's recording tours and projects I retain the colonial names from the time in which he was operating, switching to present-day names when appropriate to the period.

DISCLAIMER

Some terms used in the original writings of Hugh Tracey and his contemporaries are unfortunate and must be avoided today. They have been preserved to present a fully accurate historicized picture. Please note that all captions for photographs owned by ILAM come directly from ILAM and not from the author.

ABBREVIATIONS

AMS   African Music Society
ILAM   The International Library of African Music
NAF   The National Arts Festival
TBPS   The Black Power Station

ACKNOWLEDGMENTS

I wish to express my sincere and grateful thanks to the following people, without whom this book would have not been possible.

Firstly, deepest gratitude to the four mentors who have all given me priceless help and guidance along the way. Dr. Hélène la Rue for being the person I moved to Oxford to study and work with, and for all the music that you shared with me, always with so much love, grace, and kindness. Dr. Laura Peers for kindly stepping in to guide me through a difficult period after Hélène's passing and before I headed to South Africa for fieldwork. Major thanks to Dr. Christopher Morton and Dr. Martin Stokes, both of whom continuously give freely of their time and wisdom and of whom I could ask no more. To Jeremy Coote and Janet Topp Fargion for seeing the next levels through the World Cup. I would also like to thank the Institute of Social and Cultural Anthropology, the whole of the Pitt Rivers Museum team under Michael O'Hanlon and then Laura van Broekhoven—especially Haaz Ezzet, Helen Adams, and the much-missed Kate White—and the Faculty of Music at Oxford University. I extend my thanks also to the Arts and Humanities Research Council for awarding me a doctoral scholarship, further fieldwork funding, and for providing the general and helpful support that enabled me to complete my work. Professor Bill Tamblyn, I thank you for pointing me toward ethnomusicology. Tsan-Huang Tsai, I thank you dearly for showing me there was a door open in Oxford.

My deepest thanks to everybody at the International Library of African Music (ILAM). To Professor Diane Thram for her instant generosity in welcoming my proposal and then me, placing all of ILAM's wonderful resources and materials entirely at my disposal for a year and more. Thanks for giving me my own keys to the place so I could leave at four in the morning when I needed to. To Andrew Tracey for his unwavering generosity, kindness, and expertise, and for using the word "yes" more than any other person I have ever known. To the other staff at ILAM, in particular studio manager Elijah "Bra" Madiba, who has the respect of all, and Hilton Borewere for his wonderful voice, funny feeling, and stunning marimba playing. You can flow. To Vuyo Booi for first introducing me to the inner workings of Joza township, and in celebration of his wonderful work with his cultural group, Sakhuluntu. Great to see the New York dance companies taking note of you, Vuyo, and the youth you teach. Thanks to many other people around ILAM as well: Sabine, Geoff Tracey, Wonder, Sebastian, Khanyisa, Vuyolwethu, Zandile, Felix, Tatenda, Xhese, Koketso ("KK") Potsane, and Paulette Coetzee. Thanks also to Chris Carver at African Musical Instruments.

Many thanks to the staff and people at the Old Gaol backpackers—sadly a venue no more—for making me feel so welcome in Grahamstown upon my arrival. To Brian Peltason for creating the stimulating social environment that continually attracted everybody from experts on dung beetles to trainee game wardens. Thanks to Mhleli Ngubo for his smiling face and Mad Hatters recommendations, and to Oz Kate for being the natural and star guide around Fingo Village. Thanks to Guillaume Johnson for his friendship and help in the early stages of my sound elicitation. May the African tour happen for you and your father. To Neil Carrier for inspiring the way and chat from St. Andrews to Kenya and on. Huge thanks to Paul Mills, the kindest and most efficient man in Grahamstown—and now Johannesburg—and his wonderful wife, Brenda Schmahmann. My deepest gratitude to you both for taking me in and looking after me, for introducing me to everyone, and for the delights of the wandering Schnauzers. Sincere thanks to many other people at Rhodes University who all helped me with many enquiries, including: Peter Vale (always there with the three most important points) and his wife Louise Vale at Grocott's; Russell Kaschula for his deep and kindly expertise on Xhosa language; and to everybody at the African languages department, especially Pamela Maseko, Linda Nelani, Msindisi Sam, and Thanduxolo "Thasky" Fatyi.

I must give a big thank you to everybody in the townships with whom we have had the ongoing pleasure of spending time, and all who agreed to share extensive time and conversations and to be interviewed. This extends well beyond the list of people who have been cited in this book. Here goes: Nomtwasana Nyikilana (the finest dancer in Vukani) and Zolile Nyikilana, with Mr. Ngcongo (Seven). Jeremy Marks, Zenzo Simbao, Laina Gumboreshumba, Hlezi Kunji, Mngani, Ecalpar, Efese and Mvuyisa (Eva), Ras Kali, Anele and Apoc. Umama Joyi, Grace, and everybody at Ethembeni Day Centre, Louis

Mhlanga (perhaps the nicest star I've ever met), Udaba (Liyo, Pura, Sakhile, Dinewo and Sbo—may your band play worldwide), Mzambia (for one of the richest laughs in Joza, for walking me home, and more), and Tera Tyota and his family for all the laughs, gigs, food, and insights. Madala for the thoughts and sausages, and to Jury Mpehlo and Irene for the music and crafty tap dancing. Jane Kelele, and Mike Mati for his wonderful patient ways with busy big bags, and for introducing me to his family in Peddie. Janet Buckland and Amaphiko township dancers (especially Nomcebisi), Boniwe and Viwe, the women at Umthathi Training Project, Siyabulela Mbambaza, Kondile for leading Nyaki's Umbulelo so gracefully, uZwai, uMakhulu Florence, and Nyisha. Luntu Madinda a.k.a. MC Noize and Macabre for teaching me how to rap in Xhosa, Lulama, Silulami Lwana (Slu), Luyanda Ncalu, Sompies, and Mama Nobible for telling Nyaki that what we were doing seemed right. Madosini and Sindi, and Colin Cira—an inspiration and a man in whose hands culture and decency will always be safe: "Those kids may not know those tunes anymore," but you'll help them learn. Nombasa, Zikhona, Nox, Dudu and family, and Lazola for being interested but not quite interested enough to DJ field recordings in the township. Ras Mpho. Thembi Butana—I will always remember how you shook with delight when we listened to these recordings together—you are a vital part of keeping the music and recordings alive, and thanks for introducing me to Port Alfred townships and the joys of Richard "Grahamstown Grahamstown" Flateya. Thembi's aunt, Mama Mamnyele, Loyiso, Kwanele and Craig, Archbishop Ntshobodi. Jackson Vena for his kind and diligent guidance through dictionaries and the differences between rural and town life and values. uMakhulu Koma, Peddie oMakhulu, Cecil Nonqane, and to uTatomkhulu for the smiles and tears of joy drawn by old recordings. You all helped, challenged and enriched the recordings, the work, and myself invaluably. Thanks to Karen, Elvis, and everyone at High Corner Guest House—"Luthuli House"—in Makhanda.

Thanks also to Tisco, Rod Amner, Paul Maylham, Gary Baines, Chris Berry, Gwenda Thomas, Nina Ashton, Charles Antrobus, Julie Wells, X-Man, Jane and Karen in the Pink House, and to Richard Gayer for always looking after people and taking me on a trip to try and meet Nelson Mandela. To Chris, Jane, and family in Cape Town, and David Maskell, Clare Harris, Rupert Gill, Pete Smith, Jonathan Roberts, and the Oxford Gamelan Society, Hélène Neveu Kringelbach, Jason Stanyek, Doug Langley, Matt "take a swig of that, mate" Baker, Tom Hodgson, Jo Hicks, Ioannis Polychronakis, and Amanda Villepastour in Cardiff. Thanks to Matias Spektor, Benjamin Hebbert, Anna Stirr, Jennifer Post,

Josh Pilzer, Gavin Steingo, Andrea F. Bohlman, Peter McMurray, Tom Western, Lonán Ó Briain, Maria Mendonça, Moses Bikishoni, and Nhamburo Ziyenge.

My utter gratitude to a warm and wonderful and inspiring community of people in our new home in and beyond the Music Department at the University of Virginia (UVA). Richard Will for immaculate care, vision, and leadership and seeing and making it all happen for our family, followed by a succession of wonderful chairs: Matthew Burtner, Ted Coffey, and now Karl Hagstrom Miller. I could not ask for a better and more supportive group of friends and colleagues, with whom it is a pleasure to spend time socially and professionally, blurring the distinction. Ted, those walks in the woods and water are always real healers. Michelle Kisliuk, Bonnie Gordon, Scott DeVeaux, Fred Maus, Michael Puri, Joel Rubin, Luke Dahl, A. D. Carson, Judith Shatin, Leah Reid, Heather Frasch, John D'earth, Michael Slon, I-Jen Fang, Elizabeth Ozment, Katy Ambrose, Benjamin Rous, Nate Lee, and Peter Bussigel. Our whole department is a joy, and special thanks to Travis Thatcher (whose office I occupy more than my own), and Alicia Greenland, to Tina Knight, Kim Turner, Marcy Day, Joel Jacobus, and Leslie Walker.

UVA is a very collegial place, and my gratitude extends to many departments and individuals, not least David Edmunds in Global Development Studies; Jason Bennett, Jessica Weaver-Kenny, Gail Hunger, Hope Fitzgerald, and Judy Giering and the whole of Learning, Design, and Technology; Jim Igoe, China Scherz, and the Anthropology Department; Ellen Bassett, Phoebe Chrisman, Cliff Maxwell at Global Grounds; Stephen D. Mull, Louise Nelson, Ian Baucom, Wendy Baucom, Debjani Ganguly, Alison Levine, Liz Magill, Chris Colvin, Rupa Valdez, Joey Valdez, Matt Street, Shilpa Dave, Larycia Hawkins, and Jim Ryan. Wilson Hall is emerging as a sister space, impossible without Anne Gilliam, Carol Westin, and Julie Gronlund. The shape of the book has been improved by so many students and collaborators in a full range of Sound Studies, African Electronic Music, and Curating Sonic Ethnography undergraduate and postgraduate classes. There are too many inspiring students here at UVA to list, but special mention to Caitlin Flay, Tim Booth, Bremen Donovan, Basile Koechlin, Tracey Stewart, Justin Mueller, Stephanie Gunst, Liza Flood, Rami Stucky, Kyle Chattleton, Tanner Greene, Ida Hoequist, Torie Clark, Christopher Luna-Mega, Lydia Warren, Emily Mellen, Savanna Morrison, Sia Mohebbi, Corey Harris, Daniel Fishkin, Katie King, Eli Stine, Jon Bellona, Alex Christie, Ben Roberston, Hannah Young, Natalia Perez, Sam Golter, Becky Brown, Carlehr Swanson, Dilshan Weerasinghe, Matias Vilaplana, and to Paige Naylor and the irreplaceable Ryan Maguire. Erik "what are you working on?" DeLuca.

The MakhanduvA team grows each week, and many thanks to Lindsey Shavers, Carlin Smith, Ruthie Rosenfeld, Jessie Copeland, Jonathan Roberts, Komi Galli, Jordan Brown, Drew Buckley, Noor Samee, Noah Tinsley, Omeed Faegh, Mack McLellan, Josiah Pywtorak, Ian Sellers, and Carmen Edwards.

And the links and other professional collaborators: Nathaniel Mann, Dan Merrill, Robin Alderton, Fayrouz Kadall, Alba Colomo, Amy Sharrocks, John Peel (R.I.P.), Genji Siraisi, Sam Lee, Henry Skerritt, David Toop, Max Eastley, Colin Greenwood, Richard Elliott, Michael Bull, Lucy Durán, Ollie Wood and Chris Pedley, Piers Aggett and all the Beating Heart collective, Andrew Weatherall (R.I.P.), Jason Whittaker at Antigen Records, David Rothenberg, Michael Veal, Jane Taylor, Tony Seeger, Keith Howard, Angela Impey, Louise Meintjes, Paul Berliner, Veit Erlmann, Paul Basu, David Shankland and the R.A.I. Ethnomusicology Committee, Emeka Ogboh, Spoek Mathambo, Jo and Vic and all at OCM (Oxford Contemporary Music), Renee Balfour and all the artists at McGuffey Arts Centre, Alan Goffinski and Heather Mease at The Bridge Progressive Arts Initiative, Pikasso Swig, Banning Eyre, Nathan Moore and WTJU, Leo PaLayeng and Acholitronix, Heather Maxwell at Music Time in Africa, Lindsey Hoh Copeland, Ian Copeland, John McLean, Autechre, Tim and Chloe Meston, Ronan Quinn, Dave Beesley, Chris Brayford, Ben Kyneswood, Howard Swains, The Muppets, Matt Fenton, Andrew Lamb and the Yukons, and Louis Sarno (R.I.P.).

Lee Watkins, for all your help in navigating from the Eastern Cape beaches up to Durban and back, first with samosas and later with lemons. You constantly give and inspire and, as sure as I smell the wood burning, our home will always be your home, Lee and Eloff. Which brings me to our Charlottesville neighbors, especially Erin and Mike Garcia, Jen and Ryan Senator, and Txu and Chris Meyer, with all of their children, and Derrick Many and Alycia Yowell-Many who have supported us in a home from home. We love watching Emtee and moDernisT together, seeing Noble resting before the game, and finding owls funny by the deep water.

Inspiration from the sheer quality of people in Makhanda grows every day. Thanks to Sikhumbuzo "Sku" Makandula, Masxiole "Masi" Heshu, and Akhona "Bhodl'ingqaka" Mafani. Also to Mazibuko Jara, Bongiwe "Mthwakazi" Lusizi, Onke "Zanomhlola" Simandla, Thabisa Dinga, Daluxolo Matanzima, and all at Ntinga Ntaba kaNdoda, and Merran Roy and Mojalefa Koyana. The Black Power Station: The International Destination, a world-class space, and a community that is itself a work of art. Here we go: Professor Nomalanga Mkhize, Lindiwe

Ngunezi Madinda (a.k.a. "The President"), Andiswa "Bliss" Rabeshu, Thandazile Madinda, Lucky Ncani a.k.a. "t.o.," Efese Betela, Mxolisi "Biz" Bodla, Adon Geel, Sinethemba "Oz" Konzapi, Azlan Makalima, Lunakill, Bulelani "Words" Booi, Msaki, Rushay Booysen, Uchenna Okeja, and Mthunzikazi Mbongwana. Xola Mali, Khaya Thonjeni, Yandiswa Vara, Siphokazi Tana, Lindokuhle Phololo Madinda, Sanelisiwe Singaphi, Sinaye Jonas, Riana Meiring, One Blood, Babalwa Magoqwana, Prof. Msindo, Scara Njadayi, Vumile Lwana, Virginia David, Mkhonto Ezra Gwazela (the original man), Mawetu Zita, Tumelo Tladi, and Kholiswa Pearl Mqotyana. Mam Cethe for making uMqhombothi every time we needed it, and all The Black Power Station Ambassadors: keep on the flag of TBPS wherever you are and Amanda sisondla senkululeko yesizwe sakuthu. Thanks to the National Arts Festival (NAF), especially Tony Lankester and Monica Newton. For those we have lost during these times: Nolulamile Joyce Menzi Madinda, Sisanda Mankayi, Ayanda "Ace" Nondlwana, and Ryan Maguire. Masikhe simamele izandi zezinyanya.

I am extremely grateful to everyone at Wesleyan University Press for their commitment and support in the publication of this project, most notably editor-in-chief Suzanna Tamminen, and the Music/Culture series editors—Deborah Wong, Sherrie Tucker, and Jeremy Wallach—and the whole editorial board. I am indebted to three anonymous external reviewers who generously and insightfully helped improve this manuscript beyond recognition. For many reasons from John Cage to Punk Ethnography, I felt this project belonged here, and a very special thank you to my dear friend David Novak who is always selflessly digging to make things better for others. Sincere thanks to Alan Berolzheimer and Jim Schley of Redwing Book Services and David Anderson of IndexBusters for truly immaculate attention to every possible detail during the copyediting and production process. I would also like to express my gratitude to the African Urbanism Humanities Lab, and the Arts, Humanities, and Social Sciences Summer Research Awards, the Mellon Indigenous Arts Initiative (and especially Catherine Walden), and the 3Cavaliers Projects under the remit of the UVA Senior Vice Provost for Research, for all of the generous support enabling long-term periods of fieldwork for extended teams of people during the last decade and more. Imibulelo engazenzisiyo kwaba balandelayo, words of gratitude with no pretense to the artists at The Black Power Station who collaborated on the front cover art, which is a design based on an original concept by Xolile "X" Madinda and myself. Mfundo Ndevu was the illustrator, Azlan Makalima added colors and editing, and Efese Betela began the process for us all with his inspired drawings.

Almost finally, I must thank two remarkable friends: Nyakonzima "Nyaki" Tsana and Xolile "X" Madinda. Nyaki and Xolile, you are without doubt two of the most inspiring and impressive and wonderful people I have ever had the good fortune to meet. Your time, friendship, dedication, and all-round honor humble me every day I think about you, and it is my utter privilege to know and love you both and both of your families. Siphosethu, Siphosihle, and Lindiwe are blessed as your children. I could not have written this book without you both, and I did not write it without you both. You are my dearest and finest brothers, teachers, and soul mates, I love being by your side, and I love you both and all your families dearly. Ndiyabulela kakhulu, kakhulu, kakhulu. Siqhube sisebenze ukuqonda ubuntu kanye yintoni. Nisale kakhule, sobonana xana uQamata evuma.

The places where family meet friends and friends become family are always the warmest. Nutan and Chandu Dave for coming and seeing and for always bringing double the magic to the grandchildren for us all. Apurva and Sejal, Ishan and Anjali, it's so magic to live so close to you (by US metrics). Mum and Bob, Heidi and Paul, Thomas, Matthew, and Noah, I love you all dearly for everything and only hope that you all get to meet and welcome more of the wonderful people who helped shape all this work and time. Finally, to my wife Nomi, for being with me and for everything that makes the time always feel full of love — "You could have been doing something else with your life, but you chose to be here by my side." I knew from day one that nobody could ever model the monopod — or the moccasins — better in the townships. My wife is the filmmaker who married the DJ. Ndiyakuthanda, inkosikazi wam. Zakir and Kieran, for all your energy, noise, and serious laughter, for blending sharks, for being in such old-soul brotherly love, and for being you. You are both so constantly and deeply loved. Silapha sesfikile, sisonke, siyabulela kakhulu, kakhulu, kakhulu. Masiqondeni ubuntu yintoni, umntu ngumntu ngabantu. Camagu.

Sound Fragments

INTRODUCTION

This book is an ethnographic study of sound archives and the processes of creative decolonization that form alternative modes of archiving in the twenty-first century. It explores the histories and afterlives of sound collections and practices at the International Library of African Music (ILAM), recorded by Hugh Tracey beginning in the early twentieth century.[1] ILAM is the world's largest archive in Africa of field recordings of sub-Saharan African music, located in the Eastern Cape of South Africa but virtually unknown to most of the province's inhabitants. *Sound Fragments* explores what happens when a colonial sound archive is repurposed and reimagined by local artists in post-apartheid South Africa. I analyze Tracey's ideologies and methods for conducting his work and then examine the creative and political processes activated when contemporary South Africans make archives their own.

In 1929, Tracey, an Englishman, set out on his unprecedented and ambitious mission to map the musical memory of half a continent. Over the next five decades, he collected recordings across East, Central, and Southern Africa, seeking out "genuine" local folk music while also capturing audio snapshots of myriad forms of musical and social transformation. Through detailed analysis of a wealth of unpublished archival documents—based on more than a decade of fieldwork through ILAM and alongside local artists—I examine Tracey's recording and collecting ethos and methods, as well as critiques both from his peers and from contemporary South African artists and researchers. My aim is neither to demonize nor romanticize Tracey. I explore his contradictions—his progressive ear and his racist beliefs, his humanistic vision and his patriarchal mindset—and consider the possibilities and limits of his approach. Unlike many field recordists of his era, Tracey was not just interested in preserving and analyzing recorded sound; rather, he hoped it would benefit future generations of African musicians, whom he recognized would eventually make the archive their own. At the same time, he cooperated with White-owned mining companies, directed his outreach mainly toward White or foreign consumers and institutions, and omitted and ignored the identities, subjectivities, and direct voices of many of the people and communities whom he recorded. What is the legacy of this work to some of these communities? What is captured in these recorded sounds, and what is neglected? And how do contemporary artists and community members reimagine an old archive, as well as the concept of an archive, in new and radical ways, modes, and spaces?

In the light of growing calls to decolonize knowledge, especially in South Africa, I here foreground the perspectives and creative practices of local, Xhosa artists and researchers in South Africa's Eastern Cape, as they work through and around, inside and outside ILAM today.[2] Historian Sabelo Ndlovu-Gatsheni distills his concept of "epistemic freedom" as the "liberation of reason itself from coloniality," which is "fundamentally about the right to think, theorize, interpret the world, develop [one's] own methodologies and write from where one is located and unencumbered by Eurocentrism."[3] Independent artistry is seen and heard as a creative, political, and economic move made to explore self-possessed ownership, especially when the institution of the South African university is heavily implicated in violent processes of land loss, and, as Pedro Mzilane and Nomalanga Mhize argue, "racially segregated universities, built for spatially divided populations, formed an essential epistemic engine in buttressing segregation and sustaining the knowledge base of the white economy."[4]

While the independent artists featured in this book all draw at times from ILAM to interpret the archival record, much of their work also commits to the building of an independent arts education space for the producing, documenting, framing, and archiving of their own stories, named The Black Power Station (TBPS). Communally conceived, designed, and developed, The Black Power Station draws from institutional archiving when necessary, while also suggesting and sharing new models for inclusion in older archives. TBPS serves as a counterpoint to ILAM, both in the structure of this book and in reframing the story of Xhosa sound fragments from one about Hugh Tracey to one about X and his colleagues. Tracey's ethnographic sound fragments are amplified inside and outside the spaces of TBPS, resounding across more than half a century as unearthed archival moments. No longer bound on cold storage shelves or lost inside compression software, they grow within a range of interconnected expressive art forms and communities that speak from yesterday for today and into tomorrow.

Through avant-garde performance, art activism, and community-based interventions, the work of these present-day actors differs from Tracey's in at least three key ways. First, they emphasize human relationships over recorded sounds, redirecting the work of ILAM toward ethical and sustained collaborations with communities. Secondly, they reframe the work from "capturing sound" to reactivating it,[5] focusing on living social spaces of creative environments designed beyond an institutional library. And thirdly, they create their own, independent archives and institutions, mixing traditional practices and knowledge with soaring praise poetry and original conscious hip hop, African electronic music, and African sound art, in radical new spaces for art.

As an ethnographically trained sound curator and sound artist, I describe my own involvement and collaborations in this work, beginning with a method of "sound elicitation" that was codeveloped in 2008 to take recordings out of the archive and into local, social spaces. I show how Xhosa friends and collaborators are building their own methods of community curation, transforming ethnographic documents that often lie dormant into living experiences that channel and transmit memory and knowledge through new public performance. These methods and practices are often far removed from what Hugh Tracey imagined, and show the possibilities of reconnecting recorded fragments of history and knowledge to the larger stories and struggles of which they are a part. In these pages I seek to amplify the creative practice of independent Xhosa artists as the ultimate curators of their own sounds and expressive culture. Sometimes the artists will choose to taste and sample colonial sound fragments, decentering dominant colonial practices, collections, and stories; at other times, they choose to overlook the colonial archive altogether, but remain vigilantly aware of the history it represents, as they continually renew the call and case for independent, locally owned, and globally resonant storytelling.

Sound Fragments imagines, hears, and helps build the sound archive as something less centralized and prescriptive, something more than a preserving container for audio formats—a space with fluid ideas flowing in and out that are responsive to locally grounded modes for collecting, performing, and amplifying stories told differently. "The creative products of collaboration in the field," argue Willemien Fronemen and Stephanus Muller, "are increasingly presented under the banner of artistic or practice-based research."[6] Products from ethnographic encounters and exchanges have long emerged from historical minefields, and productive processes today try to balance experimental artistic approaches infused with a full sensitivity of what it means to find inspiration in the creative work of others. When Cara Stacey and Natalie Mason advocate "reflective openness and collaboration in knowledge creation within the academy and outside of it,"[7] they are attending to the value in creative praxis that meets both artistic and academic expectations, but remains unready and unfinished, and, as they call it, "ethically incomplete."

THINKING IN SOUND FRAGMENTS

"Throughout much of the twentieth century," writes composer and soundscape ecologist Bernie Krause, "those of us in the field were charged with carefully abstracting brief individual sound sources from within the whole acoustic fabric."[8] For Krause, sound fragmentation has been the dominant field-recording model that has endured for eight decades since the dawn of a craft, when ornithologists first focused on isolating and framing single bird calls. This perspective, he argues, favoring figure over ground, foreground over background, has led us to ignore almost entirely the interrelatedness of the human and nonhuman aural worlds. There are latent and urgent silences lurking here, and Krause has been sustaining his three-dimensional sonic mapping of environments for decades, building bigger data to show that listening to soundscapes can reveal evidence for the effects of climate change and the health of ecosystems. When listening to environments intimately we can often hear the destruction that we mostly cannot even see.

What does it mean to think of sound as fragmented, whether at the level of granular composition, the archive, or the broader cultural bedding of the soundscape? I hear, conceive of, and process sound as a fragment in at least three related ways. There is sound as a micro part that is broken—the scattered material fragments—split from, and separated off from something, detached often in readiness for inspection, analysis, preservation, and consumption. Sound that is isolated, unfinished, incomplete, the clippings loosely pasted in a scrapbook placeholder. Then there is the intransitive fragment, the sound that has no direct object, where something falls to pieces, the sound that is fragmented, collapsing under the weight of forces acting upon it. And there is the transitive, the sound that has a direct object and breaks something up or causes it to disintegrate into fragments. These are some of the properties and functions of sound—ephemeral, unpredictable, incomplete—that allow the exploratory listener "to engage through doubt in a temporary and sensorial knowing."[9] It is while listening, argues artist and writer Salomé Voegelin, that we "experience the possible slices of this world, what might be and what else there is, behind and beyond the façade of a visual reality that trades in complete images, absolutes and certainties," and that we can begin to reimagine political possibilities for effecting the truth of a community.[10] Reimagination embraces the fragments of listening as splinters or seeds from which to craft new structures of awareness.

Treating sound as a fragment of an object can clearly be traced back to Pierre Schaeffer's research and compositional experiments in 1948, as he dissected recorded audio of clappers and klaxons, hissing steam engines and clacking metal train wheels. Inventing, defining and refining a *musique concrète*, Schaeffer—"the godfather of sampling"—offered us the twin concepts of acousmatic listening and the *objets sonores* or sound objects.[11] While focusing on listening without visual access to sound sources, and on the material rather than abstract qualities of sound, Schaeffer later replaced *musique concrète* with *musique expérimentale*. He rejected the simple binary between concrete and abstract sound, when sufficient technological manipulation means "the concrete can readily be transformed into its opposite: deracinated sonic matter for composition."[12] The sound object should be thought of neither as found nor captured, but more accurately as something that was "in part machine-made; in part, a construct of iterative perception."[13] Schaeffer the composer wanted to focus on sounds standing independently of their sources and causes, "as discrete and multifaceted phenomena rather than as carriers of meaning or as effects."[14] To the listening subject his *objet sonore* fluctuates between the identifiably bounded and the imaginatively reconstructed, "balanced as it is between event-like flow and object-like individuation."[15] Schaeffer also identified the concept of the sound fragment, a recorded part that was distinct from the physical-material sound object, and referred rather to the "effect" emitted from the object and cut into a recording. In his book-length study of Schaeffer's work, Brian Kane foregrounds this crucial insight, since "the recorded fragment, not the physical source, acquired the plasticity of compositional material."[16]

In tracing here the creation, freezing, and recirculation of fragments I consider both the plasticity of the form, and also the "detachment" in attitudes that fragmentation might promote at its core. For scholar and museum professional Barbara Kirshenblatt-Gimblett, the creation of ethnographic objects is a somewhat surgical exercise informed by a "poetics of detachment," and she wonders where the object begins and where it might end. "Detachment," she explains, "refers not only to the physical act of producing fragments but also to the detached attitude that makes fragmentation and its appreciation possible."[17] Unable to carry away "the intangible, ephemeral, immovable, and animate," ethnographers choose instead to inscribe in this place of impossibility and create documents that are true to what she calls "the fetish-of-the-true-cross approach." These inscribed material fragments that we can carry away "are accorded a higher quotient of realness."[18] And the hyperreality afforded the excised fragments is seemingly often enabled by, and can reproduce, attitudes and sensibilities that detach and float free from contextual production.

This concept of the fragment allows us to think about and listen to sound archives—spaces in which sound has fragmented from its social world. As I show in this book, this fragmentation is intentional and has longstanding social, political, and economic effects. But the plasticity of the fragment also means that it can be repurposed, listened to, and experimented with in multiple ways and in other spaces across time. And it is through the malleability of the fragment that we can hear some archival practices changing since, as Carol Muller argues, we are now no longer bound to locate the archive in cultures that own technologies of repetition. Muller suggests that certain kinds of music composition should already be considered as archival practices, as "valued sites for the deposit and retrieval of historical styles and practices in both literate and pre-literate contexts."[19] When comparing "the human mind as both memory and archive" with the more conventional understanding of archives as museum-like places in which detached objects often serving political power are collected, controlled, and sometimes concealed, Muller finds a fluid, diasporic concept of the archive, and one "more suited to cultural analysis in the twenty-first century."[20] Contemporary institutional archives can be transformed into spaces that embrace and support the living archives of humanly performed memory, collecting artistic responses that repurpose and add to existing deposits.

RECORDING AND LISTENING IN THE FIELD

Field recording, once a bounded collecting procedure pinned firmly inside Victorian collect-and-classify cabinets, has long since evolved "from a description of a non-studio recording to an uneven and hazily defined subgenre." Formerly used to describe recordings made in the field by ethnomusicologists, anthropologists, linguists, and ornithologists, the practice now embraces "the recording of everything from rural soundscapes to contact-mic'd domestic appliances, industrial machinery to the sounds of pondweed, prawns or herring, distant thunderstorms detected with a VLF (very low frequency) recorder to the footsteps of ants."[21] Any field recording can be analyzed for the politics of its production, and, since it will always contain audible traces of the environment from which it was extracted, can also be used to stand in creative relationships to the environment over time.

What stories, removals, and personal pathways can be found, heard, and imagined when listening to archival ethnographic recordings? How can curators excavate around field recordings to understand their creation and composition, while also tracing active responses to recordings over years and decades, across generations and even centuries? Any sound recording exists as a rupture in time, a bounded vessel ripped from a flowing stream for inspection and audition, by a recordist often uncertain of its future audience. "The phonographer-as-listener imagines herself" writes Roshanak Kheshti, "as a placeholder for the future listener that the recording anticipates."[22] And future listeners now might just as likely arrive from noninstitutional and nonacademic backgrounds, bringing alternative ideas for creative engagement.

Scholars theorizing how or what sound writes detect in the medium the possibility for more equitable relationships. "*Listening*," argues Deborah Kapchan, "is the first step not only in translating sound into words, but in compassionate scholarship."[23] Listening links slower-burning ethnographic processes to action and activism. Engaged listening releases stories and histories, which accrue around archival fragments. In order to listen through such processes, Martin Daughtry coins the term "acoustic palimpsest" as a way of thinking about the woven layers of inscription and removals that result when sound confronts us from multiple sources. A palimpsest of layered sounds combines "the multiple acts of erasure, effacement, occupation, displacement, collaboration, and reinscription that are embedded in music composition, performance, and recording." Daughtry argues that these are all "acts that can be recovered . . . by critical listening, research, and occasional leaps of the imagination."[24]

Ethnomusicological analyses have become increasingly attentive to the negotiated—or nonnegotiated—processes inherent within recording, given that "phenomena studied in the field have also often been considered much more multivariate, uncontrollable, and unrepeatable than those enculturated in the laboratory."[25] Recording devices are no longer considered neutral mechanical objects, but are acknowledged rather to play "an agentive role in what is often a hierarchical encounter between researcher and subject."[26] Hugh Tracey standing among them, "many prominent twentieth-century sound collectors were white scholars in positions of power making a living off of performances by rural, indigenous, and black and brown musicians."[27]

Conversely, recordings have also been able to empower marginalized communities at the level of government. Examining an era closer to the dawn of recording, museum curator John Troutman has explored the relationship between Native American musical practice, phonography, and federal Indian policy in the United States between 1879 and 1934. He finds that "through access to modern technologies such as the phonograph and radio, and through music education in the boarding schools, American Indian musicians engaged not only the catalog of American popular music but also . . . the expectations of Indianness that permeated popular culture in the early twentieth century."[28] Musical performance becomes linked to a citizenship agenda, as well as the allotment and liquidation of tribal lands for Native peoples, and extant recordings provide evidence of multiple responses to ideas of Indianness, including both the embracing and shunning of Indianness in performance, as individuals and groups sought to secure their livelihoods where there were usually only limited opportunities on reservations.

Attention paid to both the processes and artifacts of recording often seems to open up a space where interpretations of recorded content can freely detach from any definitive or dominant claims. In his dual roles as both ethnomusicologist and record producer, Christopher Scales explores the intersections of live and recorded Northern powwow social worlds, "attempting to map a particular, historically specific kind of 'indigenous modernity.'"[29] He traces some of the ways that many Native Americans struggle to make sense of the relationships between powwows and powwow recording practice, and illustrates the multiple links between themes of money, reputation, and prestige and how they relate to the preservation of culture and history, the importance of new songs and originality of style, the naming and ownership of songs, and the aesthetics of sound effects. "The 'meaning' of recordings," writes Scales, and "their articulation in the flux of social life, can sometimes exist quite apart from the conditions of their production."[30]

Detachment in listening is also explored by artist John Kannenburg, director and chief curator of the Museum of Portable Sound, a "nomadic museum of sounds that exist solely as digital files that have been curated into galleries installed on our Museum Director's mobile phone."[31] Kannenburg is interested in the real conversations made possible through encounters with individual listeners, and he creates a practical dialogue between the disciplines of sound studies and museology by designing ways to prioritize listening over looking in museum contexts. When developing his idea of a museological sound object, defined for the benefit of museum practice as "a listenable sonic event generated by a physical object, animal, human, or force of nature, *independent of its source*,"[32] Kannenburg designs and explores ways for people to share their responses to sound objects by focusing on sound's portability and the personal interactions this makes possible. Developing dialogues about sound as museum practice is ultimately, for Kannenburg, intended to make museological practices less misrepresentative, and more inclusive of diverse responses, through an attentive listening process located in personal, and often individual and intimate, engagements with sound objects.

Hugh Tracey's ethnographic recordings have long been circulating as mined, reframed, and remixed sound fragments increasingly detached from their source, but arguably without the diverse, personalized, and observed interactions that practices such as Kannenburg's promote. Yawning across more than half a century, a chasm of time and space has already opened up between most of the recordings and their originating communities. The silences and omissions stilled for decades inside these recesses can be imagined and reached through creative contemporary artists operating to tell their own stories that build around archival sound. Vinyl, cassette tape, and digital files that formerly compressed and flattened dimensions of animated performance can be made available and accessible in other public spaces, studios, and independent local arts and public heritage initiatives that look different, sound different, and engage audiences differently. Recordings and their cabinet-catalogued classifications are being unlocked and challenged by lived and performed responses to archivally owned fragments. If hegemonic stories are to become decentered, challenges to the dominant account must become part of the record.

ARCHIVES GONE ROGUE, GOING RITUAL

In the age before digital proliferation and explosions of access to often unverifiable online information, historians and archivists were already questioning the objectivity of archival records, trying to understand the ways that such knowledge was produced. Where deposited documents were once treated as nuggets of truth to be unearthed, scholars now draw attention to omissions, silences, and erasures, and the ways in which records alter over time. Research pays much greater attention to "the particular processes by which the record was produced and subsequently shaped, both before its entry into the archive, and increasingly as part of the archival record."[33] For Jacques Derrida, archiving always remains a work in both memory and mourning, because "the archive—the good one—produces memory, but produces forgetting at the same time."[34] There has also been an increasing movement from the forgotten to read colonial archives "against the grain," where students of colonialism have been schooled to write more "popular histories 'from the bottom up,' histories of resistance that might locate human agency in small gestures of refusal and silence among the colonized."[35]

However, institutions usually move slowly, and a general unwillingness to expand access to archives can easily persist. Archivist Verne Harris—who worked in the apartheid-era State Archives Service and then at the Nelson Mandela Centre of Memory in South Africa—calls for the entry of deconstructive voices to dislodge the "continued dominance in archival discourse of white voices and Western modes of knowledge construction."[36] Archivists must, argues Harris, resist textual dominance "in order to open up our archives to other forms of representing in other descriptive architectures."[37] For Harris, the defining issue in transformation discourse is not merely the creation of equal access to the holdings in public archives, but rather that "they must become *creators* of users; or, in the words of the popular slogan, they must 'take the archives to the people.'"[38] Although it remains uncertain whether they can ultimately resist the commodification of knowledge, Harris categorically insists that public archives "should be transformed from a domain of the elite into a community resource."[39] Toyin Falola takes this further in his advocacy for the honoring of ritual archives— polyvalent conglomerations containing "tremendous amounts of data on both natural and super-natural agents, ancestors, gods, good and bad witches, life, death, festivals, and the interactions between the spiritual realms and earth-based human beings."[40] For Falola, the ritual archive is the only archive that keeps the invisible alongside the visible, and he recognizes that indigenous researchers are connected with knowledge-bearing locales as particular social agents "in ways that academically trained scholars lack the full capacity to become."[41]

In our information age of perpetually tracked big data, lossy compression and instantaneous file transfer, the ideas and processes constituting an archive are expanding rapidly—often nebulously, experimentally, and independently—especially when community-driven archives pop up, and then speak back to the perceived authority of institutional repositories. Performance and new media theorist Gabrielle Giannachi traces the ways in which archives evolve to absorb and activate new technologies and media, becoming a way to map everyday information. She scans their multiple platforms and sees them as a constellation of "documents (or objects, artifacts), sites, ordering systems (and administration strategies), but also as installations, cabinets of curiosity, databanks, interfaces, artworks, environments, game-spaces, network platforms, mixed reality trails, musical instruments, and motors for the economy."[42] As some archives evolve into communication strategies, many are no longer even associated with specific locations, and increasingly resemble exhibition spaces, social media, tools for re-writing history, and even artworks. Archives have gone diasporic, gone rogue. No longer just ordering systems, archives must now be open to diasporic inclusions and interpretations, creating room for "what was left out, what was destroyed or hybridized as a consequence of adverse political contexts, and . . . what has, as yet, to be found."[43] Something more than regressive tide-stemming repositories, archives can be become open, porous, and futuristic. "In spite of what would appear to be the case," writes literary and aesthetic theorist Horea Poenar, "the archive is always for the future."[44] Like art, archives "function through contamination, inter-sections, re-enactments, debts and returns."[45]

Examining ways in which new digital cultural memory, generated mostly by nonprofessional archivists, differs from print-era archiving, media and performance theorist Abigail De Kosnik detects a proliferation of "rogue archives," defined by "24/7 availability; zero barriers to entry for all who can connect to the Internet; content that can be streamed or downloaded in full, with no required payment, and no regard for copyright restrictions . . . and content that has never been, and would likely never be, contained in any traditional memory institution."[46] Whereas in the late nineteenth and early twentieth century public collective memory was the domain of the state, this memory has since flowed out and "fallen into female hands, into immigrant and diasporic and transnational hands, into nonwhite hands, into the hands of the masses."[47] Drawing her evidence centrally from Internet fan fiction archives, De Kosnik shows how the majority of community archives are "politically opposed to the concept of 'canonicity,' as they typically refuse traditional notions of hierarchy, status, and privilege, and regimes organized according to vertical logics under which their members have suffered, or from which they have been systematically excluded."[48]

In common with archival and curatorial studies, sound studies is also increasingly attentive to the incomplete, the unfamiliar, and the unheard, especially when attempting to reorient away from dominant Western centers and toward the Global South. Ethnomusicologists Gavin Steingo and Jim Sykes argue that sound studies itself is not even necessarily a useful disciplinary idea because it somewhat shapelessly attempts to link all literature relating to sound. Sound studies has seemingly begun to calcify around a narrow set of concerns, most notably "the historical development in the West of 'sound' as a concept and phenomenon separable from the other senses"—itself made possible by particular recording technologies—and "the increasingly sharp division between public and private space."[49]

If a prior limitation of sound studies was its pattern of reliance on voices about the technology of sound and recording, there has been a more recent movement toward imagining and feeling sound as experiences connecting bodies and spaces. Philosopher and curator Christopher Cox—who characterizes sound as "a nonlinear flow of matter and energy on a par with other natural flows"—argues that it makes more sense to proceed from sound as a system of flow that is both temporal and spatial, rendering us less inclined "to draw distinctions between culture and nature, human and nonhuman, mind and matter, the symbolic and the real, the textual and the physical, the meaningful and the meaningless."[50] He prefers to treat artistic productions as complexes of forces, rather than of signs or representations. Sound's dual temporal and spatial properties seem to offer the potential to outstrip written memories, somehow demarcating, describing, and then vacating spaces. "As any squirrel, whale, or architect knows," says Cox, "sound is spatially affective, interacting uniquely with the materials, shapes, and configurations of the space in and through which it moves."[51] The elusive, invasive, and evasive flows and patterns of sound and vibration compose and amplify a "discontinuous archive" allowing for spatial and temporal deterritorialization.[52] As vibrations interact, invade, and evade through spaces, artists and actors can also use sound to reterritorialize public sites and memories that extend through and beyond the stalled resonance of archival shelves.

Slivers and samples of sound can often seed newly imagined worlds for archived fragments that cannot always be reduced down into the convenience of articulated or translated language. For Salomé Voegelin, sound is generative of world making and listening is always an exploratory, physical, and continuous effort seeking to understand how to sense—and then live among and in between—things. Fragments of sound that are accessible through listening should not, she argues, be translated into visual signs, but rather remain invisible, "not to make sense according to language; to make sonic non-sense."[53] When listening to sound, Voegelin detects nothing less than the possibility of the generation of a new language and the expansion of the possibility of thinking, hearing "new connections, fabulations, fantastical things that appear impossible but which can materialize between fragments of text as unthinkable thought."[54] Scholars and artists are increasingly experiencing sounds as flowing forces that elude translation or any direct equivalence in meaning. This experiential approach necessarily takes us outside of the institutional archive, into places where sound fragments are allowed to recirculate in newly connected ways.

CURATING SOUND FRAGMENTS

The practice of curation has been simultaneously proliferating and splintering, revealing positive and negative practices, associations, and responses. Careful stewardship can just as equally lead to a reinforcement of hierarchies through rigid processes, hence the argument for a "curatorial willingness to break down traditional power hierarchies, to engage in respectful collaboration and sharing of expertise."[55] Now that we are all archivists, now that curation no longer signifies exclusive authority, and pocket algorithms can automate multiple lifetimes for an individual's listening, what place will twenty-first century sound archives occupy? What will they contain, connect, and do? When ethnomusicologists refuse to deposit recordings and other fieldwork material in institutional archives they are often resisting the associations of colonial exploitation. However, in an age of proactive archiving, increasingly driven by the postcolonial agency of people recording themselves, Janet Topp Fargion and Carolyn Landau argue that the people and places involved in expanding archival practice are changing rapidly, as are the ways in which people choose to activate archives.[56] If every music researcher is now an archivist and curator, how are these practices extending to the noninstitutional world, and how are more grassroots approaches influencing professional modes?

Curatorial discourse is marked by an awareness that as exhibition and display modes rapidly evolve, the ability to document and represent the activities and records has not kept pace. "Archive the achievements," exhorts art historian Terry Smith, because "the history of exhibitions, of museum displays, and of institutional programming is not adequately served by taking a few uninformative panoramic photographs of each room, collecting the press clippings, adding catalogues to the library, and filing the announcements among administrative records."[57] Curator Hans Ulrich Obrist agrees, noting that although curating inevitably produces "ephemeral constellations with their own limited career spans," there persists "an extraordinary amnesia about exhibition history."[58] He affirms that much curatorial history hangs as oral history, and "it's very much a story that can only be *told* because it's not yet been *written*."[59]

Artist and curator Paul O'Neill identifies a growing emergence since the 1990s of the curator as artist, from a behind-the-scenes organizer and facilitator to a more collaborative, experimental, and transformative creator. He draws attention to the web of metaphors deployed to reconcile diverse modes of practice, "ranging from medium or 'middleman' via 'midwife' to the 'curator as' phenomenon—from curator as editor, DJ, technician, agent, manager, platform provider, promoter, and scout, to the more absurd diviner, fairy godmother, and even god."[60] As curated exhibitions and outputs diversify and become more open-ended, cumulative, and durational, they no longer "prioritize the exhibition-event as the one-off moment of display."[61] Hans Ulrich Obrist scrutinizes whether a Eurocentric perspective is inevitably limiting our openness to experience. "Perhaps," he predicts, "display in the twenty-first century will come from other cultures, and will tend toward a holistic condition."[62]

Once recorded, sound is already curated and filtered by sets of framing decisions. But can sound—a flow of constant vibrational motion—really be curated? It has been argued that mixing curation with music and sound is like working with oil and water. Hearing the reduction of the phonographic recording as "something of a philosophical scandal in that it takes a moment and makes it perpetual," popular music chronicler Simon Reynolds objects to the museumification of music, especially pop music, for its dry chiseling of viscerally alive energies down into stone monuments. "My gut feeling," he ventures as he recoils from underwhelming pop exhibitions, "is that pop and the museum just don't go together."[63] However, "museums preserve art and artifact," curator Steven Lubar reminds us, "by keeping it secure, keeping track of it, and taking care of it, thus making it accessible and useful."[64] In which case, can museums and archives still become essential places or placeholders for the production of stories about sound? Any sound archivist could reel off the details of collections that would have vanished without curation, but preserving sound files is not in and of itself any guarantee of respect for human beings, living or deceased.

Moreover, the use of desirable recorded fragments can splinter opinions, especially now that ready access means increased vulnerability to theft and exploitation. In our open-source era some scholars and artists argue against overly stringent copyright laws and the dangers of starving a publicly fed collaborative commons, and it is also evident that fair use of ethnographic samples can generate respect, pride, and sometimes wealth for communities. Tracey's ILAM recordings have been circulating far away from their places of origin for half a century in academic spheres, through republishing and, increasingly, through sampling. The Beating Heart Project, a London-based label, has been licensing selected ILAM recordings and mobilizing a roster of international electronic artists and producers to work up remixes aimed firstly at the international club and festival circuits.[65] This approach has attracted both praise and criticism. I have witnessed Beating Heart's work with Malawian artists and radio producers, as well as some of their investments in community projects. I am viscerally thrilled hearing and seeing a fan video of hypercool London street choreography to Coen's slamming production around a South African sample from ILAM.[66] At the same time, sampling without critically engaging with context is problematic, especially when, as Tracey's were, the original field recordings were constructed against the backdrop of an apartheid system promoting violent racism. What stakes are at play, asks Harry Edwards, when high-profile artists sample without acknowledgment, or even awareness, of the dangerously embedded links to retribalization, and when remixes circulate with the best intentions while doing "little to engage with the full history of the ILAM" and its foundation based on the inequality of racialized power relations?[67] How can sampling avoid reproducing the extractive force of neocolonial luxury feathering metropolitan careers? At the very least, it has now become imperative to analyze and document at source all negotiations taking place, especially as local artists and community members take their rightful lead in decision-making processes.

BEYOND SOUND REPATRIATION

My training and work as a DJ-turned-ethnographer and later, as a gallery-based sound curator, has immersed me over the past twenty years in conversations and projects around the ethics and politics of using archival sound recordings. After the collecting boom of the nineteenth and twentieth centuries, scholars and practitioners increasingly came to recognize that recordings cannot sit out their lives hidden on inert shelves. One response has been to conduct sound repatriation. Inspired by the method of repatriating museum objects—notably including human remains—a growing body of researchers has been trying to return sound recordings to their sources of origin.[68] Work is being undertaken across the globe, redirecting metropolitan and sometimes smaller and personal archives back toward the communities from which they extracted their content.

Museum information specialist Robert Lancefield was one of the first scholars to identify the ethical significance of this developing method. He writes that "repatriation constitutes a tiny—but disproportionately significant—part of the global flow of recorded sound, a flow that in turn is a key component of the encompassing transnational movement of made objects and traces of intangible cultural practices." Linking past and present across time, place, and power differentials, he argues, "repatriation's enactment is complex, its effects unpredictable, its ethical grounding often dauntingly conflicted."[69] Nowadays, the process is deemed an ethical necessity, combining redress with the establishment of more enlightened models for contemporary and future practice. "The politics of Indigenous repatriation—whether it involves human remains, objects, or songs," writes Robin Gray, "requires that it be restorative so that the source community can find a sense of resolution from historical injustices."[70]

In Australia, ongoing collaborative work is linking communities in Northern Kimberley with universities and cultural centers, discovering that repatriation "may be both a means to support the revitalization of song traditions and to collaboratively redress—or at least critically reflect on—colonial research legacies."[71] Researchers and community members, with some people ideally operating as both, together attend to the living memories of the relationships that formed the recordings, considering "the extent to which, for cultural heritage communities, the cultural contracts entered into by past researchers and singers sit with recordings as metadata, unwritten but encoded in the relational performance event."[72]

Reporting on the work of repatriating sound contained in the Klaus Wachsmann collection from the British Library Sound Archive to the newly established Makerere University Klaus Wachsmann Music Archive in Uganda,[73] Sylvia Nannyonga-Tamusuza and Andrew Weintraub begin with the clear premise that communities of origin have the right to access, own, and use recordings originating from their communities. We, as music scholars and researchers, are obliged to "mobilize resources in order to repatriate cultural property to the communities of origin," initiating and engaging in repatriation as "a critical and reflexive discourse about the social relations of power in cultural representations, and a model for dissembling and potentially undoing those relations."[74]

Repatriation models can, however, still appear limited, sometimes struggling to move beyond the fetishized sound object and the point of reconnection with its source, especially at a time when some scholars are developing more ambitious activist and developmental projects. A generation ago, the polymath writer and composer Francis Bebey argued that "as far as music is concerned, the preservation of ancestral forms is meaningless unless it is part of a genuine development programme."[75] For Bebey, development was itself a goal and ethic that both preserves and "keeps abreast of the times and, in the long run, gains time."[76] Many of Bebey's proposals for development—such as the formation of companies to promote folk music, and the establishment of African instrument-making centers—have been attainable and realized among communities. But vast inequities endure and collaborative, creative, and present-day activist projects based on longstanding relationships of trust with local artists and community members reveal how to act beyond the return of a sound fragment or object.

A number of contemporary ethnomusicologists work within development- and social justice-oriented interdisciplines such as environmental humanities to explore and build tangible benefits that reside with, and are valuable to, the communities with whom they research. In her mapping of women's borderland spatialities through songs in western Maputaland, in northern KwaZulu Natal, Angela Impey explores questions of development, land claims, environmental justice, and gender. The women in western Maputaland, Impey observes, sing and act "to make visible and consequential their experiences of land, livelihoods, and conservation expansion within a discourse that is dominated by patriarchal and exogenous authority-conferring bodies, and to thus challenge their status as marginalized players."[77] She walks and listens attentively for the ways women see, hear, and experience their roles in relation to their landscape, in order to engage with post-apartheid rights-based notions of democracy. Impey provides intimate witness by walking alongside as histories are sung telling devastating losses of local land and rights wrought by the agricultural and conservation policies of a European settler economy.

Chérie Rivers Ndaliko provides insight into arts activism through film and music in the east of Congo. Her study of the radical arts space Yole!Africa shows how researchers can work alongside community-based artists and activists to help tell their stories and support their work.[78] Her approach to socially engaged scholarship stresses the importance of understanding local context and firstly giving a platform to local voices. The work of Impey, Ndaliko and others looks beyond sound objects and their return to focus instead on the broader possibilities of creative ethnography as an activist practice that is intimately aware of the possibilities of owning space.

SOUND ETHNOGRAPHY IN THE NEW SOUTH AFRICA

Decolonizing impulses search in varied directions, drawing strength from many precolonial values and behaviors that became erasures,[79] and imagine new forms of knowledge that refuse to enable the dominance of colonizing texts and languages. Decolonized knowledge systems must often appreciate and recognize issues as being both theoretical and practical. When Achille Mbembe calls out the "destructive and mendacious" ways that Africa has been described, imagined, and represented by others, he knows that the oscillation between what is real and what is imagined is not confined to text, because the "interweaving also takes place in life."[80]

Scholars from South Africa have contributed to vital ongoing work about decolonization and contemporary realities by exploring different ways in which music relates to politics in the post-apartheid era, recognizing that music and sound operate as forces that extend well beyond functional political messaging and protest. In her book written with the singer Sathima Bea Benjamin about South African women jazz musicians, Carol Muller blends living memory with jazz archives to explore narratives of dispersal and displacement across continents. In the course of the research, she began to think "more about the relationships between beauty or deeply felt emotion and social justice," searching for other fundamental musical motivations. "In a postapartheid era," she argues, "the ability to frame the artistic output of South African musicians is no longer dependent on the same kind of political message or politicized interpretation of the work with the kind of pressing urgency sensed during the apartheid regime."[81] Intimate personal conversations grown through decades of friendship are woven inside evoked soundscapes and jazz history lived for a lifetime. Working intergenerationally with musicians, Muller has continued to trace the fully human expressive dimension in South African jazz. She locates the genre's contemporary relevance since the development of the nation state in the 1990s in its power to embrace both individual and collective freedom, and "to restore narratives previously suppressed, to celebrate place, to sound local, and perhaps also to connect musically to other genres."[82]

Ethnomusicologists have also felt, traced, and witnessed whole sensory worlds in other performance styles in South Africa, detailing forms that are often difficult to convey through any singular medium. In her analysis of post-apartheid Zulu *ngoma* song and dance aesthetics performed in Keates Drift in the magisterial district of Msinga in KwaZulu Natal, Louise Meintjes evokes a remarkable force that, although born of violence and the harsh penury of wage labor, manages to enact a newly self-claimed mode of being that balances anger and praise, loss, and declarations of love. But Meintjes also detects other motivations as she watches, listens to, and analyzes the public display of the male body being pushed to its limits, observing that "most of the time, singing and dancing is more than a political act or a representation of cultural identity, even in the moments in which it plays out in the world in these terms." Such a complex expressive mode will often elude any singular translation, because, as Meintjes realizes, "ngoma does not always say something. Sometimes it is a way of being in the world that exceeds explanation. Sometimes it is just playing."[83]

The heavy electronic beats-driven studio sound of kwaito—the distinctive South African hip hop and house hybrid—has been felt as a complex form that resonates beyond recordings and nightclubs while it spins up some of its own dust. Gavin Steingo traces the aesthetics of this genre, which may not even be a genre, over the first twenty years of democracy in South Africa, and finds much to admire in the intellectual and sensory modes created by artists using music that "has been variously described as immature, apolitical, disconnected from social issues, and lacking any meaning or purpose."[84] Rather than dismissing the escapism, Steingo listens, plays, and finds an alternative multiplying of sensory realities—one that often integrates the sounds of broken hardware, cracked software, and the smell and dusty screech of public car-spinning—amounting to "a declaration of sensory and intellectual equality" by previously marginalized township artists.[85] Ethnographers of the contemporary South African soundscapes are palpably sensing deeper creative and politically expressive layers in public performance, exploring ways to adapt their modes of ethnographic representation in relation to the musical forms that so often seem to elude even the very latest documentary recording methods. Closer listening reveals more of the relationships between aesthetic structures and power structures embedded in recording and ethnographic practices, inviting curators to start imagining platforms that address, amplify, and begin to redress the inequities embedded in many prior and ongoing cultural encounters.

METHODOLOGY, ETHICS, AND OUTLINE

Every ethnographer has one or more stories to tell of how they got here. Mine traces back to a lifetime of working with recorded music, from—as my nan delighted in recounting at my and my wife's wedding—repeatedly crawling

FIGURE I-1 Man Playing *Lesiba* mouth bow, Southern Lesotho. *Photo* © ILAM.

to hug tape players when I was but a few months old, through working as a professional DJ in venues, at festivals, and on radio, and, later, as a sound artist and sound curator, designing experimental modes for experiencing sound in a full range of spaces across the globe.[86] Over time I was slowly and subconsciously drawn away from studio productions toward the ambience, environments, and textures I could hear in field recordings. I was soon searching everywhere for ethnographic sound: in archives, online, and on labels. After a period spent using ethnographic recordings in DJ sets and for sound installations, utilizing sounds ripped out of context began to me to feel uncertain, and I started to question the ethical foundations of this creative practice. I remain transfixed by the sounds—the *lesiba* friction bow from Lesotho (see figure I-1) with its scorched overtones still astonishes me more with every repeated listen—but became increasingly aware of how little I knew about them, their relevance, and their importance to the originators. Listening to any fragment I could find recorded by Hugh Tracey and many other song collectors, I quit a job at an independent classical music label in order to train as both an ethnomusicologist and a curator, focusing my work on the possible uses of sound archives. On occasions I still vividly recall the green-room conversation I had backstage at a festival in Ireland with my trusted friend and manager at the time, who advised me to enroll in an ethnographic study program while continuing my artistic practice.

In 2007 I moved to Grahamstown in South Africa, where I would be based, initially for a year, at the International Library of African Music, and I was graciously welcomed by the director, Dr. Diane Thram. This extended field research afforded me the great opportunity to listen to every fragment of sound in ILAM, and to pore over every scrap of writing from Tracey's archive containing his multiple correspondents, drafts of lectures, and myriad business machinations. It took several months being knee-deep in the archives before I was made aware that I should get outside of the archive. For this I owe so much to Vuyo Booi, the founder of Sakhuluntu Cultural Group,[87] and Dr. Lee Watkins, now the director of ILAM. I was realizing through my reading that Hugh Tracey, as expressed in much of his publicizing rhetoric, had ambitiously hoped his archive would be used by future generations of African artists, but it was Vuyo Booi and Lee Watkins who invited and urged me into the local townships to see how people might—or might not—relate to an archival collection. So began a journey that has endured for more than a decade, looking for points of connection and dissonance between ILAM and local communities who are mostly working beyond the boundaries of the academy.

My initial fieldwork based at ILAM was divided between deep archival analysis—often emerging in the very small hours to walk home to my rented garden flat beautifully situated behind fragrant frangipani—and time spent travelling with portable archival selections in the local townships, meeting an extraordinary group of local artists and their friends and families. Working side by side with the remarkable Nyakonzima "Nyaki" Tsana, together we devised, refined, and adapted a creative method to take the archive directly to people for sharing in their own homes, on their streets, and in their public spaces. This method— "sound elicitation"—was designed to share and clarify the history and long-term purpose of Tracey's archive, while witnessing and documenting a whole range of lived responses to the public experience of archival fragments. It also amplified a range of local demands for further access to, and use of, archival content, including many creative ideas for ways to make the content locally meaningful. Tracey recorded tens of thousands of songs across sub-Saharan Africa during half a decade of touring, and Nyaki and I shared dozens of songs with many artists during a year of heavy walking, but I chose to focus much of my analysis on one extremely resonant local Xhosa song—"Somagwaza"—learning a range of local responses that bring polyphonic dimensions resisting a terse label in a colonial catalogue.

It was in this process that I first met Xolile "X" Madinda, with whom I began this book and the person who has become my main collaborator, guide, and a brother to me in the years since. X and I have continued to work together since 2007 on a range of projects, both in the Eastern Cape and in Virginia (in the United States), where I am now based. X has helped me to become increasingly embedded in a number of local independent artistic initiatives that are all, in different ways, related to, supported by, or drawing from and speaking to ILAM. As our research evolved, it became less about focusing on responses to existing content in archival sound collections, and much more about considering a range of ways to perform and document Xhosa culture, tracing a radial creative network with multiple pathways and taking many shapes in and out of ILAM. I spend time with individual artists such as the radical performance artist Sikhumbuzo Makandula,[88] as well as with independent grassroots cultural organizations that intersect with ILAM, including Ntinga Ntaba kaNdoda, and The Black Power Station. This book only represents part of my work with X and others over the past decade. Alongside this research and written text, X and I have collaborated on recordings, videos, festivals, curricula, and helping to build arts spaces, as well as working together on a number of performance and sound installations in South Africa, the United Kingdom, and the United States. As the book develops, I spend time considering how some of my individual and institutional relationships have evolved, enabling ongoing modes of collaborative curation working between communities in Virginia and the Eastern Cape of South Africa.

As a White Englishman myself, I first arrived in the Eastern Cape of South Africa almost a century after Hugh Tracey moved to Southern Africa, and I was able to move freely through some of the same pathways and regions that he had previously covered. Although the oppressive apartheid regime had come and gone since his arrival, I recognized early on the pervasive and enduring inequities that have continued, and the privilege that I hold as a White man from Europe. These privileges have allowed me easy access to institutions and individuals, housing and transportation, meals and people's homes. For the most part, I have been able to go where I want and do what I want with little hesitation, and this is the very definition of White male privilege. But perhaps what distinguishes me from Hugh Tracey is a context and a moment in which this privilege is—and must be—deconstructed and increasingly refused. "In visible mode," writes Paulette Coetzee, "whiteness performs itself, displaying its own culture as symbols of superiority, while in invisible mode it acquires — or creates — knowledge of others to affirm and maintain its rule."[89] It has been my obligation and imperative to try to learn from the countless mistakes, assumptions, and wrongs of Tracey's time and to try to avoid repeating the self-same inequities in a new era. In this process, countless friends in the Eastern Cape have shown by example what it means to be antiracist and antisexist. Their trust, friendship, and the conditions for collaboration had to be earned, slowly and with genuine care, and I am extremely grateful for, and inspired each and every day by, the times and spaces we share together both in South Africa and the United States. I am also humbled to know that real relationships have developed and that our work together has taken on a shape that must be as much, if not more, theirs as it is mine.

My approach in this book starts with a colonial archive but shifts to people and their lives, putting the field recordist in counterpoint with a number of individuals working in, around, and close to ILAM today. The outline of the book closely follows my own changing interests and preoccupations, as I shifted from a focus on the recordings and the archive to an ongoing, longer-term focus on relationships, stories, experiences, and collaborations with Xhosa artists and activists in Grahamstown-Makhanda. The narrative unfolds as follows.

CHAPTER SUMMARIES

Chapter 1, "Hugh Tracey Records the *Sound of Africa*," is an ethnographic history of the *Sound of Africa* collection at the International Library of African Music, and of Hugh Tracey, the Englishman who first collected the recordings. I analyze Tracey's influences and motivations in embarking on his recording project, as well as the colonialist origins of the project and its role within apartheid-era South Africa. Much of my discussion focuses on the aims and ethics of Tracey's surveying, recording, and cataloguing practices, and the ways in which his work both conformed with — and clashed against — colonial and apartheid-era political projects. Analysis of extensive, and mostly unpublished, writings and correspondence helps build a picture of a hugely ambitious mission riddled with contradictory impulses and motives, simultaneously humanistic and progressive, patriarchal and retrograde. I analyze Tracey's identities as both collector and institution director, illustrating his romanticized quests for African theories of music and African audiences for his recordings. I then consider the value and impact of his ultimate aim to collect enough data to codify the entire range of music making in sub-Saharan Africa, which led to the establishment of the African Music Research Unit followed by the International Library of African Music, a controversial archive and research institute that is now owned by Rhodes University in Grahamstown-Makhanda in the Eastern Cape of South Africa.

In chapter 2, "Listening Behind Field Recordings," I focus closely on the sound collections, examining Tracey's methods and motivations as a field recordist, tracing the influences on his techniques and his beliefs about what could, and should, be captured in recordings. I examine the key corporate relationships that shaped his recordings, including a gentlemen's agreement with Gallo Records (Africa), and his reciprocal working alliances with mining companies, and more personal exchanges with Africanist and—rarely—African researchers and educators. I show how Tracey developed a professional standard of constructed performances of African folk music, hosted and staged on mining compounds and in villages, designed to capture examples of the finest musicianship as part of a continent-wide survey. As Tracey's ear and microphone focused on capturing short items of high-quality musicianship, I analyze his ambivalent relationship with anthropology and his aversion to immersive and sustained fieldwork. I explore the competing theories of a musicology versus an anthropology of recording by analyzing Tracey's correspondence, and increasingly strained relationship, with John Blacking, ILAM's first appointed musicologist. Examination of Tracey's motivations and recording techniques reveals through the cracks the contexts and communities that were rapidly left behind by his recording truck, small entourage, and microphone. The pitfalls of preserving African culture inside brief recordings of musical items and short catalogued descriptions are made apparent, contributing to the ultimate difficulties Tracey would face when marketing his recordings to African audiences.

In chapter 3, "Donkey Cart Curation, Xhosa Anthems, and Township Terms," I turn to focus on ILAM today, situating the archive in post-apartheid Grahamstown and Grahamstown-Makhanda. I describe the development of the method coined as "sound elicitation." As I spent increasing amounts of time away from Rhodes University and in the local townships, I developed a close collaboration with a network of Xhosa artists, in particular Nyakonzima ("Nyaki") Tsana, a professional contemporary dancer, and Xolile ("X") Madinda, a professional hip-hop artist and community arts activist. Working together, we explored ways to share a handful of Tracey's Xhosa recordings to catalyze and mobilize memory, local storytelling, and other performed responses. I show how ethnographic sounds were taken "out of the fridge" (to quote Koketso ["KK"] Potsane, a South African friend) of archival storage and resocialized in community spaces, from schools to taxis, arts spaces to old peoples' centers, from street corners to local shebeens, yards, and homes. As I discuss, the rapidly urbanizing townships of Southern Africa were key sites in which Tracey hoped and assumed his recordings would prove popular and useful. Sound elicitation emerged from the realization that local residents of the townships in Grahamstown-Makhanda had little to no knowledge of ILAM, nor did they feel that they could access its collections, despite the fact that much of the region's musical heritage was held among their communities, but had since been largely erased or forgotten. By reactivating the recordings through local social mechanisms—the spaces and media through which music and sound transmit in more recognizably sustainable and everyday ways—I show how it is possible to document and analyze contemporary reactions to archival sounds. Moving beyond practices of object repatriation, sound elicitation works by decentering, reimagining, and retelling stories about the colonial archive so that recordings are reinterpreted and repurposed by local artists and community activists within their own social spaces through their own methods of musical transmission. The chapter focuses closely on two of Tracey's Xhosa recordings, showing how oral culture and contemporary art intersect with recorded fragments to activate a web of responses that challenge the authority of institutional archival knowledge, while suggesting new and creative ways to curate and build relationships with local communities using ethnographic sound.

In chapter 4, "Art and Community Activism Around the Archive," I consider new methods for publicly performed ethnographic interventions inside and outside ILAM's archive. I present a number of individuals and initiatives affiliated with ILAM, all centered on Xhosa reclamation of the past and working to empower local artists and communities in the Eastern Cape. These groups and people include ILAM's current work with Ntinga Ntaba kaNdoda community development group; the reactivation sound projects of producer and ILAM's studio manager, Elijah "Bra" Madiba; the music and praise poetry of young artist Bhodl'ingqaka; the public history performances of artist and scholar Masixole Heshu; and the radical public performances of Sikhumbuzo Makandula, another artist and scholar. The first section builds on more than a decade of ongoing conversations and collaborations with ILAM's current director, ethnomusicologist Lee Watkins. I examine ILAM's recent partnership with Ntinga Ntaba kaNdoda, a communally owned development center pursuing sustainable local heritage initiatives linking a suite of villages nestled in the mountainous rural areas of the

Keiskammahoek region, several hours northeast of Grahamstown-Makhanda. I show how through this collaboration, ILAM's contemporary role is becoming redefined as one of community training and advice, an active developer of satellite archives to support Xhosa ethnography documented by Xhosa fieldworkers in the rural areas of the Eastern Cape. I then explore possibilities for connecting ILAM's ethnographic sound recordings more actively with the urban worlds of hip hop, sound art, and African electronic music. I present and analyze artistic work by Elijah Madiba in collaboration with a range of local poets and beatmakers who engage Tracey's Xhosa recordings as material for creative inspiration to reimagine their own productions. This work draws on, and recomposes, archival sounds and messages to create new art that speaks to pressing contemporary issues, including responsible masculinity, respect for self and environment, and education for young children. I also illustrate and discuss the bold performance modes of artists Masixole Heshu and Sikhumbuzo Makandula, both of whom deploy archival fragments within performed installations, sound art, and mobile tours in diverse spaces occupying the town center, townships, and the local physical landscapes closer to "the bush."

In chapter 5, "The Black Power Station," I focus on the work of the visionary Xhosa hip-hop artist and community arts activist Xolile ("X") Madinda, founder of Fingo Festival and Aroundhiphop Live Café, and CEO of a grassroots pan-African community arts space, The Black Power Station in Grahamstown-Makhanda. The Black Power Station is a Xhosa-owned, -conceived, and -designed initiative that produces, presents, and archives its own artworks, performances, events, and narratives, offering a community-centered alternative to the institutional ownership of knowledge represented by ILAM, Rhodes University, and the National Arts Festival in Makhanda. In this chapter I show how X's activist work evolved from local hip-hop street cyphers and festivals in the townships, to developing a community arts space with its own emerging economy for artists. In conversation with X and other Xhosa artists, I describe and contextualize X's radicalization as a hip-hop artist influenced by Steve Biko, and the development of a range of Xhosa-curated events in Grahamstown-Makhanda. I then turn my discussion to a recent artistic event addressing the contested renaming of Grahamstown to its new Xhosa name, Makhanda. I show how the process of decentering colonial heritage while honoring Xhosa warrior legends plays out live in performance, through a particular moment of original curation in which Western knowledge inscribed in textbooks is challenged by live Xhosa praise poetry. I conclude the chapter by profiling the art and stories of young Xhosa hip-hop artists, beatmakers, producers, and poets at The Black Power Station, whose curated work oscillates powerfully between deep Xhosa tradition and cutting-edge Afrofuturistic art. These artists directly and indirectly compose counterpoint to Tracey and ILAM, share overlapping concerns with cultural memory and tradition, but use radical community curation to move past the colonial project and claim, project, and assert ownership over their own stories.

In the conclusion, "Curating Sound Stories," I draw some of these dispersed stories together, discussing why it is important to critically analyze and then repurpose a twentieth-century colonial archive—rather than simply ignore or erase it—alongside a parallel focus on the creation of newly independent and locally driven archives. I consider how this narrative speaks to larger issues in sound studies, curatorial practices, and the reciprocity and ethics of listening, discussing ways that institutional archiving can partner more radical and publicly demonstrative and performed curatorial modes that support local arts scenes, enhance livelihoods, and help develop decolonized spaces, artworks, and curricula. As highlighted throughout the book, I also here suggest how collaborations between local artists and ILAM and its collections, and the ongoing curation, archiving, and amplifying of artistic responses to archival fragments, speak to the urgent issues of today, in South Africa and elsewhere: racism; gender equality; xenophobia; the reclamation of memory, history and identity; sustainable economies for the land, arts, and heritage; and the need and right to own one's own stories. In moving along the arc of changing ownership from field recording to libraries and back out into independent and public spaces, I show how Xhosa arts activism contributes to an expanding notion of what a sound or cultural archive is, where it is, and where it may resonate in the future. In an era when archives and museums are notably scrambling to collect and curate in more responsive and contemporaneous modes, while aiming to attract younger and more diverse audiences, continued sharpness and relevance can often be found speaking in the ritual archives and networks that work alongside, within, and against historical methods, collections, and intentions.

PART I

Colonial Microphones

ONE

Hugh Tracey Records
the *Sound of Africa*

INTRODUCING THE *SOUND OF AFRICA* SERIES

Mouse-hunting songs, fishing songs, songs about stage fright; songs imitating the difficulty of the long-tailed paradise bird balancing in flight; songs about rain and poverty, songs celebrating football, and songs for pulling canoes; songs that warn against European beer, songs that complain about venereal disease, songs about the sounds of unseen airplanes; paddling songs; African separatist hymns; the sounds of *likembes* buzzing and resonating on top of guitar bodies, the sounds of pauses while spittle is reapplied to moisten the reeds of a lyre, the sounds of Xhosa women outside their huts smoking hubble-bubble pipes; story songs about a mosquito overturning a lorry, about a donkey complaining it wants wages instead of maize, about a baboon that dies after repeatedly somersaulting for joy at hearing the sound of drums; commentaries on urbanization, commentaries on fighting campaigns in Burma, commentaries on working for Native Labour Associations; the sneezewood swells of massed Mozambican xylophone orchestras, the rumbling rolls of oceanic Zulu choirs, the electrifying scorches of mouth-crackling vulture quills; Ramadan town criers, hand-moistened friction drums, and a praise song for a bicycle mender.

The *Sound of Africa* is a series of field recordings that were all made by Hugh Tracey and published as 210 long-playing records.[1] The series contains over 3,100 items of music,[2] almost all of which were recorded throughout East, Central, and Southern Africa during seventeen recording tours between 1948 and 1963.[3] These tours visited Angola, Bechuanaland (Botswana), Republic of Congo (Kinshasa), Kenya, Basutoland (Lesotho), Nyasaland (Malawi), Moçambique

(Mozambique), Northern Rhodesia (Zambia), Southern Rhodesia (Zimbabwe), Ruanda-Urundi (Rwanda and Burundi), South Africa, Swaziland, Tanganyika (Tanzania), Uganda, and Zanzibar.[4] The published results cover regions throughout fifteen different countries, and include examples from 179 different language groups. Most of the languages are Bantu, but also included are examples from non-Bantu languages, including Nilotic (in southern Sudan, Abyssinia [Ethiopia], Uganda, and western Kenya); Nilo-Hamitic (from western Kenya, northern Tanzania, Uganda, Sudan, and southwestern Abyssinia [Ethiopia]); Cushitic (from Somaliland, Eritrea, Abyssinia [Ethiopia], Sudan, and northeastern Kenya); Semitic (from Abyssinia [Ethiopia], and Eritrea); and Sudanic (from West Africa).

The tours, the scale and breadth of the vision, the finances, and most of the details—right down to the holding of the microphone—were almost entirely managed by Tracey. Working against a backdrop of the rising tides of African nationalism and independence movements, Tracey improvised a pioneering career, one that he dedicated to the recording, classifying, codifying, and publishing of that which he believed to be the true expression of the folk music of sub-Saharan Africa. The story of this collector and the story of the collection are inseparable to begin with, but this book shows how the two narratives come to diverge as, reaching across decades, other voices rise and begin to challenge the dominant voice of a colonial field recordist.

Tracey's recording work began in 1929 as a private research initiative, but for much of his life thereafter he worked with some financial and technical support from Gallo Records (South Africa), and also from many of the major mining companies in South Africa, Mozambique, and Southern Rhodesia.[5] Tracey also worked as Head of Programmes for the South African Broadcasting Corporation for twelve years between 1936 and 1947, when he was based at their Durban studios. Practical insights derived from these institutional affiliations presented him with a keen awareness of the limitations of the preexisting recorded output of African music, music that he felt was purely commercial, somewhat simplistic, and only capable of appealing to the lowest common denominator. "Apart from Hugh Tracey's seminal work and the activities of Gallo and other labels," writes Veit Erlmann, "few outside researchers have shown an interest in traditional music and have thus left the field to more commercial projects of dubious academic merit."[6] Although in today's genre-mashed sound worlds, any distinction between traditional and commercial has become largely irrelevant to many, they are still signifiers that could once hold repressive power.

However humanistic Tracey's intentions may have been, this institutional support means that African field recordings made at this time come instantly wrapped in dangerous politics. After the National Party came to power in South Africa in 1948, "The new government's logic was that 'tribal' Africans were unlikely to participate in urban political activities, a belief that found concrete expression in its policy of financing any recreation that could demonstrate a link to 'tribal'/rural life."[7] Films, sport, music, and dancing were all packaged as leisure consumption for workers, as "the mines remained wedded to the racial discourse of the 'tribal' and 'detribalised' African, and spent a great deal of effort in the attempt to affirm their conception of an appropriate tribal culture for its migrant workers."[8] The collect, classify, and pin mode of Victorian anthropology could be equally applied to objects, people, and sounds, placed in the cabinets and categories where they were thought to belong.

Tracey's piecemeal endeavors and projects gradually coalesced into more formal research institutions. In 1947 Tracey formed the African Music Research Unit with the headquarters, financial support, and publication of a proportion of its results all provided by the record label executive Eric Gallo in Johannesburg. Consequently, several hundred 78 rpm shellac discs were published. Then in 1948, Hugh Tracey and Winifred Hoernlé, "the doyenne of South African anthropologists"[9]—an esteemed White South African researcher who trained Max Gluckman and laid a foundation for the work of A. R. Radcliffe-Brown and Isaac Schapera—founded the African Music Society (AMS), the main aim of which was "to preserve for future years a record of African music and indeed of African arts generally."[10] The AMS coordinated eight recording tours in the period between 1948 and 1954. In 1954, a grant from the Nuffield Foundation enabled the establishment of an independent and active collecting and publishing institution, namely the International Library of African Music (ILAM).[11] ILAM provided a headquarters for the AMS and began to produce its own publications.

Tracey wanted to record and publish the music that he believed was more reflective of the huge variety of styles and techniques that he heard and observed scattered across the entire continent below the Sahara. He began formulating a "plan for African music," identifying a niche market somewhere between the academic and the commercial. In 1965 he wrote that "although there are several minor collections of African recordings stored away in various private and public archives such as those of radio stations," there was no "major source of general and reliable information within Africa itself which . . . does adequate justice to the scope and variety of indigenous music as a distinctive and continent-wide cultural phenomenon."[12]

The *Sound of Africa*, most of which was originally published by ILAM between 1955 and 1963, is the resulting collection and Tracey's major legacy. Its sister collection, the *Music of Africa*, was published by Gallo Africa in the 1960s and originally consisted of twenty-five long-playing records that were mostly, but not exclusively, selected from the much larger *Sound of Africa* series.[13] The *Sound of Africa* was ambitiously designed to document as wide a sample as possible of the local musical styles to be found all across sub-Saharan Africa, and was intended — especially considering the cost of purchase — mainly for use in universities and by other specialists and subscribers. This is not least because, format restrictions aside, the cost of acquiring 210 LPs would have been, and would remain, well beyond the pocket of most individuals and institutions inside and outside Africa.[14] The smaller *Music of Africa* series was intended to showcase highlights, and was organized into themed albums, grouping similar instruments or albums of African stories translated into English and read by Tracey for children. This series, aimed at a more general audience and also for connoisseur collectors, was "issued as introductions to several aspects of music making in Central and Southern Africa under instrumental, geographical or 'selection' headings."[15] In 2007, an advertisement in ILAM's journal *African Music* promoted both of these series of recordings; the *Sound of Africa* was advertised as being "for scholarly purposes," while the *Music of Africa* was advertised as being "for a general audience."[16]

By the time of Tracey's death in 1977, he had published more than 3,100 items in the *Sound of Africa* series, approximately one eighth of his entire collection of field recordings. His son Andrew Tracey later added eight further LPs to the existing 210, and these additional LPs were mainly drawn from his own fieldwork among *mbira* musicians in the Zambezi valley and its environs, and also among the Chopi *timbila* orchestras in the Zavala region of southern Mozambique. The total of 210 LPs was never intended to be a final amount, but rather reflected the financial limitations of the archive and the times in which it was operating. Hugh Tracey was constantly fighting a battle to secure more funds in order to publish records. A few years before the end of his life, he wrote that "the 'Sound of Africa' series is by no means finished."[17] In 1969, by which time he had made most of his recordings, Tracey defined the limits of his recording territory as having been "primarily Bantu speaking Africa from the Equator southwards, with brief excursions into the fringes of the Sudanic and Nilotic speaking peoples as far as 3 and 4 degrees North." He noted that "this excludes Ethiopia, Sudan and the Central African Republic but includes evidence from 18 other territories southwards."[18] Later, he would make preliminary and preparatory excursions into West Africa, visiting Nigeria and Ghana and forging links with some universities in the region, but he was never able to return to the area to begin recording.

Tracey claimed to have held the microphone during the making of every recording in the first 210 LPs of the series, and that he was "personally responsible for every single item" as well as "most of the text" in his catalogue for the *Sound of Africa*.[19] The Chopi musicians from Mozambique, one of the earliest groups outside of Southern Rhodesia to be studied by Tracey, nicknamed him "Magatagata." His wife Peggy Tracey noted in her diaries that "'Magatagata'— Hugh's Chopi nickname—refers to his long, striding walk, but it has a secondary meaning, the man who goes on working all the time."[20] Tracey recorded, documented, published, lectured, broadcast, and demonstrated extensively on the general subject of African music. In 1954 he established the journal *African Music*, which remains the only journal entirely devoted to research on the music of sub-Saharan Africa. He was a regular public speaker, delivering over 240 lectures throughout Africa, Europe, and America between 1934 and 1976, on subjects ranging from the different styles of African storytellers,[21] to the use of music as a means of improving race relations in an increasingly segregated South Africa.[22] ILAM's unpublished archives include his own diaries, diaries written by Peggy Tracey—who accompanied him on many of his recording tours and helped document much of his work—an uncompleted draft of an autobiography,[23] three unpublished biographical attempts to chronicle his life and work,[24] a large amount of correspondence with key ethnomusicologists and other foreign commentators on African music and culture, as well as funding proposals and plans for the future direction of ILAM. Within these sources can be found a critical dialogue examining the developing archival project, as well as the evolving visions for the intended uses and future applications of the collection. The archival history of the collection contains within it some of the latent and predictive directions for its future use, as well as some of the flaws and reasons that it stalled. Analysis of this material reveals the motivations, methods, and ethos behind ambitions to document and codify "the musical memory of half a continent."[25] Tracey's methods, language, and beliefs constantly oscillated between the pioneering and patriarchal, the humanistic and the racist, the prophetic and the deeply retrograde.

Possessing a talent for communication and an entrepreneur's ability to forge his own path, Tracey left Devon in 1921 for Cape Town before arriving in Southern Rhodesia and joining Leonard Tracey, his elder brother, on his tobacco farm in the Fort Victoria District.[26] He arrived in Southern Africa with a suitcase, a keen musical ear, and some "well founded misgivings" from his large middle-class family. He was immediately struck by the Karanga songs that he heard accompanying the activities that filled the days of the local farm workers.[27] He began to make written records of the songs, transcribing the lyrics into notebooks, some of which are still available in ILAM's archive. Tracey first began noting down Karanga lyrics as a means of learning the language and to allow him to communicate more easily with the workers in the tobacco fields. Recording—whether by writing, or later using acetate, tape, and vinyl—was Tracey's primary method to study and learn the music that he heard and observed. Andrew Tracey recalls that his father "always kept notebooks," and that "right up to the day he died he could look at the words of those songs and sing them instantly."[28]

Tracey's entry point for Karanga culture was to listen closely to language. In a never-completed draft of his autobiography, he remembered that

> Each day the dozen or so farm hands, young and old Karanga men, from Chipika's village nearby, would sing spontaneously in the fields, especially when a task calling for concerted effort was involved, such as lifting weights, or hoeing and digging in unison with each other. It was then I discovered that while the rhythms of the music kept you going, the words of their songs opened a whole vista of African thinking. So the lyrics now began to fill my notebook, phrase-by-phrase, regardless of any convention of "correct" spelling if such existed. I wrote as I heard, accepting the age-old function of oral tradition by which all folk musics had ever been shared, "learned by heart and conn'd by rote."[29]

Tracey the collector inspected by surveying and sampling, a method that was never designed to be or become one of long-term immersion and participation, nor was it one that relied on extensive use of transcription.[30] His first experience of recording African music required him to act as a practical arranger, organizing musicians for professional recordings that could be sold to local markets. In June 1929 Tracey was instrumental in arranging what are believed to be the first recordings of Southern Rhodesian folk songs ever to be published in Southern Africa. These recordings were made by Columbia (London), a professional recording

FIGURE 1.1 Hugh Tracey recording the first content songs. Babu Chipika is fourth singer from left, Gumwie fourth singer right, ca. June 1929. *Photo* © ILAM.

company. Tracey later remarked that at that time, "no efficient recording equipment was as yet installed anywhere in South Africa," so "all master recordings had to be made by a professional team of engineers sent out for the purpose from England."[31] Having spotted an announcement in the *Rhodesian Herald* that such professional recording engineers were in Southern Africa, he contacted Harold Jowitt, director of native development and education in Southern Rhodesia, and then spent two weeks with two ex-employees, Babu Chipika and Gumure (whose last name does not seem to have been recorded), combing local villages in search of musicians suitable for professional recording work.[32] Tracey and his two assistants assembled fourteen Karanga musicians, rehearsed forty songs, and then took the men in a lorry five hundred miles south from the Fort Victoria district down to Johannesburg, in order to make some studio recordings. Sixteen items were recorded and eventually published, five of which survive in ILAM's archive.

For the recordings, Tracey adopted the role of song coordinator and conductor (see figure 1.1), developing techniques that would later heavily inform his field recordings.[33] Already he had realized the value of arranging music for "takes," selecting and presenting the most coherent or aesthetically pleasing versions—to his ears—of songs that may in themselves not be structured in the same way when played in their social context. This practice of staging music to capture examples of what he deemed excellent musicianship provided the framework for the musical content that Tracey continued to record later in the field. Tracey was attracted by the commercial appeal of selling records to help finance some of his work, and accordingly he organized his own published LPs in ways that he hoped would sell to local and other markets. Tracey was operating as the commercial markets for records in Southern Africa were expanding. Columbia and HMV were about to follow the success of Zonophone—a British label and the first European label to launch a substantial African catalogue—by establishing their own studios in South Africa in the early 1930s, and Gallo would soon build its own pressing plant at a time when "early studio recordings sold remarkably well on the South African market."[34]

Tracey observed and estimated that, beyond the communities in which the music was created, there was very little awareness of, or interest in, local and indigenous music from White or settler audiences. Consequently, he made tentative steps to present his early findings, publishing "Some Observations on the Native Music of Southern Rhodesia" in 1929, and then delivering a lecture on African music to an educational conference at Marandellas in Southern Rhodesia. As a result, in 1931, Harold Jowitt helped Tracey to acquire a small Carnegie Travelling Fellowship "in order to study the background of the music of Southern Rhodesia."[35] This $2,500 travelling grant enabled Tracey to undertake his first proper research trip, and in July 1932 he travelled around six regions of the eastern part of the Shona-speaking districts of Southern Rhodesia, again with Babu and Gumure. Little is known about this grant, although it seems that Tracey was required to link his research to local music education,[36] and that Jowitt refused to publish the results, objecting to Tracey's criticism of the destruction wrought on local music by missionaries. When Tracey began researching and making recordings in 1929, the academic study of African music amounted to little more than the work of a few foreign scholars, and a scattering of observations from travelers and explorers. Decades later, Tracey stressed "how little authoritative data has, as yet, been published for comparative purposes, and for the elementary requirements of teaching it in schools." Coordinated professional research needed centralizing, he argued, because "what information exists has been largely the work of devoted private individuals who have studied some aspect of local music within their reach in which they had taken a special interest as a hobby, but rarely on a professional or whole-time basis."[37]

Professor Percival Kirby was one of a very small number of foreign researchers interested in the indigenous music of Africa, and Tracey intended to complement Kirby's work,[38] remarking that by starting his research in the south of Rhodesia he hoped "to make it contiguous to the work of the Professor," and from then onward to "continue right through this country to the borders of Northern Rhodesia, Portuguese East Africa and Nyasaland."[39] In a conversation with his employee Irene Frangs,[40] Tracey explained that he was first motivated to record so that he could help dispel some of the misconceptions about local African music that were commonly propagated by the ignorance of an outsider general public. He reflected,

> I suppose I was driven into it (apart from a natural inclination to be interested) partly by ignorant people telling me that aspects of African music which I knew so well, were valueless. People who had no experience of how the music worked and what satisfaction it gave to Africans, would tell me the most arrant nonsense.[41]

When he had first started researching in Africa he had discovered among non-Africans "a tendency for everybody to say that whatever art Africans may have was primitive, simple and not worthwhile. Therefore, they should be taught non-African art."[42]

Much of Tracey's early period of recording and research was typical of folklorists operating elsewhere at the time, demonstrating an emphasis on collecting and amassing recorded examples at the expense of any sustained analysis or search for the perspectives of local voices. Much as folklorists collecting field recordings of blues musicians in the American South during the 1920s–'40s "focused more on making and archiving field recordings of blues songs than on publishing analytical studies about them,"[43] so Tracey also determined to amass as much primary data as he could. His work at this stage lacked any sustained framework for analysis, and he was more inclined to document and publish what he considered to be outstanding examples of musicianship. Although his interest in local music making appeared somewhat unusual for the time, there is little evidence of him developing ongoing dialogues with musicians or community members, and much more evidence of the reproduction of colonial class relationships.

Having secured his research grant from the Carnegie Corporation, Tracey travelled to England in 1932 for advice and to publicize some of his early findings to other European collectors and musicians. He presented two radio programs on African music from the BBC's Savoy Hill Studios, and lectured at Cambridge

University, and also at meetings of other societies including the English Folk Dance Society.[44] At the Royal College of Music, he was introduced by Maud Karpeles to the composer Ralph Vaughan Williams—an active member of the Folk Song Society and English Folk Dance Society—and also to Gustav Holst.[45] Tracey was strongly advised to record as much African folk music as possible and to leave the analysis for others to conduct, from their armchairs, later on. Tracey recalled how both composers assured him

> that recording would be the more important task and that musical analysis, notation, and other analytical considerations could wait till later. What was urgently needed were recordings of genuine African compositions to determine the extent and nature of their oral culture as there were, at that time, no such recordings available from the record trade, which concentrated on "popular," "best-selling" and classical items for a western audience.[46]

When Tracey returned to Southern Rhodesia, he had decided that his research for the Carnegie Corporation would "concentrate on recordings and leave the final analysis to those who in time would become capable of such work, without worrying . . . over much." He hoped that "the recordings themselves would provide the evidence and certain proof of the nature of this unexplored branch of world folk music."[47] Collecting and sponsoring institutions such as the English Folk Dance Society and the Library of Congress clearly influenced his initial recording aims. Prior to the period of his major recording tours, in 1944 Tracey had written a letter to the Library of Congress, seeking support and funds for his work. His assessment of recordings of African music was that, "the only available material other than my own is to be found in the published catalogues of H.M.V., Columbia and Singer records. . . . Of what is available, most of the music is representative of the hybrid culture taught primarily by the missions."[48] For Tracey, recording "unexplored folk music" meant mostly avoiding the popular and the emerging hybrid forms, an ambiguous and unrealizable motive given that he was also to act as quasi talent scout for Gallo. He regularly recorded in contexts and situations that were already infused with hybridity, most notably in mining compounds and in the search for stars such as Jean-Bosco Mwenda, the Congolese guitarist, who could be marketed by Gallo.

Tracey was frustrated at being unable to copy the recordings that were made during his early field trips, and when Columbia Records visited South Africa again in 1933, he decided to take sixteen Karanga musicians down to Cape Town to make a second batch of professional studio recordings. Several of these performers had previously been recorded in Johannesburg in 1929 and this time over fifty items were cut and published by Columbia as part of a series.[49] In a leaflet to accompany the sleeve notes to the record entitled "Eight Native Records by Mashona Natives of Southern Rhodesia," Columbia declared that "these native artists were selected by Hugh Tracey to represent the true type of Shona minstrel, and were taken from their own kraals in the country down to Cape Town." Recorded, and with most individuals remaining unnamed in all the accompanying documentation, the artists were then taken back to their villages. It remains unclear how—or whether—the musicians were compensated.

Upon completion of these recordings and his Carnegie-funded fieldwork, in 1934 Tracey published his first book, *Songs from the Kraals of Southern Rhodesia*. This was a collection of song lyrics in Shona with his translations on facing pages, but with no further commentary or analysis. Due to the evidently broad lack of commercial interest in African folk music from the general settler and outsider public in sub-Saharan Africa, typically the urbanizing middle class and elite that had money to buy gramophone players and other luxury items, Tracey was initially unable to secure more financial support for his work. He reported that "no further research funds were available for such a purpose," and so for the next twelve years he "took up broadcasting as a profession, taking every opportunity of introducing the elements of African music to the South African and other radio audiences."[50]

Tracey was ambitious and often constrained by the need to raise funds and serve patrons and markets. In ILAM's first bulletin in 1956, he announced that although the library was "virtually in its infancy," he hoped "to be able to publish up to 1,000 items per annum, collected from all over Africa, of which only a portion will be suited to the tastes of any one locality."[51] Two years later he announced that the library was

planning to issue approximately 60 or 70 (12-inch) Long Playing records per annum, all items being genuine and authentic examples of African Music which merit permanent recording. The Library's recordings will eventually be representative of all Territories in Africa, South of the Sahara, but at present the majority of our recordings will come from Central and Southern Africa on account of the fact that the Library's main source of income for the time being, must come from those Industrial Members of the Library who require records for the recreation of their own employees.[52]

Prominent among such industrial members were the gold- and diamond-mining companies, which were subsidizing records for recreation at a time when sinister relationships between recreation and retribalization were emerging, rooted in a belief in tribalism based on the "Social Darwinist ideal that rural Africans underwent physical and moral degeneration in the cities,"[53] despite the fact that rural areas had already been profoundly reshaped economically and culturally. Any attempt to map sound recordings onto retribalized conceptions of African people could clearly be used in the service of oppressive colonial policies for segregated control of land and populations.

To cover the cost of recording and producing records, ILAM effectively developed as a subscription library, collecting corporate and ordinary membership fees (see figure 1.2). Corporate members included a number of mining companies and municipalities of Southern Africa, and ordinary members included a range of academics and other individuals, parties, and patrons. Tracey explained his rationale to Maud Karpeles.

> Corporate Members are, as a rule, Governments, Municipalities and the larger industries such as Mines, etc. These all pay us £100 per annum. In actual fact they make a direct contribution towards the expenses of field recording, editing, processing and publishing records. No further expense, other than the cost of any records they may care to buy, is required.[54]

With the exception of a few recordings that were to be made commercially available via Gallo Records, most of Tracey's recordings were initially published only for members. In 1958 Tracey explained the limited size of the audience for his recordings.

> Records are not sold to the general public as they are only printed in a limited edition of 100 copies each. Were records sold to the general public they would cost approximately £6 per item, but there is no intention at present of disposing of Library records except to Members.[55]

By 1960, Tracey stated that "the general objective" of ILAM was "to publish within the next ten years up to 2,000 LP discs or tapes of representative African music while there is still a reasonable prospect of being able to do so."[56] In 1963 he expressed his dismay at the paucity of the material he had managed to collect by then, lamenting that

FIGURE 1.2 Hugh Tracey in the Old ILAM at Msaho, Roodepoort, ca. 1960s. *Photo* © ILAM.

we are still abysmally ignorant of the general music of the whole Continent, in fact, we don't have anything like enough music upon which African music can be detailed sufficiently accurately to write the necessary textbooks.... Our records indicate how utterly ignorant we have been in the past and the vast extent of the work still to be done, if Africa is not to be merely parasitic upon the musics of other people.[57]

In a letter written to Alan Lomax in the same year, Tracey acknowledged that his own recordings were "but a sampling of each district through which I travelled."[58] He also recognized the limits of his achievements when he listed, in a retrospective survey of the scope of the work of ILAM up until 1969, the territories he had been able to visit.

The scope of the work may thus be taken as a random sampling of the indigenous music as it appeared, much of it by chance, along the route of my recording tours. A different but equally haphazard route would no doubt have revealed equally interesting data. The fact that few Africans and almost no

Europeans could direct me to the musicians of note within their own districts adds to the random element in sampling.[59]

He continued to claim that "very little genuine African material [was] available" and that apart from his own recordings, he "could not guarantee more than a dozen recordings or so of African folk material."[60] His writings so often invoke a simplistic binary opposition between commercially available recordings and the actual "home" music made by most Africans. That people were increasingly migrating to towns and becoming "detribalized" and influenced by a mixture of urban and imported music greatly concerned Tracey. His views are intermittently reactionary, as when he dismissed commercial recordings and their bias for approximating American jazz as being "pornographic material," meaning "the great bulk of African social music remains unrecognised, unrecorded and so far as the detribalized and the pupils of the Mission schools are concerned, despised in theory because few of them have the least idea what African music sounds like."[61] He believed that the availability of commercial records merely meant that it had become "possible to obtain a representative set of the Hybrid Euro-African stuff, which frankly from a musical standpoint is very dull and sterile, being strangled at birth by the constant reiterations of the three common chords ad nauseam."[62] He blamed the record companies and European/Christian missionaries for preferring "the three common chords" rather than attempting to value or understand local and idiomatic modes, scales, and meanings. He even claimed that Gallo "at first refused to publish any item [of his] that did not have a guitar in it."[63] Consequently, most of Tracey's recordings were collected in order to publish content that was in addition to, or distinctive from, the repertoire of more commercial recordings.

In a 1959 review of the first forty-five of the eighty LPs that had by then already been published in the *Sound of Africa*, Reverend Arthur Morris Jones, a White Catholic missionary who was also researching African music, praised both the rare content and the technical quality of Tracey's recordings. He wrote that Tracey "has definitely set out to record all that is of importance in African musical culture," and "the great value of his series of records" was that "no facet of music seems to have escaped his attention. There are examples of solo performance, both vocal and instrumental, male and female; call and response choruses, with or without instrumental accompaniment; work- and non-work songs; self-delectative songs;[64] songs and music for social occasions; instrumental recordings of great and fascinating variety."[65] Jones argued that the *Sound of*

Africa represented an important advance in the academic study of African music because previously "research workers have had to depend mainly on commercial recordings," a method that was unsatisfactory because it relied on the musicianship of "detribalized" Africans.[66] Tracey also believed that the practices of commercial recording companies were responsible for creating an image of primitivism among the general public, which is an accusation that he would later come to regularly face himself. He felt that because the recording companies were focusing on urban and commercial recordings, the older more rural "tribal" music was becoming both marginalized and romanticized to such an extent that it was being reduced to simple and clichéd stereotypes. In a letter to Volkmar Wentzel at the National Geographic Society, Tracey highlighted some of the grossly simplified prejudices that people commonly expressed after listening to his recordings of "traditional" African music. He had noticed that

> everyone wanted African music to sound like *their* idea of African music, dark . . . primitive . . . and sex stimulating through that famous RHYTHMIC characteristic of all known dark-skinned people. BUT, at the same time, they maintained, it must be couched in musical terms understood by simple whites, that is *with the three common chords attached*. Educationists with the best PhD's shared the same reservations and so taught only tonic and dominant music to African students; missionaries believed unquestioningly in the "uplifting" effect of the sacred common chords and the vast superiority of a simple white hymn tune over the hordes and chords of African primitive, heathen "warriors" and "witch-doctors."[67]

Contradictions riddle the rhetoric that accompanies the recording project. On the one hand, Tracey rejected the primitivism imposed by a general Euro-American public schooled on commercial recordings and listening through Western ears, and yet the explanatory terms Tracey searched for were so often couched in his essentialized and racist language that could feed policies of separate development. He regularly critiqued missionaries and rejected beliefs that Western music was superior to African music, and yet local concepts and perspectives on music were subsumed under his own aesthetic criteria for organizing and publishing material.

His voice, which "seemed to belong to a distant era even in the series' heyday," often sounds "cringemakingly patronising today," and his views on cultural development were archaic even for the 1950s. "While organizations like the ANC were trying to foster supra-tribal African identity," writes Mark Hudson, Tracey "still saw ethnicity as the root of cultural vitality."[68] As an "instinctive populist," Hudson notes, he also furthered the careers of some neo-urban musicians such as the Congolese guitarist Jean-Bosco Mwenda, and launched the journal *African Music* that showcased some progressive musicologists, both Black and White. Tracey's recordings and his organization of mine dances largely "promoted music that encouraged an imagined tribal purity over an urban working-class hybridity,"[69] as he became established "not only as *the* expert on African music but virtually embodied white interest in African music."[70]

David Coplan has argued that Tracey's "view that indigenous pre-colonial music was both superior and more worthy of dissemination and development than urban popular hybrids . . . led him to concentrate on 'traditional' music."[71] Although Tracey did demonstrate a clear preference for those styles that he judged to be the "truly indigenous" styles of African music—by which he meant those that he believed owed little or nothing to Western musical influences—evidence shows that Tracey also recorded and presented African music as a dynamic art form. In 1959 he rejected the accusation that the African Music Society was "solely interested in preserving specimens of an outmoded art which must give place entirely to the 'modern' music of the west." Rather, its aims were "to bring to light new and complex examples of African music which are representative of the vitality of present-day indigenous composers and whose lyrics reflect the evolving scene around them."[72] It is through some of these documented contradictions that his archive appears to contain a more healthily diverse sample of music making across many parts of Africa than has been assumed by many. A superficial survey of the field recordings made by Tracey might characterize him as operating firmly within the late nineteenth- to early twentieth-century paradigm of salvage ethnography, defined as "any ethnographic study which is carried out in order to document cultures or institutions which are disappearing or expected to disappear in the near future."[73] Yet this did not entirely preclude his recording new, modern, and hybrid forms of African music. In 1966 the *New York Times* reported how Tracey had stressed his keen interest in the continuity and vitality of African musical expression, and not merely the preservation of a diminishing or decaying art form. He is quoted as saying that he and his team were "not antiquarians," but rather were "dealing with a dynamic process." A process perceived to be threatened by the immense ruptures of rural to urban migration, "African music will not remain the same," he explained, "but if we can get this project started in time, it will be possible for African music, as it changes, to retain its basic integrities, its continuity."[74] Tracey identified the field recording—the basis for his analysis, codified theories, and future textbooks—as an essential tool to bridge different listening environments, a technology to aid the continuity of musical memory.

Tracey documented many examples of emerging guitar styles, including township jive, as well as African adaptations of Christian masses and other examples of changes in local church music. Gerhard Kubik reminds us that "in the 1950s and 1960s only a handful of individuals were even taking note of the new traditions that were coming up in some of the urban centers of West, Central, East and Southern Africa."[75] He argues that Tracey was, consequently, somewhat unique in that "*he*, unlike . . . purist ethnomusicologists of that era, did not discriminate against African traditions of more recent date."[76] As Tracey travelled across sub-Saharan Africa he sprinkled his correspondence, lectures, and publications with many observations of musical change, emerging styles, and forms, and his writings and recordings indicate that he sometimes operated beyond the remit of a folk music salvager. Presenting a 1954 radio broadcast on his survey of the music of the Union (i.e., South Africa) and Basutoland for Johannesburg's SABC—while using records to illustrate the musical varieties he had encountered—Tracey wondered aloud exactly what sounds could truly represent the music of contemporary South Africa, having just established ILAM.[77] He asked of his audience,

> which sound is the most representative of present-day South African native life in our complex country? The jiving of Johannesburg? . . . The instruments of the countryside? . . . The songs of the native schools? . . . Or the hymns of the independent churches? . . . Well, who can say? I think it's a mixture of them all. No wonder it's hard to generalize about South Africa; unless you're very careful you're bound to be wrong.[78]

Any claims that Tracey only wanted to represent a static or "authentic" musical culture are somewhat inaccurate. Neil Lazarus, arguing against what he perceives to be the conservative approach of ILAM and other "traditionalist" African scholars, writes that

> the Traceys' idea of a pure traditional African music is resolutely unhistorical. Like all cultural forms everywhere at all times, African music has been ceaselessly in the process of transformation, as it has moved to assimilate, and to

accommodate itself to, new sounds, new instruments, new tongues, and new social imperatives.[79]

However, such criticism fails to take account of the inconsistencies in Tracey's methods and beliefs. Alongside myriad "traditionalizing" comments written and uttered by Tracey—whose institution he claimed specializes "only upon authentic traditional African music and only a very small proportion of what we have published contains any European influence"—there are also observations and reports demonstrating his admiration for new styles and developments in African music and new forms of urban music.[80] It was, as Wachsmann states, possible to detect "a broadmindedness" in the African Music Society's approach, "namely to rescue the riches of folk music threatened by too rapid innovation and to encourage the innovation that testified to the living quality of African music."[81] Furthermore, Kubik, an ethnomusicologist who has a long-standing association with both Hugh and Andrew Tracey,[82] praises Tracey's research methodology for being unusually open-minded for its time:

> Most important from the viewpoint of methodology was also that Hugh Tracey, as concerns the styles and instruments which he recorded, did not impose selective principles upon his nascent sample right from the beginning, as many others have done, saying "I don't record this or that," because perhaps there was a guitar which at the time was supposed to indicate a Western influence, or symbolised Western influence. Hugh Tracey recorded what existed and what exists, because he respected what exists.[83]

Archival analysis here shows multiple divergent perspectives on the criteria for Tracey's selective decisions motivating his sampling method—both from Tracey himself and other commentators— revealing the archive as a mixture of essentializing or traditionalizing, combined with remarkable glimmers of new and emerging musical innovations. His recordings become fragments that can be opened, splintered, and examined again by multiple future listeners, especially in later decades as the interpretations offered come from more diverse audiences in Africa and beyond.

The founding principles of ILAM are clearly set out in a Companies Act legal document:[84] to "study African music, its ecology and social application,"[85] to "collect in a central library or archive, and . . . classify, process, publish and issue, examples of African music and its allied arts by means of sound recording, film or print,"[86] in order to make these results available for use. It was anticipated that the main users would be "all the Governments of African territories," who would use them for "education and broadcasting";[87] "official, religious and industrial bodies" who could use them "for African welfare and recreation";[88] and "scientific and cultural societies and institutions and . . . interested persons," who would use them "for the study of African sociology, anthropology and linguistics."[89] ILAM, it was generally claimed, would "encourage the work of African composers and artists."[90]

Tracey's driven belief in the urgent need to conduct and then centralize professional research into African music was itself a racially loaded motive given the overriding influence of Western archives and academia working behind the projects. In 1954, by which time ILAM had been established as an independent institution, a letter was sent to John Blacking, Tracey's incoming musicologist, outlining his expected contribution.

> The ultimate objective . . . will be to comment constructively upon all African music passing through our hands from whatever African source: to develop ways and means of achieving accurate analysis; to consider, when we have sufficient data, the question of suitable notations, and, ultimately, to undertake the writing of text-books for the many Education Departments of Africa south of the equator, for whom no authoritative works of reference as yet exist, other than a few brief monographs from widely separated areas.[91]

Tracey wanted to discover an underlying logic for African music and recognized that this would require data to help analyze the music on its own terms, rather than translating everything in terms used in Western musicological analyses. "The African," he wrote,

> does not exist as a single entity in a musical sense, but rather as a large number of distinctive cultural units, each with its own modal preferences to which it has every right. The commonly held illusion that the western tempered scale possesses some divinely appointed right over all others cannot be substantiated. It may be convenient for western purposes but is not practical in Africa at the present time.[92]

Much of Tracey's writing throughout the late 1960s and 1970s claims retrospectively that his earlier recordings and research exist as proof of the urgent need to continue to record, analyze, codify, and publish local music. Tracey's codification primer specified that one of the main outcomes of the proposed work would be "*the establishment of accepted and logical terms suited to African phenomena,*" suggesting that he was absorbing at least some anthropological ideas. Such terms and definitions would "eventually make comparative musicology a practical study, firstly between African musics, and secondly with world musics."[93] Tracey also emphasized that his proposed research would "*provide deep satisfaction to African musicians in the future* in having their own poetry and musics culturally recognized for their intrinsic merit as never before,"[94] and that "far from being a study of obsolete phenomena," his codification would "*establish the virtue of continuity* in their artistry."[95]

Living artistry is almost always a product of hybrid forms and influences, even in communities ostensibly living in extreme isolation. Tracey wrote extensively about what he perceived to be the most significant threats to the "indigenous" music of Africa, underlining his fears about loss of "purity" and tradition, and his insistence on an imagined authenticity. He constantly published, broadcast, and lectured on his beliefs that imports of gramophone records, Western instruments, and a gathering tide of missionaries were conspiring to suffocate the genius of local musical expression. His writings regularly invoke this overly simplistic set of oppositional forces between the "external" and the "indigenous."[96] "Winds from foreign regions may bend the bough," he wrote as part of a mission statement in his 1973 catalogue for the *Sound of Africa*, but the purpose of his recorded survey was "to illustrate the nature of the tree of African music standing with its roots in its own African soil."[97] When Tracey intervened as an outsider dedicated to recording the varieties of local music making commonly overlooked by the commercial recording industry, he seemed to embrace more contradictions. He built an internationally legible career as a spokesperson for African music—as someone who could point toward, and try to translate and elucidate, some of its lesser-known principles, techniques, and styles—while binding the exposition to an archive-building structure that at its own time could never realistically allow any direct representation, explanation, or instruction from African voices.

LOCATING LOCAL CONCEPTS

Tracey lamented how it was "some measure of the actual state of the arts in Africa that the recognised authorities on almost any branch of this subject are not indigenous Africans themselves but those whose immediate origins are outside Africa." He claimed he was eagerly looking forward "to the appearance of indigenous art critics who have sufficient knowledge, integrity and wisdom to make a real contribution to African artistic life in the future."[98] In a 1964 editorial in *African Music* he announced that, although "the expounding of the theory of

African musical techniques to non-Africans will continue to have an exotic and intellectual virtue, as will the teaching of non-African musics to Africans," the real challenge, as he saw it, was

> to find a body of articulate men and women who will . . . undertake the discipline of actual performance and have the ability to convey their knowledge to Africans in terms related to African instruments, modality and circumstance. These are the foundations of the art which educationally speaking, have hardly yet been excavated, let alone constructed.[99]

"It was no coincidence," argues Garret Felber, "that Tracey had been active in engineering the 'traditional' African dances of the mine compounds and his recordings were used extensively at the SABC on Bantu Radio."[100] Given the subsequent accusations that Tracey was complicit in separate development with his interest in the purity of tribalized or retribalized music, what motivated his search for local theories of musical artistry? And why did he feel that, rather than the ideas and practice that were already established and developed locally, this knowledge needed to emerge at a later historical moment?

Tracey and John Blacking both claimed to have detected an almost complete absence of local concepts about music, although without providing any direct evidence to support their claims. Tracey asserted that "most African musicians . . . do not, and cannot conceptualise the details of their forms of music in a manner which would enable them to explain it in scientific terms and to write textbooks on the subject for example." His self-appointed role was to discover and "establish the logic of the rules which govern African music making and make them available to others who would not be able to discover them unaided."[101] Blacking, ILAM's first musicologist, reported that he found it "impossible to discuss music and musical concepts in detail with Venda informants,"[102] only later developing the insight that to understand Venda songs he must try to learn as a Venda child would learn.

Dave Dargie—a South African ethnomusicologist of Scottish descent and documenter of multiple forms and styles of Xhosa music making—claims that during the course of his research during the 1980s among Xhosa people at the Catholic Lumko Missionary in the former Transkei, he found that "traditionalists (amaQaba) and the 'school people' (abaGqobhoka), do not think in the Western way. Patterns of abstract analysis, which are made so much a part of being a Western educated person, simply are not used, and certainly not in the Western way." He wondered how it was possible that "people who use such highly-developed rhythm, harmony, polyphony, such variations in scales, who are so aware of the overtones of bow and voice, how is it that these people use no terms for these realities?"[103] Tracey claimed, more generally, that "Africans have difficulty in discussing music from an aesthetic point of view, in conceptualising the music itself and analysing its qualities."[104] Views such as these are clearly racist, patriarchal, and essentializing in their false search for equivalence. As Steven Feld notes, "wherever there is music, there is some kind of theory underlying its production and significance."[105] Dominating paradigms of "speaking for"—rather than with—people have clearly endured into the present. With so much of the "institutionally prominent literature" about African music still being written by non-Africans, Kofi Agawu pointedly rejects the hierarchical pattern and stance detected through the majority of books on African music that "are written as if there were no readers in Africa."[106] Ultimately, Tracey and other Euro-American scholars and collectors at this time were often fundamentally unable or unwilling to step outside Western intellectual superiority and value or recognize local theories, sensibilities, and views on their own terms.

At the same time, Tracey feared many of the destructive forces he saw as operating to erase African culture. Andrew Tracey noted that "a big needle for Paa [sic] was the fact that whites, the government, the missionaries, had no interest whatever in what he was discovering: Africans could have no culture, no music of any serious interest."[107] Rapidly changing social and political conditions throughout the southern half of the African continent meant that many of the patrons of local music were losing influence or position, leading to a severe decline in local music making in some areas. So "who," appeals Tracey, "will be the patrons of future musicians? Whose the responsibility to maintain their national arts? Universities? Ministries of the Interior? Foreigners? Radio? Radio is a Moloch, rarely if ever, a cornucopia!"[108]

Tracey was frequently disheartened to find examples of local musical arts abandoned in favor of Western musical forms. He felt that African educators and Europeans were overlooking African art forms, declaiming that "African town and school songs have now become the equivalent of the small carved curio figures with their vacant, vacuous features of no meaning."[109] In 1976 he warned Peter Gallo of Gallo (Africa) that "traditional music does not look after itself," because it seems that "when the social situation or custom that goes with the music changes or stops, so does the music, and there goes another piece of the cultural heritage of the country."[110] Many missionaries, it seems, were introducing nonindigenous forms and styles to African music, often with deleterious effects. In correspondence with Tracey, Robert Kauffman, who was working in Southern Rhodesia and was himself a Methodist member of the Division of World Missions, agreed that "missionaries . . . often discouraged the use of indigenous worship materials because they have not properly understood non-European art and expression."[111] Peter Mtuze explicitly calls out the inherent violence deployed when missionaries in the Eastern Cape of South Africa "plunged the amaXhosa into a crisis that has left them directionless, to put it mildly. The total onslaught destroyed their self-respect and their identity."[112] For the contemporary moment in which he was working, Tracey saw himself and others like him as the most able preservers and protectors of this music, while they left it for a future generation of "articulate" African people to delve back into the codified knowledge systems he represented, unlocking and explaining local concepts that would reveal the entire signalling and messaging systems within music making. It was assumed that articulation would inevitably require the training that would be given through ILAM.

RACE AND RECORDING

What could be mapped or coded in a song? Folk musicians, Tracey believed, acted on behalf of their entire society because they were instrumental in articulating and maintaining social mores. In the early 1950s he reported that, during the course of over twenty years of research, he had repeatedly observed how "the musicians and composers in their various societies are the recognised upholders of traditional etiquette, the mouthpiece of accepted social standards of behaviour, the critics of social excesses either in chief or commoner, and to a marked degree the political voice of the inarticulate majority."[113] For Tracey, most of the African songs he experienced in Central and Southern Africa were

> connected with human behaviour, and the problems which beset any community; . . . the problems of gregariousness, social disciplines, what is considered to be good behaviour and good manners; the problems of adolescence, sex and marriage; the problems of defence, attack and violence; the subject of fear of each other both physical and magical, of intimidation, group and political terrorising; . . . preoccupations with force and the rewards of force."[114]

In contrast, he believed that "the commercial songs of professional entertainers, particularly in these days of mechanical reproduction, fall into another category and reveal audience response rather than original artistry."[115]

Yet alongside these romanticized views there endures a patterned inability to detect African agency and power. Tracey's work was, in part, funded by the White-owned mining companies responsible for instilling violence and destroying the social fabric of local communities, the very forces that he decried in his anxiety about the loss of tradition. Contrary to his sentimental views about African culture, he was less rosy about the prospects of African liberation. When he heard subversive songs expressing unrest in Nyasaland and at copper mines throughout Southern Africa, Tracey advised P. H. Anderson, the president of the Transvaal and Orange Free State Chamber of Mines,[116] that "more attention might well be paid to the normal use of African songs and music, bringing them into the open as a natural part of everyday recreation and not allowing them to be ignored by Europeans and, therefore, [become] a nationalist weapon."[117] Tracey recorded and broadcast to help document, preserve, and promote African music to national and international audiences, and yet at the same time he warned of the dangers of local songs becoming forceful self-organizing weapons in the service of nationhood. Furthermore, he believed that African nature was inherently tribal, and that music could be channeled as a tempering force. He thus urged that the study of African music upon a continent-wide basis would "tend to restrain those fierce tribal loyalties which so quickly give place to petty nationalism before tribesmen are capable of taking the larger inter-tribal and more responsible view of the social and economic realities of modern Africa."[118] It seems that if folk songs work to transmit social realities, then control over the content of these messages would be desirable to employers of African labor.

Tracey hoped that his recordings would help produce a mass of data about African social conditions. In 1963 he wrote that his research was not primarily for musical and general educational purposes, as most believed, but was undertaken "mostly on account of the insight into the social conditions of Africa."[119] He was appalled by what he saw as the degrading conditions experienced by migrant workers in the towns and townships, and he believed that the recreation and music that connected workers with their rural roots would help alleviate suffering and feelings of a kind of rootless displacement. This view knowingly ignored the fact that mining companies could broadcast the music as a pleasant distraction from harsh realities, and as a means for workers to safely vent their frustrations. One of ILAM's primary objectives, declared Tracey in 1958, was "to provide authentic material for the immediate recreation of tribesmen who are still in touch with their districts of origin."[120] For Tracey, supplying recordings of folk music in a migrant worker's own language would help the continuity of the worker's own musical expression. He warned that for many African workers, "the change from country living to town in the industrial revolution which world pressures are thrusting upon them in some regions is such a traumatic experience for the generation which has to make the change."[121] Such humanistic concern, however, was clearly tempered by real dangers inherent in serving corporate mining interests. "Tracey's involvement in the racial separatist-driven mine dances of Consolidated Main Reef Mine and the SABC's Bantu Radio," argues Felber, "reveal a complicity in the policies of retribalisation which necessarily complicate his contributions to South African musicology with a deeply conservative notion of cultural preservation and ethnic purity."[122]

These assumptions—that the social and moral strategies of village life are superior to urban life, that they can be transplanted and continue to function in urban environments, and that such transformation can be achieved through sound recordings—have long since been challenged, and they continue to be challenged in and around ILAM today, as the later chapters in this book illustrate. "African culture," argues Coplan, "is not, as we all once supposed, something first manufactured in the 'traditional' countryside and then transported to the city where it is re-modelled and hybridised in the crucible of 'acculturation.'" Rather, "it is a 'culture of mobility,' not merely transported but in practice formulated amidst the experience and organisation of multi-sited, mobile networks of kin, homeboys and girls, and reciprocal friendships."[123] The huge changes experienced by people living in towns and townships throughout Southern Africa would be more likely to lead to entirely new ways of living that might often render the rural values and music from back home redundant in the new urban contexts. Some of Tracey's Euro-American contemporaries were already arguing against naive distinctions between "tribalized" and "detribalized" and rural and urban Africa. Max Gluckman argued that "the Rand mines and the African tribe which supplies their labour are both parts of a single social field" that the laborers were constantly traversing.[124] The *Xhosa in Town* trilogy of books also explored the complicated and interconnected processes of urbanization, compromise, and social change experienced by rural Xhosa people moving to townships around East London in the 1950s–60s.[125] Decades later, in modern-day Zimbabwe, Thomas Turino also negated any simple divide between town and country, recognizing how "indigenous beliefs remain powerful in urban, working-class townships as well as in rural areas."[126] If music and culture here is hybrid and mobile, recordings alone as sound objects might actually ossify, preserving particular moments in time within a tradition. Conversely, the collection of a series of new recorded snapshots of music made across time, as well as creative circulation of all recordings, could work to avoid freeze-drying musical expression.

Tracey believed that recording and studying indigenous African music, as well as generating increased respect for local cultures, would also improve social relations between different races. ILAM existed, he stated,

> for the purpose of improving social and industrial relations between the races of Africa—not only by making African people more aware of the importance of their contribution towards the proper recreation and culture of their own people, but also as a means of information and instruction to European personnel who hold responsibility for the social well-being of African both in town and country, and especially in urban and industrial town-ships.[127]

He acknowledged that this would ultimately mean African musicians taking full ownership of the whole process. "African music is African," he stated, and although "we whites have already provided the means for its proper study and cherishing," ultimately "it is the African students who must be responsible for its excellence or its demise."[128] He acted both to reinforce racial distinctions — through his continuing generalizations about African people and culture—and sought to erase them altogether, in language that unwittingly yet presciently anticipated #AllLivesMatter.[129] "If we act without cringing or toadying, without a false sense of guilt for being white in Africa, or a false sense of pride in being black," he romanticized, "but rejoicing in the poetry and artistry of both races it will make us the more keenly aware of the common humanity of others."[130] Paulette Coetzee is alert to Tracey's conflicting identities. She writes that, "although Tracey did not challenge white political or economic supremacy, he did challenge certain common colonial attitudes towards blackness."[131] However, Coetzee argues, Tracey's project also "had clear connections with whiteness as violence," including the constraining (and often demeaning) representations of Africans, and "as de facto agent of mining companies and colonial governments," Tracey "was directly associated with systems which relied upon routine coercion and force for their daily maintenance."[132] Almost no self-reflection on the realities of these enabling mechanisms of the excesses of colonialist capitalism can be found within ILAM's own archives.

Tracey's drive to expand ILAM and to codify the music of Africa lost some momentum when it began to run out of funding during the 1970s. Nationalist Party politics in South Africa had already begun to alienate the opinion of the rest of the world and overseas benefactors refused to fund a project that was

White operated and based at Krugersdorp near Johannesburg. With the exception of a small bursary from its education department that funded John Blacking's appointment as ILAM's musicologist in the mid 1950s, Tracey and ILAM received little support from the South African government. By 1970 Tracey claimed that ILAM was internationally recognized and that it had always made it "a cardinal point never to allow political considerations of any kind to interfere with the integrity and social worth of music to African peoples everywhere."[133] ILAM, he continued either idealistically or strategically, always dealt with "music and musicians quite regardless of their race, creed or government."[134] He noted that although ILAM was situated in South Africa, "the Library itself is a continent-wide organization with no political affiliations, and is concerned with the musics of all Africa south of the Sahara."[135] However, as Coetzee points out, while Tracey would appeal to mining companies and the Department of Native Affairs for support, ILAM was formally established under White European control by definition, and its "official constitution as a Section 21 (non-profit) company in South Africa was itself shaped by apartheid legislation." She argues that "as its racial structure under apartheid legislation did not provide for representation from independent African states on the basis provided for colonial powers, it would no longer be properly 'international' after European withdrawal from the rest of Africa."[136] Coetzee also reveals how "ILAM's correspondence files contain evidence of numerous appeals to the South African Government for support"—including an invitation to the departments of Native Affairs and Native Education to join as members—and argues that although "Tracey's attempts at enlisting membership from apartheid bureaucracy proved unsuccessful, it was certainly not for lack of trying on his part."[137]

ILAM appears and evolves within a messy network of political crosswinds. Idealistically pan-African in ambition and scope, yet Tracey remained averse to documenting and representing liberation struggles while he worked alongside governmental institutions that controlled and exploited African labor. So who or what was Tracey truly listening to?

AN AUDIENCE IN AFRICA

Throughout much of Tracey's writings, it is not always made clear for whom the recordings were intended. At times they seem designed for foreign edification, and at other times they seem to be intended purely for African consumption. In 1957, Tracey had written that his *Sound of Africa* series was going to be printed in runs of 100 twelve-inch LPs and that these records would "only be available to Corporate and Ordinary Members for recreational and study purposes."[138] A decade later, Tracey wrote—using Social Darwinist terms while assuming that social forms tend to develop toward the more complex—that the major objective of ILAM's codification project was "to provide African and not European musicians with a working knowledge of the theory of their own art and a suitable musical literacy which is essential once they are beyond the stage of composing and performing by ear alone."[139] Tracey had previously explained the difference between his two published series, the *Sound of Africa* and the *Music of Africa*:

> Our Library is now publishing its own series of long playing records for special study and for recreational purposes among tribesmen particularly over the radio and among those who come to work in the mines and other industrial areas. They are 12-inch discs and they contain more authentic African music than any other series ever published. They are not, however, published primarily for a European or white listener but for the African, so they have not been specially selected for an evening's entertainment of persons foreign to Africa as was my 'Music of Africa' Series which was published by Decca (on their London label for the States).[140]

By 1961 he had been forced to admit that the local markets and demand were not large enough to sustain the production of his recordings, in part because few could afford the necessary technology. He reported that

> The budget of the Library is mostly dependent upon grants, both on account of the fact that the demand for African recordings by Africans themselves, who possess few phonographs for their reproduction, is quite inadequate to cover Library costs in the discovery, recording, and reproduction of discs, and from the fragmentation of African languages which limits the circulation of music to within relatively small tribal units. Although the overall collection demonstrates most clearly the outlines of an established and general African musical culture, the isolationism of the individual dialects restricts African musical horizons to within strictly parochial limits.[141]

Despite these restrictions in circulation, Tracey tried to gather local African advocates for his recordings. Having secured a Ndola Lottery Committee Grant in 1959,[142] he set about distributing copies of his records, accompanied by a portable gramophone, to educational institutions throughout Southern Africa. In December 1959, writing to H. C. Finkel, director of African education in

Salisbury, to offer a set of his recordings as a free gift, Tracey explicitly requested local feedback.

> It is . . . of the greatest consequence to our work that intelligent African men and women shall have access to these recordings and, having absorbed with keen attention the complexities which they represent from the social, linguistic, poetic, physical and musical points of view, that they express their opinions of the value of distributing such a collection as a contribution towards their intellectual maturity.[143]

He explained that he had already received "a great number of statements of approval on the part of Europeans who readily appreciate the value of this work," but only a "few responses from articulate Africans."[144] Colonel Boardman, ILAM's library manager during the 1960s, even designed an exam that would help train African mine workers to broadcast selections of these recordings to their fellow workers. His exam included a series of questions designed to encourage trainees to think about the listening and recreation habits of mine workers and to relate this to the content of the *Sound of Africa* recordings.[145] Tracey was also planning to help train local musicians and artists to record themselves in order to capture the varieties in their respective styles of music. He wrote that although it was not generally known or acknowledged that Africans were still composing new music, especially since music fashions changed with the seasons and years, he intended "to instruct those who are interested in the art of cutting discs and in the finer points in 'balancing' musicians or singers to make effective recordings." He hoped that "from these local discs" he would then be able to "reproduce pressed records for educational or general purposes and thus ensure that the work of the best African composers will never go by default."[146] However, the entirety of Tracey's directorship of ILAM yields barely a single directly documented local response to recordings. The available evidence is almost exclusively only reported indirectly by Tracey and his network.

Coetzee states that "metropolitan whiteness may assume the mantle of universality without reflection"—a type of invisibility by virtue of its normalization—while "colonial whiteness can be prone to overt self-assertion,"[147] a highly and visibly performed spectacle often designed to inspire respect and fear, while in search of knowledge of others in order to maintain control. "Intelligent"? "Articulate"? Tracey's sweeping pronouncements on African intelligence must be challenged. Constructed through the gaze of this performed Whiteness that is self-portrayed as central to knowledge production and reception, Coetzee sees that "African musicians are objectified as part of the discovery, requiring Western representation and dissemination—the production and circulation of texts as cultural capital within established discourses."[148] If Tracey was targeting a particular class of African intellectual, he was also likely to be reproducing some of the class structures he claimed to be working against. African intellectuals in the nineteenth and early twentieth century, argues Mcebisi Ndletyana, "were a product of the missionary enterprise and the British civilizing mission." Often Christian converts and graduates from missionary schools, they "were part of a new middle class that the colonial agents wanted as a buffer between colonial society and the rest of the indigenous population," and "intended to become part of the civilising mission themselves."[149] Tracey again occupies ambiguous and contradictory positions, analogous to the bind he is caught in when promoting local African expression and welfare, while appealing to the government agents of repressive control for membership, support, and markets.

RECORDING SHADOWS

While seeking to document the continuity of expression and performance in African music, Tracey felt that his recordings, although never intended to be sufficient or complete documents on their own, could be invaluable resources for recreating performances and styles. He asked rhetorically,

> Is African music worth preserving? Depends on what you mean by "preserv-ing." You cannot *preserve* an oral music (you can record it). You then have to re-create it with each performance and it evolves a little each time. It is the continuity which should be encouraged, to leave open the channels of performance.[150]

Tracey wanted his recordings to be of definite practical use to African and inter-national students, and their success could be evaluated when he, or any student, reflected whether they came to "appreciate the music to the extent of being able to participate," or whether they "remain[ed] outside the magic circle, an observer but not a partner in the music making?"[151]

Later in his career, Tracey warned researchers about the limitations of re-cording. "To obtain a recording of a song or tune in Africa," he reflected, "is sometimes considered to be more significant than the creation and local use of the composition itself." Outsiders—he felt—often believed that "to analyse a recording of an African piece of music is . . . better than learning to perform the music with its creators and thus knowing it from the inside."[152] Instead of fetishizing recorded and archived sounds, we must

> never allow the recorded shadow to obscure the living object, the primary meaning of artistry within its natural or social context to be obscured by the use of a recording out of its setting, except with constant acknowledgement to the original environment and the creators of the art. If we fail to appreciate the function of the music in its initial environment we risk losing the whole meaning of its artistry, and it becomes just another form of intellectual commerce sold over the counter to titillate idle interest, a plaything to be discarded at will without further meaning or function.[153]

He urged all research personnel to be constantly aware that the "primary concern is with the African composer," and that all other "artifice . . . recordings . . . lists . . . classifications and . . . books are but a means to that end and not the end in itself."[154] Tracey had always believed that recordings were immensely valuable data that could enhance understanding of local concepts of music, and he now determined that their primary purpose was to encourage and inspire the composers who created and recreated their living art form. As early as 1954—after he had only just founded ILAM—he noted that, although there was "a certain virtue in collecting examples as widely as possible,"

> the social value of so doing will not be found upon the library shelves which house our collections, but rather in two collections outside the library; in the recognition of talent which traditional methods have brought to perfection and an understanding of the rules and methods by which social music is likely to be most effective as time goes on.[155]

One of the greatest difficulties Tracey would face in seeking to make his recordings relevant to communities in Africa was sustaining connections with local, social, and practical mechanisms to keep them circulating and being heard and used within daily life. A general sampling survey or a musicology focused on recording would continue to be challenged by other voices asking to be heard: anthropological fieldworkers and, ultimately, local demands for different types of access and use that could reimagine and repurpose an archive that both worked against, and benefitted from, oppressive and violent colonial structures, departments, and policies. A recording project that was initially marketed as "a commercially oriented enterprise, selling records to industrialists and administrators with the implied promise of producing contented workers who would not be inclined to struggle for political rights or higher pay,"[156] is also the same project that imagined African folk music elevated through international recognition as one of the great musics of the world. Can such blatant contradictions even be resolved? In the next chapter I focus in more closely on Tracey's sound collections, analyzing the influences, techniques, and intentions that shaped the content of his field recordings, while uncovering more of the forces that included and excluded particular voices. A detailed composite picture of the crucible forging the recordings contextualizes what the sound fragments do—and do not—contain. Eventually, decentering Tracey the collector and listening through the collections makes it possible to take the fragments back to some of the very people whose cultures have been mined to make them.

TWO

Listening behind Field Recordings

Warming our fronts round a log fire under the sparkling dome
of a Rhodesian night is the setting in which I heard and joined
in the chorus of the songs of the Shona minstrels, laughed till I ached at
their jokes and stories, talked gossip and discussed hut-tax, cattle, religion,
or what the world was coming to. For hours on end I have watched their
dances, and been nearly deafened yet enthralled by the drums. I have played
drums with them till my hands were numb with beating and I knew what
the elevation of rhythm really meant to one who participates and not only
looks on. While they were absorbed with the music I would slip round and
observe each player or singer, and with the recording gear all set
out on the trailer, make a gramophone record, one of my "boys"
holding the microphone in his hand near the singer, the player
or the drummer, whoever it might be at the time.

Hugh Tracey[1]

At their best, recordings act as a form of eavesdropping, where it is as if the
musician is speaking directly to you, whispering in your ear in a privileged
way that rises above ordinary experience and takes on a confessional air.

Ian Brennan[2]

Alongside practical technique, key relationships shaped Tracey's recordings, both
corporate and more personal ones. His work with Gallo Records illuminates his
links with the commercial recording industry more generally. On the personal
side, it is notable that developed relationships rarely seemed to extend to African artists, researchers, or educators. Together with his ambivalence toward
anthropological fieldwork, an absence of local relationships greatly shaped what

was, and was not, captured in his recordings. Tracey's articles, fieldnotes, and correspondence reveal a "fascinating record of sidelong glances" toward the anticolonial independence movements across Southern Africa.[3] This tendency to skate over the political context corresponds with Tracey's overall reluctance to study local social life, knowledge, and experience with any sustained immersion. With his recording lens and reporting eye focused on the search for what he considered to be the true excellence of high-quality musicianship, Tracey rarely addressed political or social life directly in any depth, which slowly became erased and forgotten in his aestheticized sound objects. Decoupling sound from motivations for other messaging in performance would most likely miss the force of the messaging. "While colonial ethnomusicology coopted 'tribal dances' for ideological domination," writes Mhoze Chikowero, "nationalists antithetically deployed African traditions as an indigenous episteme to articulate different political ideologies and conceptions of selfhood."[4] Tracey's musicological focus is reflected in the content of the recordings themselves, and the methods he used in capturing and producing them. Focusing closely on the collecting and collection with a detailed examination of Tracey's recording practices, I listen behind and underneath the recordings and uncover some of the erasures inherent in recorded fragmentation, hearing a process of slow retreat from the cultured generative soil feeding bodies and sounds. I am also searching for any evidence that will help design and establish methods and ideas for future curation, the radical reinsertion of sound back into context, and ideas for locally driven spaces for the curation of live performance in context and in situ.

One of Tracey's primary and consistent concerns was to produce high-quality professional field recordings that were always intended for publication and circulation, and for practical use within commercial, academic, and local worlds. Acknowledging that he had "only attended universities as a lecturer," and that "the bush" was really his "university,"[5] he belongs firmly among a lineage of pioneering collectors who were never officially trained as fieldworkers or scholars. Tracey's most productive recording decades — the 1950s and 1960s — represent a period when technologies and techniques were rapidly improving, at a time when musicologists and anthropologists competed to establish disciplinary legitimacy for their own favored methods. In the 1970s theory and practical technique were jostling for preeminence when, as Helen Myers argues, "excellence in technology became linked with bi-musicality through the charismatic and idiosyncratic figures of [Mantle] Hood and philosopher-musicologist, Charles Seeger," although "for scholars of anthropological persuasion, their work was theoretically weak."[6] This widening rift between the practical making of ethnomusicological artifacts and the theoretical concepts from social and cultural theory is clearly on display throughout the development of the International Library of African Music (ILAM) under Tracey, and now resonates differently within contemporary ethnomusicology and sounds studies, as some artists and scholars advocate for the validity of arguments and theories constructed and represented as, and through, sound and recording. Sounding arguments in sound.

Tracey was a charismatic and contradictory personality. His stated aims and expertise vacillated between the practical, the technical, and the scholarly, as his methods and resultant analysis operated somewhere between a more heavily musicological approach and, intermittently, a socially oriented one. Tracey's books, writings, and broadcasts display a clear interest in the behavioral and social contexts for African music. Yet the surface details and imagery gleaned from rapidly moving surveying and recording trips reveal his ambivalence toward immersive anthropological research, which would become a defining method for most ethnomusicologists following Alan Merriam's insistence that analysis of sound cannot be separated from social context.[7] The significance of Tracey's research orientation is especially evident when comparing his methods with those of John Blacking, ILAM's first resident musicologist for short periods during the 1950s. Tracey's reluctance to embrace anthropology is an unusual decision, especially considering the fact he was no armchair-bound theorist, and was based permanently in and travelled widely across Southern Africa. Tracey's research and recording project was also constantly in search of credibility and the approval of academic allies. Some ethnographers, such as E. E. Evans-Pritchard—one of only very few individuals attempting to analyze African music in context at this time—were already producing detailed studies of African song and dance as Tracey embarked on his recording career. In a 1928 analysis of the *gbere buda* ("beer dance") of the Azande people of South Sudan, Evans-Pritchard identified that "accurate work on songs can only be done with the phonograph."[8] He, like Tracey, recognized that the quality and significance of African music and dance were largely being neglected by Western scholars, and that even ethnographers tended to undervalue dance, which was "often viewed as an independent activity and . . . described without reference to its contextual setting in native life."[9] Although Tracey may have ultimately struggled to find and establish any sustained method for contextual analysis of music and dance, unlike many scholars operating at the time he devoted his ear and energies to making extremely high-quality recordings for broader circulation. And these recordings have weathered much better than some of his language and speculations.

SCRIBBLES AND SOAP:
TRACEY'S EARLIEST RECORDINGS

Tracey developed a field-recording technique that was designed to meet the highest professional standards. He claimed that he had spared no effort in making his "records of African music as effective as any studio recordings elsewhere."[10] He refined, and regularly wrote about, his recording techniques and tours that roamed across half a continent over four decades, and he argued that the true assessment of the value of his records was to be found in the degree to which they made it possible to participate in the music they contained.

Tracey began his recording career by scribbling lyrics and song texts in notebooks as he listened to Karanga workers singing in the tobacco fields of Southern Rhodesia. He quickly understood the need to capture the exact stress and tone of the words he heard and the necessity of memorizing the songs and stories in order to learn them properly. Tracey recalled how, when among Karanga musicians singing and working, he was moved by "the need to memorise exactly the vernacular words of an African song if you wanted to follow the melody and to sing it with them."[11] This was not only because of "the stress pattern of the spoken words," but also due to the fact that "the speech inflexions as well were reproduced faithfully in the flow of the melody," a common aspect in tonal languages. As Tracey became more adept at singing alongside Karanga workers, some of them would set him simple tests, for example, challenging him "to recite correctly the solo part of a well-known local song and fit it accurately into the repeated refrain."[12]

Tracey's desire to remember and participate in singing led him to make his first field recordings, most of which proved to be ephemeral. Andrew Tracey recalls that his father's first device recorded on soap: "it was a recorder which scratched a groove in a soaped disk, and you couldn't play it back, it had to be processed first."[13] During Tracey's Carnegie-sponsored travelling fellowship in 1931, he recorded over 600 items on plain aluminum discs and reported that "following on the advice of Prof. Hornbostel of Berlin,"[14] he was now "relying more upon phonograph records of this music than upon notation only, which at this stage must inevitably be inadequate and far from satisfactory."[15] He observed that, although "the rhythm of native music is such as to defy accurate transcription upon first or brief acquaintance," his own recent embossed aluminum recordings could "be played on any ordinary gramophone with fibre needles, giving very fair results."[16] However, being fully aware of the extreme limitations of making recordings that could not be duplicated, Tracey again "took Karanga musicians down south [to Cape Town] to take advantage of the temporary visit of another professional team of recording engineers."[17] At this relatively early stage of ethnographic recording, Tracey's links to publishing networks clarified for him the importance of the professional standards required for reproducibility.

Tracey's two professional recording sessions in studios in Johannesburg and Cape Town would prove to be key early influences on the development of all of his later field-recording techniques. These recording sessions taught him the studio values of arranging and directing musicians in a series of takes in order to frame and clearly present what he felt were the best examples of musicianship, shaped to feed the growing consumer markets in urban centers throughout Africa—and all ideally taped inside three minutes. Half a century later he still clearly remembered the acoustics of the Bree Street Radio Studios in Cape Town, and how he had rehearsed and conducted "his" twelve performers with a prearranged system of hand gestures.

> [T]he studio was a large room that had until recently been part of a disused theatre now draped with curtains, carpets and any material calculated to deaden natural reverberation. It was a scruffy sight when I sat my ragged singers in a circle on the floor and coached them with my hand signals when to start and when to stop their songs.[18]

Patriarchal production and the patronizing language of othering casts Karanga musicians here as adrift at the mercy of Western technology and industry. Moreover, we have no separate account of the musicians' experiences or perspectives—or even all but two of their names—in this process.

Much of Tracey's early recording career was subsidized by South Africa's largest professional record label, Gallo Africa.[19] Gallo began making mainly commercial recordings in 1932, but developed a mutually beneficial relationship with Tracey, providing him with a headquarters for his African Music Research Unit, plus some travelling expenses and the use of its press to publish selections from his recordings. Although Tracey was not formally employed by Gallo, the label's influence on his work is clear, with his emphasis on short high-fidelity items for publication, as well as his role as a quasi talent scout for the label while he was travelling through the villages and mining compounds of much of Southern Africa. Andrew Tracey claimed that, "to say . . . that my father was a 'recording engineer' for Gallo is wrong. He conducted his own research and recording programme, from 1947 under the name African Music Research, from 1954 under the ILAM. Gallo were his first, and in the early years at least, his main sponsors."[20]

Tracey acknowledged that "the interests of [his] research and the publication of commercial records for Africans" were "mutually dependent." "Gallo," he stated, had "also volunteered to house the headquarters of the Society in their new buildings in Johannesburg," and the whole arrangement meant that he could "record a thousand or more discs a year and only publish, for public purposes, a few dozen." Most importantly—for his own independent aims—this also meant that all of his records would "be available for educational purposes."[21] This arrangement was treated as "a gentleman's agreement all along,"[22] with Gallo retaining the right of first refusal to publish within Africa any of Tracey's field recordings. Mutual friends introduced Tracey and Eric Gallo to each other at a time when both were seeking to reach and expand into different markets for recordings of African music. Eric Gallo agreed to a proposition from Tracey, who would

> combine studying the incidence of African folk musics and at the same time record items for his company which he could publish commercially for purchase by the growing African clientele, mostly industrial workers in towns, who were the only section of the African community who could afford spring wound gramophones.[23]

Consequently, Gallo Africa pressed and issued a proportion of his recordings "which they considered had 'popular' sales potential," and both Gallo and Tracey "learned by hard experience how the musical taste of Africa was evolving and what the art of African music entailed."[24] Both men believed that at this time gramophone recordings were the most effective and popular format for publishing African music, and Tracey estimated that the gramophone would be increasingly important in education. In 1947 he noted that "scores of thousands of portable gramophones [were] already in the possession of Africans, and instructional matter recorded on discs [would] thus have a wide field for educational purposes." He added that "gramophones and gramophone records [were] the most economic forms of mechanical reproduction of sound, and likely to play an increasingly important part in African education for many years to come."[25] Tracey's recording aims were, from the beginning, responding to developing markets in urban centers in Southern Africa, and supported by the professional recording industry, which enabled his recorded survey of folk music to continue in villages and in mining compounds.

CONSTRUCTING "GENUINE" FOLK MUSIC

Tracey was driven to record and publish what he believed to be the genuine folk music of Africa. His was "an archive developed through a suspicion of the 'insidious forces' that were taken to 'undermine' African folk tradition."[26] He believed that a permanent record of local or traditional music from villages should be available alongside the extant and more hybrid commercial versions of urban music making. Clear parallels can be drawn with European folksong collecting and revival movements, when collectors—often middle class, White, male, and motivated by varying shades of romantic nationalism—chased a golden age of balladry, searching for rural musicians with the longest cultural memories. As musician and British folksong collector Reg Hall notes, collectors such as Cecil Sharp (1859–1924) "pointed to national airs as the potential raw material for new schools of art music to oust what was held to be the offending influence of European romanticism."[27] Hall adds that such collectors had "no intention of documenting the music-making of those rural workers and their families; the aim was to gather raw material for a minor revolution in art and popular music."[28] Although Sharp's collecting predates the method of documenting music in culture through extended anthropological fieldwork, the start of Tracey's recording career overlaps with some of these nationalist collecting procedures. Tracey regularly spoke of the need to develop national and international appreciation for a "classical" African folk music based on the strength and the varieties of local music throughout Africa.[29] In order for this to even be possible, he considered it necessary to first identify, record, map, and codify what he deemed to be the "truly indigenous" folk music of the continent.

Tracey's recording tours overlapped with, and became part of, the sharp rise in ethnomusicological collecting and publication that fed the expansion of sound archive activity in both Europe and America. In 1944 the Archives Internationales de Musique Populaire in Geneva began issuing its *World Collection of Recorded Folk Music*; in 1946 the Musée de l'homme began issuing ethnomusicological recordings; in 1948 Folkways was founded; in 1955 the *Columbia World Library of Folk and Primitive Music* series edited by Alan Lomax began publication; and in the 1960s the Berlin Phonogramm-Archiv began publishing the *Museum*

Collection series.[30] These institutional publications all attempted, in varying degrees, to document, map, and circulate the multiplicity of styles of indigenous or traditional musics throughout the world.

Although he sometimes tried to find a method of capturing the folk music of Africa within its actual settings, Tracey really began to construct something new through his recordings that were rarely intended to be wholly accurate records of social events. Certain contradictions within his writings reveal a tension between the desire to capture the "authentic" and uninfluenced music of Africa, and the reality that recording was influencing artistry and could easily distort the frame of performances and local perceptions of the value of the music making. For example, lecturing on the art of aural composition, Tracey claimed that when he went out to record he was witnessing "today's music today," and that "no one can say if it will ever be produced in exactly the same way again."[31] The finest and most complex music that he had heard and recorded had, almost without exception, "never required a conductor or been recorded inside a hall,"[32] and yet he often operated as a quasi conductor himself for many of his recordings, both in the studio and out in the field (see figures 1.1 and 2.1). He commonly rearranged and staged performances to suit different acoustic conditions and also the technical limits of his recording equipment. While committed to curating selective snapshots of local music making, Tracey, as Brent Hayes Edwards argues, does not "seem to have taken into account the potential cross-fertilization his continental archive could make possible and the radical implications it could have for musical practice, if isolated pockets of African musicians were actually able to 'hear each other' across great distances through the medium of the archive."[33]

Ethnomusicologist Anthony Seeger argues that the making of ethnographic recordings inevitably leads to the construction of hybrid products. The process involves "a number of decisions based on our own ideas about music and society," as well as "our intentions for the product," which tend to create "something that is entirely new and shaped by our own culture."[34] He notes that the field recordist inevitably makes a variety of subjective decisions, meaning that ethnographic recordings are likely to reflect his or her own specific biases and agendas, especially in an era when recording with communities was far from a collaborative or codesigned process. Surveying a wide range of collections of field recordings, Seeger reflected on the evident patterned biases:

> [P]ublic performances by adult men are the most common in our examples, followed by private performances by very aged carriers of traditions, while private

performances by children are probably the rarest. "Authenticity" and "tradition," however defined, are usually the central criteria for selection, rather than frequency of performance, cultural relevance, or something else. Only small excerpts from complete performances are usually presented, due to recording and playback, economic constraints, and the expectation of our audiences.[35]

Tracey's search for field recordings of "genuine folk music" was often designed in distinction to commercial recordings, despite his self-acknowledged ties to the commercial industry. He repeatedly emphasized that his recordings reflected a living and developing art form — not simply a decaying or dying tradition — yet he often neglected and even resisted the changes heard in new popular styles and instead sought to reinvigorate older ones. In 1956, when still in its infancy, he claimed that ILAM would aim to provide "home music" and a cross-section of the "better" music from towns.[36] Only two years later, in 1958 he announced that "home music" was difficult to obtain outside of one's own local area and that "music recorded in African towns . . . does not reflect the home music of the great majority of natives who live in the country or of those who only come to our industrial centres for limited periods on contract."[37] Tracey often stressed that he was not solely "collecting examples of a dying art." His library's first consideration, he claimed, was "not only the historical value of the recordings, but primarily their recreational, artistic, and technical qualities," and, in his opinion, African music was "intensely alive wherever African originality has not been swamped."[38] Folk music, Tracey assumed, could be transplanted on record from home into the urban centers and townships where huge numbers of male workers from Southern Africa were moving in search of employment in the mines and related occupations. His work operated within the milieu of a widening gulf between rural and urban realities, making recordings that inevitably mapped something of this in-betweenness.

ACTUALITY VS. INTERVIEW RECORDINGS

In correspondence, Tracey acknowledged the influence on his own methods of the English Folk Dance and Song Society and its salvaging approach to folk music, as well as that of some other collecting institutions. His recordings fall somewhere between "actuality" and "interview" recordings, the two main types identified by the musicologist and anthropologist Maud Karpeles, a founding member of the English Folk Dance Society who also worked as assistant to Cecil

Sharp. Karpeles was a key figure in the collection of English songs and folklore and remained in regular correspondence with Tracey until her death in 1976. She defined an "actuality" recording—or "a record of the event as it actually took place"—as being a "plain non-analytical record aimed at capturing the atmosphere of the occasion." She stated that such recordings were "particularly valuable as a record of social customs and rituals."[39] Conversely, she explained that an "interview" recording was one that was made under the specific direction of the recorder, usually during a visit to the performer's home. Tracey's recording methods often combined aspects of both of these processes, as he staged interview-like recordings, he made purely analytical recordings, and he also, less frequently, made nonanalytical and more impressionistic recordings.

In addition to technique, the intention of the field recordist remains the single most important factor shaping the recording method. Field recordists develop a range of methods and aesthetics, and some prefer "actuality" recordings, while others prefer analytical recordings. Louis Sarno, a field recordist who devoted most of his life to recording the music of the BaAka or Ba-Benjellé people in the Central African Republic,[40] contrasted the methods used to make his own field recordings with the more analytical procedures developed earlier by Simha Arom, another field recordist working in the Central African Republic.[41] Whereas Arom had advised against making recordings during ceremonies, Sarno wanted to record the spontaneity, the sounds of the environment, and the live and organic elements of improvisation that were so integral to expression. Sarno was not just trying to record music but "wanted to record how life really sounded among the Bayaka [sic] when no outsiders were present." He was looking for "the laughter and shouts and arguments of the children as they sang and played musical games for themselves, not the tame sessions they might perform for my microphones."[42] Sarno was able to make highly nuanced distinctions based on more than three decades of near permanent immersion living with the community.

Tracey's field recordist collected high-quality examples of musical excellence—as judged by his own aesthetic tastes—reflecting his background as an amateur collector and professional recordist aspiring toward academic or scientific standards. Largely self-taught, Tracey's library, scrapbooks, and published and unpublished writings reveal both a searching curiosity about all aspects of African music, culture, and welfare, and also a suspicion and, at times, rejection of anthropological methods of social analysis. His recording tours sometimes lasted for months but in reality, he rarely spent more than a few days in any particular area, village, or mine compound, thus severely restricting the possibility of developing any deep, let alone shared, understanding of the groups whose music he was recording. Reporting on his last recording tour of Basutoland, a picture emerges of short-term bursts of immersive audio tourism, where "for the short period in which the recording unit is active in the country of the tribes concerned," Tracey and his entourage would "live intensely in the atmosphere of local society."[43] Tracey was in effect taking rapid, and well-planned, audio snapshots of music, and in some of his writings he even compares his use of the microphone with the use of a camera.

Tracey knew that he was collecting fragments, and that "any sound recording is only a partial statement of the whole event." This was partly because most of the equipment he was using was monaural and therefore could "only give one sense of direction, nearness and farness, spatial but not lateral." He thus advised other field recordists that

the microphone . . . must be "focussed" like a camera to select the salient features of the music and to present them in such a way as to suggest a complete representation of the occasion. In other words, recording is an art form operating within the limitations of a frame which demands its own set of rules. The very success of a good recording is perhaps inclined to hide the fact that it is an art which conceals art. A recording, however good, is never the real thing, but a *representation* of the original.[44]

Andrew Tracey confirmed that his father's principal aim was to capture music rather than the whole event surrounding the music:

[H]e wanted to get the *music* as such. He was very concerned with the *music*, with the structure of the music, how the instruments are played, with the sounds, so that the people could learn the music. If you record in the context of a social event, you don't get a clean recording. Anthropologists in particular tend to want the *event*, and the music is secondary. But what Dad wanted was the *music*, and the event to him was secondary. There are recordings where the event is also happening, but that wasn't his aim.[45]

Such recording intentions align Tracey more closely with contemporaries like Alan Lomax. Tracey had written to Lomax in 1963, admitting that his own recordings were "but a sampling of each district through which I travelled."[46] Like Lomax, but unlike Arom and many recordists of this era, Tracey aspired toward the highest-quality musical examples because from the beginning he intended them to be for publication and circulation among different audiences.

FIGURE 2.1 Hugh Tracey recording Umakweyana bows,
probably Transvaal, 1958. *Photo* © ILAM.

When advising Willard Rhodes, a professor of music, on the type of equipment suitable for Rhodes' plans to record music in Southern Africa,[47] Tracey emphasized the importance of attaining quality, and reminded him that he had been "determined from the beginning to record in such a way that [his] published recordings could be beyond reproach if humanly possible so that the maximum use could be made of them by students everywhere."[48] Tracey also advocated a keen artistic sensibility, recommending that "the quality of the recordings must be in direct proportion to the musical sensitivity and awareness of the man at the microphone." He believed that professional recording men were not always the best judges of the quality of African music,[49] although his subjective criteria for judging the quality of the music are never consistently clarified.

Tracey believed that, aside from technical knowledge of equipment and recording, the most important factors in making successful field recordings were the ability to relate with musicians, and the ability to conceive in advance the pattern or shape of the music that the recorder was trying to capture. Tracey did at least try to establish functional local relationships in the limited time at his disposal. He felt that, before embarking upon recording tours, the essential prerequisites were both simple and personal: "a high degree of sensitivity towards the music, a rapport with the performers and an artistic discrimination which will bring out the essential characteristics of the music within the limitations of time and space dictated by the medium."[50]

Daniel Mabuto, a Karanga assistant who travelled with Tracey for many years on recording tours from 1952 onward, remembers Tracey's recording methods.

> Then he would be with them—perhaps a thousand people—just holding this microphone, if he wanted one voice he would just take the microphone and put it by that man. He could not use two microphones, because they need too much control. . . . He would put it very near the mouth of the man he was wanting. Sometimes he would tell a man not to sing. Then he would record only the instrument. He was clever in keeping the people relaxed in their singing and playing, so that they did not get stiff when the microphone was pushed in front of them. He would say, "you see this thing here—it takes your voice and makes record—when you sing, you must not be afraid of it and when you are singing just sing what you are used to. Don't try and change it."[51]

Mabuto's recollections confirm many aspects of Tracey's recording technique: the use of gestures and signals to control and orchestrate performers; the movement of the single microphone for selective highlighting and the focusing on different aspects of a performance; and also a desire for the music in the recording to seem as unstaged as was reasonably possible. Each field recording, however, inevitably became a staging, a construction, and involved a variety of editing decisions. As Tracey explained,

> For satisfactory recording it is essential that you should have already heard the music and have the general pattern in your mind. This is because the microphone is mono-aural [sic] and cannot record the usual impression of the music gained by the binaural audience at a distance. A microphone has to be situated where the relatively more important sounds are in the foreground and the less important recede into the background.[52]

A particular challenge for any recordist is identifying which perspective to capture: an individual, a group, a wider soundscape, or an idealized listener? Tracey acknowledged the subjectivity of his own framing decisions, admitting that he could not "truthfully claim that my own preferences have been altogether obliterated in the thousands of recordings of African music . . . made out in the country."[53] Indeed, he recognized that they must all have contained "some element of choice which was not African but foreign however sympathetically inclined I might have been at the time."[54] He doubted the possibility of making "actuality" recordings, claiming that it was more important to focus selectively.

> [I]t has been argued that in order to obtain a scientifically exact account of the music for anthropological purposes no control of the performers, either in time or space, should be allowed. However much one may sympathise with this point of view it would be the equivalent of demanding that every photograph taken for ethnological research should be a complete panorama.[55]

If any central thread of consistency can be detected within Tracey's recording perspective it would be his vision of imagined future audiences—gathered around gramophones, tuning into radio, and listening in classrooms overseas and at home. His selective frame and the quasi-academic packaging meant that his published recordings would be much more likely, at least for the immediate future, to reach listeners other than the local African communities that his rhetoric repeatedly claimed he intended for them to serve.

METHODS AND TECHNIQUES
IN TRACEY'S FIELD RECORDING

A detailed picture of Tracey's general fieldwork and specific microphone techniques—and consequently, what he thought it was important to capture—emerges through analysis of his writing and correspondence. Rosily rhetorical in nature, his lectures, letters, and radio broadcasts, oriented primarily toward Western and academic audiences, conjure up romantic images of pioneering travels through sub-Saharan Africa at a time when such movement was relatively straightforward for those who could afford to move freely through colonial networks. His self-reporting sometimes contradicts the content of Peggy Tracey's diaries and more of his own claims made elsewhere. At times their respective writings reveal contrary claims about his policies of paying musicians, the relative cooperation and resistance of some musicians, the person that held the microphone, and even some of the methods used to inspire and channel performances. A lyrical diarist and author herself, Peggy Tracey often characterized her husband's field technique as serendipitous and instinctive. Together, she wrote, they "were looking for music, the kind of music the African peoples themselves make . . . a merry troll-like sound coming across the water."[56] Conjuring colonial hunting imagery where songs replace game in a Dark Continent, she remembered that when recording in the country, you can never count on a performance being repeated twice. You have to be there at the crucial moment to catch it, snatch it . . . photograph, record, or film it, the rainbow and the cuckoo's song never come together again. Next day the performers will have melted away into Africa, or gone to the market or next village, or they will simply be too tired or have lost interest; or maybe it just isn't done to do it, whatever "it" is, all over again.[57]

In contrast, the picture that emerges from Tracey's own writings is the development of a planned and highly professional recording technique, using devices to inspire performance where necessary, and gestures to control musicians, most of whom he believed could not be expected to have any microphone technique. Tracey argued that it was "never possible to ensure that African folk will in fact sing for you . . . since there is a great difference in their relative musical abilities and willingness to perform."[58] In an interview in 1966 he claimed that he had never experienced any difficulty getting people to record as long as he first approached them in a friendly manner and paid courtesy calls on local chiefs. However, Tracey revealed that there was sometimes a need to trigger or catalyze performances.

[I]n the early days, for instance, before my loudspeaker was any good, I'd travel with two or three Africans, whom I paid. We would sit down on one side of the fire, and the people we wanted to record would settle themselves on the other side. And then we'd have a competition. We would sing a song, they would counter with one of theirs, and when I heard something I wanted, I'd get up, ask them to repeat it, and record it.[59]

Similarly, Tracey revealed that the use of playback would often lead to more performances (see figure 2.2), for example when people from a particular community would choose to compete with recordings from elsewhere, or would simply delight in hearing their own performances being played again, and would then respond to them.

[F]or most recording purposes in Africa, a loud-speaker playback system is essential or the performers will feel disappointed. Hearing themselves on a loudspeaker is such patent pleasure that the performers are not only delighted, but will frequently volunteer excellent material which would otherwise never have been brought to light.[60]

FIGURE 2.2 Hugh Tracey photo of Mbuti Pygmies listening to playback of their music he had just recorded. *Photo ©* ILAM.

Once a recording session was up and running, Tracey employed a system of selective microphone focusing in order to follow what he decided was the most important musical aspects of a given performance. He advised that

> by hand-holding the microphone it was possible to follow the main interest of an item, for instance if the soloist changed, or by focussing temporarily on different instrumental or vocal parts. Standing in amongst the performers made it possible to estimate variations in the intensity of the sound during the course of a song and react accordingly. Placing a microphone on a fixed stand was out of the question as the performers with no knowledge of recording could not be expected to relate their performance to it.[61]

Tracey also advised working with one ear against the microphone so as to be able to hear the live music itself rather than the recording, detailing that when recording players in intimate proximities he could often feel their breath.[62] He used a system of hand gestures to orchestrate performers and ensure that they kept to the time limits imposed by his recording equipment. For simple practical and economic reasons, Tracey would limit the length of performances and, whenever he felt it necessary, would prevent undue musical repetition. In order to prevent "over-long intervals in between verses of a song," he suggested that making a sign by plucking at your lips has the right effect. To one who is singing too much so that his accompaniment cannot be appreciated, holding one's hands across one's mouth is generally enough, or a sign to concentrate on the instrument may help. Turning the outstretched hand over may help to bring on another variation in a tune which is stuck in a rut.[63]

Similarly, in order to make sure that a performance would fit into the allotted time limit of the recording apparatus, he described the theatrical conducting gestures that he used to bring a performance to a close, and which he imagined as "universally" comprehensible to local performers.

[T]his I do by raising one arm to shoulder level with the hand in front of the face. Then, as the last verse is ending I make a wide slow sweep of the arm outwards and downwards, at the same times bending the knees. This bending of the knees is a universal African gesture and never fails to indicate the ending. It almost always evoked the correct musical ending to close the recording.[64]

Tracey's experience of professional recording techniques in studios and with mobile industry recording units gave him a clear idea of the ways to control the acoustics for outdoor performances, and he also had a keen and controlling ear for certain sounds that he felt should not be included in a field recording. He explained that, in general,

recordings of African music are usually made in the open air. For this purpose a suitable site in the village or centre is required, in the shade and out of the wind. A verandah or open shed generally makes a good "studio" and the interior of a thatched hut or cottage is also good for quiet songs and speech. Halls, on account of their high reverberation, are mostly unsuitable for the recording of African music.[65]

He also advised against recording in marketplaces, "on account of the great activity and chatter associated with such places," which would more likely result in an "actuality" recording "with market and other noises in the background."[66] Tracey preferred using selective recording techniques, both to exclude sounds that he felt did not record well, and to emphasize what he heard as key areas of interest within the music. The field recordist, he warned, should have a clear idea of the types of sounds that are likely to modulate or otherwise will not record well,[67] and so "unexpected piercing whistles or other surprises" are to be avoided.[68]

Likewise, the recordist should be aware in advance that trying to record, for example, the sound of Victoria Falls will give bitterly disappointing results that can sound no more impressive than the running of bath water.[69] Tracey openly acknowledged the artifice in his technique, admitting that "recording is *an art form of meaningful sound surrounded by silence* like a photograph within its frame."[70] "Sound recordings," he said, "can be very good liars."[71]

Tracey managed to refine his field-recording techniques to such a professionally repeatable standard that before travelling to mine compounds to make selections of recordings, he would distribute circulars to mine owners advising of his methods, preparing the ground to ensure well-organized recording sessions that would encourage the prior selection of the highest-quality musicians. His ideal content for these recordings was well worked out in advance of his tours, while not only Tracey but also mining officials were given key roles in interpreting local aesthetics. In precirculated notices full of the language of record label talent scouting, Tracey asked mine-compound managers themselves to collect the best musicians and prepare them for recording. He provided the following recommendations to the compound staff:

> [M]ay we suggest that all kinds of social music and song, and particularly instrumental music, and songs sung to indigenous instruments, usually make the most effective recordings. Dance music, either country dances or town music, however interesting as a spectacle, are usually not so effective on records, largely on account of the deafening amount of sound produced by the performers and singers. We always take examples of such dance music wherever we go, but we would like to stress that these are not usually the most important recordings for future recreational use. Good guitarists are welcome, but not to the exclusion of the players of indigenous instruments. Any singers or musicians of merit will be given a hearing, and if up to standard we will record their items.[72]

Tellingly, it is mining managers who were invited to make these aesthetic determinations. With one ear on the music and an eye on foreign and commercial audiences and publication, Tracey's memorandum also requested the "services of some knowledgeable African interpreter for each tribal group." But these roles were limited to little more than helping interpret song titles and content, identifying the correct local names for instruments, and quasi censoring to "ensure that undesirable phrases which might be intruded by thoughtless performers would not be included in published records."

Tracey promised that the moment a record had been taken, the performers would immediately hear their own items played back to them through loud-speakers, a practice that "they find most gratifying, and as a rule, leads to a great number of volunteers for further recordings." Addressing the mine managers, he stated that all items recorded at their compounds that proved to be "technically worthwhile" would be made available "in pressed record form for future recreational purposes in your Compounds."[73] As noted in chapter 1, these collaborations with the White-owned mines were designed to be mutually beneficial. Moreover, Tracey's field-recording techniques—pre-planned, orchestrated, and heavily stylized—were collected by a single microphone guided by an outsider, and all designed for publication, clearly privileging fragments of musical sound over social context or concerns. Within the entire archive there is little, if any, evidence of plans to stay in contact with individuals or groups of performers, with all further analysis and interpretation to be conducted by Tracey, John Blacking, and other ILAM affiliates.

FORGETTING CONTEXT

Tracey's recordings occupy a third space between realistic representations of folk music—comparable to the way music would normally be performed away from the reach of the microphone—and highly staged productions, carefully framing performers and sounds so as to take maximum advantage of the acoustic conditions outdoors in the villages and on the mine compounds of Southern Africa. Some of his recordings were entirely analytical, wherein he isolated individual parts of instruments or ensembles for demonstration purposes.[74] However, the vast majority of his recordings were in principle supposed to be closer to everyday performance. Many of his field recordings were intended to circulate via the mining companies—indeed much of the route of Tracey's recording tours can be mapped onto mining areas, and as noted, these companies were among his major sponsors. His visits to the compounds often resulted in full-day recording sessions designed to capture some of the best examples of musicianship from all the major language groups across sub-Saharan Africa.

These recording sessions highlight key contradictions inherent within his recording project. Tracey often waxed lyrically about the unspoiled rural realms of Africa in which traditions were allowed to flourish, yet he apparently saw no conflict between this search and his close relationship with White-owned mining companies. He repeatedly wrote about the importance of recording local music "uninfluenced" by foreign forms and styles, and at times he even wrote that "detribalized" musicians in towns and urban environments were diluting musical expression by mixing with different ethnic groups—an argument unmistakably close to the later policies of separate development pursued by the apartheid regime. Remarkably, mining companies were directly responsible for the social upheavals that he elsewhere decried. Moreover, as a result of their economic displacement, musicians on the mining compounds were almost guaranteed to mix with new forms of music and other ethnic groups—to become "detribalized" by virtue of their working and living conditions. The majority of these musicians lived for most of the year in urban townships or in mine compounds, far removed from their families and home areas, and their music making was inevitably shaped by these new experiences and interactions. In an analysis of the ways that many rural migrants in KwaZulu Natal relate to kinship hierarchies in homesteads, Jason Hickel traces some of the ways in which urbanization and democracy have "rendered everyday livelihoods increasingly precarious,"[75] and in effect demonstrates how townships would increasingly become areas for state control of people. The Housing Act of 1920 and the Natives (Urban Areas) Act of 1923 had "provided for the establishment of African townships and required that Africans entering urban areas report immediately to registration officers to be assigned accommodation in either official hostels or a series of planned 'native villages.'" Control of labor, movement, bodies, and even leisure went hand in hand. "Recognizing that urban Africans—who were needed as labor—could not be 'retribalized,'" writes Hickel, "and fearing that social anomie would give rise to political unrest, the state undertook to forcibly relocate slum residents into segregated planned townships, where they could be 'civilized' for the purposes of control."[76]

If not the ominous political threats, Tracey, with assistance, was a meticulous documenter of the more immediate factual details accompanying and helping classify his recordings, and he constantly urged other recorders to document as much as they could at the time of recording, aware of the dangers of quickly forgetting important observations. He advised:

> [P]erhaps the most exacting task in the course of a recording session is that of writing down the detail of each and every item on a card or in a book kept specially for this purpose. It may well be said that one cannot write enough, and said with equal truth that one never does. Time, place, date; name of item, of singer; his language, dialect, and origin; the type of song, of instrument; its local name, its tuning, structure and its social function.[77]

Much of the responsibility for the written documentation of the music lay with Peggy Tracey, who reported that

> every musical item we collect and record must be identified by a corresponding card while every conceivable piece of information connected with it must be duly written down and checked. It is checked by Hugh, by our interpreter, by our recording engineer and anyone else of authority and standing, subsequent items of information are added, and finally a fair copy of all this is typed on another card and added to the files in the library. At the end of it all, the original cards look like valuable palimpsests which have spent a long time underground.[78]

In his search for the "genuine" folk music of Africa, Tracey was aware that much local music had a social context and function, and reported that it was "often worthwhile . . . to record the activity which normally goes with a particular song or tune." For example, in the case of a dance he would ideally "hold aside some of the dancers to do the singing while the others dance, in order to make sure the item does not flag for lack of an active moment."[79] He saw value in recording music in its specific place and context wherever possible, for example claiming that in instances where women use pounding songs, the women usually sing better "if a pestle and mortar are on the spot," because "the clank of the pestle added to a voice a little short of breath makes a far better recording than the same song divorced from its occupation."[80] While he acknowledged that recordings should be made where local people would most likely hear the song themselves, his primary motivation was in creating the clearest balance in recording sound. Tracey's attempts to capture or accurately document the context of music making were mostly classificatory for catalogues. Although he often acknowledged that much music was embedded within dance and domestic and other activities, his attempts to incorporate such contexts remained cursory and secondary to the musical items themselves—items over which he exerted great aesthetic control. This rationale is most clearly revealed through analysis of Tracey's attitude toward anthropology, exemplified in his correspondence and changing relationship with ILAM's first musicologist, the anthropologically trained John Blacking.

Tracey's major recording tours were never designed to allow him to spend more than a few days in each area because he was aiming for a broad general survey rather than an in-depth study of particular areas. Much of his life's work was devoted to proving the necessity of developing more recording units in order to eventually document the entire musical content of sub-Saharan Africa. He knew that the music he was seeking was often not the music experienced by travellers and tourists, and also that it took time to find. He was also aware of the advantages of advance planning and research before visiting communities for recording. He recommended that "if a good anthropologist can go ahead of the recording team and note down the persons who are normally considered to have talent, hours and days of unnecessary waiting can be avoided."[81] He also regretted that he simply could not find many people suitable to staff his projects, lamenting "in how many places in Africa is there a musically sensitive anthropologist?" Overlooking other articulations of African expertise and knowledge beyond the musicianship and performances he recorded, he claimed that he had been lucky enough to "find only three or four in twice as many years." Consequently, he believed that ultimately "the serious recording of African music must be left to local units who have both the time to spare and the enthusiastic confidence of the local people."[82] Local recording units were to be coordinated centrally through ILAM.

In 1954 he formally employed such a "musically sensitive anthropologist," John Blacking—another Englishman—but as soon as Blacking began to develop innovative fieldwork techniques during extended research among Venda communities in 1956,[83] Tracey became increasingly dissatisfied with his output. Tracey's initial formal job offer to Blacking is instructive, as the desired research methods focus on listening to recordings, and at this stage Tracey seemed more receptive to methods for social analysis. In 1954, when he first wrote to Blacking to offer him the post of resident "anthropologist/musicologist," he stressed the necessity of "empirical methods" since so little of this type of collecting work had been done before. He specified,

> We would like you to devote your time initially to acquainting yourself with the sound of African music, in particular by making a close study of the many records already in our collection here, and those which will be coming to us from time to time. As you become more familiar with the music, we would

like you to assist us in its proper assessment in its relationship to social usage, its technical analysis, and in any other way which the unfolding of the study may suggest.[84]

When ILAM was formed in 1954, Tracey still considered that the most effective method of studying African music was to analyze its sounds. Blacking would gradually come to doubt the value of making and transcribing recordings, and as he engaged in periods of intensive fieldwork he came to realize the importance of concentrating on in-depth studies of smaller music areas, and he began to develop close relationships with people in the community. Comparison of the sounds of Blacking's field tapes with Tracey's reveals a completely different approach to documenting African music. Most of Tracey's field recordings are refined, with many extraneous noises and events removed because they are designed to present clear audio pictures for both academic and commercial publication and circulation. In contrast, Blacking's recordings sound much more like amateur memos and contain blurs of activity and movement, and, at times, even include bursts of his own over-the-shoulder commentaries and observations. Unlike Tracey, Blacking claimed that he never requested musicians to lay on a special performance for him, as he, like Louis Sarno, felt that such a request would bring about "a certain lack of vitality in the performance."[85] Blacking, who operated mostly on his own, admitted that "collecting data has often been a hectic business" when he explained his recording method.

> I have had to decide whether to take cine or still photos, make recordings, write notes, or join in the dancing, playing and singing. At a number of ceremonies, especially at night, I combined notes and recordings by giving a running commentary on the tape, which I later transcribed.[86]

Blacking soon came to doubt the primacy of recording, finding much less value than Tracey in the technique of sharing playback in the field. In 1956, after experiencing a litany of problems with his own tape recorder, he wrote:

> I am hardly using the machine at all at present, as I have completely lost confidence in it and it has caused so many embarrassing situations. If I note the songs down direct, singing them back on the spot to the performers, I cannot possibly let people down, and in addition the novelty of a European trying to perform their music is an added incentive as well as a deterrent to requests for

money: a recording machine automatically conjures up pictures of Johannesburg and big money; and when it breaks down or plays back the music badly, as it invariably does, they feel cheated.[87]

Blacking's preference for notating and singing back in the field instead of recording both mirrors and develops the first techniques Tracey used in the Karanga tobacco fields before he came to privilege the duplicating function of recorders. In addition to what he saw as the economic benefits, Blacking also decided that a more immersive and empathetic fieldwork technique was possible by putting the recorder away. Blacking argued that "to attempt to understand Venda music, it is not enough to learn about novel rhythms, melodies and scales, nor is it enough to observe carefully and analyse afterwards." This was because in the analysis of Venda poetry and songs he felt that his own interpretation was "insufficient" and that somehow or other he "must find out what the poetry means to the Venda themselves."[88] He expressed his frustrations with many of Tracey and ILAM's methods, and so he began to develop new ways to study Venda music through direct and intense participation in local social life. Blacking explained that he "felt the inadequacy of [his own] methods of research, going from kraal to kraal taking recordings, making notes, collecting texts, and then analysing it all as if in a vacuum." He decided that it was necessary to try to approach Venda music "as if he were a Venda child, to absorb the music and poetry from the bottom upwards."[89] Blacking, in paving the way here for a new style and method of research among musical scholars, was arguably "the first scholar to complete an extended 'anthropology of music,' making a detailed study of music in one area as a professional anthropologist and participant in the music-making experiences of a community."[90]

Blacking's immersive research techniques diverged distinctly from Tracey's more musicological surveying, and understanding the differences in approaches explicitly highlights what Tracey thought he was capturing. As early as 1955 Blacking had already begun to question Tracey's focus on recording clear musicological items. He had found that "the transcription of African Music [was] almost always a slow and laborious task, even with the help of the Repeater Tape,"[91] and he decided to step up out of this library armchair analysis to improve his listening, and to discern more closely the relationships between musical structure and the social environment.

The transcription of music for instrumental ensembles is particularly difficult; it is almost impossible to pick out every note played by each musician, and so many transcriptions of such music are inevitably rather sketchy. Another deficiency in any analysis made solely from a recording is that one can only account for what reaches the ear, and, moreover, an ear trained in Western musical traditions. This armchair method of studying folk has been found adequate by many students who elect to analyse purely musical characteristics, neglecting the social setting of the music and the physical properties of the instruments used. The purely musical qualities of many of my first set of instrumental transcriptions can be analysed after a fashion; but in my opinion such analysis is insufficient and of little value.[92]

As well as doubting the value of amassing recordings isolated from their social context, Blacking came to reject ILAM's entire approach of making general surveys of areas. His 1957 report to ILAM, purporting to describe "the role of music in Venda culture, as a feature of the social, economic and religious life of the community, as well as a source of entertainment," is clear advocacy for an anthropological method for analyzing music and culture, and is also a method that clashed with Tracey's recording focus. Blacking's realizations reveal a major divergence in fieldwork technique as he sought to bypass the folksong-collecting method favored by composers and song hunters. Blacking readily outlined both the limitations and potential within his own methods.

[M]y chief mistakes in collecting data were making a general survey before settling in one area, and going out of my way to observe everything, to the extent of neglecting interviews with informants. In making a general survey, I was adopting the normal technique of the folk-music collector: I reckoned that I might be able to understand sooner the overall pattern of music making in Vendaland, which would suggest problems to be examined in greater detail. The result of this was that during my first three months' work I learnt a considerable amount about individual music making, but very little about communal music. Ironically enough, I learnt far less about the overall pattern of Venda music as a result of a general survey, than I would have done if I had concentrated first on one small area and then worked outwards, in accordance with the field-technique of many social anthropologists.[93]

Tracey was initially reluctant to publish Blacking's reports and never published any of his recordings. His own assessment of Blacking's work was that his "views and methods of procedure are sociological with special reference to music, rather than musical with special reference to sociology,"[94] and that his work contained "little indication of the aesthetic qualities of Venda music which would enable one better to assess its relative value as one of the African folk musics."[95] Tracey gave no indication of the criteria by which "aesthetic qualities" could be measured or analyzed, and he elicited feedback on Blacking's unpublished reports from two other White ethnomusicologists, the Reverend Arthur Morris Jones and also David Rycroft, a South African. He was advised by the former that Blacking's report was "really not a musical treatise but an anthropological one . . . a report on musical practice from the anthropologist's and not the musician's point of view."[96] Jones recognized the importance of the social context provided by Blacking, but advised that this was "essentially BACKGROUND information rather than specifically musical information."[97]

In an interview decades later, Blacking recalled being with Tracey on two expeditions to KwaZulu Natal and Mozambique, helping him record music while himself learning recording and field documentation techniques. He admitted that he "became frustrated by the kind of Cook's tour we were engaged in. Things were not inducive to in-depth musical study."[98] After a year's fieldwork conducted through and for ILAM, Blacking resigned but continued working with support from a small scholarship granted by the Royal Anthropological Institute in London. In the same interview, Blacking claimed that nobody knew how to do ethnomusicological fieldwork in the 1950s, and stressed that he had sought to break from the tradition of collecting data as exemplified by Maud Karpeles, Percy Grainger, Bela Bartók, and Constantin Brăiloiu, choosing instead to explore more immersive methods focusing on smaller areas.

For Tracey, the wider social and contextual analysis carried out by Blacking seemed to be at best a subsidiary concern. Tracey believed that a musicological focus on sound recording and analyzing music as an abstract system should be the starting point for African music that would enable comparison with Western music. His surveying approach retained much in common with the work of many other nationalist folksong collectors such as Alan Lomax, Maud Karpeles, and Cecil Sharp, while his recording route was heavily influenced by the operations of the mining companies of Southern Africa. During many of the recording sessions hosted within mine compounds, large pools of migrant workers would readily perform, as well as providing potential markets for the recordings. The speed at which most tours and recording sessions operated meant that Tracey inevitably gleaned a quick impression of musical styles and instruments before moving on, a thinly described report of music occasionally sprinkled with fragmented backdrops of local social life.[99] Tracey rejected the anthropological method of functionalism that aimed to study function as part of social structure, believing that the more engaged anthropological research of John Blacking was compromised by a reduction in the quality of musicological analysis.

Analysis of African music can never be reduced to function or form or context alone,[100] although formal analysis as favored by Tracey can always reveal structural depth and complexity. Martin Scherzinger argues that "even if we believe that, say, 'thickly describing' the social context of a piece of African music stakes a closer claim on an African reality than does an abstract formal music analysis," we should not ignore "the socio-political use to which a formal analysis, however fictional, might be put in that context."[101] And we know that a major use for Tracey's recordings and analyses was to support the policies of mining compounds. Conversely, Tracey also sought to extract and publish abstract examples of "authentic" musical excellence before corrosive social and political forces rendered their creation too late. As Brent Hayes Edwards argues, Tracey feared that "the tectonic shifts in the African political landscape in the independence era, like the more gradual forces of labor migration and urbanization, imperiled the supposed authenticity of musical traditions on the continent, breaking the 'continuity' of the music's relation to a particular local culture."[102]

Archival documents detailing the processes of creating Tracey's African field recordings bring to light some influential counterarguments that doubted the validity of folksong surveying projects. And as one anthropological voice chips away at the purpose of field recordings mined from living traditions, the ground is slowly paved for other local voices to participate in the archival project and its future life. The local African voices that are always excluded by the reproduction of colonial class relationships may have been invited to listen to playback sessions and imagined as future audiences and markets for their recordings, but their voices and responses to what has been preserved on their behalf remain key to appreciating what is also missing from these records of musical excellence. The absence of these voices is glaring.

In these first two chapters, "Part One: Colonial Microphones," the historical, social, and political contexts for the methods, techniques, and intentions of ILAM's founder and his field collection have been established. Aspects of the archive in contemporary context are explored next, focusing on the stories and initiatives of artists, scholars, and activists in the Eastern Cape of South Africa today, where ILAM has already been situated for more than four decades.[103] As the rest of this book shows, community curation picks up where the colonial project stops.

PART II

Local Voices

THREE

Donkey Cart Curation, Xhosa Anthems, and Township Terms

Back then it was not a matter of access to libraries;
it was access to elders and who we know.

Sibusisyo "Sbo" Mnyanda (2008)[1]

INTRODUCING SOUND ELICITATION

Elicitation as a method in anthropology and museum studies searches and probes through sensory experiences, becoming "a way in which to seek informants' reflections through the use of a prompt rather than by asking direct questions."[2] Photographs, material objects, music, and even smells can be shared to stimulate responses, although the use of sound is less common.[3] The reintroduction of recorded sound into performative contexts, however, often releases latent aspects of the medium that can unlock memories and histories in vibrantly personal ways. "Sound memories," according to anthropologist Anna Harris, who attends to the sounds of hospitals and public history, "are not replicas of what has come before, but rather change every time they are remembered; they are messy and fragmented, collages of impressions."[4] So, what happens when messy and fragmented memories mix with the latent human transactions within field recordings, the documents of the performers and places that "bring together lore and life"?[5] Bringing Tracey's recordings into the present by listening to the live conversations and relationships triggered by archival fragments serves to foreground Xhosa voices, memories, oral histories, and knowledge. An immersive focus on two archival Xhosa recordings demonstrates how field recordings—when dislodged from shelves and reactivated within local, social worlds—can open up multidirectional lines of historical and predictive inquiry.

My sound elicitation case study focuses on Xhosa musicians, artists, elders, and youths in the local townships of Grahamstown-Makhanda in Makana District in the Eastern Cape of South Africa, the province where the International Library of African Music is situated. Among over 25,000 field recordings made by Tracey that cover 179 different language groups, there are 201 Xhosa recordings, all made during one tour of the Transkei and Ciskei in 1957. Xhosaland—*emaXhoseni* ("at the place where the amaXhosa are")—is, broadly speaking, a coastal strip separating South Africa's inland plateau from the Indian Ocean. The Eastern Cape of South Africa is a predominantly isiXhosa-speaking area. AmaXhosa number over eight million in South Africa and form the second largest language group after amaZulu. Under the apartheid regime they mainly inhabited the former Ciskei and Transkei homelands that were notionally independent, and since 1994 the majority of Xhosa people remain in what is now the Eastern and also the Western Cape provinces.

"The Xhosa people today," according to Jeff Peires, "think of themselves as being the common descendants of a great hero named Xhosa who lived many hundreds of years ago."[6] AmaXhosa are an Nguni-speaking group, Nguni being the groups of people who "live mainly below the high plateau of the interior, between the escarpment of the Drakensburg and the sea, and stretch, in a long broad belt of hundreds of tribes, from Swaziland right through Natal far down into the Cape Province."[7] It is thought that amaXhosa may originally be of East African descent.[8] AmaXhosa are properly Cape Nguni people, or "the southernmost Nguni tribes," a group of people who speak broadly the same language but with some regional variations, and are "an example of related tribes . . . represented by the Gcaleka of Willowvale, the Ngqika of Ciskei, and smaller tribes like the Ndlambe, Dushane, Qhayi, Ntinde, and Gqunkhwebe."[9]

AmaXhosa are divided into at least twelve different chiefdom clusters, all of which trace their lineages back to different chiefs and regions. Tracey only recorded the music of four subgroups of amaXhosa; the Gcaleka, Mpondo, Ngqika and Thembu peoples.[10] Many of the amaXhosa people in the Grahamstown-Makhanda area self-identify as Gcaleka or Ngqika, broadly speaking because migration patterns have brought them here from the western regions of the Eastern Cape. The abaThembu are typically located further east and, properly speaking, the amaMpondo are a different group who reside even further east.

Nicolas Jacobus Van Warmelo noted that the numerous tribes and clans of amaMpondo are

> ruled over by several independent chiefs. The Mpondo are again distinct, in some respect.... They are divided into a great many clans, of which the largest though not necessarily the most important in rank are, amongst others, the Bhala, Kwalo, Gingqi, Kwetshube, Nyawuza, Khonjwayo, Nci, and Ngutyana.[11]

These distinctions prove important when considering differences in regional uses of, and responses to, Gcaleka, Ngqika, and Mpondo recordings.

Most of the fieldwork for this book takes place in the local townships in Grahamstown, also known as the City of Saints, iRhini (Xhosa), Grahamstad (Afrikaans), Settler City, and, most recently, Makhanda. Grahamstown is a frontier town in an area still often known as Frontier Country. Comprising approximately 70,000 people, the town is strongly identified with Rhodes University, which dates back to 1904,[12] and the annual National Arts Festival (NAF), established in 1974 and today the largest celebration of the arts on the African continent.[13]

The city is also steeped in deep, contested, and ongoing historical struggles. "Built on the site of Lukas Meyer's farm, De Rietfontein," writes Thomas Rodney H. Davenport, "Grahamstown became the focal centre of the British 1820 settlement after the decision had been taken to make it the administrative capital of the eastern districts in 1828."[14] After twenty thousand Xhosa warriors under their chief Ndlambe were expelled from the Zuurfeld in 1811, Governor Sir John Craddock established a headquarters for British troops on the site of the present Church Square as a frontier against the amaXhosa, naming the headquarters after Lieutenant-Colonel John Graham (See figure FM.1). In April 1819, during the Fifth Frontier War, the Xhosa chief Makana attacked,[15] and was defeated by, the British at the Battle of Egazini ("the place of blood"). The Frontier Wars (1779–1879) dominated South African history in the nineteenth century as amaXhosa resisted wave after wave of eastward-moving White pioneers or "Trek Boers."

On June 29, 2018, after receiving recommendations from the South African Geographical Names Council, South African Minister of Arts and Culture Nathi Mthethwa published in the *Government Gazette* the approval of renaming "Grahamstown" to "Makhanda." When the name was officially changed just over three months later, on October 2, 2018, Mthethwa's rationale immediately circulated online.

The town formerly known as "Grahamstown" is named after Lieutenant Colonel John Graham whose role in the Frontier Wars was to exercise the "maximum degree of terror" on the Xhosa natives and who was and is still infamous for his methods to "break the back of the native" by employing the most savage means imaginable including liberally employing the "scorched earth policy" against those he conquered—burning their homes, their crops, their livestock and homes, before murdering the warriors he met in battle, and butchering even women and children in a mass extermination of a people—whose descendants can still be found in the area.

"The name of John Graham," Mthethwa continued, "is one that evokes unimaginable pain." Moreover, he impressed,

what South Africans ought to know, is that the name change of the town to Makhanda is the fulfilling of the prophecy of "Ukubuya kuka Nxele" ("the return of Nxele"). Makhanda was a warrior, war doctor, philosopher, and prophet whose heroics in the Frontier Wars included an attack on a British garrison at the locality. Makhanda ka Nxele was imprisoned on (and would later die while escaping from) Robben Island a few years shy of some 100 years before the founding fathers of South Africa's liberation.[16]

Debates over the renaming of Makhanda, alongside broader struggles for the right to own and tell Xhosa stories—and how best to express and keep them— will come into sharp focus throughout the next three chapters.

TOWNSHIP SOUND TRANSMISSION

When I first moved to Grahamstown in 2007 to research the history and contemporary resonance of the Hugh Tracey collections at ILAM,[17] the sound artist, musician, and DJ in me was initially drawn by ethnographic sound fragments, professionally recorded sonic snapshots of local music made in villages, on mining compounds, and during other staged performance settings across much of sub-Saharan Africa. The anthropologist and sound curator in me was most animated by what these sounds might mean, if anything, to the communities whose ancestors had been recorded. More than fifty years after Tracey's death and almost a century after he made his first recordings on the African continent,[18] his field recordings still remain by far the most significant material in ILAM and one of the world's most important ethnographic collections of African music. In 1978, ILAM made the transition from a private initiative to being owned by Rhodes University, continuing as a research center and archive. Housed in a purpose-built single-story building at the end of a dipping rocky lane at the edge of campus in Grahamstown-Makhanda, ILAM is quietly tucked away from view. The walls and floors of most of the rooms are hung and illustrated with an extensive display of hand-built instruments collected from all over sub-Saharan Africa, mostly by Tracey and his son Andrew. *Lesiba* mouth bows nestle alongside kudu horns,[19] paraffin tin guitars and *uhadi* bows.[20] Visitors can play some of the instruments, such as the beautifully carved Chopi *timbila* xylophones from Mozambique with their amplifying resonating calabashes suspended under keys made of sneezewood.[21] The building hosts an active community of students from Rhodes and further afield, researchers, musicians, occasional tourists, and—much less frequently—local artists from the townships.

Most of the local producers, hip-hop artists, and other musicians and community artists and activists I came to know lived in the townships rather than in town, and very few identified with, or had even heard of, an archive that was tucked away up in town behind the fisheries department toward the outer edge of Rhodes University. As Tracey himself had intended, ILAM is known to academics and institutions around the world. It is, however, virtually unknown to most of the Xhosa residents of Grahamstown-Makhanda itself. The enduring legacies of apartheid mean that almost none of the local artists and performers I met had ever previously set foot in ILAM, despite it being an archive that includes some of their own recorded past, housed in their own town, and in some cases recorded very nearby. As I came to spend more and more of my time in the local townships—in Grahamstown East or "ezilokishini"[22] as the more marginalized parts of town are known to locals—I found myself moving through a vibrant and noisily mixed sound environment. During daily travels I would hear South African and American hip hop and house, gospel, dancehall and ragga, Euro-American house, and ceremonial Xhosa music all in close, and often overlapping, proximity. By 2016, the cool and slow jackhammer heavy beats of *igqom* were slamming down everywhere, spilling from taxis and houses, children's phones and shebeens. Townships were some of the primary places where Tracey hoped his recordings would be used to bring rural snapshots alive in urban environments, and while hanging out with more and more artists I began to wonder how it might be possible to curate sonic pathways from archive to township and back.

As I came to forge friendships in the townships by spending increasing amounts of time there with local artists and musicians, I witnessed firsthand the chronic lack of resources, facilities, and employment in these areas. I came to learn more about the everyday hustling realities of township life, which seemed to be a mixture of town and village life in sprawling peri-urban areas that had sprung up very rapidly, and often with little planning or infrastructure. Many inhabitants were originally from nearby farms and rural areas and had moved to Grahamstown in search of employment, finding themselves in a very different, and often much bleaker, social and economic environment. Nearly everyone seemed to have to hustle to get by. Over time, more and more people had been born in the townships and had little connection with the rural areas anymore, contrasting sharply with earlier reports from the 1940s that suggested that many migrant workers did not become "detribalized" but regularly returned home.[23] Many of the forces that Tracey believed were threatening indigenous culture and music remained destructive in urban South Africa. Most of the townships around Grahamstown-Makhanda are impoverished, disenfranchised, and still mostly segregated. Townships are almost entirely populated by the local Black and "colored"—or mixed race in local categorization—communities,[24] and these groups of people typically live in townships separate from each other. On the surface, at least, there seemed to be relatively little "traditional" music making.

The more I was invited into and became immersed in local, everyday music making—during ceremonies and in shebeens, at hip-hop cyphers and street fora, sharing sounds inside taxis and makeshift studios in township bedrooms—the more people asked about my own intentions and, subsequently, the purpose and history of Hugh Tracey, ILAM, and its recordings. My role soon evolved into becoming a translator and mediator for a colonial and institutional archival project. Moving within, and listening to, the vastly divergent worlds of township streets and institutional archives, I looked for points of connection and disconnection, and the possibility of creating and curating shared listening spaces. A starting point would be to enable the recordings to be heard. Although there are renowned performing Xhosa artists and musicians—such as the late Miriam Makeba, the multi-instrumentalist Madosini, the Ngqoko Ladies performing group from Lady Frere District in the Transkei, and the singer-songwriter Msaki—the more academically recognized experts on Xhosa music, such as David Rycroft, Deirdre Hansen, and Dave Dargie, are all non-Xhosa and White. Almost nothing was known, or even heard about, what amaXhosa think about Tracey's Xhosa recordings, even though ILAM is in an isiXhosa-speaking region and is close to several large Xhosa townships.

I chose to limit the focus of my sound elicitation to some of Tracey's Xhosa recordings and the local Xhosa communities in and around Grahamstown. This was influenced by many factors, not least that in early trials and listening experiments working with a full range of recordings from many areas and countries in Southern Africa, it was soon apparent that most people did not seem to offer many specific observations beyond asking about related dances, and typically requesting instead to hear more of their own Xhosa recordings. ILAM exists under the radar even locally, on a campus which is based in a small, nonindustrial city buried in the hills of Makana district in a relatively remote part of the Eastern Cape. Tracey's Xhosa recordings from 1957 are snapshots of forms of music making already in change and flux, and rather than restudying or repatriating sound, I preferred to find ways to share the sonic fragments as part of people's daily lives, and to listen to individual and collective responses, performances, and ideas for future curation. I was already aware of the potentially impossible task of locating musicians that would remember being recorded by Tracey, although I did manage to spend some wonderful time with a few, including the captivating jazz musicians "King" Jury Mpehlo and his wife, Irin. In her master's thesis investigating the issues of copyright, access, and potential royalties due from the sale of Tracey's recordings,[25] ethnomusicologist and music educator Boudina McConnachie noted that, "although Hugh Tracey was a meticulous record keeper, many of his field cards for his recordings do not specify who the individuals on the recordings were."[26] McConnachie demonstrates how difficult it could be even to trace a performer who had been personally identified by name, illustrating how she attempted to trace Iris Mjekula, a singer from Tuku's location in Peddie District in the Eastern Cape, who Tracey had recorded in 1957 singing *ngoma ya bantwana* ("song for the children").[27] McConnachie showed that the lengthy process of failing to find the correct Iris Mjekula incurred expenses that amounted to over ten times the sum of the royalties that were due to the performer. "How," she asks, "do you compensate a group of people you will, in all likelihood, not be able to find and therefore contact?"[28] and especially in ways that are appropriately valuable and respectful?

Compounding this problem are the general difficulties associated with using recordings for research. Reflecting on the way that "ethnic" music is usually packaged and marketed beyond its source communities, Laurent Aubert has argued that, as soon as a recording is exported, the listener is confronted with referential structures of music normally anchored in another time, place, context, and reality. "According to a certain point of view," he argues, "its transfer implies a shift that can be considered in itself a kind of deception, or in any case a distortion in relation to the music's everyday playing circumstances."[29] Tracey knew that recordings could be "very good liars," and while recordings inevitably distort or shift the frame of the live music they represent, both Deirdre Hansen and Dave Dargie have shown that the sound of Xhosa recordings can be particularly misleading and deceptive. Hansen's research in the former Transkei between 1969 and 1972 was originally inspired by discovering Tracey's field recordings. As a preliminary to fieldwork, she copied and transcribed all of his Xhosa recordings, and soon became aware of their limitations when she realized that "a basic principle of Xhosa music is that *all* music is accompanied by some form of physical activity, whereby the basic metre and tempo of the music is expressed or at least indicated."[30] Dargie similarly acknowledged the limits to understanding Xhosa music through recordings alone, noting that Xhosa rhythms are highly developed—partly because vocal rhythms may not appear to fit in any obvious way with the bodily rhythms of dancing and clapping—and are thus "very difficult to analyse by ear alone from tape recordings, and in fact also difficult to grasp even when experiencing a live performance."[31] John Blacking had already identified similar limitations of relying on recordings during his brief stint as ILAM's musicologist in the 1950s.

What is the nature of the space that opens up between a recording and its source? There was inevitably going to be a distance between the historical sound recordings and the reality of music making in the townships half a century later, especially because there was already evidence at the time Tracey was recording that, even in the rural areas, some of the music was changing and, in places, declining. Hansen, for example, reported the apparent extinction of a distinctive clapping style called *umngcutsho* that had been recorded by Tracey in 1957 and used to be performed by young amaMpondo married women.[32] She also reported that of the many indigenous Xhosa instruments listed by Percival Kirby in 1934, very few were still being used. "Only the bow instruments (*uhadi* and *umrhubhe*) are found in certain areas,"[33] she observed, "and even these are slowly falling into disuse."[34] Hansen also pointed to the growing influence of Western instruments (the guitar, accordion, and harmonica) and the importance of modern sounds such as *umbaqanga* and jive and the growth of *isawundi* (plural: *amasawundi*) "sounds" or neo-Xhosa music influencing both urban and rural groups. Similarly, Dargie reported on the erosion of traditional Xhosa music and instrumentation, observing that "perhaps the most popular instrument in the Lumko district these days is the radio." Indeed, the first time he went looking for *uhadi* he was told by one lady, "I don't have to play *uhadi* any more; now we have the F.M."[35] Decades later, Andrew Tracey advised a student who was planning to research music in the townships around Grahamstown to expect to hear the music of choirs and diviners, but he regretted that "this area is not at all rich in music of the more traditional type."[36]

The townships are also fertile places to assess—especially by listening to and collecting oral histories—the local significance of what Tracey thought were relatively "pure" forms of traditional music, largely uninfluenced by Western music. Infrastructure and culture in such areas mostly appear to be a mixture of the urban and the rural. Martin Miller studied Zionist religious services in these local townships and concluded that "township culture is in an embryonic and unstable stage of development," leaving the township dweller occupying "a world characterized by anomie, rootlessness and discontinuity."[37] Similarly, in a study of the *amagqirha* (traditional healers) in Grahamstown, Manton Hirst observed that there has been "considerable adaptation and accommodation between traditional religion centred on the domestic cult of the ancestral spirits (*iminyanya*) and Christianity with its concept of God (*UThixo*)."[38] Hirst also stated that, despite the large body of social and economic research on local conditions generated by Rhodes University, "very little is known about the oral history of the townships."[39] South African township culture more broadly observed and imagined has been celebrated as vibrantly hybrid, a tribute to "the cultural and spiritual vitality of black South Africans, who humanised a wasteland of oppression and neglect,"[40] and clearly the most important testimony comes from the very people whose families, communities, and lives are most strongly embedded in these places.

SHARING SOUND ON TOWNSHIP TERMS

Mpho Molapisi,[41] a museum anthropologist who lived in the townships while working at the Albany Museum in Grahamstown,[42] and I were sitting in his office listening to some of Tracey's Tswana recordings that had been recorded close to Molapisi's original home near Mafikeng, capital city of the North-West Province. He paused. "There is that sad feeling that comes into my heart as soon as you open that first song, because I see myself as a stranger to this," he said. "I have an assumption that it belongs to me, maybe indirectly so at this stage, because there is no tangible network that can link me to what we have been listening to." Molapisi suggested that the only way for sound recordings such as these to connect with local communities was to consider using local resources and networks, because "if you look for . . . existing mechanisms in those environments for how to take this back to them, they will appreciate it, they will have time for it."[43] Molapisi could clearly hear and feel the rupture, the space between archived history and contemporary practice, and immediately saw the potential for these recorded fragments to be shared among communities.

Many local respondents also agreed with Molapisi and preferred access to recordings on "township terms." When I asked people for the best way to circulate Tracey's recordings, I preferred to ask them how they would do it themselves if they were in charge of the resources. Not a single person suggested digitization, contrary to the current academic emphasis on this process.[44] However, many people suggested playing them on radio, copying them onto cassettes and playing them in homes, and taking them into schools and telling children stories about them. The most common suggestions included the need for a general forum for these recordings, the necessity for people with knowledge to bring the music and information alive, and the need to start performing and teaching the songs and instruments to the younger generations again. It was much less a matter of format and much more about socially situated sharing and performance. Many people said they wanted the recordings and related resources such as a studio to be located in the townships, not just at ILAM. Artists such as Boniwe and her brother, Tera Tyota, both reiterated that most people in the township felt that resources in town and at the university were not available to them and some even felt that they were for White people only.[45] Perceptions and also hard realities of disenfranchisement prevail in the space that grows between communities and archives. Especially since in this archive, as Alexa Pienaar notes, there is very little information about most of the communities who created the music in the recordings and their relationship to them. Inevitably, to date "the story of Hugh Tracey, and not of the creators . . . lives through the archive."[46]

One afternoon in early 2008, shortly after I arrived at a local community hall in Albany Road Recreation Centre to hear a friend's band play gospel songs,[47] I met Nyakonzima ("Nyaki") Tsana, a professional artist, actor, and dancer who was from Grahamstown and lived in Phumlani township.[48] Nyaki was on stage working with the Bionic Breakers and teaching the group of young breakdancers how to choreograph their moves, drawing from his experience as an artist trained in ballet, physical theater, and contemporary and traditional dance. Extremely warm and graceful, devoted and energized, Nyaki immediately impressed, and drew me in. At the end of the workshop I introduced myself properly and we walked back toward town together. I invited him to ILAM to hang out and listen to some music, and we soon began to spend a great deal of time together.

Listening in the archive together with Nyaki instantly changed my awareness of the potential uses for Tracey's Xhosa recordings. Nyaki recognized most of the items we listened to, which mainly included ceremonial songs and Xhosa instruments such as the *uhadi* and *umrhubhe* bows. He could easily translate most of the words in songs, and was also able to assess from personal experience whether the songs were still currently known, valued, and performed locally. I asked whether people would want to hear these recordings and, if so, how we could make this possible. Nyaki didn't think that most people would choose to come to the archive for headphone listening appointments, then the preferred mode for students and researchers. He told me that one of the most effective networks for sharing sounds and ideas was via the public performance spaces and art practices that people had already chosen to create for themselves: hip-hop cyphers, DJ sessions, and street theater. He suggested that we would get a strong response by hiring a donkey cart and wandering the townships with a group of young artists, because this was exactly the type of music event people in the townships would notice and choose to attend. In these spaces there was usually a sense of something happening, a reason to announce things, and, most importantly, the lively and sociable sounds of the streets buzzing. Several months later, on a dusty afternoon in June 2008, a group of fourteen local artists walked through the extensions of Joza township, playing Tracey's recordings, singing and calling for people to participate as they moved through Joza location.

After a few weeks preparing with this network of artists, listening to Tracey's Xhosa recordings, and learning some of the songs and sounds both at ILAM and in local houses, a collective decision was made to develop a kind of living archive that would move through the township streets, led by Nyaki and friends. Xhosa recordings were to be mixed within a spectrum of live poetry, storytelling, and hip hop and house DJ-ing. With a brilliant blue band tied round its twitching ears, our donkey for the day patiently pulled a light wooden cart forward carrying artists, a PA system, and a portable tape player. Young men and women walking on either side beat oil cans, empty water tanks, and a few small hand drums, while starting to sing as tapes broadcast the sounds of Tracey's Xhosa recordings. A moving crowd gathered almost instantly, many watched and some walked alongside the cart before it was parked outside Bra ("Brother") Pet's mechanic's shop. A PA system was then set up to play more of Tracey's Xhosa recordings alongside hip hop, house, ragga, poetry, and other live performances. Archival

FIGURE 3.1 Donkey Cart Curation, Joza Streets, with Nyaki fourth from the right. June 4, 2008. *Photo by the author.*

and contemporary sounds could be heard across the street in the yard of a local old people's home, children came out of the public library opposite to participate, and elders arrived and expressed surprise to hear young artists DJ-ing Xhosa field recordings alongside other forms of South African electronic music. Some of the gathered audience publicly shared stories and memories of growing up hearing the sounds of the archival songs, others asked whose music this was, where it came from, and how they could hear more. The audience grew to number more than a hundred people. People stood and asked questions about the unexpected archival sounds amplified from inside the silver MacBook Pro attracting more and more dust and scratches while resting on the street outside Bra Pet's store in Joza township.

Unprompted, Mzambia, a local artist and friend of Nyaki's, stood up with a microphone and talked about Tracey's archive, inviting people to come forward and share their knowledge of Xhosa music.

Namhlanje size apha ngomculo wesingqi, ngomculo wakwantu, ndifuna ucele oMama ukuba beze ngaphambili basixelele kutheni benga sixelele ngemvela-

phi yethu ngoba nezinye intlanga ziyafuna ukusazi isiXhosa, njenga amaZulu naBasotho.

(Today we came and gathered here because we want to learn our ancient indigenous music. I would like to ask kindly our mothers to come up front to give us the reasons why they don't want us to know about where we come from, and who we are, and our history, because other nations would like to learn and know us as the Xhosa people like the Zulu and the Sotho people.)[49]

Many people came forward and volunteered their clan names and where they originated, and began to talk about the history of their own songs and the need to bring them back. An elder man spoke up from the back of the crowd and said that he was born in Mount Frere (in the former Transkei), that his father had come to Grahamstown looking for work, and that his family was here in Joza. He said that the songs we were playing reminded him of Transkei. He identified himself as being Thembu, addressed his ancestors by name, and said that he had not heard this music for a long time, and that it made him remember his friends, most of whom he had now lost. He said that he felt lost and useless in the township.[50] Some of the residents in Ethembeni, a nearby day care home for the elderly, overheard the DJ-ing, performances, and conversations while they were sat outside in the yard opposite Bra Pet's. They sent one of their helpers over to our street gathering to express their approval, inviting us to go and play recordings to them in person. This resulted in an emotionally charged listening session a week later where more than thirty elders gathered and told stories about the music, danced, and sang other songs with us.[51]

As we developed this method of sound elicitation together—finding ways to design and share listening experiences within local social mechanisms—Nyaki and I responded to the ways that artists and community members themselves wanted to use and experience the recordings. One June afternoon in 2008 as we were all listening to archival sounds in the house of Zolile and Nomtwasana Tsana (Nyaki's aunt and uncle) in Vukani township,[52] Colin Cira, a neighbor and Xhosa elder, walked confidently through the front door, shoulders up and smiling. "Those kids don't know these songs anymore," he announced and sat down. The listening session, which had begun with shots of brandy poured by Zolile on the thresholds of the house as offerings to the ancestors, was one of our first inside a family home and immediately drew people in from the street outside. Colin then took the lead in a highly animated conversation, demonstrating dances that accompanied specific songs, and insisted on hosting further listening sessions

FIGURE 3.2 Xolile "X" Madinda, Nyakonzima "Nyaki" Tsana,
and Luntu "MC Noize" Madinda, DefKamp, Fingo Village.
July 17, 2008. *Photo by the author.*

in his own house, for which he rounded up more elders, and young children whom he wanted the elders to teach. From this day onward, Nyaki and I would spend hundreds of hours with groups of young artists and other community members sharing archival Xhosa recordings from ILAM, and listening with people debating the morals, messages, and sounds in the songs. We followed the momentum almost anywhere it took us, as archival sounds began to be broadcast in yards and school classrooms, shared in shebeens, played in taxis, DJ-ed in clubs, discussed in libraries, and played in many homes, on street corners, and in other communal spaces. The tape player's gathering momentum would soon lead us into Fingo Village township and the door of DefKamp, the home and studio of hip-hop artist and community activist, Xolile "X" Madinda. X would push this method forcefully in new directions, and the story of his remarkable work drives chapter 5.

The most common general response to recordings was for people to identify the social reason for, or ceremonial context of, the music and, where applicable, the dance that accompanied the songs. Most people would also tend to classify songs according to clear gender or age-group divisions, demonstrating their interpretation of the "ownership" of the songs, or the specific groups allowed to sing particular songs or play particular instruments. There were often contrasting, and sometimes contradictory views on these issues, including a variety of opinions on the correct times and places for the specific uses and performances of music. Many people also expressed strong views on the correct social order and moral values that could be demonstrated and reinforced through the music and songs. The verbal, physical, and emotional responses of local amaXhosa began to add newly activated layers of interpretation to Tracey's historical Xhosa recordings, most of which remained on the storage shelves and classified with very limited contextual information.[53] The many different creative responses catalyzed by close listening to two Xhosa songs carefully selected from Tracey's *Sound of Africa* collection were transformative.

MHLAHLO WELCOMING SONGS

Flip through a stiff and fading red card-bound paper catalogue or search online and you will find that Tracey recorded three versions of the song "Mhlahlo," including a version in 1957 in Released Area 32 in King William's Town District, Cape Province. The item is listed as the "name of a dance" and as a Xhosa/Ngqika party song "for young people, with clapping" by "five young Ngqika women and girls." During the song, as described in the catalogue, "the hands are first struck together and then struck on the skirt or lap," while "the singers were all sitting on the ground in their traditional yellow or red ochre cloth skirts and shawls." The singers told Tracey that the song "was typical of those sung by young men and women at a party to accompany their dance called *Mhlahlo*."[54] Tracey also recorded two other versions of *Mhlahlo*, one sung by a group of Xhosa/Gcaleka people, and one sung by a different Xhosa/Ngqika group.[55] Tracey explained that the Xhosa/Gcaleka version "may be sung on any occasion by the older folk," and that "every ceremony or 'occasion' is opened by the singing of 'Mhlahlo', which really means a 'beginning' or opening song."[56] He also explained that the third version of *Mhlahlo* was a "song for the *mhlahlo* dance, with clapping," by a "group of Xhosa people, young and old."[57]

We chose to play the first of these *Mhlahlo* recordings during listening sessions partly because Nyaki identified it as a "beautiful song" that he remembered his aunt loving, and it was clear that here was a song, or type of song, that had been sung by different groups of people for different reasons. The song is a call and response between one girl and a small group. It flows with an easy and unrushed tempo, as dry and crisply clapped beats fall like the first deepening drops of a slow and heavy rain. An unnamed leader sings about Amantakwende clan names, and builds a fragmented and cryptic story about two boys, Namatha and Walaza. Toward the end of the song, the leader addresses the *Mhlahlo* song itself and claims something is wrong.[58]

A very common response, especially from women but also some men, was to stand up, or remain seated, and physically demonstrate the dance associated with the song in the recording. Nearly every time Tracey's recording of "Mhlahlo" was played, for example, women would join in, clapping their hands together in front of them for the first beat before clapping their right hand against their right thigh in time with the next beat. Thandeka Budaza, a teacher and the leader of a young girls' performing dance group, explained that this gesture highlighted the near sacred nature of the female lap that had to be respected for its importance in child-rearing.[59]

In many cases the information that accumulated from different people's responses was complementary and gradually contributed to a more composite understanding of the recordings and associated ceremonies. Colin Cira, the elder who had grown up in the rural areas in the nearby Peddie District, whom we had first met in Nyaki's family home, cried out almost disbelieving in joy upon hearing "Mhlahlo." "I remember my mother," he beamed from under his white sun hat, saying that she would be wearing her *isikhakha* (traditional Xhosa dress from head to foot) while she sang this song, which was only sung by *oMama* (married women) when there was *umthayi*—one of the biggest ceremonies and one that required a lot of *umqombothi* and brandy,[60] but no slaughtering.[61] "'Mhlahlo' is when women mostly sing together with neighbors to celebrate, it has to be sung then," he explained.[62] In a separate interview, Sompies, an elder woman who had also grown up in the surrounding rural areas, recalled that "this is a big song for the ancestors when there is *umthayi* ceremony and then there is a slaughtering of the cow. This is a big song for the home, you never just do it [for no reason]."[63] She described how *oTata* (married men) would be wearing "shorties" (short trousers) and would have their own blankets and beads covering their bodies, and how they were supposed to carry two sticks during this ceremony.

As well as giving the purposes for songs, people often explained the type of individual or group who had a right to sing particular songs and identified their correct position and function within ceremonies. Many people claimed that only women sing "Mhlahlo" while men listen, dance, and encourage them. Indeed, men would often shout encouragement over the top of the recording, typically using deep guttural breathing underneath exaggerated hisses with sharp intakes of breath blown back out through their teeth, as they demonstrated their own relationship to the song when in ceremonies. "*Ima mama, isiko lakwaXhosa alinofa sisekhona*" ("Please stop it there, Mama, the Xhosa culture and heritage will never die while we are still alive"),[64] a gleeful Colin Cira shouted over the top of the recording as the brandy flowed in a listening session in his own house in Vukani. uTatomkhulu, another elder, repeatedly shouted "*yima, ntombi, yima*" ("wait, girl, wait") over this same recording, showing another typical improvised response by men that was used to encourage the singing during ceremonial performance.[65]

Kondile Tsana, Nyaki's uncle and an elder who often conducted ceremonial proceedings, listened to "Mhlahlo" and explained that "*le ngoma inje, ayivunywa kungekho mcimbi*" ("the thing about this song, you don't just get up and sing it anyway or anywhere you like without a ceremony"), and that it must only be sung by aunts and other *oMama* who are married to men in the family. He said that it was often used as an opening song in ceremonies to prepare for the next round of singing when other people could sing anything they chose. He added that in "Mhlahlo" clan names have to be sung in order to address the ancestors, and pointed out that during a previous ceremony that he had conducted at Nyaki's father's house, the women did not include the Tsana family clan names, and this was, he felt, because they were no longer fully aware of the correct family songs.[66] The "Mhlahlo" in Tracey's recording was sung correctly, he said, because he could hear that the women were addressing clan names.

Mike Mati, a local dancer and arts company manager in his thirties, explained that "Mhlahlo"-type songs usually announced the beginning of ceremonies but could be sung by anyone, not just women. He said that such songs are games designed to involve everyone.

> Just like a ceremony is on the following day, these are songs that people would sing to wait for that day to come, they sit the whole night, they pass jokes, just like there is something you want to say to your husband, but you do not have a right, so you sing and then the husbands sing in response. You may tell a story and the children ask what happened by singing . . . it could be jokes, it is just entertainment passed around people. This kind of singing has no regulations, but fortunately there is no swear words — it is family music — kids can sing with their grandfathers and their elderlies.[67]

Mary Kelele, a woman in her thirties who had previously worked as a local radio presenter, responded to most of Tracey's recordings with a strong and palpable nostalgic yearning. She agreed that *Mhlahlo* songs welcomed people to ceremonies. She compared the singing in "Mhlahlo" to the "traditional work"— ceremonial celebrations—that her family performed back in the Port Elizabeth area.[68] She explained how during the celebrations, which often lasted from Friday to Sunday, her mother would start these songs.

[W]hen we go there my mother would sing one of these songs and knock on the door and she is singing and she doesn't say anything. Then everybody wakes up and everybody knows that she is the one, and then she is going to wake everybody up, and then she is going to sing, and she is going to start to dance, and everybody is going to clap their hands. It is like a welcoming song, no? And everybody knows it . . . and everybody will come, from early morning right through until late.[69]

Another common response was for people to add their own interpretations of the lyrics in the recording, and also of the context and reasons for perform- ing the song. Archbishop Tshobodi, the head of an African Zionist church in Joza township, explained that "Mhlahlo" was "a song for customs that is sung by *oMama* when they go near the kraal for the slaughter of the cow." He stated that *"yingoma ehlanganisa izinyanya ndingathi ngumthandazo wakaXhosa"* ("This song is for bringing and gathering together our ancestors, I can safely say it's our Xhosa prayer").[70] Tshobodi explained that the *oMama* are singing for the home and are also encouraging the young men of that home. He pointed out the fact that the *oMama* used the word *umfana* ("boy") and this means that they are inviting young men to join them, and "the reason why they call boys is because they want them to learn how to behave at home."[71] Tshobodi also claimed that this song teaches young men how to dance, is not difficult to sing and understand, and unites young and old people by sharing knowledge.

People would often explain how songs articulated broader social or moral messages. Listening carefully to the lyrics of the recordings, Thandeka Budaza emphasized the importance of their song lyrics in general, proudly pointing out that Xhosa people "have got the talent of telling you things without you under- standing it." She claimed, "we can compose a song telling you that you are ugly and bad without you understanding and yet you are enjoying the song. . . . If you don't listen to the words you will be stupid because the song is about you."[72] In this recording of "Mhlahlo" she heard women criticizing Namatha, a man who has done wrong. She explained that this could be specific criticism of an individual or more general criticism of the community, and believed that it was more likely to be emphasizing that such ceremonies should be led by a strong and upstanding man.

[W]hen you are doing this type of a ceremony there must be a very chosen man . . . you don't just take any man, this man must be a man who is married, not a divorcer, not a man who is drinking a lot or sleeping with girlfriends. No, a man who is with dignity, who has got cows . . . [who has] a really strong name in his family, no conflict, peaceful in his life. . . a man who can support a family, motivate people, solve when you have got a problem.[73]

During one listening session we played Tracey's recordings to Ecalpar, Mngani, Nombasa, and Zikhona, a mixed-gender group of young artists, none of whom had heard much of this type of music before, either in ceremonies or from recordings. They all paid careful attention to the lyrics and songs and reflected on the scenarios evoked in the recordings. Zikhona pointed out that the women in the recording of "Mhlahlo" were "complaining and . . . praising."[74] Ecalpar agreed that the women were complaining and suggested "there might be a pregnancy involved and maybe the father is responsible . . . the influence comes from the girl's mother . . . it has something to do with claiming parenthood from the father for the baby."[75]

Varied responses to and interpretations of "Mhlahlo" would sometimes reveal clues and information about some historical lineages and migrations among amaXhosa groups. People would often speak at length about the correct way to use a song within a particular ceremony, explaining how the ritual should proceed and usually seeing the two as almost inseparable. Jackson Vena, a retired Xhosa historian and librarian, confirmed that people still sang *Mhlahlo* songs in a way that was similar to Tracey's recording, claiming that it was also known as *Ndlambe*.

[I]t is still the same, it is sung in the same way, it is one of the important songs that relate more especially to this area when Ndlambe was in charge as a chief, some people call it Ndlambe.[76] It is a royal song, that is why it is called "Mhlahlo" . . . it is . . . sung at very important functions . . . where people slaughter an ox to celebrate the reincorporation of a spirit of a man who has passed away, and when there is a pot of beer which celebrates a big occasion in the family . . . because it invokes the spirits of the family's dead people. It is also supposed to include the invocation of the spirit of chief Ndlambe as the chief of this area. . . . "Mhlahlo" is a divine service held at the great place and the song sung becomes a sacred song. . . . "Mhlahlo" is the sacred song which chiefs tended to own, but it has been adopted for sacred services—beer drinks, and ox slaughter for rituals by different families.[77]

Vena even took the trouble to open a dictionary in front of us to support his claim. He quoted:

Umhlahlo: a meeting ordered by a chief in case of sickness, to find out by divination and dancing, of a witchdoctor the person who is suspected of causing the sickness.[78]

Vena's identification of the Mhlahlo songs as Ndlambe—named after a Xhosa chief—shows that the song was used by some families in the nearby rural areas to honor a particular chief whose ancestral regions seem to have been disputed. "Ndlambe," according to historian Noel Mostert, "emerges from both oral accounts and the written record as a wise, restrained chief of considerable personal integrity" as well as a particular military genius.[79] Ndlambe's defeat by his nephew Ngqika seemed on the one hand to draw a permanent line along the Kei River between the Gcaleka and the Rharhabe and other amaXhosa living nearby. However, historian Julie Wells argues that Ndlambe and Ngqika should not be seen as trapped in a fatally flawed personal power struggle, but rather that their story is "the struggle of the amaXhosa to define how to respond to the British presence," standing more as "a story of unity of the amaXhosa than a tragedy of divide and rule."[80] After the 1796 war between the amaGcaleka and amaRharhabe, when Ngqika drove his uncle Ndlambe into exile, the uncle and nephew continued to coexist in a royal hierarchy, an ancestral pattern persisting today.

Collecting responses through close listening to archival songs slowly transforms the fragments into catalysts for new stories, debates, and performances often grounded in oral histories. The archival records become more than just audio snapshots of a historicized moment frozen in time, and start to emerge and sound more like the beginning of new understandings.

"SOMAGWAZA": A XHOSA ANTHEM

Nyaki leaned back in the wooden chair at the library desk in ILAM, pointing at the laptop screen, his eyes gleaming. "Yo"—still pointing and smiling—"this is our Xhosa anthem" he announced. "This one everyone will know, everyone still sings this."[81] We had been working our way through the 201 Xhosa recordings made by Tracey, and had just arrived at "Somagwaza." Translated as "father of the stabbing," this recording of a Xhosa/Mpondo praise song performed by Khotso and a group of Mpondo men and women with clapping and five drums was made at Quakeni "Great Place" in Lusikisiki District, Cape Province, in 1957.[82] Tracey classifies amaMpondo as a dialect of Xhosa,[83] but the Mpondo are more accurately an Nguni-speaking group from the former Transkei between the Mtata and Mtamvuna rivers and have a different lineage to the amaXhosa. Tracey lists "Somagwaza" as "sung in thanks to the Chief when he has killed a beast for them."[84] The sounds of the song are full and joyous, rolling forward through call-and-response variations underscored by an insistent and leathery-sounding drum, while individuals harmonize around the phrase "Somagwaza, hi a yo-ha" with variations singing around the name.[85]

"Somagwaza" is the song that consistently elicited the most animated responses in our listening sessions, principally because it is one of the few songs recorded in the archive that was still sung regularly, especially at a specific point during an *umgidi* initiation ceremony.[86] It is also clearly a song that has travelled far, acquiring and inspiring a healthy variety of uses and interpretations. *Somagwaza* has more recently been traced further within literature and among focus groups, revealing how a male initiation song has been secularized, and when reimagined as a popular song, adapted by Stompie Mavi, has also been feminized in places.[87] Who or what or where was *Somagwaza*, and what could a recording of *Somagwaza* be, or mean, or do? A praise song? A modern composition? The sounds of a myth, a warrior, a surgeon? A secret song for male initiation, or a mobile call-and-response communal epic shared by men and women, moving and meeting between the bush and the home, between childhood and responsibility?

Peter Mtuze, a writer and authority on Xhosa culture, categorized *Somagwaza* as a "post-initiation song" and added that it was formerly a war song. He explained:

> Few people realise today that *Somagwaza*, the song sung when young men come out of the initiation school, was actually a war song sung to celebrate victory. This and another song called *igwatyu* used to be sung when able-bodied young men leave home to drive some courage into those who are obviously scared to go to war.[88]

He also acknowledged that the use of the song has changed, but does not explicitly state whether or not women sing the song, merely referring to their practice of ululating to welcome the men home.

"Somagwaza" is a song that is well known by every man who has gone to initiation school. It used to be sung strictly when the "boy" came home but can also be heard when the boys go to school these days. On the return of the boys, their mothers who had not seen them since they went to circumcision school would come out of the houses, throw their blankets on the ground, ululating vociferously.[89]

Fundile Majola, in a post detailing his own memories of circumcision in his bush-school outside New Brighton near Port Elizabeth, remembers Somagwaza featured a lot in the teachings, as "a rather mysterious, if not mythical, forefather who invented circumcision as a means of passage into manhood for amaXhosa."[90] In an analysis of the widespread Xhosa circumcision ritual based on fieldwork in Mchubakazi Township in Butterworth, Eastern Cape, Andile Mhlaho reports that *Somagwaza* features at different stages and "is the traditional song that is used when taking boys from the 'bush-school' back to the community. It is also used when men accompany a boy to a traditional surgeon for circumcision." He describes how it involves "men singing, carrying fighting sticks while escorting a boy who is covered by a blanket."[91] The song is performed as a symbol of victory and is characterized by stick fighting.

However, it is also clear that the song and its meaning move and change according to different people and places. Examining the role of Xhosa male initiation in moral regeneration, Luvuyo Ntombana listened to stories about Somagwaza among men in Mdantsane, a township fifteen kilometers from East London, and nearby areas,[92] and concluded that Somagwaza was a "mythical ancestor." In Mdantsane, one elder identified the ancestor as a respected but lapsed leader who, after raping a woman without punishment, decided to cut off his own foreskin out of repentance and guilt.[93] Caciswa Nombembe has traced the song's use further afield among an amaXhosa/amaMfengu diaspora in Matabeleland in Northern Province, Zimbabwe, where uSomagwaza—meaning "father of the spear-fighter"—is given as the biological father of the initiate in the *ukwaluka* circumcision ritual.[94] Nombembe distinguishes between the ritual song "Somagwaza" for men only, and "Itsho Magwaza," which is more openly shared.[95]

The song has long travelled even further afield, especially during global anti-apartheid movements. In the 1970s, African American composer Dr. Bernice Johnson Reagon, leader of the women's activist a cappella group Sweet Honey in the Rock, was inspired by freedom songs from South Africa, including "Somagwaza," which she learned from Pete Seeger, who himself had learned it from a book of transcriptions titled *African Folk Songs*.[96] Reagon, feeling the structure and four-part harmony, sang "Somagwaza" as an anti-apartheid protest, without being aware of the lyrics or meaning until she met South African ethnomusicologist Elkin Sithole.[97]

"Somagwaza" was, almost without exception, the first recording we played to people to begin the listening sessions, chosen as a familiar entry point, and also because it was clearly open to interpretations of disputed stories. Usually we simply played the recording and invited general responses, before providing the few lines of limited information from Tracey's catalogue, including its function for the amaMpondo group in the recording. Everyone recognized the song in the recording, and almost everybody we spoke to shared an opinion on some aspect of its style, relevance, or origin. Everybody recognized the melody and opening line of "Somagwaza" instantly, and most people offered their responses without listening to the entire recording. Thembinkosi Butana, a local professional musician whose artistry blends both traditional and modern styles and instruments, remarked that "everyone in the township knows this song; it includes you."[98] Likewise, Xolile "X" Madinda claimed that "if you . . . stand on the street and sing 'Somagwaza' . . . most of the people in the yards will sing along with you. It is a song people all know; a little kid will know it, because he has been to *umgidi*."[99] The fact that the song was so recognizable to male and female elders and youths led to a wide variety of responses, ranging from some men struggling to speak through nostalgic tears of joy,[100] to a professional guitarist plugging his electric guitar into an amp and improvising on top of the central melody of the song's refrain.[101] Many people gave detailed memories and stories to demonstrate the correct version of the song, explaining where and when and for whom it was appropriate to sing "Somagwaza."

Some people claimed that the song in Tracey's recording—made more than sixty years earlier—was almost identical to the way it was still being sung in the townships, while others identified clear differences in instrumentation, style, tempo, and the gender of singers. Tracey's Mpondo recording of "Somagwaza" was sung by both men and women and included the use of five drums. These details, whether noticed automatically or provided by us, prompted Xhosa listeners to offer many different opinions on the correct way to perform the song. While everybody recognized and claimed the song as their own—a Xhosa song—hardly anybody accepted Tracey's catalogued explanation. However, most of the people we spoke to were not Mpondo but self-identified as coming from different Xhosa subgroups. The amaMpondo are a group of Nguni-speaking peoples, and their homeland was one of the largest parts of the former Transkei, which was itself an independent Bantustan established under apartheid-era policies of displacement and land redistribution. The Transkei was dissolved and partly reincorporated into the new Eastern Province in 1994. Most amaXhosa in Grahamstown still knew and used the same song that Tracey recorded, but usually for different reasons than amaMpondo.

Jackson Vena, a male Xhosa elder who had grown up in the rural area of Salem near Grahamstown, offered his very precise opinion on the correct way to perform "Somagwaza." He disagreed that this was a praise song for a chief or that women were allowed to sing it, explaining that it was only for men to sing when the boys returned from their initiation ceremony in the bush after circumcision. He added that the returning male group would be met by women who could ululate and sing a different song, but who would not join in and sing "Somagwaza." Vena explained the difference:

> There is the one they call *umyeyezelo*—that is the ululation song. They [the women] are not supposed to join in what the men are singing. The moment the men stop then the ululation song takes over. The moment they [the women] see the boys, the mother of the child starts it and says, "now my son is a man." That's the one, those are two different initiation songs. One is for the men when they come back to be hosted, that is the reincorporation song; the other is the welcoming song from the women. So that's what the difference is.[102]

Other people also agreed that "Somagwaza" should only be sung by men. For example, Cecil Nonqane, an elder man and acting director of the Albany Museum in Grahamstown, recalled that he had been "brought up with this song around and it was done only by men bringing back the circumcised . . . but it is not meant for women."[103] Jackson Vena also explained why he believed women were not originally supposed to sing "Somagwaza":

> These days I find it very odd that women . . . are allowed to sing it. . . . [I]n the olden days they were not supposed to sing it because it relates to death and women are not allowed because they carry babies—future warriors—they are not supposed to celebrate the fall of a man.[104]

However, some people explained that the use and the meaning of the song had changed even during their own lifetime. Sompies, an elder woman, claimed that "Somagwaza" was originally "just for *oTata* [married men] only but nowadays *oMama* [married women] sing it as well."[105] Similarly, Mama Nobible, an elder from Fingo Village township, agreed that "Somagwaza" was a song for initiation (*ulwaluko*) and said that women now had a right to sing the song because women today know more about what happens to men in the bush.[106] Although gender restrictions on singing the song "Somagwaza" are clearly varied and evolving, it was still possible to find more conservative views on the correct use of the song. During an interview with Thembinkosi Butana and his aunt in a township in nearby Port Alfred,[107] Butana's aunt happily got up and danced and sang along with the recording of "Somagwaza." However, despite speaking freely about some of Tracey's other recordings, she became awkward and very reluctant to comment on the content and use of this particular song. A few days after the interview Nyaki explained to me that

> her body language shows she was shocked here, probably because it was the first time for her to be asked about this song [because] she grew up in the era when "uSomagwaza" was a man's song, and as a woman you are not supposed to talk about it. We gave her a license to talk about the song. . . . She knew more than she told us.[108]

People also responded with other strong beliefs and even prescriptions for the correct way to sing "Somagwaza." Some people claimed that the song could not just be sung randomly because it only made sense during a circumcision ritual. For example, Mzambia, a young musician and artist from Joza township who had previously worked with Andrew Tracey at ILAM, explained that "you can't just sing the song 'Somagwaza'; you can't just sing anytime anywhere; there is a ritual that is going with that song."[109] However, others argued that there were many different ways to present the song and that it could just as easily be adapted, arranged, and modernized. For example, Udaba, the group of young musicians from Fort Hare University who occasionally performed at ILAM,[110] included the first line of the refrain from the song "Somagwaza" during their live performances that mixed traditional and modern sounds, including both live and sampled Xhosa instruments.[111] The Ngqoko Women's Ensemble, a professional performing group of Xhosa women from Lady Frere District in the former Transkei, include a version of "Somagwaza" sung and played with *uhadi* on their CD *Le Chant Des Femmes Xhosas*.[112] Furthermore Player, a musician in his thirties and lead guitarist of the Vibrafarians,[113] a local Grahamstown band, explained that they often modernized "Somagwaza" using extra instrumentation when performing throughout the Eastern Cape. He claimed that, "nowadays you can change it and modernize it with some instruments. . . . Songs like this you can add some modern instruments like keyboards . . . you can play it in gigs, this song."[114]

Although many people claimed that Tracey's recording was very similar to the sound of "Somagwaza" that they knew and sang themselves, others disagreed. Hleze Kunju, an actor, musician, and ethnomusicologist, claimed that he did not think much had changed "from what is used there and what is used now."[115] However, other people claimed that there were now many differences in the way the song was sung. Some noted that the rhythm was much slower in the recording than the rhythm they would themselves use. Sompies, for example, felt that "they have changed it completely [today] because in the olden days it was slow."[116] Likewise, Nomcebisi, a young choreographer and ethnomusicology student at Rhodes University, noted that the song, although familiar to her, also sounded very different because she was used to hearing it being sung at a faster pace in the townships. She remarked that in the recording they sounded "slow or something, but now it is fast with the energy that they give."[117] For Nomcebisi, the change in the speed of the song nowadays reflected wider cultural changes in the practice of the *umgidi* initiation.

> In the olden days the boys from the forest they would be accompanied by older people, but now you get like a twenty-year-old accompanying them and it changes the rhythm because the older people will sing differently and they are slowing down the song. . . . Now the twenty-year-olds, there is a change with the energy.[118]

The generational shift here is evident, where a Xhosa teenage girl was able to offer observations on changes in the sound and speed of the song, in contrast to some elder women who felt unable to talk freely about what, to them, was a song sung by, and for, men.

Group listening sessions proved to be a very valuable means of collecting different opinions because people would often begin to debate among themselves about the sounds of the recordings, reflecting their own backgrounds and how they had been exposed to, and learned about, the songs. Silulami "Slu" Lwana, a local actor, and Luyanda Ncalu, a local radio DJ, engaged in active debate about "Somagwaza" and the other recordings.[119] Slu had already claimed that the song was not heard much anymore in the townships during initiation ceremonies, contradicting the responses of most people. Slu stated that to his knowledge "Somagwaza" was now rarely used in *imigidis*, but instead it was more commonly used by *amagqirha* (traditional doctors) for healing ceremonies.[120] During a joint listening session later the same day, Luyanda disagreed with Slu, claiming:

To be specific that song that you have just played there, "uSomagwaza," it is not a song for the *amagqirha*, that is a song that amaXhosa played when there is a young man from the circumcision. . . . [W]hen the young man has passed the test from the bush and you go and collect him, we used that song to celebrate that he has passed the test that he has come back home. . . . [I]t is an old Xhosa theme.[121]

Luyanda added that "Somagwaza," as he heard it locally, was still similar to the song in Tracey's recording, stating:

There is not much that has changed in that song . . . but the difference . . . this song now it has got the beat behind it [in the recording] . . . there is a beat and you rush with the beat, otherwise the version of the song is the same, we can switch off this thing and sing this song and it's the same thing.[122]

Disagreeing with others—and especially elders such as Jackson Vena—he explained that while men are returning from the bush the women are actually waiting at home singing and they then change their song at a specific point to join "Somagwaza."

The old ladies have *ingqongqo*, it is old zinc, and they will put it outside the yard, and they will hit that while the elders are fetching me as a boy. They will remain here—the old women and the mothers—they will take the old zinc and they will hit it, and immediately when they see us coming back, they will change whatever they were singing to "Somagwaza." Yes, they will change that tune because they know that tune we sang there, so they will use the same song and they will hit it on the zinc.[123]

In the session with Luyanda, Slu remarked that, unlike the amaMpondo in Tracey's recording, people nowadays did not use drums to accompany "Somagwaza." He speculated that this might mean that the song could have originally been borrowed from elsewhere.

If you listen to this song it is being sung by old ladies with a drum, mind it was being recorded fifty years back, so my opinion is that this song was not meant for *umgidi* . . . but what we did was as Xhosas we stole the song and said, "ok, we will use this for someone who is coming from the bush."[124]

Collecting responses to a recording of a song that is very familiar to most people can produce some consensus on its use and style, along with much debate and disagreement—as with any form of oral music making—and there can often be as many interpretations as there are listeners or performers. Listening to "Somagwaza" draws many different responses even within a relatively small local area. These responses ranged from the highly precise prescriptions of elders on the correct way to use the song, to examples of younger musicians claiming that it could be modernized, reinterpreted, and even remixed to be used in new ways that are more resonant with their contemporary world. Colin Cira claimed that "Somagwaza" was an *igwijo*—a song that fits with any ceremony—and that it was also used by *amagqirha* and by boys going to stick fights against other villages.[125] Other people claimed that the song was a war song or that it could be sung for many other reasons. Tracey's recording and catalogue notes claim that "Somagwaza" was a praise song for the amaMpondo group that he recorded, and there may well have been a similar diversity of responses from different amaMpondo groups in the 1950s, as well as at any time since. Unlike the recordings of "Mhlahlo," Tracey did not record a version of "Somagwaza" by any other Xhosa groups.

As Nyaki continued to skilfully broadcast and weave the recording of "Somagwaza" through his communal artistic network, many people began to speak about or question the origin of the song, the lyrics, and the reasons for its use, along with other associated stories. Some people commented on the different lyrics that were used today in the townships. For example, Tera Tyota—a musician whose father had been an *igqirha* (traditional healer) who had met Tracey and also worked with Andrew Tracey—remarked that the song sounded very old and unusual to him, because people in the recording did not add or improvise words to the basic refrain.[126] The lyrics in Tracey's recordings are simple and repetitive, effectively just repeating the name with variations:

> Somagwaza, Somagwaza, ha-ho-yo . . . Somagwaza, Somagwaza, gwazele hi ho ha

Today most people sang the lyrics,

> Somagwaza ndizakugwaza ngalomkhonto (ha yo) (Somagwaza, I will stab you with this spear [ha yo]),

and the latter version includes the expanded lyrics that most people sang when accompanying the recording. Nyaki himself remarked that for him, apart from these lyrics, there was little that distinguished the content of the recording from the song as he knew it, although he said that he had never witnessed it being played with a drum before.[127]

Some respondents developed the point that "Somagwaza" was used to inspire courage in men both to help endure the physical pain of circumcision and life in the bush away from their communities and families during the circumcision school, and also to inspire the courage to assume the responsibilities of manhood upon being welcomed back into the community. The musician Player said that men sing this "traditional song" when a boy is on the road to manhood and "they used to sing this song to appreciate him, to make him proud of himself."[128] He explained that "'Somagwaza' is the title of the song, *ukugwaza* is to stab so maybe *uSomagwaza* is this spear?"[129] Thandeka Budaza explained:

> They usually sing this song to give the young men power and to chase away the fears because it is painful to be circumcised because there is no anaesthesia there [in the bush], there is nothing. But to prove that he is a very strong man he must go there without injections or anything. They sing that song "Somagwaza" because they want you to be firm and strong, so if you sing that song you feel proud of yourself and you're not gonna feel the pain.[130]

She developed the idea that circumcision was part of the battle to enter manhood, with the clear link between the spear and the blade that was used to circumcise the male. She explained that the song was still used as a victory song, namely the victory of having successfully undergone a painful exclusion from the community and the hardship of life in the bush, before the raw physical pain of circumcision.[131] Nelson Mandela vividly recalled in his autobiography the very moment when he felt "as if fire was shooting through my veins; the pain was so intense that I buried my chin in my chest. Many seconds seemed to pass before I remembered the cry, and then I recovered and called out, *Ndiyindoda!*"[132]

Interpretations of "Somagwaza," or any of Tracey's other recordings, depended to a large extent upon where, and when, and how a person had grown up, which greatly determined the types and frequency of ceremonies and songs they would have experienced. Jackson Vena grew up in the rural areas near Grahamstown where traditional ceremonies had been, and still remain, much more common and often lasted for much longer than ceremonies in the townships. He readily gave a lengthy interpretation of who he believed Somagwaza was, and explained that much of the detail came from his grandfather, who had himself been an initiator, or man who performed the circumcisions at *imigidis*. "My version is," he said, "this song has got history behind it."

Somagwaza was a person; he was one of the chief's warriors and he was responsible for the circumcision of boys; he was the chief's surgeon. So what happened, they went to battle and then he fell in battle. Now the other warriors came back and on their way back home they said they decided to sing this song to make . . . an announcement to the other people in the village . . . that Somagwaza fell in war.[133]

Vena thus agreed with Peter Mtuze that "Somagwaza" was originally a war song. Thandeka Budaza, however, claimed that Somagwaza was the first Xhosa man to have been circumcised. Consequently, she argued, the song was now used as "a song of support . . . as you are going to feel pains there but you must be able to tolerate the pains as those pains are going to prove that you are a man."[134]

Cecil Nonqane asked to hear what other people had been telling us about "Somagwaza," and he disagreed with some of the responses that we had already collected.[135] He referred to the story of Magwaza as told in the isiXhosa book *Umkhonto kaTshiwo*,[136] and identified Magwaza as the man whose conscience prompted him to kill himself with his own spear.

Magwaza was a man and this man didn't like people that are accused of witchcraft, so whoever has been accused of witchcraft has to be destroyed because he wanted a pure nation. . . . And if you are accused of being a witch you are taken right into the bush to be killed. So Magwaza was the one who had the spear, or what you call *assegai*, to stab the one who has been appointed as a witch. . . . Now this carried on until somebody came along with a child and said she was accused of being a witch and said, "okay save myself or save my child." And they decided to save the woman and the child, and they put them in a shelter, and while that was happening this Magwaza took the spear and put it here and fell on the spear and then he killed himself.[137]

Nonqane believed that there were a lot of false beliefs about who Somagwaza was, and argued that "people are misusing that [story]" because "Magwaza was not killed. With circumcision there is cutting . . . and still over those things he was not killed so he [the person being circumcised] is not like Magwaza, who killed himself."[138] Nonqane's version resonates with the versions Ntombana (2011) collected in Mdantsane (near East London), especially the belief that Somagwaza used a spear to punish himself in shame.

Nonqane also remarked, referring back to Tracey's recording, that amaMpondo people did not go to circumcision schools until relatively recently in their history, and so the use of "Somagwaza" as a song during a circumcision ceremony is much more likely to be a Xhosa practice than a Mpondo practice. He claimed that using "Somagwaza" in initiation ceremonies "could not have come from the Mpondos; this could have come from the Xhosas . . . it is my own analysis."[139] Thus it is quite possible that Tracey's description of "Somagwaza" as being a praise song for an Mpondo chief was perfectly accurate for the group he recorded. However, we do not know who his informant or translator was, and he did not provide any other versions of the song or accounts from other groups to compare and help confirm or contradict this interpretation. However, collected responses can be compared to each other and related to ethnographic research. For example, in 1931, at the time Tracey was beginning his research, John Henderson Soga wrote:

> Tribes of the Aba-Mbo origin, such as the Pondos, Pondomise, Xesibe and others, as well as many Natal tribes have never practiced circumcision. At present time, however, circumcision is gradually making its way into Pondol-and and gives evidence of becoming an institution in that country at no very distant date.[140]

Later, in 1974, Virginia van der Vliet wrote that "all Cape Nguni circumcise except the Bhaca, Mpondo, Xesibe, and Ntlangwin," but also claimed "the Mpondo used to have initiation schools with circumcision rites."[141] However, despite almost every Xhosa respondent claiming "Somagwaza" as their initiation song, back in 1931 Soga made no mention at all of this song in his extended description of Xhosa circumcision ceremonies and their associated dances. Instead, he claimed that:

> The *dancing songs* of the *aba-kweta* are primarily the following three: 1. *Um-Yeyezelo.* 2. *Ingoma ka-Mhala.* 3. *Um-Qolo weNamba.*[142] A few others less well known are also sung. The above three are of Xosa [*sic*] origin but have been adopted by all tribes of South-Eastern Africa which observe the custom of circumcision. The first of those songs mentioned has to cultivated ears no music in it whatever, and yet to the Bantu it is the most commonly used of all.[143]

Is it more likely that this song was not used at all among the Xhosa as an initiation song at this time, or simply that it was not in use among the groups to whom Soga referred, if Soga's otherwise relatively comprehensive accounts are assumed to be a reliable source? Soga's omission of "Somagwaza" is likely to be significant—especially because he gives a full explanation of the origin and use of "Mhlahlo" as a divination song, as well as describing its performance and words.[144] Despite this song being, in Nyaki's choice of words, a "Xhosa anthem" known by most people, its meaning and use also seemed to be extremely varied, fixed for some and fluid for others, and often highly localized.

THE ANCESTORS WELCOME RECORDINGS

The style, significance, and use of a song like "Somagwaza" can clearly vary according to a person's birthplace and cultural upbringing. Active exchanges between amaXhosa and some of their historical recordings elicit and grow layers of awareness around the content and meaning of a recording, and also highlight the extremely varied, and often personalized, meanings of particular recordings. This opens up productive lines of historical inquiry whereby archival recordings play an active part in tracing the origins and transmission routes of performing techniques and styles of songs. By inserting archival sounds into living social spaces and interactions, old recordings can be reactivated and release relevance and meaning for listeners today. As Koketso Potsane, an ethnomusicology student at ILAM, asked rhetorically one day during a listening session, "What is this music doing in the fridge?"[145] The process of doing this—of taking the recordings out of the fridge and onto the streets—was nearly always exhilarating and sometimes elusive and exhausting in its seemingly boundless possible directions and pathways. Although Nyaki could usually anticipate the reactions people might have even before we played the recordings, the animated forces of many of the live responses—majestic dancing displays of shimmering upper-body control, lengthy debates on cultural vitality, and young artists choosing to write plays drawing on the moral messages they heard transmitting in the songs—was palpable, powerful, and mostly personal. New ceremonies were triggered by sharing MP3s through laptop speakers, and people started to arrive at ILAM's door to make their own requests. And slowly, Nyaki's own status within his family and community changed.

Nyaki was one of very few people locally in the townships who had managed to earn a living as an artist by exploring and performing his own Xhosa culture and identity. This was unusual in an area and community where there were scarcely any such paid roles and almost everyone hustles. As Nyaki began to be seen to be conspicuously taking his own Xhosa culture and identity seriously, he was allowed to sponsor family ceremonies for the first time, and to begin to build stronger relationships with his elders. Nyaki was sure that his ancestors supported our work together and also that the ancestors were present in Tracey's recordings, and therefore that it was important for him to pursue this work. Reflecting on our first period of fieldwork together, he told me that

> the archives that you bring to them, these recordings are not just coming with us. There are two of us and I am telling you we are with the good spirit of the ancestors. . . . When that thing happens it shakes my body, I feel the energy . . . the energy that was there. We were not just there with uColin and my aunt and the others; we were there with the good spirit of the ancestors.[146]

Shortly afterward he began to have dreams and to experience signs that indicated to him the need to sponsor a traditional ceremony at his father's house.[147] He had noticed that his father, who had been the responsible head of a large extended family, had begun behaving strangely and seemed to have stopped teaching his children their Xhosa values. After seeing his father in regular difficulties out on the street in Hlalani township,[148] Nyaki realized, "this is not right. It is time to act—he used to look after many but the ancestors are not with him at the moment." Nyaki decided to ask his elders to let him sponsor a ceremony and he said that he wanted to include some of Tracey's Xhosa recordings. "I will learn how these songs are made," he promised.[149]

Nyaki explained that learning about, and then using Tracey's recordings during our sound elicitation had given him an understanding of some of the reasons why many of the rural Xhosa songs and values were no longer being transmitted in the townships. He saw the pattern happening in his own family.

> [M]y father does not allow me to sit down with him and talk about the family rules and regulations and how they were using them to do their ceremonies. . . . He is my responsibility now. I must do something so that he must follow me, and I will start to learn when he is there at the kraal talking with the ancestors. I haven't learned a lot of those things.[150]

Nyaki believed that it was vital that young people openly expressed curiosity in ceremonies, and almost a decade later he still held the same conviction: "It will be the kids' responsibility to go into traditional ceremonies outside in the location," he said, "and then make more research, and each and every time there is a ceremony the kids will be so curious what is happening here, why these songs are being sung."[151] Elders needed to witness again the interest of the youth, "so elderly people can see that our kids they still know and they still want to know more about our culture, because our culture is extinct it is going—*iyaphela*—it is going, it is dying."[152]

More than a decade later, Xolile "X" Madinda was in conversation with eth-nomusicologist and ILAM's studio manager, Elijah Madiba, as they co-taught an interactive class linking studios and spaces between ILAM and the University of Virginia in April 2019. X reflected on the value of this sound elicitation as he saw it.

> And I think one thing that was amazing when Noel was here many years ago, we took a CD to the street and then we played it to elderly people, and the way they responded to the music it was like, it made them feel younger, it has a memory. . . . Even when we played the song to those old men they actually stood up; they are like very older men but they know what needs to be done when that song is played. They stood up and then they started, they were, "hey, you are younger than me but you don't know this song." So it transcends to generations because you can tell a story by listening to it. I wasn't there, I don't know that history but still when that music plays, I have a connection with it.[153]

COLLECTING LIVING OBJECTS

Tracey's focus on collecting and preserving sounds seemed primarily to create legacy for ILAM, in contrast to his later claims that actual living traditions were more important than what could be filed on shelves. Pioneering a collection and building an archive, at his time, was a process that became almost instantly detached from the people recorded, in part at least because of the brief and ex-tractive nature of the survey tours, and the absence of anthropological attentive-ness toward local modes of musical transmission and preservation and, crucially, relationships for collaborative exchange. Sustained engagement between a local community and audio snapshots of their recorded heritage can become possible, and it is itself a method and mode that requires invitation and collaborative and iterative design from the outset. Elicitation often reveals that what is valued lo-cally is the human relationships—actualized, imagined or heard—within the recordings, the individual and communal connectivity to regulatory social tissue, which for many people includes their ancestors. For ethnographic sound archives to resonate, the people recorded can remain connected with recorded material, both in and out of the archives, so that the archive becomes "an institutional-ized vibrant space in which different agents provide and borrow information from the sound archive."[154] Contemporary theorists and practitioners in sound studies explore sound as a complex of forces and experiences that evade and elude the most sophisticated of microphones, and these insights can be mixed productively with immersive performance modes that convey and map human and nonhuman interactions with their environment through sound and movement. Imagining how to curate future collections that contain, reflect, and retransmit the multidimensional relationships between the sounds and the lived and moving gestures creating them, may require an imagined archive born and housed within an entirely different type of space. When Toyin Falola remembers, values, and analyzes ritual archives, he includes the "non-world," and "forces that breathe and are breathless," alongside "shelves on sacrifices and shrines, names, places, incantations, invocations, and the entire cosmos of all the deities and their living subjects among human and nonhuman species."[155]

More than a decade after first hearing the sonic fragments Tracey recorded, the artist, anthropologist, and curator in me still listens to these noninstitutional ideas for different ways to transform possible experiences of the knowledge systems contained in archival recordings. For a long time, Tracey's unique recordings of Xhosa music from a particular time and place had seemed destined to remain reduced, flattened as items for pinned preservation, too separate from the lived humanity and values that give the charge to the original performances. Collaborative curation that translates between local artistic practice and institutional archival processes has triggered more animated sound stories that grew around the mined archival fragment. The lived responses can then be collected as part of a multimodal archive designed to embrace new stories responding to, and standing on, colonial collecting products and procedures. As the archival record expands to include contemporary responses and new performances and narratives, an ethnographic sound curator will continue to ask how archiving can adapt to—and be molded to include and enhance—the lived world of communities whose expressive culture was documented, then taken, sampled, and pointed somewhere else.

FOUR

Art and Community Activism
around the Archive

The basis for this archive is the recording, the object, and one radical aspect
of it would be to reinsert the song back into the context and to record the
context itself and to engage with the participants on their terms.

Dr. Lee Watkins, director of ILAM (2018)[1]

New directions come with new directors and, since 2016, ILAM has been South
African-led for the first time. Once most of ILAM's holdings had been fully
organized and digitized under the leadership of Diane Thram,[2] archival conditions had become more primed to return sound to communities, while enabling
broader policies of awareness and access to open the archive to more radical
ideas for activist community curation. Successful community partnering requires
interrogating notions of heritage both from within and outside the archive, a
process made possible through the changing focus of music studies taught and
researched through ILAM. This requires reconceiving ways to curate performance
practice that suspends the fetishization of music, sound, and the recorded object,
questioning and expanding the very core practices of a sound archive. Given that
in South Africa all universities are public institutions, current ILAM Director Lee
Watkins argues that "the community pays us and so for example the research we
produce belongs to the community broadly conceived."[3]

The international awareness of ILAM's recordings may well obscure the reality that ILAM is a small and precarious building and operation, as good as hidden at the outer fringes of the campus of Rhodes University in Grahamstown-

Makhanda. With a small permanent staff of three, the archive has, since its founding in 1954, fought a continuous battle to survive, often relying on the goodwill of volunteers to help even with core business. "Security issues at ILAM became rather urgent," reported Watkins, noting that "there was no protection against fires, books were being smuggled out, and traffic was not being monitored."[4] Despite these restrictive realities, ILAM manages to initiate original projects and models for the study of African musical performance. At ILAM, Watkins continued, "words such as the 'decolonial' are not mere rhetoric but a part of its lived experience from one day to the next."[5]

This chapter focuses on a range of new initiatives for publicly engaged sound and heritage activation in and around ILAM's archive, enabled through the quietly generous guidance of Lee Watkins, a South African ethnomusicologist searching for ways to connect communal heritage collectives with archival processes, while broadening the range of sound and music influencing ILAM's collections to include hip hop, African electronic music, and African sound art. As repatriation and remix projects through ILAM connect collections with communities in multiple countries in East, Central, and Southern Africa—many initiated under Diane Thram—Watkins has deliberately decided to concentrate energy and resources on projects in the Eastern Cape. He envisions deepening long-term engagement with local Xhosa artists and organizations, and the originality of his approach lies in three key areas: community collaboration; diversifying the archive's genres and modes of sound and performance; and decentering the dominant story and identity of Hugh Tracey. This chapter illustrates how these three approaches work together by focusing first on shared archiving and curation processes with Ntinga Ntaba kaNdoda, an innovative Xhosa heritage collective based in nearby Keiskammahoek, and then analyzes the original and increasingly radical artistic interventions made by South African producers and performance artists who gravitate in and out of ILAM's spaces and holdings. Spending extended time with contemporary artists who hear, imagine, and create their own archives in their own spaces, and researching and listening to the creation of Tracey's archive, identified some of the ways and places in which it has remained previously unheard.

As a number of scholars have noted in the context of Black American music, performance, and recording, heavily racialized lines are routinely enforced and sensed through attending to the ways that people convey what they imagine others to be saying, performing, and acting. Race is constructed in part upon what we choose, or are allowed to hear and listen to. Drawing from a multimedia archive including early sound cinema, radio drama, and folk and blues in America during the period 1845–1945, Jennifer Lynn Stoever argues that "The inaudibility of whiteness does not mean it has no sonic markers but rather that Americans are socialized to perceive them as the keynote of American identity." Furthermore, she states, "while never seeming to speak its own name, white sonic identity imagines itself against circumscribed representations of how people of color sound."[6] This argument is readily applicable to the "performed Whiteness" of Tracey's patriarchal documentary project, which creates its content only by reproducing colonial-enabled relationships, imagining and narrating the more traditional sounds of villages as a keynote of African identity. In the twenty-first century, Beyoncé herself—despite working with creative partners in Nigeria, Ghana, and South Africa on her latest visual album "Black is King"—has been criticized for showing images of Africa that some consider clichéd: horses and huts rather than skyscrapers.[7] Contemporary African responses to representation by colonial sound fragments have now been seen and heard as sites of personal historical inquiry, and as calls for reengaged ownership.

In his work tracing the history of notions of "primitive," "savage," and "Africa" in the transnational public discourses of the 1930s through the 1950s, David Garcia notes the powerful forces linking, on the one hand an elitist intellectual privilege in thinking, speaking, and acting about Africa, and on the other hand a shared resistance to oppression, where "Africa as Western civilization's Other afforded musicians, dancers, activists, and others to retrace, usually subversively, modernity's decipherings (temporal, spatial, epistemological) of Africa."[8] His work remains alert to the deep and historical problems facing expressive Black culture that performs a reimagined ownership of African roots, while a listening White audience that so often occupies the privileged seats dispenses the endorsements for what makes origins sound truly "African."[9]

While coining the idea of the "audio-racial imagination," Josh Kun argues that the act of listening to music opens critical space for acknowledging cultural differences and challenging simplistic hegemonies that normally elide, blur, and bury any possibility of nuanced conversations. Throughout the incendiary American culture wars that rage across multiculturalism and diversity, Kun argues that "race and popular music have always been experienced not alongside each other, not as complements, supplements, or corollaries of each other, but through each other."[10] For Kun, music and songs, whether klezmer, hip hop, or Latin rock, can be "audiotopias," experienced not just as sound but as "a space we can enter into, encounter, move around in, inhabit, be safe in, learn from."[11]

Much of the work of the book now is to continue to listen beyond the recorded fragments to consider the occupation and expansion of the spaces in which archival recordings can be heard and made to sound differently.

SPACE FOR RADICAL ARCHIVING

I first met Dr. Lee Watkins late in 2007 when he was the resident ethnomusicologist at ILAM. Propped for long periods behind the heavy brown-flecked library desks, I was becoming more and more consumed inside the spilling stacks and piles of paper in the ILAM archives—Tracey's typed correspondence, field journals, lectures and fund-seeking rhetoric—while also listening to everything else Tracey had recorded, broadcast, and produced. I was absorbing every scrap of every written and spoken word and music and sound I could find. Watkins was busy teaching, reviewing books, and researching local heritage trails, and one afternoon in the side office he shared at ILAM, as we were slowly getting to know each other better, he generously advised me: "Get out of the archive and out among people, find out what is happening out there and what people want."

Watkins was a lecturer in ethnomusicology in the Department of Music and Musicology at Rhodes University, and was spending much of his time researching and writing at ILAM inside the room that was mainly dedicated to storing books, boxes of field cards, and some of ILAM's print archives that were yet to be digitized. Having studied ethnomusicology at the University of KwaZulu Natal and the University of Hong Kong, he was pursuing hybrid interests in the music of migrant Filipino musicians in Hong Kong, ongoing research into the origin and evolution of South African hip hop, and an emerging interest in localized concepts of heritage and heritage management. Watkins was working closely with digitization projects under the directorship of Diane Thram, an American ethnomusicologist who was leading a major drive to digitize and organize all of the collections at ILAM with collaborative projects supported principally by the South African National Research Foundation.[12] During this period, Watkins was gradually becoming more familiar with Tracey's recordings and the historical development, and potential future trajectories, of ILAM.

A decade later, in September 2016, during an emotive and moving talk addressing a packed room in Wilson Hall at the University of Virginia's African Urbanism Humanities Lab, Watkins recalled how he was drawn into the world of archival sound recordings.

I must say when [having returned from Hong Kong] I started out at Rhodes in 2007, I was on a contract basis, and I didn't have much interest in ILAM or Rhodes or Grahamstown or South Africa . . . but I thought "let's see what comes up." . . . But I was compelled to digitize and [produce] metadata and a whole world opened up, and since then I have been hooked on these recordings. . . . [I]t is a different space, it is beautiful, not to romanticize the collection or the archive.[13]

Prior to becoming director of ILAM in 2016,[14] Watkins had left South Africa again for several years to work in Hong Kong before returning to Rhodes University and becoming head of the Department of Music and Musicology. During this second period back and working in the Eastern Cape, he had become much more focused on community heritage projects, at a time when he felt increasingly displaced within the discipline of musicology. In a public forum at Nelson Mandela University in Port Elizabeth, Watkins shared some current ideas for reimagining ILAM through decolonial mindsets that refused to privilege Western concepts of time or space, but rather aimed to be more responsive to the demands of local communities for enhanced access and ownership. He boldly confirmed that "answers do not come from within the academy or from the curators but from the community."[15]

Building on insights drawn from a background as a long-standing community activist and a scholar of both traditional and popular music, particularly in its mobile and transnational forms, as director, Watkins is developing a new model for ILAM through local curation, focusing in depth on the Eastern Cape and partnering with local community organizations.[16] Through all his collaborations he actively explores what it means to share resources, notably in helping develop the capacity for establishing satellite archives, at various scales, that support and empower local researchers and fieldworkers, offering advice on archiving, documenting, and disseminating material. As Watkins's predecessor Diane Thram continues to develop international repatriation projects through ILAM, returning copies of Tracey's recordings to selected originating communities in Kenya,[17] Zanzibar, Malawi, and Uganda, Watkins works daily to increase ILAM's capacity to resonate first within the local Makana district and then further afield throughout the Eastern Cape. He recognizes that, "in the Eastern Cape there are a lot of stories that are not being told,"[18] and to this end he welcomes and amplifies different voices within ILAM. He reflected to me more recently:

Thinking of the archive, it is kind of a quiet space. . . . [T]here is not much traffic, apart from Mondays when there is a lot of teaching, so it tends to be quiet.
But when the hip hoppers arrive you just hear the whole building vibrate. . . .
[I]t's fantastic because so much of the university is still elite, it is still retained
by privilege, and here they come to one of these buildings and they just take
charge. It's fantastic—Hugh Tracey must be loving it.[19]

Within this archive that surveys and maps diverse music making and sounds
collected widely across Southern Africa, Watkins detects a progressive humanistic impulse that animates the collections, values that can transcend the methods
and story of the collector. As a Black South African, Watkins refuses to identify
primarily with any particular group based on color, but "would rather identify
with a class that is the underclass, because our struggle is more class-based than
race or color."[20] He hears in a constellation of localized recordings the emergence
of a grander statement of humanity.

What appealed to me about the collections was two things: one is a sense of
nostalgia, there is a kind of beauty of yesterday—it is kind of like this is what
music was like then. . . . The second thing for me was that it's pan-African . . .
you know, the problem in South Africa is xenophobia which surfaces now
and again and is quite volatile and that is where one of the strengths of the
collection lies—it speaks to a pan-African sensibility almost . . . it doesn't say
"of the Ndau" or "the Chopi musicians" or "Ashanti" or "Baganda" or whatever
perceived ethnic group: it is the music of all of Southern Africa. And you look
at all these borders—it is a colonial legacy—and you look at all this xenophobia,
and here you have a collection of music that almost challenges these issues of
xenophobia and borders and nationalism. So for me it is a very progressive
aspect to the collections, not the person himself but the collections.[21]

These insights immediately give a much wider-screen view in counterpoint to
the narrower lens of my own sound elicitation built on close and deep listening
to a few fragments of archival Xhosa sound.

Watkins is driven by an impulse to radicalize the work and space of the archive
while acknowledging that, "it is very difficult looking at repatriation for ILAM
because it is a new thing, what models do we emulate, which paradigms do we
follow?"[22] One response has been to listen to alternative concepts and percep-

tions of heritage from voices that have typically been excluded from the archive. Stressing the importance of consulting collaborators in the community, Watkins also argues for the need to change external perceptions of an institutional archive, its holdings and mission.

> To define ways in which the music, how these recordings can help return some kind of esteem, some kind of dignity . . . I think that is a huge undertaking for any archive . . . but it is possible through partnerships with the community organizations. . . . How can we radicalize the relationship between the archive, the community, and the sound object? I think that is one of the next stages we should be going through . . . and also to remove the mystery around the academic world because many people feel like it is an alien space for community members.[23]

Removing mystery, as Rose Boswell and Francis Nyamnjoh argue, can work while developing "reasonable" over "high" theory.[24] According to Watkins,

> there is not just only one interpretation or understanding of heritage or archive or curation; it is discursive terrain. Let's say look at Hugh Tracey, Andrew Tracey investing so much in traditional music, Diane [Thram] focusing on traditional and jazz. Well, I am also compelled to look at traditional music but I am also willing to look at hip hop . . . and pop music.[25]

Within this move to broaden the range of genres studied and archived at ILAM is an intention to break down elitist notions of knowledge production, especially in the context of the powerful student-led "Rhodes Must Fall" and "Fees Must Fall" protest movements beginning in 2015, demanding the decolonization of the curricula and an end to institutional racism in the spaces of higher education in South Africa. "Just because you have a PhD or you are a director doesn't mean that you have sole monopoly of knowledge or sole authority," says Watkins, who prefers to see himself as "just one of the custodians for this time" and someone who is "supposed to move on."[26]

Watkins believes that much academic and archival work remains too self-referential and closed, and that without necessarily being in opposition to Hugh Tracey's idea of the archive, "it is almost the most natural thing to move from what he [Tracey] understands as the archive to bring it to the community to get the domestic workers' understanding of the archive—what does it represent, what could it mean, what should it mean?"[27] The problem of archival accessibility is the same as the problem of knowledge hierarchy in general in South

Africa—which "is still too exclusive, it is still too elitist" and forces us to ask, "how then does one make the archive the space of . . . an imagined egalitarianism in terms of the holding, the curation, the management of the archive?"[28] Elitism easily exacts its own violence, both epistemic and physical. "The colonial and apartheid curriculum in South Africa has," claims Savo Heleta, "promoted white supremacy and dominance, as well as stereotyping of Africa."[29]

Decolonizing—an ongoing and multiply strategized philosophy and movement—necessitates "rejecting the centrality of the West in Africa's understanding of itself and its place in the world," and is also about "'re-centering' ourselves, intellectually and culturally, by redefining what the centre is: Africa."[30] Watkins, and the other artists and actors featured in this chapter and the next, are all asking through different modes what could make this international archive an African archive, as distinct from an archive in and of Africa.

Focusing on the context of the Eastern Cape, it is impossible to ignore the local realities in an area where economic segregation is entrenched, deeply demarcated along color lines, and where some districts regularly suffer from water shortages, load-shedding of electricity, and are even intermittently rendered quasi bankrupt. "The socio-economic context that we live in or work in is dire economically—social development and economic development, those areas are lacking,"[31] laments Watkins, echoing Bebey's vision from a generation earlier that "it is imperative that the future of African music be based on the idea of development and not merely upon preservation."[32] Linking cultural archiving to development becomes a logical and ethical necessity, requiring the ability and willingness to consider "how does the archive serve—or the university itself by extension—how does the archive serve and how can it contribute to social and economic development, so we are not just thinking musicologically?"[33]

NTINGA NTABA KANDODA AND
COLLECTIVE COMMUNITY DEVELOPMENT

How can and does a university-owned sound archive operate "beyond musicology"? Watkins's collaboration with a local cultural group illustrates the practice and possibilities of this move. Since 2012 he has been leading a project linking ILAM and the School of African Languages at Rhodes University with the local heritage and community self-empowerment initiative Ntinga Ntaba kaNdoda, which is located a good two-hour drive northeast of ILAM.[34] This initiative—hereafter referred to as "Ntinga"—is a collective developing heritage, education, climate justice, and food security programs, near the town of Keiskammahoek in a rural corner of the Eastern Cape. Many of the roads through this interlinked network of villages are unpaved flattened rocky tracks that dip and weave through a dust-raising area of stunning mountainous beauty clothed in indigenous forest, part of the Great Escarpment. The area is in the former Ciskei, part of the disastrous experiment in Bantu-governed homelands, and contains multiple heritage points and monuments symbolizing Xhosa heroes and history, many of which have been doubly buried under vandalism and neglect.

Ntinga is a "vibrant rural community movement that mobilizes for rights, democracy, land reform, and sustainable rural development," striving to "build and nurture collective community solidarity, critical consciousness, and democratic practices."[35] The organization focuses on building programs for community arts, heritage, and culture, a sustainable solidarity economy, quality public education, youth leadership, and rights-based participatory democracy. With its headquarters housed inside several rondavels located on a four-hectare site gifted by the nearby Rabula village, it takes its name from an unyielding site symbolizing African resistance to colonialism, the mountain Ntaba kaNdoda. Ntaba kaNdoda, "one of the iconic mountains that constitute the Amathole mountain range in the Eastern Cape," is "historically a venerated symbol of amaXhosa nationhood," and a site that poets, authors, and others have identified as a symbol of unity for all Black South Africans.[36]

Ntinga was founded in September 2002 with members originally pooling from a collection of thirteen villages, fueling further ambitions to link all forty-two villages around Keiskammahoek. Mazibuko Kanyiso Jara, Ntinga's executive director, approached ILAM in 2011 and invited them to participate and present at their annual heritage festival. Watkins accepted the invitation, although he felt that ILAM had little to present or offer at this stage. However, when he saw the wealth of local Xhosa tradition celebrated by multiple practitioners, and witnessed firsthand evidence and accounts of decline in local resources such as *uhadi* instruments and indigenous forests, he instead proposed a collaborative audit and documentation project. Jara and Watkins began to imagine and explore possibilities for collaborative heritage curation.[37]

When explaining why the collaboration with Ntinga became so important for ILAM's future directions, Watkins points to the significance and symbolism of waiting to be asked and invited to work with established community-owned structures, rather than trying to initiate another top-down project. "It fits in with the ethical approach to research," he says, because Ntinga "approached us and asked us to do research with their community. . . . Many times as researchers we go and ask for permission, but here it is the other way round, and to have someone like Mazibuko, one of the managers of Ntinga, who is not afraid of the gown, the space [at ILAM] and so on, so that makes it easier."[38] For Watkins the collaboration is a chance to interrogate institutional concepts and practices of heritage, making sure that together they do not focus on "just music but we look at how people perceive heritage, how do they perceive culture?"[39]

I travelled through many of the villages and projects linked by Ntinga several times during 2017–2019, accompanying Watkins, Jara, heritage expert Daluxolo Matanzima, and other local fieldworkers. I witnessed the collective initiatives to develop music, culture, and farming tied together under a framework of local heritage sites where the stories are told by tour guides drawn from local villages and trained by Ntinga. The Keiskammahoek area yields many sites of both local and national significance, including: a memorial to Maqoma—the most renowned Xhosa chief in the nineteenth-century Frontier Wars; King Ngqika's grave; and the Ntaba kaNdoda mountain itself, named after Ndoda, a Khoi chief and rainmaker, and the site of fighting between the Xhosa and British during the War of the Axe (1834–1835), the War of Mlanjeni (1850–1853) and the War of Nchayechibi (1877–1878). Within these proximities, ecotourism and community heritage initiatives designed to document history and generate income are emerging, such as the Cata lodge, heritage trail, and museum. The Cata Museum is unique in South Africa, being "the only museum that tells the story of rural land dispossession, and the community's successful struggle for restitution."[40] Travelers and tourists can choose to stay in Cata chalets, communally owned three-star self-catering lodges that were built by pooling collective money dispensed by governmental compensation for the apartheid-era "Betterment" projects that had forcibly removed local land rights. The chalets can only be approached on foot or in robust vehicles driven cautiously up steep winding tracks that curl closely between houses and rondavels, unleashing at every turn sweeping views across valleys. Looking out at night, distant home fires dot the blanket-dark hillsides, while excited winds roar their whistling songs that threaten to rip through the thatched roof above you. Trails starting at the lodge reach into indigenous forest shrouding gorgeous waterfalls and providing a home for the rare Cape parrot. Homestead stays can also be arranged, marketed as chances to experience Cata daily life and to learn isiXhosa.

ILAM's collaboration with Ntinga has already led to the successful hosting of heritage festivals in 2012 and 2013, support for ecodesign architects building the Ntinga office site, and the establishment of a significant shared archive. "We have accumulated," reports Watkins, "a substantial number of recordings of performances of music, dance, *imbongi*,[41] *ntsomis*, *ntlombe*, and other rituals, and interviews with local community members on cultural and social matters that lie close to their heart."[42] With members from each organization regularly visiting each other's spaces, Watkins reasons that "members of the community will be learning more about storing digital content, and will also have greater access to the virtual archive and its management."[43] Meanwhile, some members of Ntinga travel within and beyond South Africa building networks of support for their work. In 2018 Jara and musician Bongiwe "Mthwakazi" Lusizi were hosted in the US at the Arcus Center for Social Justice Leadership at Kalamazoo College in Michigan,[44] and then flew to Charlottesville courtesy of the African Urbanism Humanities Lab at the University of Virginia (UVA).[45] Speaking at the interdisciplinary Global Grounds space to a room packed with students and faculty from music, global development studies, and beyond, Jara explained how the movement's approach since 2002 has been a mixture of "with, beyond, and against," and that "at the heart of it all is how do you build the power of ordinary people, so that it is people themselves who drive, who decide?"[46] When Jara introduced Mthwakazi, a self-styled "Xho-opera" singer-songwriter who is in charge of establishing Ntinga's Creative Academy, she shared her own vision as a self-appointed "rural activist." "I do want that exchange," she said holding her *uhadi*, "I want these instruments to be seen on the street like you see children carrying their violins and their 'cellos. This is what I want to see."[47] Jara and Mthwakazi then flew west the next day to speak to other partners in California.

For Ntinga and Watkins, this research exchange must be both collaborative and mutually equitable. For example, Watkins reports that it can often prove difficult for amaXhosa to talk about the past in the former Bantustans, given the history of violent displacement of Black livelihoods, identities, land and communities, and also to understand what a privileged institution like Rhodes wants to gain from their engagement. In the early days of the collaborations when the community hosted repeated visits of groups of students and faculty from Rhodes, Watkins realized that the community wanted explanations for why fieldworkers kept coming back, and he responded by returning the hospitality.

[O]ne time we arranged a trip for them from Keiskammahoek to the archive [ILAM] for them to see this is what we are doing—collecting and recording and retrieving things, and we catalogue it and we put it on the server and

[add] metadata . . . and one of their first reactions was, "we feel our dignity is being restored."[48]

Watkins then realized that a primary motivation—or justification—for repatriation beyond the ethical and practical was the need for emotional healing, "especially people's reaction to the [Ntaba kaNdoda National] Monument when you go and sometimes you ask people what happened under Lennox Sebe's rule,[49] they don't want to remember so you need to push and sometimes you need to be very obnoxious almost, you need to be very insisting."[50] Jason McCoy similarly recognized through his work providing the de facto censored songs of Simon Bikindi to survivors and witnesses of the 1994 genocide in Rwanda that musical repatriation "is not always a simple, unilateral exchange free of controversy."[51] Emotional and physical trauma can both be documented in, and then released from and through, recordings and other artifacts. For Watkins, helping document local stories at the same time as sharing archival Xhosa recordings from ILAM constitutes repatriation, which "is almost like dealing with the damage, trying to heal, it's not only ideological," but rather is addressing personal and communal realities still riven by deep trauma.[52]

An informal network in the Eastern Cape connecting Ntinga, ILAM, and independent artists has begun to collect, archive, and publish some of these unearthed and performed stories and histories. Ntinga supports Amava Heritage Publishers, an independent Black publishing house established by Themba Ngada, that has published several books on the Xhosa chief Maqoma, and actively encourages children to engage with heritage. Amava works to reclaim the heritage of Black people "by researching, packaging, debating and publishing our stories. Stories that tell of our economy, our justice system, our governance structures and our heroes. Stories that prove there was life before the colonial invasion, before we were forcibly turned slaves, before we lost our self-worth."[53] Meanwhile, Watkins has also worked closely with performance and visual artist Sikhumbuzo Makandula, arranging fieldwork excursions to Keiskammahoek, as the artist searches for ways to blend an ethnographic and ethnomusicological sensibility within his fine art performance practice.

Almost anyone travelling through the nearby villages will at some point catch glimpses of the concrete curves of the Ntaba kaNdoda—the National Monument of the Republic of Ciskei—reaching upward in faded grandeur, stunningly unexpected once seen and felt in the rural areas between Burnshill and Dimbaza (see figure 4.1). Built in 1981 and named after the eighteenth-century Khoi chief

FIGURE 4.1 Ntaba kaNdoda (National Monument of the Republic of Ciskei), Dimbaza District, Eastern Cape. July 14, 2019. *Photo by the author.*

Ndoda, the memorial was erected to remember the Xhosa chiefs who were killed in the wars against the British. On a typical day it now stands empty and unattended, the wind often whipping through the empty concrete rooms and structures that are tattooed with rain, graffiti, art, and occasional grazing cattle. The concrete structure is dominating, with vast horn-like columns curving upward together into the sky, fronting an amphitheater area that was originally designed to hold eighteen thousand people. It was commissioned by Ciskeian President Lennox Sebe to inaugurate a new identity during the tragic homelands Bantustan separatist era, and the nearby "Heroes Acre" houses the remains of the nineteenth-century Chief Jongumsobomvu Maqoma (1798–1873) that were disinterred and transported back to the Eastern Cape from Robben Island, where he had been imprisoned and died. This drab grey monument resonates with competing histories, some of which have been chipped through its concrete. For a long time willfully forgotten, the monument has more recently been scratched over and sporadically reactivated by artists and festivals.

Artist Thando Mama has created several photographic and video works asking whether structures designed to preserve the memories of the Xhosa past "can serve any meaningful memorializing purpose and whether they are impervious to the erosion of amnesia and shaping of selective histories."[54] His *Remember-Dimbiza* work uses ninety packets of soil to reference the graves of those killed in the vicinity during the first two years of forced relocations between 1967 and 1969. Seventy were children. Mama's *Forgetting Ntaba kaNdoda* exhibition at the Albany Museum in Grahamstown-Makhanda in February 2018 mounted multi-layered photographs of the artist performing before the Ntaba kaNdoda Monument,[55] designed to "counter the passing of time that has eroded our memory of this sacred place, and acknowledge the negligence that have [*sic*.] robbed us of our heritage."[56]

Performance artist Sikhumbuzo Makandula also makes work that reclaims this space using video, photography, and ritualized performance. In his series of untitled prints from 2016,[57] the monument appears centrally as a character alongside, in front of, and behind Makandula, who is at times wearing a balaclava and robes seemingly to symbolize both authoritarian control and anonymized resistance to oppressive forces. In his performance video "Isigidimi" (The Messenger, 2016),[58] Makandula is dressed in robes and a conical hat and proceeds throughout the deserted building, burning *impepho* (incense) and performing an unidentified cleansing ritual "as he moves methodically and rhythmically through the space."[59] Curator and writer Nancy Dantas sees the monument as a "carcass, like those of other monuments of division," which "still occupies the landscape, and the Eastern Cape's visual horizon, despite the fact that Sebe's bust has been dethroned." For Dantas, the monument both embodies and represents "the persistent physical marks, etched into the landscape, of a past with no immediate undoing."[60] Mama and Makandula both choose to insert their bodies and make their work centrally within this divisive monument and landscape.

In Mama's *KaNdoda-I* (2016–17), a black-and-white inkjet print on photographic paper, the artist's head and upper body are framed inside an artificial Polaroid-style white frame, set against the dominant rising backdrop of the rear of the monument, which now appears to grow brutally from his head like a massive concrete crown. According to South African artist and writer Rachel Baasch, both Mama and Makandula "engage directly with their own lineage and ancestry and consider how it connects to the history of the site in KeiskammaHoek."[61] Thando Mama's visual art, argues Leibbrant—specifically referring to his *Of Nationhood/Desolation* exhibition hosted at the AVA gallery in Cape Town in 2015—questions whether the Ntaba kaNdoda National Monument can "actually convey any remembrance of the 'Xhosa chiefs who died in the clashes with the white colonizers in conflicts for land.'"[62]

The range of voices and perspectives engaging with heritage, monuments, and remembered trauma in this area is steadily building layers of localized understanding that are all being documented, and often performed, as acts of reclamation. As the sustainable sharing of skills, labor, and cultural content between ILAM and Ntinga builds a collaborative archival project that empowers local fieldworkers and artists to collect, document, and tell their own stories that continue to resonate within their localities, Watkins simultaneously welcomes and guides other original repatriation projects. He is committed to sharing ILAM's resources, including professional studio time, to incentivize creative collaborations with young Xhosa beatmakers and poets in and around Grahamstown-Makhanda. This is most notably evidenced in the work of Elijah Madiba.

ELIJAH ("BRA") MADIBA AND STUDIO CURATION

Elijah Moleseng ("Bra") Madiba—ILAM's studio manager, ethnomusicologist, and a consummate and highly versatile musician, producer, and recording artist—is centrally and uniquely placed to understand the history and future of ILAM's collections, curatorial projects, and future directions. Originally from Phalaborwa, a copper-mining town close to Kruger National Park in the Mopani District of Limpopo Province, Madiba first came to the Eastern Cape to study music and technology at Nelson Mandela University in Port Elizabeth. Since 2002 he has worked at ILAM as a sound engineer, studio manager, and project manager with responsibility for overseeing major digitization projects. Having spent significant time working with three different directors—Andrew Tracey (son of Hugh), Diane Thram, and Lee Watkins—his on-the-ground technical, practical, musical, and scholarly knowledge of the realities and priorities of curating ILAM's sound collections is second to none. He has listened closely to the majority of the holdings across decades, and during this time he has worked constantly to deliver the sounds to meet a wide range of requests to broaden access to the collections. He has personally introduced Tracey's recordings to Ludwig Göransson—composer of the score for *Black Panther*,[63] the Marvel Studios blockbuster directed by Ryan Coogler—to Michael Baird for his remastered series, "Historical Recordings of Hugh Tracey" on SharpWood Records,[64] and to the Beating Heart Project, which more recently began to license recordings from several countries for international producers and artists to sample and remix.[65]

I have been privileged to spend time with him as he shares expertise and stories with preeminent African musicians, including Louis Mhlanga from Zimbabwe, as well as South African stars Zwai Bala of TKZee and Themba Mkhize.

"I played bass guitar, sax, and keyboard," explains Madiba, "but since I came to ILAM I've learnt to play so many more instruments," including the *uhadi*, *umrhubhe*, and various *mbira*.[66] He is a highly accomplished multi-instrumentalist, at ease performing in neo-soul bands, traditional marimba ensembles, and experimental jazz bands, as well as being an in-demand producer working across multiple genres from hip hop to gospel. As manager of a studio where the everyday sonic environment oscillates between ethnographic preservation, hip-hop production, and full band recording, Madiba continuously shapes and blends these musical styles while also being heavily involved with outreach projects in the community, especially as a board member of Sakhuluntu Cultural Group, established by Vuyo Booi in Joza township.[67] As a musician who has toured overseas and who plays regularly in venues throughout town and the townships, as well as on campus at Rhodes University, he is constantly able to gauge the relevance of an archive of African field recordings to diverse local audiences. He has also witnessed, supported, and often helped document and archive an array of repatriation and musical conservation projects.[68] A sustained and intimate immersion inside Tracey's collections has enabled Madiba to conceptualize and build diverse links between ethnographic recordings and contemporary musical landscapes and communities.

Madiba has, since 2016, been developing his own sound-curation project, part of which was submitted as a master's thesis in ethnomusicology at Rhodes University in December 2017.[69] He has long been involved in community outreach projects, and, across more than a decade, has seen their importance grow. "Not many South Africans come to this place to listen and enquire," he observed back in 2008, but instead "people from outside come to know." At that time he was already regularly recording township musicians in ILAM's studio and helping them to market and promote their own CDs. He said that, although he was driven to help township artists, he realized then that "most do not want help and art; they just want money."[70] Over time, however, as he witnessed and participated in the repatriation projects expanding through ILAM, he saw how to develop his own research and practice in a way that would be most meaningful to local artists. Reflecting on the intentions of his research—when co-teaching my class in African Electronic Music at UVA with artists Xolile "X" Madinda, Andiswa "Bliss" Rabeshu, and Mxolisi "Biz" Bodla from The Black Power Station—he situated his work along a continuum with Tracey's, explaining how digitization and recent technology have made repatriation a much more locally viable proposition.

> What we couldn't do before [digitization] which was Hugh Tracey's wish— when he went out to do these recordings he wanted them to be returned to the places where he recorded the music because he felt that . . . the communities where the music was recorded must have these recordings to at least mark a certain time in history so they can always have a point of reference. . . . But he never managed to do that mainly because the technology didn't really allow.[71]

"As the sound technologist," he explains in the introduction to his thesis, "I had various duties and as I became more involved in the outreach activities at ILAM I realized that many learners from local and provincial schools who visited ILAM had little to no knowledge of the music in the archives. It became apparent that the archived music was not accessible to people in Grahamstown nor elsewhere." Yet digitization and technology should, according to Madiba, be making more of an impact, given that "it is easy now because we can put the recordings onto cellphones, we can put it onto anything so we are able to return the music to people who would be able to use the recordings."[72] Madiba's project and evolving research methods came from his own embedded position as a musician, engineer, and producer whose daily work and patient and generous personality have made him extremely well known in Grahamstown-Makhanda, throughout the Eastern Cape, and further afield. Over time, he has gradually redefined his own curatorial role as a cultural broker for ILAM, dedicating his research time to finding ways to expose the recordings to local musicians, poets, and artists in Makhanda and nearby Peddie and Port Elizabeth. He has been exploring the potential for archival sounds to be used creatively on a continuum somewhere between repatriation and revitalization of local music making. Building on revitalization work already undertaken through ILAM by Gomolemo "Pinkie" Mojaki among a Bangwaketse community in Botswana,[73] as well as developing models that improved upon the limitations of my own initial sound elicitation experiments, Madiba sought to "not only create an awareness of the existence of these recordings but also to stimulate use of the recordings in ways that appeal to the youth."[74]

Fully aware of the postcolonial debates and critiques of Tracey's codification methods, Madiba takes a practical and action-oriented position on use of the collections, preferring to demarcate a clear line that detaches the collector from the collection. He reasons:

I work at ILAM and many people have asked me how I felt about the fact that ILAM was established by a man who is viewed by many, in retrospect, as a colonialist. My response has always been that if Hugh Tracey had not taken his time and made it his life mission to record this music, we would not have this archive and we would have lost a great part of our history and heritage. I do not care what he was because I cannot change it. I can merely be grateful for the music he preserved.[75]

Madiba released ILAM recordings throughout the local artistic community during the course of more than a year, allowing a long creative gestation period for the sounds to gradually influence music making. As a trained sound archivist steeped in, and central to, the history and mission of ILAM, he was already well aware of existing preconceptions about ILAM and Tracey. He reported that some of the musicians he approached were reluctant, due to the fact that ILAM was founded during colonial times, and that there were still unresolved questions surrounding the motives and ethics of how the instruments and recordings were acquired by Tracey. For some artists, decolonizing the archive meant not even touching it.

An enabler who works very closely with many undergraduate and graduate students in music and ethnomusicology, Madiba intimately witnesses on a daily basis the stark reality of the town/gown divide and how township artists remain extremely marginalized. "One major challenge of this research and my role as a 'culture broker,'" he stated, "was finding locations such as libraries or youth centers in the community where the public will have access to the music."[76] Madiba experiences and knows the mistrust that institutions, especially those perceived to be predominantly White-owned, are met with among disenfranchised communities and individuals, who often prefer more informal and noninstitutional modes of access and engagement. Madiba was aware of the irony of the danger of being perceived himself as the colonialist by association, and so addressed this issue up front before working with anybody. Rather than simply testing the relevance of recordings through people's responses, he was primarily interested in supporting practical outcomes.

I wanted to give the music to people who I knew would do something with it, not just listen to the music and it ends there—that's why I gave it to . . . different kinds of musicians who do bands and hip hop and all that. . . . And I wanted also to give it to people who are into dance and drama, just everybody who can be able to use the music.[77]

Madiba first consulted widely with friends and artists before circulating the recordings—all 201 tracks from sixteen albums of Xhosa music in the *Sound of Africa* series—hosting community discussions and working closely with the Fingo Festival organization in Fingo Village township, an initiative founded by Xolile "X" Madinda, as well as inviting artists into ILAM in order to publicize and make available the institution's own resources. He gave the music to more than twenty musicians from Grahamstown-Makhanda, King William's Town,[78] Queenstown,[79] East London, Port Elizabeth, and Peddie with an invitation to use the archival recordings in their own work and according to their own schedule.[80] All of these towns and regions are places Tracey had travelled through and recorded in or near. Madiba simply asked the musicians to let him know when they were working with the music so he could visit them to observe some of the creative processes, as and when this was welcome. Madiba explains his consciously open-ended instructions:

> I stated that the recordings belong to the amaXhosa people, their people, and as such, they had every right to use the music in any way they pleased. I also said that because they were working artists, making music and poetry in different genres, I hoped that they would use the tracks in any way to produce something that would be beneficial, both financially and musically, to themselves. Finally, I asked that I could be part of their creative endeavour. I had wanted to record both the process and the music. The musicians welcomed this freedom and my request.[81]

Madiba organized a workshop with Fingo Festival in 2016, designed to share and discuss the sounds and context for Xhosa traditional music. which was mostly attended by hip-hop artists from Grahamstown-Makhanda and neighboring towns. Poet Yakim led discussions about access to ILAM and the sampling of recordings of traditional music in relation to copyright, and beatmaker Adon Geel gave a live workshop showing how to turn one of Tracey's recordings into a new track.[82] He demonstrated how he immersed himself in archival Xhosa sound and spent much time cutting the sounds into smaller segments to fit his own compositional structures.

Over time, Madiba detected a pattern of interest that shaped his focus, observing that of all the musicians he met, "it was the poets and hip-hop producers that were most engaged with the early recordings and who worked diligently with them."[83] From the outset, Madiba was able to offer enticements for exchange that worked for artists, including free studio time and professional production, together with ongoing training in studio recording and production techniques whenever required. Madiba's in-demand talent as a producer and studio manager not only meant he had already earned the respect of other artists, but also that he was able to offer a real opportunity and tangible resources to artists as his research unfolded through a network of genuine exchange. Significantly, the studio itself becomes a productive space for research, musical production, and mastering, and a free environment for clarifying, sharing, and adapting ILAM's mission. Madiba explains:

> I opened the ILAM studio for them to use as both an educational opportunity and an opportunity for me to watch them work because there is a lack of recording studios in Grahamstown. Artists furthermore lack money to pay for studio time and therefore have no experience in this line of music-making. This worked very well and most of the musicians made use of the facilities and learned a lot about recording and producing and I, in turn, was able to watch their creative process.[84]

For example, noticing that among artists in the Eastern Cape "most beatmakers use only a computer and maybe an outboard sound card in their bedroom studios,"[85] Madiba shared his expertise in studio recording techniques with the artists, including, for example, teaching the beatmaker Mthibazi ("Ongidaro") Tatana how operating a digital mixing console was different from his own recording process working with a sound card.

Generous exposure to studio time and expertise proved equally valuable for the poets and self-styled "language activists" as well. "For the poets," said Madiba, "it was mainly the experience of working in the studio, learning to be professional by coming prepared, knowing and understanding their voices, and how to project and use their voices to portray certain messages."[86] Most of the poets were previously unfamiliar with the process of studio recording. The shared exchanges in Madiba's research are tangible and audible, as his curatorial approach brings the dual mutual benefit of exposing to artists the archival recordings and the institutional resources that houses them. Meanwhile the co-productions in ILAM's studio become the active research exchange and the creative mode for the professional recording of new music through ongoing sharing of studio time and skills. Madiba's research method evolves by helping to create, and then follow, productive spaces for artists to choose to work and record in. He is able to engage with a wide range of creative processes at the intersection of archiving and contemporary composition, ranging from beatmakers struggling to work with drifting time signatures in software that is usually designed to accommodate Western rhythmic units, to poets interpreting obscure isiXhosa words in archival song titles and lyrics and settling on their own translations.

Archival fragments fed into the local process of isiXhosa language activism. For example, Siphelo "Nqontsonqa" Dyongman[87] is a thirty-year-old poet from Grahamstown and graduate of Walter Sisulu University who performs his poetry in isiXhosa to address "social issues such as absent fathers, education, love, and divided churches."[88] Madiba reported that, after being given access to ILAM recordings, Nqontsonqa "then made ILAM his second home. . . . He sits at ILAM to write his poetry, does research on the ILAM recordings and has since released an album featuring some of the ILAM recordings given to him called 'KULE' (khawuve, uthando lwalaph'engingqini, hear the love here in our space)," which he produced together with beatmaker Ongidaro.[89] "Unotshe, asoze ndixolise" (Never, I won't apologize) is one of the poems written by Nqontsonqa and was inspired by the ILAM track "Ingeji yam" (My engagement ring), sung by the Zwelitsha Choral Society and recorded by Hugh Tracey at King William's Town in 1957.[90] In Tracey's recording, a girl sings about hearing a young man saying "give me back my engagement ring," lamenting that she doesn't know why she has been jilted.

Madiba's research highlights both the potential and problems of working with archival Xhosa recordings. Some poets, such as Bhodl'ingqaka, heard and then created further resonances between the archive and their contemporary practice. Madiba noticed that when the poets heard the recordings from ILAM "they are the ones who felt this goes with their poetry, the story they are trying to tell, because . . . they write their poetry in isiXhosa and . . . they are . . . language activists, they use their poetry to highlight the beauty of the language, so it linked very well with what they are doing."[91] However, Madiba also noticed a practical problem that needed to be bridged to enable the beatmakers to work more closely with archival sounds, which were often not well suited to the sampling parameters and functions of software such as FruityLoops.[92] Madiba also identified a pattern among beatmakers whereby few had any prior prolonged engagement with archival sounds and their ceremonial or everyday occurrences. According to Madiba, the major problem for the beatmakers was that

they are not really able to connect with and use them because [the sounds] are not really what they are normally exposed to. When you ask them "do you hear this?" they say "no, I only hear this when there is *umgidi* and then after that nothing else." But the rest of the music they hear every day—radio, TV, everywhere—so that becomes the question: do you retrain the ear to listen to an African song?[93]

Madiba's use of Tracey's recordings to catalyze new songs and artworks deployed an open-ended and potentially sustainable method of allowing musicians the time to absorb recordings, and to find a place for them within their creative process. It also worked by offering valuable and desirable returns, especially the access to recording and production facilities within a professional studio. He focuses on the ways musicians use repatriated recordings to spark new poems, stories, and tracks, paying attention more to "the contemporary musical results than the process or the pedagogy."[94] As a producer, studio manager, and artist who is deeply embedded and connected within the local campus, town, and township music scenes, Madiba already knew well that ILAM had resources to offer to artists beyond repatriating recordings, so he decided to extend his responsibilities, recognizing that "as an engaged ethnomusicologist one must be prepared to create opportunities for the artists to learn and improve their art form."[95]

Madiba also helped create the conditions for other new forms of work, including isiXhosa storytelling for children. Lonwabo "Adon Geel" Phillip—a hip-hop producer, rapper, and studio manager who is from King William's Town and, at the time of Madiba's research, was based in Port Elizabeth—works part time in Grahamstown-Makhanda for Fingo Festival, which commissioned him to manage an isiXhosa storytelling project. Madiba reports that Adon Geel chose to use ILAM tracks as background music for some of the stories and then decided to work directly with a musician who sang and played traditional Xhosa instruments. Together, they created and recorded to CD *uJakalashe usomaqhinga* (The trixie jackal), a trilogy of stories about a jackal who tricked other animals. Their stories variously use ILAM recordings featuring the *uhadi*, *umrhubhe*, and an *mhlala* (a cry, call, or summons). The first story, "Udyakalashe [*sic*] neMfene" (Jackal and the baboon), samples Tracey's recording "Inkulu into ezakwenzeka" (Something very bad is going to happen).[96] Adon Geel uses Tracey's archival recording to begin their track, and then continues with the recording as background music to the story, which is narrated by Pura, a Xhosa musician and anthropologist who plays both *uhadi* and *umrhubhe* and was a founding member of the band Udaba whom I first met at ILAM and Fort Hare University in 2007. In the second story, "uJakalashe neNgwe" (The jackal and the leopard), Adon Geel and Pura used the Tracey recording "Nyakumtyela egageni" (You will eat it out of doors).[97] In the final story, "uJakalashe neNyamakazi" (The jackal and the animals), the song was inspired by Tracey's recording "Mama ndaswelindawo ngendaba" ("Mama I lack accommodation on account of the news"),[98] but this time small samples and new recordings inspired by the track were created by Adon Geel and Pura and formed a sound bed for the story.

This trilogy of storytelling—created by an established hip-hop producer in collaboration with an anthropologically trained Xhosa musician versed in both tradition and avant-garde experiments—illustrates the varied and subtle ways that Tracey's recordings can be used and reused by individual artists: as historical reference points, quasi-ambient background flavor, or as a sonic starting point for newly composed Xhosa music and narrative designed to engage young children through stories. This work is also created and then shared within the distinct but loosely related spaces of ILAM and Fingo Festival, and ethnographic sound fragments begin to oscillate again in places between the archive and the townships simultaneously. The performance practice of three young local artists involved in these creative processes working through increasingly mobile spaces around the archive illustrates how archival fragments are being amplified and owned in spaces outside the archive. Some of these artists and fragments will sound again within a new creative arts space explored in chapter 5, The Black Power Station.

AKHONA "BHODL'INGQAKA" MAFANI
AND YOUTH PRAISE POETRY

Akhona "Bhodl'ingqaka" Mafani is a twenty-four-year-old poet who performs in isiXhosa and "comes from a collective of poets called Imin'Esisdenge,[99] who have been reciting poetry in and around Eastern Cape."[100] Bhodl'ingqaka—which roughly translates as "the one who burps cream" (i.e., "the one who speaks quality")—was the first person to use some of Tracey's recordings within his own poetry during Elijah Madiba's research. He had met Madiba through their mutual friend, Xolile "X" Madinda, at Raglan Road Library during the PUKU isiXhosa Storytelling Festival.[101] Bhodl'ingqaka had been commissioned through Fingo Festival by the Recycling and Economic Development Initiative of South Africa (REDISA), to write a poem about conservation, and then, when he was given access to Tracey's Xhosa recordings, he wrote a poem entitled, "Londoloza Indalo" (Protect the Creation) in which he used the track "Ndoyika u-Ntusangili" (I am afraid of Ntusangili) as a basis for a new poem.[102] Madiba reports that

Bhodl'ingqaka "decided to use this music as a background for his poem, but instead of writing a poem about love he wrote about littering: what is bad about it; why we keep ourselves clean and then about ruining the environment by littering."[103] For Bhodl'ingqaka, the connection between the archival recording and his own poem came from his realization that the woman in Tracey's recording was afraid to express her feelings. He responded by choosing to address contemporary everyday issues and confront people directly through praise poetry (*izibongo*), inspired by his own determination to face up to difficulties through expressive art.

In 2017–19, I shared time together with Elijah and Bhodl'ingqaka, both at Fingo Festival and in the studio at ILAM, and was instantly impressed by the vision, energy, and sense of purpose and social responsibility possessed by the young poet, who was originally from Vukani township, an uphill walk past Fingo Village leading further away from town. He spoke passionately about his ideas for documentaries, festivals, and other film projects, and had just officially launched his first album at the National English Literary Museum in Graham-stown-Makhanda. The album is titled *Iintonga Zetyendyana* (Fighting Sticks of a Young Boy) and Bhodl'ingqaka describes its content as "musical poetry with a traditional African twist," representing "a snapshot of life on the dusty streets of Vukani where I grew up."[104] He had previously recorded at Shizzo Manizzo, a label co-founded in 2007 by Siphelo Dyongman and which works with several local artists, operating from Lonwabo "Dezz" Gwente's backroom shack at his mother's house.[105] Shizzo Manizzo has since grown into a respected local music label, and, as one journalist reports, "now has three laptop computers to record with instead of the antiquated desktop machine they started out on. But they still record local artists in Gwente's back-room mud home."[106] For Bhodl'ingqaka, recording *Iintonga Zetyendyana* at ILAM was his first time to work on a full album in a professional recording studio.

Bhodl'ingqaka acknowledged that when he was introduced to the recordings by Madiba, like many of the other invited artists he was uncertain of what to make of, or do with, the sounds. He admitted that, "when he first did this, no one paid attention, in fact we just took the music as he gave us CDs which had this music so we had to go home and to look and see if we could make this music . . . so it took time for us to realize we need this music."[107] Gradually, he began to feel that he wanted to write poetry over the top of Tracey's recordings, rather than using "modernized beats." "I got impressed by the songs," he said, and "I never even used the modernized beats that we use—I thought you know what, let me just do the poem on this song." The workshop at Fingo Festival and dialogue about ILAM hosted by Madiba with Xolile "X" Madinda and other artists was instrumental in revealing the potential of working with archival recordings. Bhodl'ingqaka explained:

> I was approached by Xolile Madinda calling from REDISA recycling development initiative . . . situated in Cape Town—they wanted a piece making a point that you are taking care of the environment, so I wrote a poem. We worked with Madinda and when he was editing I did not know that he was going to use the ILAM songs underneath, but when he did the editing he said to me "come listen," and I was very impressed. So that has been the motive for myself to use the songs more and more. . . . [S]o that was the video, it was about nature preservation, taking care of the environment.[108]

In the video for *Londoloza Indalo* (Save Nature/Protect the Creation),[109] filmed and edited by Blah ze Blah and produced by Fingo Festival as part of the PUKU isiXhosa Storytelling competition sponsored by REDISA,[110] the young poet is seen wearing his backpack and walking in the Botanic Gardens in town before he addresses the camera directly. The piece opens with Tracey's recording of women singing over the dry sounds of clapping, before Bhodl'ingqaka's poetry begins to flow. As he continues with solid and steady urgency, the camera cuts to shots of discarded rusty tin cans and rills of muddy water snaking at the edges of tracks in the townships, juxtaposed and contrasted with views looking back across the high street toward the cathedral and the leafy Botanic Gardens with their ornamental ponds inside Rhodes University's campus, seemingly a world away from the townships. I asked Bhodl'ingqaka about the poetry and imagery used in his poem and video, and he explained:

> In this poem I am motivating people, it is more about preservation, so I am say-ing, "let us preserve nature let us make that we keep the environment clean and nice," because I feel that the places that we live also determines ourselves. . . . For example, if I am living in a house that is dirty—*yebo* [yeah]—people are bound to see to me as someone who might be dirty too. . . . So I am saying that I am motivating "let us keep our places clean," as we know that some diseases can just come out of the dirty places and children are growing up and they play out in litter and all that. So I am saying, "let's be responsible." So the message must be addressed specifically to the parents—the old people—let them be responsible so that their children can also benefit, can learn to be responsible.[111]

Young, hip, and fond of wearing popular labels, Bhodl'ingqaka usually performs dressed in traditional Xhosa material and beads—exactly as he appears on the cover of his *Iintonga Zetyendyana* album (see figure 4.2)—and was first inspired to remain in touch with his Xhosa roots "through his late grandfather, who was a respected traditional healer."[112] He began to hear and feel the value in some of the social messages revealed within Tracey's recordings, and recognized that the way to ensure they remained relevant was to reframe them and use them within new songs and poems, creating messages for both younger and elder audiences.

Bhodl'ingqaka also wrote other poems to layer on top of Tracey's recordings, turning the ethnographic fragments into quasi backing tracks, including "Mazibuye" (Let them return), which he wrote using one of Tracey's recordings of "Mhlahlo," the welcoming song that Nyaki and I often played in our sound elicitation project.[113] Elijah Madiba interprets the new poem as addressing "the wrongs that occurred in the past where black people were robbed of their land, cows, and other belongings. He is saying that what was taken from them must

FIGURE 4.2
Akhona "Bhodl'ingqaka"
Mafani (l) and Nyakonzima
"Nyaki" Tsana (r), at ILAM.
July 19, 2017.
Photo by the author.

Art and Community Activism around the Archive **153**

be returned."[114] For example, in one verse Bhodl'ingqaka calls for a respect for Xhosa cultural tradition and self-knowledge.

> Mazibuy' iinkomo! mazibuy' iinkomo zoobawo
> Apho sikhoyo sikwavula zibhuqe
> sidad' ebugxwayibeni sirhubuluza ngamapeqe
> Mazibuy' iinkomo ngale nyanga yenkcubeko,
> Ngale nyanga yokuzazi, ngale nyanga yamasiko

> The cows must come back. The cows of our forefathers must come back.
> We are in a state of no laws, rules, and regulations.
> We are swimming in the deep end of dirt with our brains.
> They must come back in this cultural month, a month of knowing self,
> A month of our traditions, a month of sticking to our roots.[115]

Bhodl'ingqaka, who was inspired by the *imbongi* tradition when he first saw performances at the National Arts Festival at the age of ten, claims to be inspired to write by everything happening around him. "So if for example," he says, "I'd seen something done wrong by the people, or whatever it is, say some sort of abuse from a parent to a child or whatever it is . . . I find a reason to write about that."[116] In conversation with Elijah Madiba and myself, he explained how he really wants to "accommodate" more of the archival recordings, and hopes to find more "patient" producers and people who can help out, who can study and work hard to craft ways for the archival recordings to fit with the more "modernized beats." "There are challenges," he said "because we are coming from a hip-hop background, so sometimes it's kind of hard for our producers to manipulate them in the software."[117] Accordingly, one of his responses has been to simply leave the original recordings as soundscape beds for his improvised poetry, setting up a new call and response as both come in and out of focus and the fragment is reinserted into a broader contemporary and modernized sound field.

The linked work of Bhodl'ingqaka, Madiba, and Watkins shows that it is the spaces for breathing new creative life into archival recordings—bedroom studios, ILAM's professional studio, performance workshops, and community heritage centers—that prove to be at least as important as the actual sharing of archival sounds. Lee Watkins's collaborative work conceives of the archive as a space with radical potential to explore communal ownership, and Madiba's studio-based interventions place the contemporary artistry of township youth at the center of a reimagined and remixed archive with production values. Bhodl'ingqaka, who has been writing and performing since the age of fourteen, frames archival sounds inside roaring *izibongo* praise poetry, as well as neo-soul, hip hop, and other popular forms, widely performing locally and on national TV.

Meanwhile, new forms of radicalized and mobile performance art targeting contested public monuments in Grahamstown-Makhanda are transforming archival practices into highly original performance modes that engage knowledge from the streets and the land. As I shared a deepening engagement with the formal and informal arts scenes in the Eastern Cape across more than a decade, I came to experience the mobile public work of Masixole ("Masi") Heshu and Sikhumbuzo ("Sku") Makandula, two vitally insightful young South African performance artists working to activate and interrogate the public reclamation of history. Both artists studied at Rhodes University and have been creating work that moves fluidly around and across historical sites in the spaces between town and townships, and in and out of archives such as ILAM. Though mostly working independently of each other, both artists blend sound, dramatic performance, and vibrantly original narrative modes to activate archival material and inhabit living stories in situ at public monuments and in spaces of deep historical significance.

PERFORMING TAXI TOURS:
MASIXOLE HESHU AND MOBILE HISTORY

Are conversations about the ownership of monuments, spaces, and histories inevitably doomed to be dragged into partisan and polarized opposition? African American artist Titus Kaphar is perhaps best known for his ongoing "Monumental Inversions" project, a series of sculptures that confront the competing histories and reputations of America's forefathers. He is renowned for the way he reworks and reimagines historical paintings and sculptures, crumpling, stripping, breaking, ripping, remixing, and "torturing" art works as he reconfigures historical narratives. "Publicly," he states, "we're having a very binary conversation about these sculptures, and it's by and large one group saying keep it up and the other group saying take it down." Kaphar believes there are other ways to communicate, and he works outside the boundaries of these binaries and dichotomies, imagining "a possibility where contemporary artists are engaged to make public works that stand in the same squares as these problematic pieces that we are forced to walk by daily."[118] It is one thing to tear down Confederate statuary, and another thing for Kehinde Wiley to install his own "Rumors of War" statue outside the Virginia Museum of Fine Arts, as a direct response challenging the message and legitimacy of the Confederate statues that line Monument Avenue in Richmond, the former capital of the Confederacy.[119]

Art historian Brenda Schmahmann shows how activist artists in South Africa also create something more polyphonic, articulating "opposition to values associated with commemorative public art from colonial and apartheid eras . . . without involving desecration or removal."[120] Alongside a history of defacing, removals, and erasures of colonial monuments in South Africa, she finds more persuasive traction in artistic interventions, such as the Kultural Upstarts Kollective's *Untitled Intervention* (2007). When a vuvuzela, giant sunglasses, a cape, and a *lekarapa* (a reworked miner's helmet denoting sporting allegiance) were placed on Marion Walgate's statue of Cecil John Rhodes — erected at the University of Cape Town in 1934 — the guerilla artistic act countered the imperialist aura with "the ironic effect of turning Rhodes from a magnate surveying his lands to a fan surveying a soccer match." For Schmahmann, Rhodes has been reoriented, and retold, so that "rather than seeming to gaze acquisitively towards Cairo, his look is implied to be simply at the sports field in front of him."[121]

I first met Masixole ("Masi") Zinzo Patrick Heshu in June 2017, thanks to the creative networks linking Nyaki and Xolile ("X") Madinda with many other artists, many of whom were gravitating in and out of the drama department at Rhodes University and also, though admittedly less frequently, through ILAM, itself nestled at the end of a curling lane that begins almost directly opposite the entrance to the Drama Department on Prince Alfred Street. I came to know this vicinity, with several cafes and bars visible nearby, as a hub and meeting point, especially for artists and students. At the time, Masi was a master's student in the history department, working closely with the Isikhumbuzo Applied History Unit,[122] having previously completed his undergraduate degree in drama and politics at Rhodes. I already knew Masi's mum, Ntomboxolo "Nox" Donyeli, having been introduced to her by Nyaki in 2007–2008 when we were sharing ILAM recordings with local artists in Grahamstown. Nox is an extremely talented, charismatic, and well-known actress and performer, regularly appearing in leading stage roles during the National Arts Festival with Ubom! and other theatre companies.[123] Nox began her career in the 1970s as a young female artist at the height of apartheid and did not have the opportunity to go to university. She recognizes that "those who went to university get better opportunities than people like me who have had years of experience, so even now I'm not treated equally as an artist."[124]

Growing up as a "born free" and immersed in theater since he was very young, Masi began his performing career at the age of twelve, and remains one of very few artists from the townships to graduate from Rhodes. Nyaki urged me to witness Masi's distinctive take on publicly performed mobile history, and we began to spend time together in the studio at ILAM, in rehearsals in the drama department, and while hanging out with mutual friends. The first piece written and directed by Masi that I attended was *Iimfazwe* (Battles), an intimately captivating taxi tour performance that composed and connected live stories, songs, and oral histories within mobile journeys to historical sites. On a mildly windy early July afternoon in 2017, fifteen of us crammed into a minibus taxi for a tour that began outside the Albany Museum at the edge of the Rhodes campus where the university begins to meet town. As we drove away from campus and down High Street, which was humming with the sprawling energy that the National Arts Festival brings to Grahamstown-Makhanda every June and July, some of the passengers gently surprised us as they subtly revealed themselves to be actors in the role of tour guides. As songs, stories, and questions emerged and unfolded, the "tour guides" intermittently interacting with the travelling audience, the taxi continued right up Raglan Road, cutting alongside Fingo Village and other townships, while stopping at selected monuments and sites of historical significance.

A performed conversation took place between "tour guide" Thandazile Madinda, a renowned artist and *imbongi* (praise poet), and other actors in the taxi bus. Madinda played the role of uMkhulu (Grandfather), telling stories to other artists inside the taxi, loosely based on the stories Masi's grandfather had told to him. uMkhulu continuously drew the rest of the audience-passengers into the conversation, interrogating our awareness of indigenous concepts and Xhosa names and histories, drawing attention to the remnants and remains of colonial brutality and the local monuments. We drove alongside a statue on High Street and caught sight of the splashing red paint lines of graffiti that announced "iRhini," a Xhosa name for Grahamstown (see figure FM.1). Songs—mostly laments—broke out sporadically, and at several points we disembarked to watch performances staged at historical sites. Thandazile and the other artists climbed out of the taxi to join a small group of young actors who were already waiting for us on rocky outcrops in an area closer to the initiation "bush-schools." We watched two youths playing a board game that might have been chess inside a stone-rimmed circle, as two young boys in black capes danced toward each other, honoring cattle wealth and other Xhosa symbols.

uMkhulu addressed the hills looking back across town and up toward the apartheid-era 1820 Settlers Monument and beyond: "I thought I knew this place. Mountains and hills, they never speak. But they know better," he declaimed, while reciting the litany of foreign and Xhosa names that identified the hills and land for miles around.[125] As the wind whipped at our ears and all the gathering screens of angled smartphones, uMkhulu continued: "My sight is blinded as my feet collide with the soil. It is hard to trace the past." We headed back in the taxi to Egazini (The Place of Blood) Monument, where a group of young school-girls performed songs and dances in a circle, mixing Xhosa songs with popular recordings. They danced to "Change the World" by Lira (Lerato Molapo), and then moved us along to a village scene staged under trees where three women, one of whom was Masi's mother, Nox, told stories from the Fifth Frontier War and how their husbands and male relatives never came back. Nosipho, another local artist, played *uhadi* over the refrain of laments, as Nox fought to speak through tears. "I had to answer questions" she said. Nosipho, now in the role of a child, looked at the ground and turned to Nox, asking with urgency, "Mama, uphi uTata noMalume?" (Mama, where is father, where is uncle?). "Bayeza" (they are coming), Nox tried to reassure the child, as a man's checked jacket and fad-ing dark trousers hung loosely from a tree, fluttering in the devastating wind as flimsy symbols of the West and the absent bodies that would never return. We moved on to the final site, the Old Gaol, which took us back to a place opposite the tour's starting point.[126] A desk had been placed outside the grey igloo-shaped cells, facing the imposing reach of the tall, concrete-slabbed and windowless walls bounding the former prison. Seated behind the desk was another young actor telling stories accompanied by a singer from the taxi tour. "I fear that I am losing the power to direct my own stories," he confessed. "I fear silence." The performance then ended when Masi, who had not been on the tour, appeared by the desk to thank us and ask for us all to provide our gift by offering feedback.

The piece was remarkable for its gradual and powerful shift from the everyday mode of the taxi journey between town and township—a route taken both ways by many workers daily as part of a year-round lived routine—combined with its moving reclamation of Xhosa songs and stories that were actively shared inside the taxi and trailed out into the landscape as prayers for the soil, mountains, and the amaXhosa who had walked, farmed, and fought for their land in these places before. A few days after the piece, which would go on to win a Standard

Bank Encore Award, I spoke with Masi in the drama department at Rhodes. He explained how the theme had evolved from his own family histories and then crystallized through his realization that more and more people felt as if they did not know their own histories as amaXhosa. "What happens in the taxis," explained Masi, "is that a grandfather is taking his grandson on a journey to share the history with the grandson about all of these sites, especially Grahamstown which is part of the Zuurfeld," as the Albany District—the rural hinterland stretching inland from Port Elizabeth—was named by migrating Boer farmers in the late eighteenth-century.[127] Masi explained that a key moment—when uMkhulu addresses the land and says that he thought he knew her—grew from his own visceral reaction to the times when historian Julie Wells, director of the Isikhumbuzo Applied History Unit at Rhodes, had taken him around some of these sites and shared histories that he himself had not previously known. Masi wanted to create work in direct response to this dawning realization, especially since this moment took place at a point in the landscape where Xhosa initiation schools stand close to more recent monuments, mostly now neglected or vandalized, at the very place where Makhanda stood with his warriors before attacking the British Army at the Battle of Grahamstown on April 22, 1819.

"In oral societies even more than in literate ones," writes Jeff Peires, a historian of amaXhosa, "it is the victors who record the history, particularly if the losers become reconciled to their defeat."[128] Peires had traced a stark decline in Xhosa oral modes, and claimed that the world of the traditions was becoming very unreal to the Xhosa, and "difficult for them to visualize," now that "chiefs approximate more to the local bureaucracy than to the fighting leaders of a hundred years ago, and the presence of the white West permeates even the remotest corner of Xhosaland."[129] And whereas Leroy Vail and Landeg White argue against the simplistic dichotomy between the oral and the literate—rejecting as an ahistorical simplicity the "dehumanized stereotype known as 'oral man'"[103]—it is possible to trace a renewed vigor, power, and splendor in Xhosa oral performance, exemplified in the work here of Masi, Thandazile Madinda, and of Bhodl'ingqaka and other language activist poets and local artists who are all visibly and audibly performing their pride in Xhosa orality.

Masi's motivation for writing and staging Iimfazwe was to present an oral mode of history as performance art, and to help banish local inferiority complexes. He still felt it was a battle for orality to be taken seriously, remarking that "even though it may not be accepted by academics, there are still a lot of people who practice that oral tradition and it becomes a pillar to young people."

He also spoke of the fears of inferiority that ran high in the townships. "There is that fear of a township kid at high school and maybe they want to study at Rhodes, but there is that fear, they come from a poor background." As both a performer and scholar of public history, Masi feels that "history is written in a way that makes us look inferior in what we do," and believes that "at least if we do a tour we can have a conversation about that and move on from that." While writing Iimfazwe, Masi soon realized that few local people knew much about the history of Grahamstown-Makhanda. "What we are doing is a simple thing," he said, namely "taking the knowledge to the people."[131]

Masi further explored the notion of Xhosa erasures in his next major production, Xhosa Chronicles, a play that premiered a year later in July 2018 at Victoria Girls' School Hall, also as part of the National Arts Festival, and which was later adapted for staging inside The Black Power Station.[132] Written and directed by Masi with a small cast including Nox, as well as Masi's uncle and friends, the play represents scenes from life in a village, focused around a kraal placed center-stage within a family homestead where family elders meet to speak with their ancestors. In the fictional village of Magwala, the Xhosa residents seem to live in a state of fear of the unknown, and the village elder, Mgolombane, tells stories to the community that recall the first visitors from overseas, and how they infiltrated, and ultimately violated, the land, the women, the children, and the cattle. Appearing in Xhosa browns and blues, clothed with headwraps, beads, and animal skins, the performers establish dialogue with the ancestral past (kumanyange). "The play," reports Thandolwethu Gulwa, "addresses the tools which have been used to distort the truth about amaXhosa and isiXhosa," and sets up "a disjuncture between amanyange and the new generation," in order to present "an image of how foreign belief systems have influenced the youth."[133] Xhosa Chronicles, "a lament for lost stories,"[134] adds a deepening theatrical engagement to expand on Masi's work to find the modes and styles for performing Xhosa stories in ways that reflect and meet local Xhosa modes of transmission, successfully engaging mixed audiences at Rhodes, on the streets in town, and in the townships.

PERFORMING MONUMENTAL INTERVENTIONS: THE RADICAL RITUALS OF SIKHUMBUZO MAKANDULA

Sikhumbuzo ("Sku") Makandula was born in De Aar, Northern Cape, and is both a visual and performance artist who works between Cape Town, Johannesburg, and Makhanda. He studied Fine Art at Rhodes University and holds a master's degree in Public Spheres and Performance Studies from the University of Cape Town. His series of visual prints at the Ntaba kaNdoda Monument serve as an example of ways he seeks to reinsert identities, bodies, and media within historical sites and landscapes. His practice focuses on media such as live art, photography, and video art, with interests in public culture, public and social history, heritage studies, and conservation of built environments in Southern Africa. He works intimately with sound, poetry, photography, video, ritual, movement, and sculpture, and much of his work is performed live at monumental sites, using sound, gesture, action, and symbolic movement to unearth, question, and displace received dominant histories. In many of his performed works, religious symbols and clothing are repurposed, rendered ambiguous, and sometimes destroyed. Makandula speaks of experiencing a calling, a need to trace back his lineage, which ironically came from the staunch Anglican religiosity of his mother's side. "I discovered that I come from a family of practitioners, of healers," he explains, "something that in the family . . . a Christian family, was silenced actually. It was never spoken about, even till today."[135]

In an article entitled "Reimagining Our Missing Histories," Makandula is in a conversational partnership with Ugandan artist Eria Nsubuga Sane. He discusses the value of his own work alongside his contemporaries, which he sees as being a form of "self-authorship of our own narratives as we write our own history by revisiting, remapping, and reimagining our collective identity and social history."[136] At Sane's invitation, Makandula explains the broader artistic intentions behind his work.

> My work is simply an attempt to revisit black people's erased and silenced histories. Importantly the performances serve as a collective memory in questioning who is remembered and why, and in negotiating spaces and places where spirits of those who did not have a proper burial need to be properly positioned in the world of the ancestors.[137]

Makandula's 2016 performance piece *Ingqumbo* (Wrath)[138] is a collaboration with violinist Christopher Jardine. The artist staged a series of rituals at public historical sites in Grahamstown-Makhanda, and finished the piece by carefully handing flaming weapons to the audience outside Drostdy Arch, which both marks the main entrance to the campus of Rhodes University at one end of High Street, and becomes the place where people remember Makandula hanging a noose. The title of the piece references the classic 1940 literary masterpiece *Ingqumbo Yeminyanya* (The Wrath of the Ancestors) by A. C. Jordan. The performance began in front of the main entrance to the Cathedral of St. Michael and St. George on High Street in Grahamstown, *impepho* (incense) burning inside an artificial human skull as the artist rang a bell held up close to the sides of the faces of the mostly White audience members. Makandula describes how the piece progressed from here.

> I then proceeded with the audience to a Settler statue opposite the Cathedral, which commemorates the Battle of Grahamstown in 1819 and signifies the spot where Colonel Graham and Captain Stockenstrom decided upon the present site of the City of Grahamstown in 1812. Here I inscribed the words "Nxele, Ndlambe, Umhlaba" on the blank side of the statue, registering that which was occluded from the historical narrative of this statue. Nxele led members of the Ndlambe regiment, who were fighting for their stolen land and were displaced by the British Settlers. The performance ended at the top of High Street by the Drostdy Arch, where I hung a noose. Placing the artificial skull beneath the rope I linked the histories of terror and killing of the two sites. Finally, I handed Molotov cocktails to the audience as a way to remind viewers/participants about the systematic violence that characterized our collective history and memory.[139]

During the performance—which included a visit by the police in response to alarmist reports—Makandula also gave the audience members whips to lash the wall near the swinging noose. Makandula's work here exists as both an active refusal of dominant histories and, at the very moment when the #FeesMustFall protest movement—the student-led protests demanding free education and government investment in universities—was escalating on campuses across the country, exemplifies "a peculiar socially engaged turn in art" in South Africa.[140] Art critic Athi Mongezeleli Joja reads this particular work as being much more than just "performative simulation of exotic rituals," but instead as "a history lesson, bridging the gap between the sensual and the political. A visual travelogue, that though it transported us to a time seemingly lost in the historical passage, it conjured those moments not as dead archival material to be simply studied but as part of a persistent structure that frames the present."[141]

Makandula's diverse corpus of work is visually stunning, meticulously researched, sharp and distinctive, and usually unsettling. He appears in photographs looking at times priest-like and other times dictator-like, and can also be seen greeting a drawing of a crane as it appeared on the flag of the former Ciskei, drawn by artist Buntu Fihla on the grey concrete wall inside the Ntaba kaNdoda Monument.[142] His pieces are always active inhabitations, live creations of historical presence and memory. The 2014 piece *Barongwa* (Messengers),[143] commissioned for Blind Spot as part of the National Arts Festival in 2014, was written and performed with Mohau Modisakeng.[144] Makandula here leads a silent march from Fingo Village to the Egazini memorial, the site of the 1819 battle between the amaXhosa and the British colonial settlers, and one of the sites occupied during Masixole Heshu's *Iimfazwe*. Makandula explains that this particular historic site—one of the most important for symbolizing Xhosa resistance—is tragically overlooked. Here there was an "attempt by the amaXhosa to claim back the land stolen by settlers. The spirits of many who died in the battle were never brought back to their people nor was there a ritual done as a way to connect them with the living-dead."[145] During the performance, headed by Makandula, who is clothed inside ribboning green robes, a silent marching band moves along Raglan Road from Fingo Village to the vicinity of Egazini Monument. Gleaming brass instruments lay on the roadside and are picked up—but remain silent—as the band marches. There is merely an occasional drum roll. Makandula then unfurls a flag at Egazini and conducts an *intlwayelelo* (sowing) ritual to connect the living with the spirits of the dead, handing beads to audience members. The marching band strikes up only after the ceremony is performed, after the ancestors have been acknowledged.

Makandula's work is self-conceived as being a "living archive," an interrogation of how space has been historically governed. In its search for a reflection of the self in the archive he looks for the erasures and blind spots that are always created by narratives of domination, whether through sonic investigations of the emancipation of slaves in nineteenth-century Cape Town in *Zizimase*,[146] or repurposing the hymns of the nineteenth-century intellectual and priest Tiyo Soga, working alongside musicians including Mthwakazi from Ntinga Ntaba kaNdoda.[147] When he reflects on his own work creating new archives driven to recover forgotten histories, Makandula—whose full name means "Be the one who reminds the nation"—speaks eloquently of what he identifies as the Black archive as being something that is co-created.[148] "I see myself as a writer," he says, one who has "a responsibility to myself, to my parents, to my clan, to the people that I am born with and also to the people who are not yet born."[149] He explains that he uses everyday sounds, such as songs and church bells, and creates repetition to explore the attainment of rapture, all the while asking what rewalking a landscape that holds violent erasures might mean to a younger audience that may only have a "post memory" of a battle in 1819. "A lot of the time, I don't consider the people that I am creating for as an audience," he says, "I always consider them co-creators because by virtue of witnessing the work it also means you have responsibility to complicate the work further, to ask more questions."[150] His is not an archive for passive witnessing. In his performances, observes artist and art historian Nombusa Makhubu, "one generally does experience it as a ritual, it is something that you are undergoing, it's a spiritual experience, it's in the way he uses music, it's in the way he gets people to participate. You become part of the society that's trying to change something."[151]

In Makandula's work, activation and interrogation of archival fragments within living spaces and landscapes typically start at home, in areas that resonate with violently displaced stories. He locates the importance of The Black Power Station—where he regularly performs, including at the venue's official opening— as being an "intergenerational space for ideas to germinate, to be created, but also to be experimented with." Its liberated mode is real and actualized because "it doesn't come with the burden of 'there is a knower who is better than the other knower' . . . but it becomes an intergenerational space that allows us to come with equal voices." For Makandula, The Black Power Station is an incubator that "allows experimentation, it allows silences to be welcomed and silences to live alongside noise, and within that it also allows people to contemplate what it is they are witnessing and what it is that is co-created within this space and time."[152]

These living histories directed and performed, independently, by Sikhumbuzo Makandula and Masixole Heshu, create embodied narratives actively inserted into the landscapes at monumental sites that privileged other stories, reflected dominant histories, and that have erased collective memory to produce forgetting. Their primary focus is rarely simply on extracted archival fragments, but rather on live and performed action occupying landscapes and monuments as dynamic new frames for the fragments, tugging at their roots to allow and make them face different directions. Through their live narrative modes, the practices of both artists elude and resist most institutional archival practices, situating the curation of knowledge firmly inside and between people deliberately occupying spaces. Privileged as I am to have spent rewarding time with both artists over the last few years, sharing their ideas, creative practices, rehearsals, and performances, I am struck by how much they both ground their work in archival documents. They constantly return to collections at ILAM, the Cory Library at Rhodes, and the Bodleian Library in Oxford, as well as drawing from oral memories and living histories, as they refine their own processes for public performance to add inhabited layers to the archival records.

As the artistic work of the various individuals and collectives herein presented illustrates, ILAM increasingly exists within a dynamic context of art activism, as communities in the Eastern Cape grapple with their complex historical struggles. Establishing the connections linking the institutional archive to artists writing these multimodal currents of work—art that flows in and out of the archive—allows for new relationships to be built and new stories to be told. For some, this work of decolonizing archives and histories also means building alternative spaces and independent institutions for the incubation and amplification of the intergenerational artistic knowledge of Xhosa communities. Enter The Black Power Station.

FIVE

The Black Power Station

My name is Xolile, it means "at peace." I know who I am and what I must do.
I must make sure my daughter, Lindiwe, does not grow up angry
at the things I did not change.
Xolile "X" Madinda[1]

When I first met Nyaki's friend X as part of the Grahamstown arts scene in 2007, Nyaki and I had already spent dozens of hours visiting people in their homes and yards in the townships, as well as DJ-ing archival sounds as part of street theater and in clubs and bars, taxis, and schools. We worked with many young artists to share sounds publicly, and when we linked up with X, he immediately wanted to walk with these sounds through the everyday street life he lived and understood. We spent many days walking together from town to Fingo Village, the township where X grew up, and back. With town receding behind us, we strolled with Tracey's recordings playing on cassette, moving along Raglan Road where the potholes plunged deeper, alongside riverbeds ribboning with rubbish, past Jackie's corner store where X regularly hosted street cyphers, and into the small public spaces of Fingo Village. X would approach almost anyone to try and engage them with his tape player: women sitting and selling fruit on the street; people waiting in vehicles; others heading back from farms in vehicles with goats purchased for ceremonies; and old men drinking outside the jagged iron leans of corrugated shebeen walls. He always looked for ways to strike up conversations with the people who he felt were the most marginalized.

For X, anything that works as a creative catalyst for prompting dialogue was worth exploring within his community, and he felt that sharing archival Xhosa recordings could both help create a conversational space and dispel some prevailing negative perceptions about the youth—especially hip-hop artists—among elders. The value seemed to be in the mutual public display of a desire to engage with Xhosa cultural histories in the present. As he said at the time, "the music, it might be a formula for old people to gather 'round to talk about themselves so they can start stepping away from these negative things, they have this knowledge but they don't give it to the people."[2] The motivation chimed with Nyaki's own move to ask to sponsor family ceremonies, and the idea and image of a young hip-hop artist sharing archival recordings in public was both novel and helped banish some negative stereotypes that can drive a fissure between generations. After speaking with a group of elders sitting in front of a shebeen in Fingo, X observed that "they were surprised . . . the youth in these days don't make them think that we are interested in our own culture."[3] X made it clear through all of his work and practices that physical space matters, patterns of movement around town matter, and so do spaces for listening where connections can be made, youth can meet elders, and Black, "colored" (mixed-race), and White South Africans can gather and share voices.

How do archiving and curation become revolutionary acts? This chapter features many young Xhosa arts activists who are repurposing the archiving and curation of their own culture as radical tools for expression and action in the Eastern Cape today. The central focus is on Xolile "X" Madinda, the musician, artist, and community activist who opens and finishes the book. For almost three decades, X has been creating a new model of arts activism, purposefully building on his own history, tradition, and the past for present and future empowerment through self-possessed understanding. Driving a suite of initiatives under his umbrella organization Aroundhiphop, X and others use sound, music, and performance as ways to reconfigure the space of Grahamstown-Makhanda itself. While the town has long been dominated by Rhodes University and the annual National Arts Festival, under-resourced yet extremely driven community activists are taking back space for themselves to redress historical wrongs and imagine new futures.

As Jennifer Lynn Stoever argues, color lines—hierarchical divisions between Whiteness and Blackness—are marked out audibly as much as visually.[4] Any visitor standing outside the 1820 Settlers Monument in Grahamstown-Makhanda and looking across the city inside a valley cannot fail to see the racial and economic segregation laid out before them. For Masixole ("Masi") Heshu, raised as a young boy in the monument's shadow, its existence cannot be avoided, and it "represents a symbol of a [sic] domination and control, and its unique physical location makes it a true surveillance, camera. . . . It stands high in Makhanda watching every building, every movement of people, peeping into private affairs of every conceivable variety."[5] Any person walking between town and township can also hear these divisions, where despite some advances, isiXhosa is yet to be embraced as a first language on campus at Rhodes University.[6] In this formerly frontier town in the Eastern Cape of South Africa, artists such as X and a collective of allies are subverting the established color lines drawn across and through their historical legacies with actions that seek to create a new "listening ear" for young Xhosa people today. They do this together by building new communally curated spaces for listening and for being heard and recognized through their own art and in their own language. Resonating with the work of the language activist artists heard in chapter 4, X's actions here seek to amplify isiXhosa language and philosophies using hip hop, theater, poetry, sound, and visual art that reclaims Xhosa identities and histories in public spaces. His work is firstly and always intended for local audiences, while his recordings, productions, and documentations are all framed through The Black Power Station, imagined and built as "the international destination." In a town where most opportunities are disproportionately owed to Rhodes University and the National Arts Festival, artists at The Black Power Station all work tirelessly to subvert these established color lines, and aim to generate an independent economy for Xhosa artists. The vision is ambitious enough to aspire to uplift the entire province of the Eastern Cape as a center for artistic excellence, a truly independent vision remarkable for its achievements in the face of almost no financial support or safety net.

X's work over the past few years has coincided with ongoing clashes over history and public space in Grahamstown-Makhanda. In 2017, this debate hit a new height over a South African ministerial decision to rename the colonial frontier town to reflect its precolonial history and Xhosa identity. This act of renaming "Grahamstown" to "Makhanda" generated a slew of oppositional voices from predominantly White residents, as well as artistic responses from young Xhosa activists. Engaging these debates, X has created new forums for community curation, bringing together differing voices to stage performed conversations. At the same time, he has continued reclaiming abandoned or forgotten spaces in order to redraw the lines of his newly renamed town. The Black Power Station, a formerly derelict electricity generating plant, has become a remarkable repurposed and self-driven creative home to an expanding collective of young, local, and independent Xhosa artists. Revolutionized through recycled, donated, and locally sourced materials and supplies—and almost entirely self-funded—the space changes incrementally every day according to its needs. Some days, dona-

FIGURE 5.1 Xolile "X" Madinda securing padding for new seats at The Black Power Station, Landfill Site, Makhanda. June 18, 2019. *Photo by the author.*

tions of books might arrive, and on others X might travel to the local refuse-tip to source padding to make new seats (see figure 5.1) There is nowhere quite like it in Grahamstown-Makhanda—if anywhere else—as its work increasingly reaches outside the Eastern Cape province and overseas to amplify the sheer quality of the Xhosa arts and creativity it incubates, produces, broadcasts, and archives.

X had been looking to occupy or build his own arts space for years. He knows the local landscape as well as his own voice, and in finally securing permission to develop this derelict industrial space, he had found a space that—vitally—was neither university owned nor in the townships, where the noise and the hustling demands of daily life could often be too distracting. There seemed to be good reasons to transport an artistic idea of the township all the way to the other side of town, along the way passing through and past the spaces and resources owned by Rhodes University and other businesses in Makhanda.

"MY JOURNEY STARTED WITH A BOOK": FINGO FESTIVAL AND INDEPENDENT XHOSA ARTS PROGRAMS

Fingo Village is the oldest township in Grahamstown, the one that is closest to town. X was born into this township named and known for independent thinking, and one with its own history of violent displacement. Fingo Village was started by the British as an attempt to assimilate African people through European-style urban spatial planning, while the name Fingo itself refers to groups of clans originating from KwaZulu-Natal who fled the Mfecane wars in the 1820s and 1930s,[7] moving west from Natal and arriving in the Eastern Cape. The name amaMfengu was derived from the term "ukumfenguza," meaning "those who wandered seeking help." According to historian Nomalanga Mkhize, "these 'Mfengu' refugees were initially integrated into Xhosa society but later groups moved off to pledge allegiance to the British Crown and eventually became amongst the first groups to be deliberately settled into Western-style settlements such as Fingo Village."[8] The Western-style "Victorian" town planning can still clearly be seen, Mkhize observes, in the wide streets, square cottage-like houses, the adjacent cemetery, and freehold titles.[9]

"'Fingo-ness,'" it has been argued, "sprung from a movement, both literal and symbolic, away from the centers of Xhosa authority." Fingo people often sought to accumulate and consolidate wealth and power outside the existing frameworks of authority of Xhosa chiefs, through more independent agriculture and trade, and "consciously or unconsciously they aspired to a greater autonomy, at either the homestead or the individual level."[10] "Siyamfenguza!" — supposedly the cry the Fingo used to announce their arrival in Xhosaland — "can translate as 'we are hungry,' 'we seek work,' or 'we want something.'"[11] Later, freehold settlements were given to amaMfengu partly as reward for serving on the British colonial side during the Frontier Wars of 1846–47 and 1850–53. However, after the Group Areas Act of 1950, racial zoning was slammed onto Grahamstown and Fingo Village was declared a "colored" area, meaning many Xhosa and amaMfengu were displaced into the separate homeland of what was then known as Ciskei. As with the forced "black spots" removals elsewhere in South Africa, extreme deprivation was experienced: "the violation of the rights of freehold title holders; the long periods of uncertainty; the complete lack of choice for the people concerned; and, of course, the nihilistic destruction of an established community."[12] Nomalanga Mkhize urges that instead of ethnicizing the township, it is important "to write the history of Fingo Village as just the history of a place, not a history of a people,"[13] especially because there are other areas in the region relatively nearby, such as Peddie, where Mfengu identity is much stronger due both to the pledging of allegiance to the British Crown and the mass forced relocations.

X, who is Xhosa and not Mfengu, has long been aware of these histories, and observes that Fingo Village has always been a community of mixed backgrounds. Raised from a very modest background, he lived for much of his life in a small hand-built one-room building he named "DefKamp" (see figure 3.2), cropped next to a tavern named "Welcome." When I first met him, he was spending all of his time and resources arranging public education events in Fingo; usually hip-hop cyphers on street corners giving platforms to local artists, or isiXhosa storytelling competitions for children. Young and neither married nor a parent, he would often give the little spare money he had to help other families pay for their children's school fees. When xenophobic riots blazed through the townships of Johannesburg during a global economic plunge in 2008, X and his friends took to the streets in their own townships and urged people to resist this reactionary xenophobia, and to remember and protect the people who were—and still are—their brothers and sisters from elsewhere in Africa. DefKamp was a creative haven, a refuge, a thriving multipurpose bedroom studio and hangout space constantly occupied by beatmakers, rappers, and poets. It was "a place where people came to learn to rap. . . . [M]ost MCs that might have come out from Grahamstown came from DefKamp."[14]

X's purpose as a young artist was transformed the moment he was introduced to Steve Biko's writings on Black consciousness by his uncle, Alistair Maxeg-wana.[15] X explains:

My uncle didn't like what I was doing, he didn't like hip hop, he didn't like anything I was doing that was including hip hop, so he started teaching me about Black consciousness and how he was afraid that I was going to become like an American, you know—lose my identity. So he gave me a lot of books . . . he gave me Steve Biko's book and when he gave me the book he said I must go and read it for a week and come back to him.[16]

"Merely by describing yourself as black," wrote Steve Biko—the radical Xhosa martyr to Black Consciousness—"you have started the road towards emancipa-tion, you have committed yourself to fight against all forces that seek to use your blackness as a stamp that marks you out as a subservient being."[17] It is hardly possible to overstate the influence of Biko and the evolution of a Black Conscious-ness movement locked on overthrowing apartheid and all forms of injustice. While "a standard criticism of Black Consciousness is that it was an 'American import,'"[18] Biko and other radicals resisting the White supremacist National Party controlling South Africa from 1948 onward promoted their politics and philosophy as a right to their own way of life, challenging "all those tradition-ally excluded from full citizenship in South Africa to realize that liberation was central to consciousness of self."[19] Liberating the self, refusing self-hatred, and empowering Black initiative and responsibility were the keys to an alternative political awareness that could appropriate power to the powerless.

After reading Biko, X and his group DefBoyz, co-founded with beatmaker Mxolisi "Biz" Bodla, "realized we needed to start rapping in Xhosa," and this gave birth to the initiative that would become Fingo Revolutionary Movement. "Fingo," notes X, "were seen as people who look for places, so for us we look for open spaces that are in the township that will make a statement about the issues in the community."[20] Fingo Revolutionary Movement acted from the start with a shared philosophy of inclusive conversations that were available and accessible to all in their own language. X explains that one of the rules at their events is that if you create a play or any form of art, "you must stay and the community asks questions, even if you are a child you have a right to ask a question." When asked what needs to happen to create social consciousness in South Africa among the youth, X answered, "I think most of these conversations are happening in English and when we talk especially to young Black South Africans in Xhosa now you are being lazy [speaking in English]—people when you speak their language they start to be conscious of their surroundings and all that is happening."[21]

As X's political consciousness grew, he became increasingly aware of the historically distinct place that Fingo Village occupied within Grahamstown, and he and his friends formed Fingo Festival,[22] a direct response to the dominance of the annual National Arts Festival (NAF). Held annually between late June and early July, the NAF traces its origins back to 1974 when the Settlers Monument— parked like a stranded concrete ship slammed inside the hillside overlooking Grahamstown-Makhanda—was officially opened as a living memorial to the 1820 British settlers. The festival, billed as "Africa's largest and most colourful cultural event,"[23] doubles and sometimes triples the population of the city every year.[24] Grahamstown-Makhanda "completely transforms and explodes across 90 venues to become Africa's largest multiarts festival, attracting more than 200,000 visitors, who are here for more than 2,000 performances on a programme of more than 600 events."[25] The festival was renamed the National Arts Festival in 2002 and is now an independent company with "an unrivalled reputation as the leading African showcase of local and international creativity," as well as being "a significant driver of the economy of the City of Makhanda and the Eastern Cape Province."[26] According to Bryan Schmidt, who cites an economic-impact study made in 2017 by the South Africa Department of Arts and Culture, "the festival contributes R94.4 million (about $7 million) to the local area annually and about R377.15 million ($25.36 million) to the Eastern Cape province."[27] For the vast majority of artists living in Grahamstown-Makhanda, the festival has remained one of their most important economic and creative opportunities. The NAF hosts and promotes some truly remarkable local and international acts, ranging from Madosini—"SA's National Treasure"[28]—to globe-trotting comedians, from Ladysmith Black Mambazo to the inclusive physical theater of Unmute Dance Company,[29] from Mira Calix to theatrical adaptions of *The Gruffalo*.[30] The festival also supports a vibrant Fringe Festival, where many local and other artists develop work for a range of venues, such as the 2016 Ovation Award-winning *Falling Off the Horn*, which tackled the issue of xenophobia in South Africa from the perspective of a local spaza (convenience) shop.[31]

The NAF has been regularly criticized for its distortion of the local economy, which leaves local artists vying for work during an eleven-day annual window, but with little residual infrastructural investment to promote artistic livelihoods beyond the festival. Schmidt even reads *Cape Mongo*—a street performance in 2013 by Grahamstown-born artist Francois Knoetze, who intentionally roamed away from the heavily curated western side of the city while inside "a giant antelope-shaped suit made of cardboard detritus"—as an emblem of the racial, aesthetic, and economic fault lines that can be steadily reinforced by a festival that still draws most of its traffic toward the wealthier parts of town.[32] The festival, claims scholar and arts administrator Brett Pyper, "has amply demonstrated both the strengths and the limitations of arts festivals as vehicles for cultural advocacy, celebration and critique, as well as the social and economic development for which they are looked to by many in their host communities."[33] Pyper critiques the NAF for a lack of curation that reflects deep cultural research, although he acknowledges the deep-seated reasons for this, including "an unease among some festival decision makers about the legacies of colonial ethnology in South Africa, with which ethnomusicology is (rightly or wrongly) associated." These curatorial decisions, claims Pyper, also reflect "a general sensitivity in the public sphere at large in contemporary South Africa . . . about the ways in which the performance of what is colloquially referred to as 'indigenous traditional music' or sometimes 'cultural music' maps onto reductive and divisive apartheid-era notions of ethnicity and 'race.'"[34] The NAF, it is argued, exhibits much power and influence both over the local economy and how arts in South Africa are curated and received, and sits in orbit over an extensive pool of extremely talented local artists who seek and need to survive all year round.

In contrast, Fingo Festival has its roots deep in post-apartheid politics. It was started in 2011 with help from the Khulumani Support Group, an organization founded by people testifying in the Truth and Reconciliation Commission.[35] Beginning with a modest initial grant of 40,000 rand aimed at keeping youth away from crime by fostering social spaces,[36] Fingo Festival features locally curated events and performances within the townships. Each year the festival is themed to engage locally with national issues, including the philosophy of standing up for yourself (Vukuzenzele, 2011), celebrating the hundred-year anniversary of the African National Congress (ANC) in 2012, and forty years of youth struggle, marking the anniversary of the 1976 Soweto Uprising (2016). As part of Fingo Festival 2017, local DJs working under a giant curling red mollusk-shaped tent dropped cutting-edge *gqom* beats in the middle of the afternoon, as young school children competed to display their dance moves on stage. This celebration of the legacy of ANC hero Oliver Tambo happened alongside a launch for a book about liberation stories co-edited by a local journalist, with plenty of other free activities and free food for children. Always designed for township residents, Fingo Festival faces a constant battle for funding, given that all events are free. It was supported by the NAF in 2012, though it remains independent and moving toward full sustainability. "We don't sell anything," explains X. "Everything is free. People don't understand; they think it's a waste. But then, how do you charge; who do you charge? Even though they visit, our target is not the buying audience that is in town."[37]

Grahamstown-Makhanda's artistic economy is disproportionately geared to the eleven-day window of the annual festival, when tourists and companies come flooding in from out of town and across the continent and "every hall or large room becomes a theatre, parks and sport fields become flea markets, normally quiet streets have to be managed by an army of temporary traffic wardens, and every available bed in the city is booked."[38] But, as journalist Zaza Hlalethwa asks, "what happens after the fest?"[39] Fingo Festival aims to create sustainable opportunities for local artists throughout the year, including an annual "Business Beyond the Festival" program that conceives of ways to grow business and opportunities beyond the NAF window. Fingo Festival also builds programs to provoke dialogue, asking "what have young Black South Africans been able to build twenty years into democracy?" Its organizers interrogate the reasons why most of their halls are not ready to stage more events, why taverns and shebeens have not developed spaces for artists to perform, and why the NAF has not yet come fully to the community. These dialogues always seek to include people from all generations. According to historian Nomalanga Mkhize, the real significance of Fingo Festival is that as well as being Black owned, "it also has a very high standard of expectation for what community art should look like, but at the same time without leaving the community behind. . . . [I]t has grown from the members who are in the community," and "it takes art for children seriously."[40]

"If you look at our community," X observes, "visually it is not uplifting." Part of the problem, he feels, is that in an area when most people rely on informal employment, "art in the Black community is viewed as passing time, it is not viewed as something that can sustain you."[41] After receiving a social investment grant in 2018, Fingo Festival was able to expand,[42] including further initiatives such as sponsoring the creation of original murals on public buildings, walls, and bridges, both in the townships and in town. For X, the aim is to reclaim past practices and present spaces.

> [O]ur culture still matters, our language still matters, and our streets still matter. We have to heal our own broken communities with our art so this is a part of that—the move to heal our own community with our art, with our people. . . . The term is cultural, but for us we are more like "how did the people live, how did people have fun?" So we want people to come and bring their own ways of living to the art, like you have cultural dances that when people perform they will relate, "this is how we used to do, this is how our dance goes." . . . There are some modern dances that are popular, so by showing kids the art that is within their culture as Black people, they will start to relate to being African, to being South African, because you can't be South African if you don't embrace Africa. So we are trying to say, "see what is happening within your community—this is the art we have," before you embrace a culture that is foreign to your own self because your culture guides you, how you see yourself and how you see your community.[43]

As Fingo Festival grew in stature, X decided to shift his own practice from hip hop and music to curation and community building. As one of the most influential rappers in the Eastern Cape, he came to realize that rapping about social issues wasn't enough to make the changes he envisioned. "I used to rap a lot," he explained, but "doing a CD, it was not enough, I needed to do something physical like put people on the street and discuss, 'let's do something, formalize things,' and as a community we must say 'let's do things for ourselves, build ourselves.' For me, I read Steve Biko and then I wanna apply it."[44] He decided, at a young age, to all but retire from stage performance, preferring to enact the vital changes that he felt, up until then, were too easy to simply rap about without making sure they actually happened.

AROUNDHIPHOP LIVE CAFÉ AND THE
BLACK POWER STATION

X was excited to share the news when he called; after all, it was decades in the making, and we had not seen each other for a few years. He had his own space to develop now, and told me he was on his way to pick me up because he wanted me to see the place for myself. It was 2017 and I was back in Grahamstown, spending time at ILAM and catching up with local artists and other friends. Once the festivals were over, X drove me away from town and the locations behind, past the wealthy private schools, over bridges swept with murals painted by local artists from Fingo, and turned into the industrial area toward the peeling husks of the buildings marking the old power station on Rautenbach Road. The approach is slow, rocky, and bumpy. Cars wheel around a contagion of potholes pitting into the dusty track, alongside scrubby land where sheep roam and a few small businesses operate.

I first became aware of the power station through a video X sent me that was produced by Sinethemba Oziris ("Oz") Mzwali, a dynamic young local producer and owner and CEO of the Blah ze Blah production label focusing on music and video.[45] Oz filmed the video inside one of the derelict buildings. Beatmaker Adon Geel wanders with his headphones in a cavernous room while the Xhosa rapper Lunakill prowls, picking and kicking at rubbish strewn on a concrete floor roughly punctured by plants and grass. He recites "Hooks over Points," his "intellectual rhyme scheme that sounds complicated to your ears," a calling for rappers to nurture and hone their messages before their hooks. It's a "Don't Believe the Hype" for the twenty-first century. The year is 2016 and Lunakill coolly raps straight to the camera.

> You should never hate on anyone's hustle
> and you should never throw certain insulting remarks
> which is why it's fact over hate when I say rap is confusing nowadays
> 'cos all they care about are hooks over points
> so they leave us with question marks.

Lunakill's voice is rich and baritone, his poise and confidence the mark of an artist in control and with a message to share. He understands and works pace and meter, letting the empty decayed resonant space of the power station shape his words. "I paused," he says, and the watching audience is now inside his hands. "'Cos I can guarantee you that fifty-two people didn't think that a question mark was shaped like a hook over a point." The image flickers and glitches. Chilled instrumental hip-hop beats tug in the logos for Aroundhiphop and Blah ze Blah as Lunakill walks off stage while Adon Geel stays and stares stonily at the camera, defying people to question the remarks. The video was designed to promote Lunakill's then forthcoming mixtape, *The Bigger Picture*,[46] while also announcing the development of the new space: Aroundhiphop Live Café, soon to become The Black Power Station (see figure 5.2). While X had spent a long time readying the space, Oz quickly encouraged him to start producing and promoting the space as a creative brand.

Entering the space for the first time a few months later, I walked into a cavernous concrete room full of DIY local art and furniture. Hip-hop painting was propped up against a wooden stage made from recycled pallets. A green room was being constructed behind a heaving iron door, while a corner area framed on one side by a heavy black chimney was transforming into the Book'ona, a reading nook stocked with literature on Black Consciousness, Black history, and creativity. X pulled strongly down on a screeching rusty metal chain to open a

FIGURE 5.2 Andiswa "Bliss" Rabeshu and Ta Sky, outside eKabini at The Black Power Station, Makhanda. June 30, 2019. *Photo by the author.*

The Black Power Station **177**

rolling garage door, letting light flood into the dust-darkened space. We then wandered around the whole complex of the old power station, while X shared the particulars of his vision for an outside stage built on the back of a truck, skate parks in abandoned water-cooling ponds, and an open-air kitchen for cooking traditional food in pots hung over fire. We walked up to the blue shell of a long-abandoned phone booth and looked across the rusted skeleton of the nearby railway line over toward the locations and town. Leaning back inside the phone booth, X pointed out the proximity of the prison, a police store for stolen items, and a few other local businesses, including a restaurant, gym, carpentry company, and an international school for leather. "You see what is nice here — the sound. It is quiet, but you can hear a car passing by the National Road, the dog, the goats."[47] It was clear that X was anticipating that Grahamstown-Makhanda was a slow train rolling toward this destination.

The quiet in Waainek, this decaying industrial suburb created in the 1920s, comes from being hidden in the hills beyond the outskirts of the town. The coal-fired power station was created in 1922 to serve the White side of town and was further expanded in the 1960s, but it closed in the 1970s after the national grid was extended and the station ceased to be competitive. In the 1980s the building complex was leased and used by craft groups who worked with an NGO called the Social Change Assistance Trust (SCAT), which aimed to protect Black-run organizations against politically motivated evictions. According to a report written as part of a proposal to regenerate the complex by a company owned by the NAF, "the complex is rare as most other buildings built similarly for the generation of electricity in South Africa in the first half of the twentieth century have been demolished."[48] Tony Lankester, CEO of the NAF for twelve years up until 2019, has called it "an iconic monster of a space — structurally unsound in many places, barely habitable for the rest."[49]

X had long been looking to find a space in which to develop, curate, and promote his community projects. He had already been refused permission to use the abandoned train station on the opposite side of town and closer to the edge of the locations, and first became aware of the potential for this empty space in Waainek in 2012. Two years later, he visited the US as part of an artists and social change exchange in 2014, during which he was exposed to collectives like Busboys and Poets in Washington, DC — "when I saw that place I was like, I want this in my hometown"[50] — and Warehouse 21 in Santa Fe, New Mexico.[51] He remembers his first visit to the US well.

The last place I went to was in New Mexico—Warehouse 21. That place just blew my mind, where young people under the age of twenty-one were creating their own programs, having their own printing station, printing their own t-shirts, having their own radio stations and a small theater. For me, that felt like "this is the dream." Being South African—like were a South African to wish for this in their community—because we lack that, we lack a place that gives hope to young people. Remember that in South Africa we have a broken society, it is broken for families, and this is continuously happening from the legacy of apartheid.[52]

Tony Lankester granted X and Aroundhiphop a lease to develop part of the space in Waainek, when "they asked for nothing other than the opportunity,"[53] and as I stood with X excitedly admiring the space it was clear that hundreds of hours had already gone toward transforming it. Artists in white masks swept and reswept years of collected dust away from the building, then carried a large tree trunk inside and carved and shaped "Sombovane"— rendered as "the great everlasting ant" by X—a shared seat named in honor of the ant colony that had to be evicted from the tunnels they had chewed through the wood. Paintings were exploding onto large white canvases and left leaning against walls, as chipped paint pots, dripping aerosol cans, and clotted brushes mounted up on the floor. The dank walls were clothed with a heavy-hanging dark green paint, reaching down to the stylish Book'ona corner, under the watchful eye of a painting of liberation hero Oliver Tambo by the artist Banele. A playback session for *We Got it From Here . . . Thank You 4 Your Service*—the latest album by A Tribe Called Quest—was hosted. Local rappers "wanted a space to interrogate the album and we had a listening session, so we just came, just made fire, and we sat and listened to the music . . . and it just became a space for artists, it became a space for people to just hide away when they are doing their art."[54]

Aroundhiphop Live Café was formally opened on June 24, 2017, and would soon be unofficially, and then officially, renamed as "The Black Power Station." The program was headlined by the renowned Eastern Cape singer Msaki. Msaki, who had spent time with X when she was a student at Rhodes University, was back in town to perform at a house show and was already familiar with Aroundhiphop Live Café via Facebook updates, where she would follow this industrial space slowly being cleaned and prepared by local artists. She urged X to stop cleaning and to formally adopt the name "The Black Power Station," and then she invited everyone at her house show to come to the space afterward. The opening event reflected the space's aims of teaching, reclaiming tradition, and creating new art that serves as a living archive of past practices. Sikhumbuzo Makandula performed his research on the songs of Tiyo Soga, the nineteenth-century Xhosa missionary and hymn composer, while local artists Lunakill, Azlan Makalima, and the multimedia Uhambo Collective shared their hip hop and poetry.

By the time I returned to the Eastern Cape a year later, in July–August 2018, thousands of creative hours had been poured into transforming the space. X and myself had been planning to interrogate the resonances between the violent clashes over monuments and histories that were taking place in both South Africa and the US, especially since the 2015 #FeesMustFall student protest movement in South Africa, and the armed violence swarming around Confederate statues in my adopted home of Charlottesville, Virginia. We invited two undergraduate students from the University of Virginia (UVA)—Lindsey Shavers, a computer science and entrepreneurship major, and Carlin Smith, a global development studies major—to come and learn about local heritage projects in the Eastern Cape while working as part of X's team at The Black Power Station. For their introduction to Grahamstown-Makhanda, X insisted on driving them around town and up to the hilltop housing the 1820 Settlers Monument. From here you can view and almost touch the whole of the Rhodes campus directly below, see across town and past the cathedral and over to the townships crowding up the hills on the opposite side of the valley. Looking down, the social and economic divisions of the town are always palpable. Starkly visible. "The design of this fascinating city," writes Eusebius Mckaiser, "carries important historical pain," and when standing atop most of the hills cradling the place you "can see what apartheid geography looked like, because the design is that visible and that crude, courtesy of the racist urban planners of Grahamstown."[55] From our elevated viewpoint, X shared his narration of the histories of division and exclusion that have continuously shaped the town.

The Settlers Monument, designed by Jock Sturrock, sits imperiously like a late Brutalist ship, its hull crashed through the mountainside. Completed in 1974, it was built to serve as an "active participant in our developing nation, and commemorates the contribution of the 1820 settlers, and other English speaking immigrants, to the development of South Africa."[56] Rededicated in 1996 by Nelson Mandela, the monument, which includes statues of a settler family right outside on the approach road, was designed to draw "particular attention to two areas of British Settler heritage that benefit all South Africans—the English language, and the democratic tradition."[57] With the wind whipping at our ears and recorders, X stood immediately outside this building—which also houses the NAF offices during festival season and hosts and promotes other shows and festivals throughout the year—and told stories sharing his reckoning of local history, questioning whether most South Africans in his community had benefitted at all.

I knew X well enough to know the irrepressible scale of his arts activist vision, and I realized that here at The Black Power Station I was privileged to witness the growth of a new independent arts education model that, while almost entirely self-funded, was deliberately designed to balance and redress the dominant stories of power and ownership in Grahamstown-Makhanda. Located neither in town, nor in the townships, nor on the campus of Rhodes University, The Black Power Station is firstly a home for local artists to incubate, develop, and promote their practices and knowledge. Visitors and guests, whether students and faculty from Rhodes or the University of Virginia, festival-goers, or other tourists, are invited to share in a series of locally curated performances, lectures, classes, readings, and festivals. There is a fluid, responsive, live and improvisatory mode to the programming, which I have often seen changed at the last minute to accommodate a group of actors from Wits University or a traditional beer-and-song ceremony to serve a particular need for a community. Everyone is free to contribute to the creative atmosphere, and outsiders and guests are almost always invited to open or close a session with a Book'ona reading (see figure 5.3), which requires the invitee to select a book, let it fall open, and then read whatever text appears before them for as long as they are moved. Literature is sampled and performed live, and White guests will often find themselves performing perspectives from Steve Biko, bell hooks, or Aimé Césaire. At almost every event, young children and elders are present. "It's remarkable—it works like an open-source space," reflected my friend and colleague Jason Bennett, an instructional designer and maker space specialist who visited in 2019 as part of a team working on a "sister spaces" concept linking The Black Power Station with communities and spaces in Virginia.

The creative working mode of The Black Power Station speaks to many of the current developments in archival and museum practices, where community accessibility and real-time documentation of more current issues is a requirement for our instantly twitching and pointing social media age. In the South African context in particular, there is an ongoing call for an inclusive archiving to reflect everyday realities. "With the dawn of democracy," writes Mpho Ngoepe, "the archival scene in South Africa was supposed to transform and reflect

FIGURE 5.3 Siphosethu reading in the Book'ona, The Black Power Station, Makhanda. June 22, 2019. *Photo by the author.*

the diversity of the country, but it is still mainly the Western-dominated global mainstream."[58] As vital moves are taking place to decolonize the archives and create more open-ended "archives without archives," Ngoepe identifies the importance of participatory archives, decentralized curation, radical user orientation, and—under the prevailing rhetorical slogan of "taking the archives to the people"—argues for the need for public repositories to be "transformed into social space for storytelling rather than be equated to stillness in the graveyards."[59] A relentlessly fluid stream of productive work at The Black Power Station already operates within these self-liberated modes, while also developing an idealized festival for inclusiveness that is created and enacted every day.

"South Africa's turn to festivals over the last quarter-century as a means of redressing apartheid's legacy of structural racism and inequality," argues Bryan Schmidt, "relies on framing creativity as a uniquely inclusive form of productivity that is both sustainable and measurably impactful."[60] With videos, images, and recordings constantly buzzing through WhatsApp, Instagram, YouTube, and Facebook, alongside emerging plans for more formalized archiving under advice from ILAM and other institutions, the work of The Black Power Station is already its own participatory archive, as its artists and audiences collect, perform, and self-document their art, telling their Xhosa stories that had remained mostly untold and unheard in the local and global context. A full palette of art designed to educate is showcased in a space where "the highest currency is a book,"[61] meaning that those that cannot afford to pay entrance at times when there is a cover charge are simply encouraged to donate a book to the collective instead. The space, the programming, and the atmosphere are all always conducive to informality and improvisation. During the last few years, isiXhosa has clearly and rapidly become the main language for expression, and the performance mode blends a township street vibe—sounding true to where most of the local artists still live—with Xhosa family-style conversations inside an art gallery framing, all of which is combining to attract more and more students and professors and artists from Rhodes and further afield to experience and become part of the learning.

"GRAHAM'S LEGACY, MAKHANDA'S FUTURE"

In August 2018, barring legal challenges, Grahamstown was on the verge of being renamed Makhanda. As early as May 2005, President Thabo Mbeki had questioned the controversial association of this city's name with an agent of colonial violence. Mbeki asked, "Why do we celebrate a butcher? This place has got a name; it's called iRhini. But, we celebrate a butcher!"[62] More than a decade later, changing the name of Grahamstown to Makhanda—intended at once to honor a Xhosa warrior hero and to render more explicit the colonial violence exacted by the British general—was celebrated by most of the Black Xhosa community, and met with resistance from others. Some of the skeptics seemed largely sympathetic, but also believed the name change to be symbolic and a distracting waste of money that could be invested in more pressing needs like improving infrastructure in the townships. Other objectors, such as the Keep Grahamstown Grahamstown (KGG) campaign, who had vigorously contested the proposed change since the issue arose in 2007, mobilized more than six thousand supporters to argue that the name change ignored due consultative process. Advocate Jock McConnachie argued that the decision was in conflict with the South African Constitution, and complained about "a spirit of retribution rather than reconciliation."[63] The KGG website includes the multilingual banner tag line, "*Makana + Grahamstown = Reconciliation / Rekonsiliasie / Luxolelwaniso*," stressing "the importance for the purposes of Reconciliation of retaining the names Grahamstown and Makana in combination as together they symbolize the coming together of opposing histories."[64] By December 2019, the court application to overturn the renaming decision had failed, when a judge ruled that art and culture minister Nathi Mthethwa "had acted in strict accordance with all consultative and other requirements before deciding to change the name."[65]

X had decided to host a creative event to interrogate these debates, and called it "Graham's Legacy, Makhanda's Future." Hip-hop artists, poets, *pantsula* dancers,[66] actors from physical theater, DJs, elders, and a professor of history at Rhodes University were all invited to contribute to the debate, as were people opposed to the name change. X also devoted several mornings to driving around to schools in the townships and encouraged teachers to make sure their students could attend, offering wherever possible to help provide transportation and food. Intergenerational discussion was essential, and the space itself had been designed to be futuristic, traditional, and communal. X's mother, Nomhle Joyce Madinda, brewed the Xhosa beer *umqombothi*, which was served from a large metal vessel in the green room, and *iqhilika*, a fermented honey drink, was prepared on a local farm and served to adults. On the day of the event itself, performances unfolded across four hours of a mid-August afternoon, mixing from the professionally staged to the fully improvised. The audience, ranging in age from six to sixty, was mainly school children and artists from the townships, as well as a few people from Rhodes University, including some journalists, and Elijah Madiba from ILAM.

The first performance was by Masixole "Masi" Heshu, who introduced himself as a storyteller. Masi spoke of how his great-grandfathers were from Grahamstown, and how history could be difficult to read and know in a city that has, he reminded us, many names: Settler City, City of Saints, iRhini, Grahamstown, and now Makhanda. As he spoke with a deliberately considered and pausing theatrical pace, another poet, the "artist, hustler" Wamkelwa Nkhone,[67] from the town of Uitenhage, sat on top of a carved and painted wooden chair, singing broken melodic lines and counterpointing her own poetry that broke like insistent waves overlapping with Masi's spoken words. She declaimed:

I grew up in this land
I am the seed of this land
The tree of this land

I am Black, and I am strong
I am the heartbeat of the African soil
Trees of the African soil listen to me

The local poet Bhodl'ingqaka from Vukani township—the artist discussed in chapter 4, who has repurposed some of Tracey's recordings in his own work— performed hip hop from his album *Iintonga Zetyendyana* (Fighting Sticks of a Young Boy), rapper Blaqseed arrived from Port Elizabeth, and X himself welcomed everybody and gave a rare public performance including versions of several of his early hip-hop tracks. Lindsey Shavers and Carlin Smith contributed self-penned poems exploring names, identity, home, and belonging across continents, almost a year to the day that White supremacists had violently and fatally descended upon their college city of Charlottesville, Virginia.

Masi encouraged the audience to respond throughout, eliciting their opinions on both the art and the meaning of the name change. The afternoon was full of charged moments, perhaps none more so than when academic history was met by improvised *izibongo*, or Xhosa praise poetry. The historian Julie Wells—author of *The Return of Makhanda*, "an attempt to reconcile both the popular and the written histories surrounding Makhanda and the battle of Grahamstown"[68]—had been invited to talk about the history of Makhanda, the person and the name. She spoke for almost half an hour, sharing insights from historical sources that explored the relationship between Makhanda and other Xhosa ancestors, advocating the reclamation of his legend as a heroic and popular Xhosa freedom fighter. Makhanda had famously led the failed attack on the British at Grahamstown in 1819, "the most ambitious undertaking in Xhosa military history aimed at eliminating the colonists from the area."[69] Wells reminded the audience that five hundred people were at this very time still opposed to the name change, and if the majority who favor the change didn't speak up, "those 500 might still rule the roost" through pending legal challenges. "If you hear anything interesting today," she urged those gathered, "take this outside and talk to people so there can be no mistake they can be proud of the person who said, 'I want to restore the dignity of my people.'" Masi then took the mic, thanked his professor, and began to address the crowd again, observing that "for us creative people, in the way that we have rescripted and reclaimed our histories through our own expression, it simply comes in a performative way because this language [i.e., isiXhosa] is not spoken by many but a few." At this very instant, *imbongi* Thandazile Madinda sprang up from the back of the room and strolled forward within the audience with energy and purpose. As he declaimed, he roared from his feet up through his throat, and walked directly over to Julie Wells, shook her hand generously, and proceeded to prowl the open areas of the venue. Thandazile kept improvising lashing waves of Xhosa poetry inside swirls of whistled ululation rising and spilling out of a highly engaged and supportive backing audience, who constantly called out encouragement and approval. His performance was an interrogation of Eurocentric histories and written texts, delivered instead in powerfully poetic isiXhosa idioms.

Months later I asked X to reflect on this particular moment when different understandings of histories met live in his performance space. He explained:

> [T]hat moment was very profound and very significant for Thandazile to get up at that point of time, to actually disrupt a conversation in a beautiful way of saying, "there's two dimensions in the conversation of the name change and the history that it carries." . . . And also in the powerful words that Thandazile delivered, he was basically saying that we have an oral way of knowing this tradition, we have an oral way of knowing who we are, and this has been our way. . . . Thandazile was bringing the traditional way and the emotional impact that Makhanda had to his people. The amaXhosa and Black people in particular hold the value of Makhanda, not just because . . . of a book written by a historian who happens to be in the room at the time.[70]

X, and most of the audience, responded to Thandazile's performance as a powerful embodiment of the name-change process itself, a reclaimed validation of their own modes of transmission, in their own language and expressive modes recognizable locally and nationally, where the praise poet has the right to interrupt anyone, including the president, as the voice of the people. Jeff Opland and Patrick McCallister present the *imbongi* as a liminal figure and trickster, a sacred mediator who both upholds the status of the chief or king while acting as a social critic for public reflexivity, and who "in performance was accorded the licence to speak his mind as he saw fit in the language of his choice," and who could voice "criticisms and comments that could not otherwise be articulated in public, at times trenchant and explicit, at times sly and oblique."[71] Opland states that the *imbongi* "also enjoys the license to criticise with impunity persons in positions of power," and suggests that these licenses "seem to be acknowledgements that the imbongi in performance is not to be held responsible—perhaps *is* not responsible—for what he says."[72]

X elaborated:

[S]o the poetry, or let me say the point of view shared by the *imbongi*, was more of like a wake-up call because—if you remember—it changes the mood of the room, him shaking the hand was merely to say, "Hi colleague, I recognize you but this moment I take, I lead as a poet, as someone who represents a feeling that just came right now to acknowledge my own existence and my own heritage and my own people who fought for liberation." . . . So Thandazile came forward strongly, saying, "We are here and we can speak for ourselves and we can speak about our history for ourselves and we acknowledge you, but we are here, we will deliver, we will defend our history and have been defending our history. . . . As much as these things are written, we know how to teach our people beyond the books, beyond the research that is written by *abelungu*, meaning White people."[73]

Thandazile's intervention in an instant physically revolutionized the atmosphere in the space by radically changing the communicative mode. X explained, "You could feel what was pumping in his blood when he was thinking of this. . . . [H]e took over the platform and delivered in Xhosa. . . . You felt an energy delivered, you felt a takeover of a space after that because an *imbongi*, that is what his purpose should be; he takes over and shifts the dimension to say, 'don't forget we know these things.'"[74] In their analysis of oral genres as constructed and historicized maps of experience, Leroy Vail and Landeg White recognize that "the image of the *imbongi* confronting the king with the demands of the people is an attractive one,"[75] although they warn against placing too much emphasis on the role of an individual *imbongi*, arguing that "it is *not* the performer who is licensed; it is the *performance*."[76] However, X argues that the individual poet and what the poet says amount to the same thing as custodians of history, since every *imbongi* must necessarily also be a researcher of clan names, language, and history. Remembering his performance in response to Julie Wells's presentation on Makhanda, Thandazile would later reflect:

What made me stand up and recite that poem, I was trying to emphasize . . . what is important is what we have, how we define ourselves, no matter it is relevant to those who know these things—who are from the West by the way—but I was trying to show what is important is for us to define ourselves as we like to show the world, because now is the time for us to identify ourselves as people who are civilized, as people who can be among the other nations in the world.[77]

More performances followed, and X rounded out the event with a DJ set including a number of Tracey's Xhosa recordings, which had all been transferred to him during his enabling of Elijah Madiba's creative research working to reactivate the recordings and revitalize local music practice. X seamlessly worked recordings, including "Somagwaza" and "Mhlahlo" (explored in depth in chapter 3) and others, alongside contemporary hip-hop sounds as young artists and small children stayed and danced in the space. X DJ-ed Tracey's recordings in their original and full form, choosing not to sample or loop or process them, but rather to simply present these documents through a good sound system designed for beats and live bands, demonstrating that they belong next to live and studio-produced sounds. Although beatmakers such as Mxolisi "Biz" Bodla and Adon Geel regularly sample slices from the Tracey archive for their own productions, this time X presented the recordings in equivalence to the latest tracks from Emtee and other major South African artists, by virtue of playing them with exactly the same technique, presenting them for listening and dancing. The field recordings register a different sonic space, especially given the near total absence of bass and any studio production, in what was by now a booming dance floor, but people still danced, and continued dancing when hip hop and house returned. A decade scrolled past as fragments on a playlist moved from cassette players on township streets and into a driving PA system inside a reclaimed industrial space.

Where scholars and artists continue to debate the nature and function of the sample and the remix in hip hop and broader popular culture as something operating beyond intertextuality, ideas and critiques even circulate about sample culture as a form of performance magic or supernatural time travel conjuring phonographic ghosts and illusions.[78] In this DJ set, X explored and unpeeled multiple layers of Xhosa sound history by including cutting-edge Xhosa hip hop—some sourced via friends working in the music industry in Johannesburg who were at the event—alongside tracks sampling Tracey's recordings, as well as playing some of the original field recordings in full, while young hip-hop artists and praise poets added live vocal improvisations. The sound aesthetics were designed to align with the exploration of overlapping and competing histories experienced when Thandazile took over from a more overtly academic mode, turning the lecture page into a roaringly improvised poem.

Diane Thram, ILAM's director from 2006–2016, has continued to advocate for proactive repatriation of its holdings, "moving them out of the archive and into the public sphere in as many ways as possible," in the process combining "restudy of the original recordings with their return."[79] Repatriation delivered in The Black Power Station pays intimate attention to the design of spaces for the transmission of sounds, moving beyond libraries, seminar rooms, and even studios to invite a young Xhosa audience to connect archival recordings with the ceremonies they often know and the hip hop and house that most of them also choose for today.

A few days after the event I sat in the Book'ona of The Black Power Station with X and Andiswa "Bliss" Rabeshu, an MC, poet, and the resident visual artist, to share their reflections on the name-change event. As X noted, "no one has had a public discussion. We are the first ones to have a discussion, and that public discussion was not with bureaucratic people. It was with us as artists." He observed:

> For me the event—as the title puts it—is that the town you are in now is called after a man who murdered a lot of Black people and he was honored and given the name after he has done his work well. So . . . we realized as artists we have an option either to keep quiet or to raise the awareness of the discussion in a way that allows people to feel free as artists to engage in the topic. Because you realize the topic is engaged by those who don't want the name, and those who want the name, and those people who are in these categories; it's either businessmen of Grahamstown who control the economy of the town, and secondly it might be political people who have political benefits when the name is changed. So ordinary artists have not seen if the name is changed, and how they will benefit. . . . The content that artists such as us will produce politically, it will be around Makhanda. We will raise his name with a different perspective, so by having artists discuss this we might come up with a better solution for people to understand these two worlds.[80]

For both X and Bliss, the central importance and significance of this event lay in the large number of school children who were driven from all over the townships to come and witness the performed debates over the naming of their own heritage. Children as young as six were able to see, hear, and celebrate Xhosa hip hop, physical theater, and sound art, as well as some of Tracey's field recordings. The children also saw and heard an English-speaking history professor being met and equaled by a Xhosa praise poet working in a style and language infinitely more recognizable as their own. All of this was MC-ed by Masixole Heshu, another young Xhosa artist and one of only very few to date to make it from the local townships to study history to master's level at Rhodes University. Masi showcased how he works to increase the visibility of publicly

performed Xhosa history both within academia and on the local streets closer
to where it originates.

XHOSA HIP-HOP ARCHIVES

Hip hop remains one of the most important recent inclusions within institutional
archives, both in the conventional sense where its architects and practitioners
move to define standards and classics — placing hip hop in the canon — and also
in the way that hip hop's creative processes already work archivally to constantly
recycle, remix, and reengage musical and social histories. The rapper as griot,
the mixtape as instant archive. 9th Wonder, a Grammy Award-winning artist,
producer, and professor — the Harvard Hip Hop Fellow — gets the heads of both
Kendrick Lamar and Dr. Henry Louis Gates Jr. visibly nodding, while he develops
the art form's profile as an archive.[81] Hip-hop educator and media producer
Martha Diaz collaborates with first-generation genius Nas and other thinkers
to develop hip-hop curricula and the Hip Hop Future School. The archiving
of hip hop is increasingly happening both institutionally and independently,
documenting the histories and evolution of its scenes, places, sounds, samples,
and its media. The mixtape, the free and cheaply distributed "street album" that
today is often indistinguishable from label-produced albums, "emerged as a
personally expressive and privately distributed object in the mid-1970s when early
hip-hop DJs taped their live sets."[82] Mixtapes have grown into global ubiquity,
especially through their influence on the reigning playlist curation culture led by
Spotify, SoundCloud, and YouTube. The medium of cassette tape was originally
both innovative and broadly accessible and, dually available as prerecorded and
also as blank cassette, "was one of the first sound recording media conceived and
marketed with consumer participation, even creation, in mind."[83] Collecting,
remixing, erasing, and rebuilding were built into the medium and the art form
of hip hop, allowing personal archives to proliferate. When X first named his
company Aroundhiphop, he was grounded behind, while looking beyond, two
turntables and a microphone, choosing to work with and document all of the art
forms that were "around" or true to the creative, self-liberating, and repurposing
spirit of hip hop.

The philosophy and practice of X's collective is to pursue ways to perform and
archive Xhosa culture, remaking the city as "a living gallery."[84] The crew combine
deep respect for Xhosa tradition with the latest electronic production techniques,
creating their own documentary archives of everything they make, stage, and

perform. This usually all happens spontaneously and quickly. A few days before the Makhanda name-change event, we were all hanging out at The Black Power Station, while a group of around twenty artists, including the rapper Lunakill and producer and label owner Oz, were gathered for another video shoot. Oz, who was originally from the Eastern Cape but had moved to Johannesburg where he works in the music and creative industries, had already been shooting footage for Lunakill's videos to accompany tracks from his "The Bigger Picture" mixtape, as well as for some more recent work. Blah ze Blah's videos for Lunakill are always cool and sharp, as the music deserves. They showcase young Xhosa artistry while referencing and paying homage to both African and American hip-hop history, and are clearly aimed at both local audiences and also the cutting-edge big-city markets in Joburg, Cape Town, Durban, and further afield.

Lunakill had just written a new track, called "Premonition."[85] He had been suffering from dreams about his father that dealt with his own anxieties about making it big in the music industry, and he had decided to seek guidance, which traditionally means consulting Xhosa elders and ancestors. Oz wanted to turn this into a filmable moment, so old wooden pallets were collected and a fire was made, lit, and stoked in the yard just outside the main entrance door leading into The Black Power Station. A small group of young Xhosa men gathered round the fire, including X, beatmaker Mxolisi "Biz" Bodla, dancer Simamkele "Crankydy" Xako, Nyaki, and Lunakill. As the fire warmed the circle of men on a dark winter night with few stars, a group conversation evolved discussing what it means to be a responsible Xhosa man, to be a Xhosa father, and to guide people through their own culture. Individuals spoke in turn, all offering Lunakill advice. Artists shared highly personal examples from their own experiences of feeling guided by their culture, as live hip-hop art sought the embrace of traditional Xhosa cultural knowledge. Simamkele Xako reflected on the strength he felt in being raised by a very strict grandmother, and X spoke about how a township upbringing typically required a suppression of emotions behind a tough masculine mask. He turned and asked me to retrieve a copy of Frantz Fanon's *Black Skin, White Masks* from the Book'ona. "There is something we started . . . two days ago, when we were here," he explained to Lunakill. "We would ask someone to pick a book to read, just open it and read the paragraph that you see in front of you and from there it is entirely up to you how you interpret it. . . . When you open that, there is something that will resonate to what you are talking about. We are here to be responsible."[86] Lunakill was handed the book. He let the pages fall open, and then began to read aloud a passage of Fanon's writing detailing how Black men are forced to behave differently and exist at all times in two dimensions when among White people. Lunakill's rich and deeply eloquent voice flowed Fanon's urgencies onto the night: "subjugation is beyond question," he pronounced, and "what matters is not to know the world but to change it." Artists leaned through their shoulders into the fire and, nodding into the spit-crackling flames, felt and gently shared their agreement.

Meanwhile, inside The Black Power Station a similar-sized group of women were gathered by the brick chimney fireplace in the Book'ona, talking about their own role and experiences as women, and especially the prevalent culture of rape and sexual assault in Grahamstown-Makhanda and South Africa. The women's conversation inside was urgent, given the tragic suicide of a prominent young female student that had very recently rocked the city. Lindsey and Carlin, our two undergraduate students from the University of Virginia, were part of this conversation, and Lindsey was later moved to share how consuming this experience was. "Some of our conversations were heavy, but all in all we talked about womanhood and our personal experiences both in Makhanda and back in the United States. I really bonded with everyone during our conversation,"[87] she later shared with an undergraduate class at UVA.

Taking place simultaneously, these two gendered conversations reflected and honored some of the structures of Xhosa family debates that take place in the homes and kraals and especially during ceremonies, where there are often moments of clearly demarcated gender dynamics, creating spaces for men and women to discuss matters independently of each other. It remains true that gender issues can be as problematic in the Eastern Cape as anywhere else. As Kholisa Gogela observes, although there is a clear drought of research on women in relation to amaXhosa initiation ceremonies, gender divisions are increasingly being resisted in some ceremonies and in recent years there have been "pockets of women rising and speaking against the values and norms of *ulwaluko*," the male circumcision ritual that has been criticized for reproducing and reinforcing patriarchal structures.[88] However, inside and outside The Black Power Station on this evening, women had actively created a space to talk about sexual violence with and for women and without men present, while young Xhosa men in parallel were debating for hours how they could become more responsible role models for themselves and others in the townships. Some of these moments then became part of the creative videos and productions that are posted almost instantly on affiliated YouTube channels and other social media,[89] ensuring that the values that are preserved and taught in family ceremonies are also speaking in the online spaces through the phones that almost every young Xhosa person uses to connect with other people.

In the official "Premonition" video that dropped on August 17, 2018, two days after the name-change event, Lunakill can be seen rapping with friends and other artists on the grounds near the tennis courts and in the gardens of Rhodes University (where at the time he was also a student). He raps and sings fluently about money, the industry, and the problems of ignorance. His delivery jumps, speeds up, and slows down as his voice flows across samples of spoken definitions of "premonition." Staccato word explosions give way to warm melodic singing as he leans back into the support of his young friends dancing in the video while holding a Bluetooth JBL speaker, moving and mouthing the messages. Then, suddenly at 3 minutes 15 seconds, the scene cuts to the fireside conversation for the last minute of the video. The beat continues and the fire pops, crackles, and crumbles underneath as Luna speaks in a mixture of isiXhosa and English. His words appear subtitled in the fire.

> I wrote this track because my father didn't know I make music
> And that's basically me sending a message to him
> That I'm suffering from a premonition
> And that's me blowing up and being in the industry
> And the reason why I call it a premonition is because
> I know that, in the industry there are a lot of problems that are awaiting me
> And that's why it's not like
> A good thing that I foresee
> That's why I call it a premonition
> Because a premonition is usually associated with an event that you foresee,
> But that event isn't necessarily positive.[90]

"So uyaboniswa?" asks X, "so you are having visions?"

The cut to the traditional Xhosa male conversation in the "Premonition" video fits a broader aesthetic cut-up pattern in Lunakill's videos where a stylish youth Xhosa culture mixes the voices of local artists and students at Rhodes, blending hip hop and the spoken word of individuals within an intensely rooted local setting. In "New Rules," which had dropped a few weeks earlier, the video, also filmed on the Rhodes campus, foregrounds vignettes of Black students speaking about resistance, cutting them in and out of the flow of Lunakill's rapping.[91] The track works as a call to follow music and art if you feel drawn, and not to get sidetracked by the persuasion of other pressures. The cool edits pull from students speaking their ideals back to Lunakill throwing his on-message rhymes, at once mixing homage to Public Enemy and his South African brothers and sisters. For Lunakill, Oz, X, and the other artists, their own hip hop, electronic music, and dance are vehicles to connect with Xhosa tradition, language, and communal values, while reorienting their messages through the contemporary pulse. Their conversations interrogated and blended together traditional Xhosa dialogues and hip-hop aesthetics. Male and female dialogues held inside and outside The Black Power Station mirrored the way some conversations would typically be structured in homesteads, as young artists start to voluntarily assume some of the responsibilities of being elders. Fragments of Xhosa praise poetry, Xhosa hip hop, sound art, and recordings taken outside of ILAM and placed back in DJ sets for beatmakers and as backing music for collective Book'ona readings all filter together and are kept alive on the air in the collective spaces around the fires. And all the while someone is filming and recording to create short documents of all the creativity, ready to push it into Final Cut Pro and then online to reach and inspire the next artist to come and be part of the conversation.

CONVERSATIONS FOR XHOSA CURATION

What does it mean to be a living archive? How can sound, music, and performance be curated collectively? How can they also be given life and value outside of galleries and institutional spaces? Drawing on a range of indigenous knowledge systems in South Africa, Nigeria, and beyond, historian Toyin Falola is animated by the potential reality of "ritual archives" and "pluriversalism" as a possible answer to the problems of the inequalities in intellectual knowledge production. By ritual archives he means "the conglomeration of words as well as texts, ideas, symbols, shrines, images, performances, and indeed objects that document as well as speak to those religious experiences and practices that allow us to understand the African world through various bodies of philosophies, literatures, languages, histories, and much more."[92] Valuable for the knowledge shaping that exists between the visible and invisible worlds, Falola insists that we "never lose sight of that dimension of archive that is never (fully) collected but retains power and agency in invisible ways,"[93] stressing the need for indigenous researchers and "the insertion of the entire range of vernacular epistemologies into formal educational institutions."[94]

The name-change event at The Black Power Station shows how alternative arts spaces can lead to creative and radical new approaches to performing and curating local Xhosa culture, including the direct interrogation of formal academic knowledge production. Archival recordings from ILAM are neither fetishized nor neglected, but rather valued and broadcast as the equal of contemporary, and more popular, Xhosa hip hop, such as Emtee's "Thank You," a massive tune by a huge artist that celebrates *ubuntu* (humanity) and the love and support of a community of friends and family, where "*umntu ngumntu ngabantu*"—"a person is a person because of other people." When X drops tunes such as these alongside ILAM recordings, whether in The Black Power Station, or in his car driving back to town down the dipping hills at night, people listen and forge their own connections. "Emtee, man," volunteered Oz. "These artists have the power to influence a generation."[95]

Although the audience for the name-change event was predominantly Black— of perhaps a hundred people in attendance, only four where White—it had been widely advertised on local radio and Facebook, and in *Grocott's Mail*, the local newspaper, and people who were known opponents to the name change had been invited to participate, although few attended. For the Xhosa artists, the turnout illustrated the ways in which space and sound are still highly segregated. How many White people listen attentively to Xhosa performance? How many would respond to Thandazile's *izibongo* in the ways in which the Xhosa audience did? The Sonic Color Line—the concept Jennifer Lynn Stoever adapted via W. E. B. Du Bois—along with the limited range of the "listening ear" that demarcates racial lines, also clearly operate to reinforce racial hierarchies just as powerfully through what is not listened to. Stoever warns us against the "willful white mis-hearings and auditory imaginings of blackness" that have canonized a White male historiography of sound studies,[96] challenging us all "to consider black artists as theorists and agents of sound, rather than solely as performers or producers."[97] When Thandazile praises the leader Makhanda, he changes the live performance mode from a preceding history lecture into prowling praise poetry that reaches from the roots to the roof as it physically and audibly fills the space. The already powerful and historical medium of *izibongo* in this instance draws even more strength by interrogating, and in the moment replacing, the authority of lectures and books that are often not primarily intended for isiXhosa speakers.

For Xhosa artists such as X, Bliss, Thandazile, Lunakill, Masi, Nox, Sku, Nyaki, and others, a distinctly Xhosa way of curating and archiving already exists. For one, as Thandazile demonstrated, the isiXhosa language itself needs to be fore-grounded, with its distinct tonal palate of clicks and its subtle, lyrical, and often near untranslatable metaphors. Western ideas are often best challenged through languages other than English, as another recent event at The Black Power Station illustrated. For the first film screening in the space, the collective chose *Black Panther*, the Marvel Comics superhero film that became a cultural phenomenon for being the first mainstream Hollywood film to feature "a virtually all-Black cast, a Black director, a Black soundtrack and a Black African storyline."[98] The language spoken in the Afrofuturistic fictional land of Wakanda is a version of isiXhosa, and the film's score was influenced by Tracey's recordings, after Swedish composer Ludwig Göransson visited ILAM to spend time listening and researching alongside Elijah Madiba. This screening in The Black Power Station was "aimed at the youngest kids in the community of Makhanda," and "since the movie was in Xhosa, we wanted to see how the kids would relate to the language and to the movie."[99] Before and after the film, X and his friend Sanele read from books on Black Consciousness and translated them into Xhosa for the children. As X said later, "the most important thing is trying to interrogate things in Xhosa first because it allows you to gain control of the subject, and to be able to articulate in your language, and to be able to see the relations between things and how they go back to your society and the possibility of it relating to things of the past, the present, and the future."[100] Xhosa children delighted in identifying aspects of the film and language that felt recognizable while casting doubt on other themes, such as the lack of respect shown by the character Killmonger to elders, that felt too far from the reality of home.

Xhosa artists also recognize the existence of archiving practices within their own traditions, through ceremonies and everyday practices. These locally rooted ways of remembering at times intersect with Western-based audiovisual archiving, and at other times do not. Some cultural archiving is only transmitted clan to clan, and only through particular ceremonies. X explained:

> It has not been written down that OoGaba—which is my clan, people of the water—we know that when you enter the kraal you do not put your shoes on, and when you slaughter an animal there are certain things that need to be done. Those things are not written down, they are shared via practices as rituals happen and people learn. . . . [I]t is shared information from leader to leader. The one who slaughters the cows on behalf of the family, he is the one who is the bearer of knowledge, so when he passes away there is someone else who picks up the stick.[101]

X has always moved between deep tradition and the futures that are being written by artistic youths, and he recognizes that his culture points in many directions. As someone who has been promoting literacy for decades—teaching English and Xhosa through hip hop, book drives, and children's theater and poetry sessions—he remains hopeful "that everybody is able to read, everybody is able to access the Internet," and that "we need to move to a written form . . . because in the next generation, everybody will be able to read. So if we share the material right now we guarantee that in the future the culture can be saved."[102] Xhosa ownership of the documented material being shaped in ceremonies, and also being produced in artistic spaces such as The Black Power Station, are transforming the archival model a long way beyond codifying musical logic from music recordings. By placing the local Black artistic community first as owners and bearers of their own culture, X is gradually trying to develop an independent arts-driven curriculum that resonates and collaborates with ILAM, Rhodes University, and NGOs and other partners overseas, provided that the agenda and ownership by The Black Power Station is honored first. To do this, he consults traditional Xhosa elders and ancestors in ceremonies, and he also consults young and cutting-edge producers making waves and tracks in the music and media industries in Cape Town, Durban, Johannesburg and beyond, ensuring that there are points of conversational connection between the generations. When plays are written reimagining Makhanda's military strategies against the British, the researchers speak to elders in the communities, collecting stories from the longest cultural memories, while also poring over books and documents in libraries at Rhodes. At The Black Power Station, X then curates by creating the events and documents in community-owned spaces that keep different generations in conversation with each other. With a clear emphasis on intergenerational teaching, it is also obvious that The Black Power Station aims much of its messaging at. and appeals greatly to, a Xhosa youth audience, recognized as the most important demographic for nurturing the transmission of knowledge.

At the time of these exchanges, X had just returned to South Africa after an arts residency at the University of Virginia in November 2018.[103] As we were preparing to finalize his visit, he explicitly asked not to visit the US in December because he was required to devote much of the month spending time in the bush with young male initiates undergoing *ulwaluko* circumcision rituals. X explained how this mode of knowledge training is experiential and not learned through textbooks.

[H]ow do we curate our own culture? It is already happening in a sense at this current moment, the whole thing of circumcision. I just came back, I spent time there, and you know you need to be part of that system to feel it. Our culture as Xhosa people, it is so powerful in that it embraces a young man's mind to know that "I am a man now, I have responsibility." And that is not being taught via a book, [or] someone standing in front of you and explaining things [in a classroom]. . . . [P]art of this thing is embedded in your system as a person that you should remember why this should happen.[104]

X talks freely about the work "in the bush" and its importance in training young men into modes of responsible adult behavior, occasionally sending me images taken by himself in the middle of the night, but always asks me not to share them any further. For X, and many in his community, there is little point archiving a recording of "Somagwaza," a song that is always sung in these *ulwaluko* ceremonies, without respecting, shaping, and tending to the deep Xhosa learning rituals of which the song is only one part. The revealing of secrets containing moral guidance for young men must be earned and granted via clan and communal lineages, and much of this requires transformative physical experience guided by the permissions and conversation of elders. And these realities can also be self-staged and represented, as when X, Nyaki, and Kwanele Butana (another local artist) performed "Ndiyindoda" (I am a man) at the NAF in 2007, debating aspects of Xhosa masculinity at the point of initiation into manhood. Some aspects of these rituals have even been explored more publicly in Nelson Mandela's autobiography, as well as in magazines,[105] features on Al Jazeera,[106] and in *Inxeba* (The Wound), a controversial, award-winning feature film.[107] Despite some alarmist outcries, especially following documented deaths from the traditional circumcision surgery, much of the practice is deliberately kept out of textbooks, recordings, and films. An age-old tradition, the *ulwaluko* is easy to mystify and also to misunderstand. One outside observer who gained the trust of initiates and attended *ulwaluko* ceremonies reported that the practice is "a mystical, secretive ritual that occurs far away from the eyes of the public, and virtually the only information non-participants and non-family members ever have about it is the disturbing death toll from what the newspapers call botched circumcisions."[108] He concluded with insights that are much less commonly reported in the press, notably how much he "loved the warmth and comfort shown by the community of men," and how he had "never sat in communion around so many fires, and seen children and adults work together so effortlessly for a common cause." It seemed that "all had their role and all had respect for one another."[109] Perhaps the only way to collect and document here, if even at all, is through oral histories from those who feel it is right to talk and want to document, and where permission is granted from within the community. Curation—the care taken to protect and then ethically disseminate knowledge—takes place firstly through the channels of clan and familial permission to attend initiations, and in the pedigree of the elders who reciprocate and share their own experiences as initiates while being present to train the young men.

It is increasingly obvious— indeed vital—that archival materials should be "taken to the people." In her extensive analysis of South African music archives, Lizabé Lambrechts compares commercial, radio, ethnographic, and personal archives, observing that "archival practice in South Africa is still mainly defined in terms of custodianship, physical material, and places of custody."[110] The seared wounds still burning from apartheid patterns of oppression "left a fractured record reflecting a minority culture that sought to control what was known or knowable about its other," leaving major gaps and silences that must be popu- lated.[111] Specifically addressing ILAM, she sees "inserting other ways of knowing into the archive" as an imperative for people to "challenge the authority of the archival system and material,"[112] especially by placing equivalent value on more ephemeral and embodied repertoires. Considering Lee Watkins's claim that the truly radical things for archivists and curators to do would be to reinsert recordings back into contexts, and to record the context itself, while engaging with participants on their own terms, it is possible to see how independent, original, and predictive are the performative curatorial modes designed and deployed by artists like X, Nyaki, Elijah Madiba, Masixole Heshu, Nox, Sikhum- buzo Makandula, Andiswa Rabeshu, "Oz" Mzwali, and Lunakill. Artists of this caliber think and move beyond the bounded frames of extractive recordings, building and maintaining creative living spaces and expanding practices for the live transmission of arts and language activism. Their creative work often builds around an archival fragment, whether an ILAM recording or a self-documented moment, and constructs productive frames using contemporary elements of hip hop, poetry, music videos, and sound and visual art. Little of this fits or sits easily in cataloguing systems: Xhosa hip hop that spits against hate, youth praise poetry asking for respect for the environment, and walking sound art that suspends the sounds of colonial marching bands until deceased ancestors have been ceremonially honored. Curating such living galleries requires and demands the creation and occupation of more independently owned and run arts spaces exerting control over their archives. These are the communal spaces for performing and housing differently owned stories that can challenge the dominant histories that endured while only a few people recorded and wrote and accessed their versions of the memory of nations.

The ethnographer, the archivist, and the curator can no longer act with belief in an omniscient observation, documentation, and explanation. Ethnographic work can, however, as Carol Muller suggests, embrace a more ambient poetics as "a way of conjuring up a sense of a surrounding atmosphere or world."[113] We might, she argues, rethink ethnomusicological representation beyond conveying cultural context solely through words and through reading, reimagining the work as "the constitution of witnessing through sound" while developing inclusive listening publics.[114] The creative work of all the South African artists shared here calls others to witness their stories, their poetry, their performances, and their performance modes, increasingly crafted and made public in their own language, and in spaces within a renamed landscape that is being reclaimed, renewed, and remade. The conditions for getting anything to change in the society we live in "will only come about," X offers, "when people start to work together *intsebenziswano* with the spirit of *ubuntu* in the center. . . . *Sithemba kubawo kumdali kuyokowenzeka camagu.*"[115]

CONCLUSION

Curating Sound Stories

At the memorial service for Hugh Tracey held at Saronde Farm in Krugersdorp on October 26, 1977, Denis Etheredge, a mining magnate, predicted that people would take a long time to realize the value of what Tracey had preserved: "I believe, of course," he said, "that those who do not understand now the value of keeping this African music, will certainly in fifty years' time."[1] What neither Etheredge nor Tracey could properly hear was how the structures and practices inscribed in such recording, classifying, and codifying maintained an archive that would remain fundamentally detached from the people whose ancestors Tracey asked to play and sing for him. With the passing of half a century, a colonial archive only becomes a postcolonial archive when it breaks down its own reproduction of racially constructed power imbalances, and actively builds new and equitable partnerships for decolonized and anticolonial exchanges. This book began by reconstructing the archival record of Tracey's colonizing recording exchanges, in an attempt to better understand the broader social and political environments shaping the extractions, before offering the recordings with their dominating histories for local artists to freely interrogate, request, repurpose, or reject. Their choice.

Colonial opportunist, humanistic visionary, exploitative settler, or prophetic emancipator? Hugh Tracey's crusading work and beliefs will continue to polarize many commentators and observers. "By paying serious attention to African music, Tracey was a generation ahead of his time," state Leroy Vail and Landeg White, referring to his analyses of the music of Chopi orchestras in Mozambique. They also acknowledged the limitation of his musicological orientation. "He was equipped," they claim, "neither as a literary critic nor as a historian to examine the meanings of the songs he transcribed." If his explanatory notes could frequently be illuminating, "his general comments range from the whimsical and patronizing to the totally erroneous."[2] Mhoze Chikowero pulls fewer punches, arguing that Tracey's egregious problem lay in the promotion of tribalism, achieved through the sponsorship of cultural difference, a context in which for decades "Tracey and others found ready support from the state, western institutions, and international capital, including record companies such as Gallo . . . to research and resuscitate African interest in 'their own' music and cultures."[3] He spots the familiar watermark of latent racism embossed in colonial collectors and collections, a prejudice that would not dissolve. "If Tracey eventually became intellectually and culturally competent to listen to African music," says Chikowero, he still "chose to hear the 'tribal drum' over the contemporary (political) concerns of African laborers."[4] Paulette Coetzee similarly hears the dangers of racist practices ringing through his collecting, which was always enabled by old-boy networks of privilege, and she warns of the dire damage that could be enforced when blanket statements are thrown to stifle further free expression. "Tracey's recording project was not merely undertaken within an oppressive context," she writes, but it was also "conceptualized and structured to advance a colonial capitalist agenda . . . selling records to industrialists and administrators with the implied promise of producing contented workers who would not be inclined to struggle for political rights or higher pay."[5] Close examination of the ways in which the recording work was conceived and implemented clearly shows that some of Tracey's thinking embraced retribalization, but conversely that he also imagined some future uses beyond the contexts of apartheid specifically and colonial control more generally.

A first step toward relinquishing hegemonic and hermeneutic control over the archive is to seek or create new ways for the archive to be shared and listened to, amplifying local and contemporary responses and the voices clamoring to express their own struggles. When Toyin Falola argues for the need to amplify ritual archives, "to apply the techniques and resources of academic archives to rituals so that there can be greater preservation and valuation,"[6] he is resisting the prior forces of control displayed when "the colonial archive has been imposed and given prominence over the ancestral ritual archive, leading to the erasure and degradation of indigenous perspectives and local talents."[7] In resonance with these ideals, this book illustrates work that so far has been made to decenter a colonial archive in three phases: it critically examines the methods and aims of a White collector of African culture, before refracting fragments of the archive through contemporary Xhosa audiences in the Eastern Cape of South Africa to challenge, reimagine, and remake the catalogued cultural classifications. And in the present, it witnesses, and sometimes includes the invitation to co-create and make work with, some remarkable South African artists, all of whom are developing innovative ways to publicly perform and archive their own stories, reimagining what archives can sound and look like, and where they can resonate and be reclaimed.

As this research and practice have developed over the past decade, moving increasingly further from Tracey and closer to the contemporary artists, academics, and activists of Makhanda, an ethnography of a collector, his collections, and an institution transforms into an ethnography of alternative archives happening next door and nearby. Along the way, it has often been asked why the International Library of African Music matters to this story at all. Isn't this a story about artists in Makhanda and not about ILAM or Hugh Tracey? ILAM and Hugh Tracey are part of this account because the gatekeeping that both represent, and that has continued to fascinate and persuade many outsiders, has often been simplified and misread, whether romanticized or rejected. Some of the predictive future uses for the collection can be found in the archival record, as well as some of the jarringly dangerous threads of retribalized thinking. The story of the collection is followed through to today not just because of the singular importance of some remarkable and often unrepeatable recordings, but because almost every single artist encountered in the Eastern Cape asked for further access to the archive, holding their own ideas about what it might mean and how it might be used. It was the pressing demand from Xhosa artists, once initial awareness had been raised, to use their own Xhosa recordings that made it evident that relistening to fragments need not necessarily become retribalizing, but could instead nurture seeds for reimagined modes of storytelling.

IMAGINING DECOLONIZED LISTENING

Once fantasies and imaginaries of populations are created through recording, they can become instruments for the subjugation of populations. In apartheid-era South Africa, music and sound were used by the state to represent and essentialize Black and "colored" (or mixed heritage/biracial) people. Radio Bantu—which was established by the South African Broadcasting Corporation in 1960 to broadcast in local languages to ethnic groups in designated areas—followed the separate development policy made law by the Group Areas Act in 1950. Recording teams were aggressively sent out to "native" reserves to actively produce the idea of ethnicity through sounds. "Corporate practice was institutionalized as a matter of state," writes Grant Olwage, and "recording ethnicity for the state was primarily for ideological reasons — to naturalize the idea of the tribe and the ideal of the homeland."[8]

Sound recording and separate development became mutually reinforcing, and colonial collectors such as Tracey have often sailed in, or close to, these lashing winds. Historian Mhoze Chikowero has examined the ways that music and song operate as sites that can be both oppressive and subversive — depending on who is recognized as the authority — and argues that any external focus on ethnically demarcated music functions as nothing more than primitivism. "The colonial state," he argues "conceived 'tribal dancing' as a performative instrument for articulating a self-justifying discourse of conquest and domination in a process that produced the African 'Other' as a lesser, 'tribal' being with no claim to 'modern' rights."[9] Chikowero hears in the patriarchal collecting of Tracey, whose "aestheticized primitivism and self-interest hardly veiled the racism of the shared settler idiom,"[10] little more than a prejudiced and "tribally jaundiced listening."[11] Beginning in the tobacco fields in 1920s Southern Rhodesia, Tracey's work, however admiring of indigenous expression, could never have been a genuinely mutual project because "colonial survival depended on cannibalizing African autonomy."[12] Chikowero names this exploitation. Tracey and his brother Leonard's extraction of both settler land and then indigenous culture relied on, and profited from, the oppression of subjugated labor. "By controlling the colonized Africans' cultural expression," Chikowero argues, "Tracey helped deliver them to capital and empire while amassing a fortune for himself and his family. To him, Africans' labor and cultures were both gold mines."[13] The danger of an extractive recording project working closely with the mining companies of Southern Africa to continue regulating leisure time through sound is a bitterly obvious irony.

In a study linking race, gender, and recording in the emerging American global music industry, Roshanak Kheshti also sees and hears the rampant incorporation of fantasy in recordings. She argues that through the pursuit of fidelity — literally the accuracy with which an electronic system reproduces the sound or image of its original signal — field recordings have always been complicit in creating imaginary listening objects and events for the future. Making a faithful field recording "requires that all parties acquiesce to the power of the archive and the power of sonic continuity by remaining silent while a recording is under way and by allowing the performers to do their imagined 'thing.'"[14] If the recordist encounter typically reinforced preexisting hierarchies between the recordist and recorded, then future listeners can be given access to the histories of these encounters, and can choose to change the ground and places where they occur, and in refusing to replicate these power dynamics enable the telling of different stories. "Treating the archive less as a dominant reference and more as a living and changing subject," suggest Frank Gunderson and Bret Woods, "can help us rethink how and why archives take shape."[15] People think, act, move, and perform in different ways depending on whether they are on the street, inside a reclaimed power station or a studio, or in a museum or library, both as a function of the affordance of the spaces themselves and the histories hanging through them. And the ethnographic fragment can sound very different when activated within spaces that people can make their own. "The real aim of colonialism," writes Ngũgĩ wa Thiong'o, "was to control people's wealth." Of all the human aspects, the most destructive domination always occurred through oppression of "the mental universe of the colonized, the control, through culture, of how people perceived themselves and their relationship to the world."[16] So liberate yourself through the arts? "This is a space which seeks to encourage freedom of thought and the expression thereof. We exist on the edge of the Makhanda Waainek Industrial Area, away from the daily noise that distracts the mind. We are a place of healing, recuperation, and learning," welcomes the homepage of the website for The Black Power Station.[17]

Some of the work in this book has been to try to imagine possibilities for a decolonized listening, for a colonial archive to be better understood in postcolonial contexts, imagined differently, and decentered through contemporary artistic responses. With a massively energized global surge in support for the Movement for Black Lives, monuments to racism in South Africa, the US, and the UK are rapidly being toppled, as "protesters have dethroned, decapitated, defaced or otherwise targeted public representations of some of the most venerable members (deceased) of the Great White Canon of Conquest."[18] Iconoclasm reigns, and we should remember, argues Verity Platt, that "monuments are only as powerful as the human will that keeps them in place."[19] As the work of the artists, organizers, and activists illustrated in this book shows, neither recordings nor heritage nor ILAM itself are any longer conceived solely in terms of Tracey or other powerful individuals who spoke with authority over "African culture" for so long. Rather, it is individuals such as X, Bliss, and Nyaki, Lee, Mthwakazi, and Elijah together with their collaborators who are today reclaiming new modes of listening, expression, and public memory.

While listening to local stories that speak of people's pasts, presents, and futures, we see how an archive could be differently constructed, owned, and made more locally meaningful. I recall and honor daily my training as a sound curator with the late Hélène la Rue, who always encouraged contemporary artists to remix and reclaim the Victorian collections boxed in Oxford museums. I still love the story about an artist who chose to leave a wooden crate of fresh lemons on top of darkened glass cabinets in the Pitt Rivers Museum. Art or air fresheners? No one was really sure. Hélène was. "These are what we should be collecting," she would say, "the responses." However, neither the anthropologist, artist, or sound curator in me could have predicted at the outset that one of the most constructive curatorial moves in one particular South African context would be to help hire a donkey cart and sound system to roam rocky streets playing tapes at township cyphers. The confidence that this would work and resonate came from Nyaki, another remarkable South African artist. This explosive reclamation of sound and public space created energy and a vibe on township street corners, and promised a momentum that was owed and attracted a strong following. Donkey cart curation worked for many locally resonant reasons, probably the most important being Nyaki's own determination to take hold of this archive and bring it alive on his own streets. Witnessing creative responses, and collecting in innovative modes when there is permission, allow for a layered archival texture to grow, a more ritual archive. Over time, artistic responses will be critically interrogated, adapted, and built upon — much as Tracey's own modes and methods continue to be — and there will also be much to learn in due course when artists listen differently to scattered sound fragments across sub-Saharan Africa without an "anticipation of Xhosaness."[20] Xhosa artists and artistry are not limited by the need to listen to Xhosa archives alone. The Black Power Station is a deeply rooted space for Xhosa art, sound, poetry, and being, but is also self-imagined as an international destination, a pan-African space, and has welcomed and honored artists and work from Uganda, Egypt, the US, Europe, and beyond.

Critical engagement with witnessed or collected or co-created responses to "Xhosaness" animate the next stages of The Black Power Station and the search for creative liberated spaces. Communal and collective projects can often be utopian and threatened at the same time. As Viv Golding observes, if the term curator can hold a range of positive and negative associations and powers, so too can the notion of community. "While *community* is most often used to describe positive aspects of a group," she writes, "a community can also be exclusive, serving to divide and marginalize."[21] In an interactive online lecture-presentation titled "Creative Economies: Centering the Margins," historian Nomalanga Mkhize and

X together presented some of the histories, future plans, and lessons learned from working to build The Black Power Station. The talk was part of "Arts Activism," a collaborative January Term class hosted at the University of Virginia. As well as demonstrating principles of Black community art as self-expression and an exertion of autonomy, and the vital importance of funding artistic opportunities for Black children, Mkhize and X were also alert to the problems of communal creative spaces. They shared stories of activism burnout, jealousies, beef, and rivalries, differing perceptions of what "communal running" and "communal ownership" means, and the sheer hard work of finding sustainable funding for autonomous, improvised, and collective arts education spaces. Art, they both shared, can create many burdens beyond the work itself, and can easily be falsely imagined to be the way to solve all social problems.[22]

Decolonization, writes James Clifford, is "an unfinished, excessive historical process," a type of "recurring agency, a blocked, diverted, continually reinvented historical force."[23] He finds much to admire in local examples of cultural endurance—in the face of patterns of invasion, dispossession, and resistance—that often unsettle more dominant modernist stories of human survival. Clifford's analysis of what it means to "become indigenous" in the twenty-first century requires from all of us neither romantic celebration nor knowing critiques, but an attitude of critical openness and "realism." He recognizes that half a century after the wave of postwar liberation movements, conditions for sovereignty and self-determination may now be "less a matter of independence and more a practice of managing interdependence, inflecting uneven power relations, and finding room for maneuver."[24] He also notices patterns of role reversal, where "scholarly outsiders now find themselves barred from access to research sites, met with new or newly public suspicion," while anthropologists have now become stereotyped and defined as "a negative alter ego in contemporary indigenous discourse, invoked as the epitome of arrogant, intrusive colonial authority."[25] For real and alternative pathways forward, ethnographers await an invitation that may now never be offered, and if it ever is, they must negotiate to collaborate, and think and act creatively to avoid repeating cycles of neocolonial extraction.

The central argument in this book has been that liberated archives are created in independent spaces when artists and protagonists decide and set the terms and modes for their engagement. The archive—"the tangible collection of intangible heritage"[26]—often seems to be recognized as valuable through its material tangibility, its concrete legibility, its institutional validity. When listening through these pages to the essential work of South African artists and scholars actively performing and curating stories about their own heritage, I am constantly reminded how fetishistic it is to focus only on the object or fragment of the field recording. "A possessed listener, someone addicted to the wonder of exploring the sounds of elsewhere," writes collector and producer Ian Nagoski as he excavates and curates global sounds from the "inscribed sound stones" of 78 rpm discs, "thinks of them as containing galaxies and miasmas of beauty, each one potentially magically charged with the possibility for inward transportation and contact with humanity in extraordinarily elevated form."[27] This respectfully warm utopian sentiment almost perfectly describes how I felt as a listener and artist first discovering ethnographic fragments online, a feeling of transport I still recognize every time when listening to Tracey's recording of "Mhlahlo" or "Somagwaza" or the *lesiba* mouth bow, wherever I am located in the world, and however I am listening. But this is also a mode of privileged consumption. Such imagined contact with humanity today—the elevating epiphanies of aestheticized and distanced listening—remains physically and ethically fragmented, and often uncomfortably close to the hoovering colonial recorder, the "white man's microphone" pointed by Tracey.[28]

Throughout this book, the listening has really been focused on the spaces activated by local South African artists themselves listening to colonial sound fragments and making their own work that I have been invited to witness. My analysis seeks to understand what a contemporary reclaiming of Tracey's recording project can reveal about ways in which sound recordings create and deny, obscure and idealize particular perceptions, images, and relationships. If sounds collected in colonial Africa have inevitably been split and fragmented from their originating communities, diluted by their removal from several generations across half a century, portable copies of the sounds can also easily be made available again, proactively, to serve the preferences of any community requests. Active spaces for enabling shared new listening exchanges can be built in ways that shift the authority of a colonial archive, inviting communities to express their own responses parallel to the clashing histories of extraction heard.

DECOLONIZING ETHNOGRAPHY

How far have critiques of twentieth-century modes of archiving, displaying, studying, and Othering brought us? At a time when many in academia are again questioning with some urgency whether we as individuals and as collective disciplines have managed in any way to transcend the past modes exemplified by Tracey, how much has the pattern of White ethnographers studying people of color really changed? "Not admitting that ethnomusicology remains a colonialist and imperialist enterprise," argues Danielle Brown in her open letter on racism in music studies, "is part of the resistance to equity and justice for Black, Indigenous, People of Color."[29] Does my own positionality here differ in any fundamental ways from Tracey's, or have I simply reproduced the epistemic violence of Eurocentrism again? As a White English researcher based in America, I have greatly benefited from the resources, support, and legible and transferable identity afforded by association with Oxford University, the University of Virginia, and Rhodes University, as well as connections with an international art world—all powerful institutions with their own histories of domination and erasure. As a sound curator who trains and works both through and outside these institutions, I have tried to listen carefully to some of the ways that power is constructed, and especially how it sounds. This requires thinking and practice that resists privileging field recordings as the most authentic documents, valuing other ways of documenting and sharing performances of local culture. How much ethnographic fragments matter is so clearly contingent upon whether the documents can be used to build and teach and nurture healthier, more equitable relationships for all of the people whose history they field. Any roles created, played, and occupied in fieldwork today must, as Samuel Araujo argues, become "more politically articulate."[30] An intensely participatory mode of musical ethnography is one in which collaborators "negotiate from the start the research focuses and goals," including the data sought, the demands of a community, collective authorship, and new forms of diffusion.[31]

The ethnographer's role should always be evolving and can no longer claim to be omniscient, definitive, or panoramic, if it ever really could. The phenomenon of the collector tapping and draining colonized sound from the field still exists, but it is also steadily being replaced by self-documenting communities working with a full range of technologies to suit different local realities and requirements. Songs are mapped and shared on Saharan cell phones while MP3s of *gqom* beat stems flow through WhatsApp groups and other locally driven sites online and offline. Such practices allow performers and producers to redefine and control the recorded encounter, choosing when to engage record labels, and reversing a century of being silently consumed. Within this multiplicity of voices and recording channels, there can be no singular or definitive postcolonial tradition.

As Rose Boswell states, "the 'post' in postcolonial does not mean that colonialism has been overcome." Rather, she urges, there is a need to produce "multiple forms of knowledge to empower those previously marginalized."[32]

Boswell argues that this type of knowledge production might prove more possible "with assistance from 'reasonable' theory as opposed to 'high' theory."[33] Her call is to work alongside—and ultimately replace—the dominance of Euro-American high theory, long deployed as an exclusive and distancing weapon for reinforcing hierarchical elitist structures. Similarly, Francis Nyamnjoh makes the case for a more intimate anthropology, one grounded in "convivial scholarship." Nyamnjoh values conviviality as a disposition that privileges conversation over conversion, moves us beyond tolerance, and emphasizes good fellowship and feelings of security "imbued with a spirit of togetherness, interpenetration, interdependence and intersubjectivity."[34] A conversational togetherness becomes possible when ethnographers relinquish authoritative modes, attending to the compassionate listening that might hear and help document new and alternative stories that can expand understandings of existing archives while further amplifying locally owned ways to self-document. "Had Euro-theory known a little more of Africa, past and present," write Jean and John Comaroff, "perhaps the idea of a more complex notion of human personhood, one grounded in a multidimensional space-time, might have commended itself a long time ago."[35]

It is also possible to modulate and transform the text that engages these processes, especially when we remember that writing and other seemingly muted media can also sound. David Toop has written convincingly about the soundscapes of silent paintings,[36] and while some artists and ethnographers reject the limitations of text as a medium to convey the three-dimensional depth of sonic performances, other writers strive to also make text sound, crackle, and move on the page. In her listening ethnographies of authors including Zora Neale Hurston, Gayl Jones, and Ralph Ellison, Nicole Furlonge notices that while nationhood in America so often seems bound up with the ability to speak, to have your voice heard, to declare independence, the opportunities for speaking are rarely evenly distributed. "Black literature sounds," says Furlonge, as she illustrates the ways acoustics permeate African American and Black feminist literary criticism.[37] And we can continue asking how opportunities for speaking might become more evenly distributed, especially among marginalized communities, and whether there are ways that ethnography can be made to sound differently.

In his book *Hungry Listening*, Dylan Robinson—a xwélméxw (stó:lō) or First Nations writer in Canada—"sets out to understand forms of Indigeneous and settler colonial listening,"[38] in the wider context of a significant increase of Indigenous participation in art music since the early 1990s. Robinson powerfully advocates for "disciplinary redress," calling out mischaracterizations of Indigenous knowledge and exhorting "non-Indigenous scholars [to] amend their citational practice to prioritize Indigenous writers, knowledge keepers, and artists."[39] He pointedly includes devices to change the tone of the academic monograph. The text is predictive, notably through the inclusion of an epigraph "written for a readership yet to come, for future generations of fluent Halq'eméylem readers and speakers, of which there are currently few."[40] Following this epigraph, Robinson deliberately creates a space for Indigenous sovereignty, deploying an injunction asking settlers not to read the subsequent section which "is written exclusively for Indigenous readers."[41] His conclusion then features an "improvisation on Decolonial Listening and Action," an extended conversation between two different "settler scholars," Deborah Wong and Ellen Waterman, "intended to complement the Introduction's written space of Indigenous sovereignty."[42] The dialogue calls out the critical problem of White possessiveness, which, as Wong diagnoses, "can be most fully on display when settlers claim the right to dislodge the problem—to claim authority, including the authority to assert they're no longer part of the problem."[43] When Waterman suspects that truly ethical collaborations based on deep listening can only start with invitations from indigenous artists, Wong embraces a radical willingness to claim no knowledge, no authority, and no expectation to be invited inside. She wonders whether "elevating collaboration as the ideal terms for encounter isn't another kind of hunger."[44]

Real collaboration means the equalization of terms, beginning with all parties retaining the free choice over whether or not to collaborate. In my work with X, we have spent much time and energy learning how we can both bring complementary qualities to the table for each other. In high-level meetings about the potential purchase of expanded buildings and land for The Black Power Station, for example, X knows local realities well enough to calculate that he would often be given more information in meetings if he were accompanied by a White collaborator perceived to be connected to institutional funding streams overseas. We speak and message every day, often multiple times a day, sharing ideas for work and love for each other's families. He and I have been through this entire book together, word by word when we read it aloud over our dinner table in Charlottesville, Virginia. X has read the text and has improved and approved the accuracy and content, as has every artist whose work is included in the second part of the book, although of course any enduring errors are entirely my own.

But an academic monograph alone will rarely stand as a medium for equal collaboration, and so we remain dedicated to a full range of outputs and creative opportunities that support and amplify each other's work. Sharing each other's spaces as much as possible feels and seems right, and during the last few years we have been co-teaching multiple classes in Virginia—often linked over Zoom even before Covid contained us all online inside a socially and physically distanced world—and X has already flown over twice for artist residencies in Virginia.

In South Africa, intrusive and imported ideas of authority are being widely and forcefully rejected. The violence, injustices, and inequalities wrought by South Africa's apartheid government still burn fiercely in many places, not least in the spaces of higher education, where the fight for universal access and for the very idea of African universities, rather than European transplants, "goes as far back as the 1860s and 1870s."[45] The Rhodes Must Fall and subsequent Fees Must Fall protest movements that swept through South African universities began in 2015 and 2016 at the historically White University of Cape Town, and soon developed into a network embracing "different sites of decolonial struggles that were targeting diverse offensive immediate issues" including colonial/apartheid iconography, economic exploitation of workers, and the name itself of Rhodes University, the institution that owns the International Library of African Music.[46] The student-driven protests gained international traction as they forcefully highlighted major inequities propagated by these "institutions that opened their doors to all South Africans after 1994, but failed to dissolve their colonial infrastructures."[47] The protests were initiated by student hostility to the stark realities of epistemic violence lived and experienced while "two decades after the end of apartheid, the curriculum at South African universities is still largely Eurocentric, rooted in the colonial and apartheid dispossession, looting and humiliation of Africa and its people."[48] Might the anger pulling down colonial statues, bureaucracies, and art works also be directed toward colonial collecting projects such as Tracey's any day soon? Can the archive that Chikowero hears as built on "tribally jaundiced" listening and economic subjugation even be part of current-day decolonized listening and compositional practices, and become an African archive in Africa that sounds like, looks like, and really is something more than transplants from the Eurocentric imagination?

Posing the question "What is an African Curriculum?" Harry Garuba proposes that the first step toward an answer must be "to recognize the cultural and scientific production—the knowledge—of previously devalued groups of people." He argues for selecting the middle ground, a contrapuntal analysis that "takes into account the perspectives of both the colonized and the colonizer, their interwoven histories, their discursive entanglements—without necessarily harmonizing them or attending to one while erasing the other."[49] Jean and John Comaroff also propose reversing dominant Western perspectives when they argue that Euro-America is evolving toward, rather than away from, the Global South. Refuting ideas commonly held in the Euro-modernist narrative that the South is tracking the North, they instead find "radically new assemblages of capital and labor" in Africa that prefigure the future for the global North.[50] Meanwhile Sabelo Ndlovu-Gatsheni, in a conversation about the future of African studies with Duncan Omanga,[51] argues that Northern epistemologies have already been exhausted. Coloniality—the perpetrator of the crimes of epistemicide, linguicide, and culturecide—is named as a "death project." A theory of life requires a noncolonial way "which underscores that all human beings were born into valid and legitimate knowledge systems and recognizes the various and diverse ways of knowing." Decolonization does not merely seek inclusion in the system, or an Africanized validation of the European game, and instead demands deep structural change. "The decolonization of the twenty-first century," states Ndlovu-Gatsheni, "is to question the rules of the game, not to be part of it."[52]

SIQALA APHO BAYEKE KHONA
(WE START WHERE THEY ENDED)

"The thing that makes me angry about ILAM," said X, "is that it makes it look like we chose to forget."[53] Tracey took on the familiar role of imagined savior and protector of what he saw as a lost culture. But as X asserts, no Xhosa person, no Black South African, no colonized person ever *chose* to lose their culture, their identity, their ways of knowing and being. This loss was the result of centuries of abject violence inflicted upon people who never asked to be colonized and who fought and struggled endlessly to maintain their social worlds and sense of place and dignity. X's statement incisively shows what Tracey was unable to fully see: the agency and inner lives of the people whose music he recorded. None of the artists and activists in Makhanda working in The Black Power Station ever chose to forget. The Black Power Station stands as testament to their work, with its mission to "uplift the province" by empowering local artists through a collective hub that creates opportunities to build community, work, and income for everyone involved. Inclusivity is modeled in the range of experiences and backgrounds represented, and where academic and other professional qualifications and titles are treated as no more or less important than a young teenager producing her own isiXhosa comics.

When I first saw the derelict space in Waainek, X extended an invitation to me to be part of this process and I have been privileged over the past several years to share time and ideas and to work alongside these brilliant and cutting-edge artists. In this process, we have experimented with ways to collaborate and build community across the Atlantic. When X visited Virginia in 2018 during one of his arts residencies, he asked to work with musicians who could help rearrange some of his old rap songs for a small pick-up band. We fixed rehearsals with three jazz musicians in the music department and organized a performance at The Bridge Progressive Arts Initiative, a local community arts gallery.[54] A year later, in April 2019, we co-designed "Makhanda at Dawn," a live arts link between The Black Power Station and The Bridge.[55] The same pick-up band improvised live in Charlottesville as they watched and listened to a canvas being painted live by Andiswa "Bliss" Rabeshu in Makhanda. Multiple laptop video calls enabled microconversations to take place between the spaces as sound experiments, sketches, and improvised music were exchanged in real time between the countries.

In the spring of 2019 we hosted a live collaborative class designed to place thirty undergraduate students in my "African Electronic Music" class in creative multimodal exchanges with Elijah Madiba, who was hosting X, Bliss, and Biz from The Black Power Station at ILAM. The interactive Zoom class linked several studio and art spaces in both countries, enabling the live creation and swapping of beats, rhymes, song lyrics, and visual art in response to some of Tracey's Xhosa recordings.[56] As slices of ethnographic samples and original beat stems flowed between producers in studios linking both countries, Elijah demonstrated the playing techniques for the Xhosa instruments *uhadi* and *umrhubhe*, and he and X simultaneously led a joint conversation on the history and ethics of sampling African field recordings. The discussion took place synchronously as ILAM recordings and other beats were being sampled live. During part of the class conversation, X was already reflecting on the process with students who were curious to understand the reasons and terms for our collaboration, for which we had been preparing together for months.

I think what is the beauty of what is happening today is these three stages that we have: there is *bhuti* [brother] Elijah explaining how the music was acquired, and now we have Biz at the back—he has made a beat out of the samples and on that side [UVA] there is Ryan [Maguire] and others at the studio,[57] and there is Bliss on the other side [outside the studio at ILAM] doing the artwork. So I guess the experiment here is how do you actually continuously tell the story in different forms. . . . How do you continuously tell the story visually—because Bliss she is drawing—and we are here busy trying to talk about it and actually find ways.[58]

X acknowledged the important role played by Elijah, who "started by giving the samples to us as people that are into hip hop—and anyone else who wants to transform the music that was recorded—in any form that they please, but with respect."[59] By the end of the class together we had created new beats, sketches of Xhosa instruments, poetry, and song lyrics, all framed by a live conversation considering the historical and ethical realities underpinning our collaborative process across continents. "When you leave today," X encouraged the students, "please ask yourself what life are you building beyond your classroom?"

FIGURE C.1 Lindsey Shavers and Xolile "X" Madinda in the Book'ona working on coding for The Black Power Station website. August 7, 2018. *Photo by the author.*

Siqala apho bayeke khona. The phrase and translation are held in striking yellow and white over an image of three young Xhosa children crouching in a small absorbed huddle, captivated. Looking down, six small hands are feeling for the grass and earth, just outside The Black Power Station. One of the children is Lindiwe, X's daughter, "The President," as she is only half-jokingly known. This beautiful and emblematic photograph is revealed as you scroll through a website coded by Lindsey Shavers, who was working alongside X and Bliss, partly written in The Black Power Station, during two separate visits, and partly back in Charlottesville, before being passed to Lwandiso Gwaburana, another talented website developer in Grahamstown-Makhanda (see figure c.1).[60] Lindsey's visits to Makhanda later inspired her to program and curate a "Transatlantic Turn Up" at the Urban Hang Suite in Richmond, Virginia, as part of Black History Month in February 2020,[61] when both X and Bliss were our guests in the US for a joint arts residency. Marking four hundred years since the first enslaved Africans arrived in Virginia, two hundred years since the founding of UVA—a school that did not admit its first Black student until 1950—as well as two hundred years since White settlers first arrived in South Africa, the event brought X and Bliss together with other hip-hop artists and writers and poets from Virginia.[62] In her press release for the event, Lindsey recalled how welcomed she felt on her first visit to Grahamstown-Makhanda in 2018, when she stayed in the Rosa Parks House that had been decorated to celebrate Michelle Obama. "The conversations I had with people I met in the townships and at The Black Power Station," she writes, "taught me more about Black history than I learned in grade school."[63]

As this text hits the page in Virginia, I am watching a looped video banner chosen to feature at the top of the drafted template for The Black Power Station's website, a rich mixture of Biz's laptop beats, improvising electric guitar, and laughter on repeat. *Lost Conversations*, the first Black Power Station visual presentation, has just gone live online, developed during the virtual National Arts Festival, a Covid-19–enforced shrinking of a major arts festival back inside the digital domain.[64] Written by X and produced by Adon Geel's production company The Groove RPBLK, this play stars local actors Thandazile Madinda as "King Makhanda" and Lucky "Tolo" Ngcani as "Chief Mdushane." Everything is filmed on a single camera in a stylish black and white, turning The Black Power Station into a stage set, lit only by candles while *impepho* burns.[65] Archival research is combined with newly collected oral histories, original compositions, and small fragments of Tracey's Xhosa recordings, as the crew reimagine how military strategies were developed in the days before the amaXhosa army would attack the British garrison at the frontier town in the Battle of Grahamstown on April 22, 1819, during the Fifth Xhosa War. Previously dismissed as a superstitious betrayer of his people and also idolized as immortal, Makhanda is now cast as a strategist of some genius, an unsettler of settler history, a liberation hero fated to die at Robben Island and see his legacy resurge two hundred years later. "It's our own version of history, our own version of starting conversations using history moments,"[66] claims X. *Lost Conversations* is already planned to become a series of productions,[67] researched and written around other scenarios, including missionaries arriving to try and convert Makhanda, and a visit from a Virginian to explore connected legacies of slavery. The format is open-ended. Actors research characters and rehearse with beatmakers and other musicians who write and produce the soundtrack alongside them. "The only rule," X affirms, "is we are not going to show Black people as not intelligent, because that is what the previous people have done when they are producing something on Makhanda; they make him look like he was not learned."[68]

My phone buzzes night and day sharing fast-flowing streams of video clips, images, and sound recordings, updates dropped in WhatsApp documenting the writing and production processes in Makhanda. The creative work for *Lost Conversations* was also beginning to inform more collaborative research linking The Black Power Station with a network of artists in the UK for other commissions for a virtual Xhosa soundscape, originally to be hosted at Tate Modern (London) in late 2020. The original idea for our composition—which would blend fragments of drumming and *igqhira* and *sangoma* healing songs, poetry, and performance invoking knowledge from water—was to produce a version of the "Sound Galleries" immersive ethnographic installations I have been developing in collaboration with UK- and Spain-based artist Nathaniel Mann, originally through the Pitt Rivers Museum in Oxford.[69] We immediately extended the invitation to The Black Power Station, intended to amplify the work of a former power station reclaimed by art inside the "monumental brick shell and interior steel structure" of the Bankside Power Station in London,[70] another power station reclaimed from redundancy and now a global mecca for contemporary art.

Before advancing any work together, X and I talk and talk and talk at length until the idea of the work takes shape, changes, and emerges in soft and hard focus. I often remember preparing together for an academic conference when X was in Makhanda while I was in Europe. It was late for us both and we were on

FIGURE C.2 Used with permission,
© The Black Power Station.

Skype, nine thousand miles apart, imagining what we might share together the next morning in a conference whose theme was collaborative ethnomusicology. "My brother," decided X, "we will improvise a conversation." We both knew from experience that we might easily lose the internet connection when it was time to present live. I had already recorded some of our conversation as back up, but X was cool. "We cannot hide the connectivity problems," he knew. So what about collaboration, then? "*Mfowethu*, I want the group to think about collaboration. What happens when a powerful institution collaborates with a smaller institution that has more powerful ideas?" he asked, already knowing. Self-possession and, from the start, the conditions for change. Camagu.

EPILOGUE 1

Sikhona siphila phakathi kwenu

In June 2020, The Black Power Station invited artists, faculty, students, and community members in Charlottesville, Virginia, to contribute content for their programming.

With a permit to perform essential services in Makhanda, The Black Power Station (TBPS) will be hosting collaborative virtual productions addressing the theme *Sikhona siphila phakathi kwenu* (We exist, we live among you) as part of this year's virtual National Arts Festival. As the pandemic year 2020 marks 200 years of Settlers, we invite people to consider how people live locally in spaces and leave legacies for others, exploring some specific ways in which history is present in their own lives This year the creative productions at TBPS will be designed virtually, there to be enjoyed and interacted with online. Expect beatmakers and praise poets to work alongside actors and visual artists. Reimagine with us through play the quality of Makhanda's resistance strategies and how they resonate within the land today and in future.

The Black Power Station invites you to imagine and then create your own part of this conversation, as we seek to collect recorded fragments (90 seconds maximum) of video, conversation, field recordings, beats, and poems. *This invitation is being sent to individuals with personalized content to respond to, chosen by* TBPS. We will then produce and mix a two-hour collaborative conversation that asks us to embrace *ubuntu* across the continents. *Umntu ngumntu ngabantu.* The Black Power Station is the international destination. *Sikhona siphila phakathi kwenu.* Peace.

EPILOGUE 2

Conversations around Hip Hop

They both research around hip hop, but in very different ways. In 2019, Dr. Lee Watkins formally invited Xolile "X" Madinda to join ILAM's advisory board, diversifying the guiding circle and including a representative voice for local Xhosa communities. Already, some foundations are being laid to establish an archive of local hip hop at ILAM, alongside a festival and documentary about hip hop in the Eastern Cape. On August 4, 2020, Lee Watkins, Xolile Madinda, and I discussed ILAM's legacy and future. The triangular conversation took place over Zoom between Grahamstown-Makhanda and Charlottesville, an artifact enforced by Covid-19 virtual realities. Selected from the conversation, we share here a small fragment.

NOEL: What's your take on the future of creative decolonization of archival fragments and history?

XOLILE: It's not just about the archive, it's about finding something that's not dying, that is present, that makes people move, makes people feel something. How do we take what is already recorded and make it accessible and also make it make sense in the present time? What I like about ILAM now is they want to be relevant and current. The archive is not something standing still that doesn't move; it's something that can relate to the present time.

LEE: I can reflect on what X said about the archive being about time and space. I think there's some kind of ambivalence with the archive. By their nature, most universities or institutions are inherently conservative. They speak transformation, they use all the right language, but it doesn't reflect in the everyday practice of the university. On the other hand, it is the prerogative of ILAM to push the boundaries. The archive is at once very conservative because it hoards things, it collects, and it puts them in the freezer or digitizes. But like X was saying just now, the archive also has to be an agent. It's got to find a way of working within a conservative mode and find ways of radicalizing the space. Radical means to interrogate ideas of knowledge, participation, like the university is being an exclusive or elite space. And also we can't think of the archive as just a building or a repository, so the idea of archiving shouldn't just be about the building, the university, the institution.

XOLILE: I think you're right. A building can also intimidate. But there's this illusion that if things go digital they're accessible, but that's not true. They're accessible for those who are far away but who live in that space of accessing material that is online. My fear for TBPS as we're building a new archive and new ideas, we don't just want to be a building, we want to be a living space that people can access from a phone call.

I imagine that ten years ago I wouldn't be speaking about ILAM the way I do now, because of how ILAM changed its accessibility to the people. When I was young I wanted to record [there] but I could not, I was told "no." So I feel that the archive should relate back to people. These things are made by people, which is the problem with universities with knowledge: they make it look like it's produced in the university, although they go to the field [laughs].

NOEL: If you think back to ILAM and Tracey's project, it's clear that a lot happened there but a lot was left out. That's changed in the work you're doing, but from both of your perspectives in the current archival moment, what do you think is still being left out?

LEE: Lots of work is being done to create access and to return recordings and to sell the idea of ILAM to make it more present, more visible, more participatory. So, the challenge is, it's not about just the building itself and the collections, it's also about developing the archive as an agent, and that's what those with the authority and the resources, that's something they can't see. I think what's also left out is more participation, like there's a board but there should be broader representation of the community, a lot more stakeholders of the community broadly conceived. I think that's a critical omission that I didn't think of 'til now, which X is there to remind me of in the future. Instead of having too many academics on board.

XOLILE: Wow, I support what he's saying. I think the vision of whoever recorded that, they never envisioned Black people participating in that. It was his [Tracey's] journey, a selfish journey that now we're trying to make not selfish. What I think is missing in the acknowledgment of every archive is that there should be a declaration that this music or whatever is kept comes from people, and as it comes from people, it belongs to people. And the ownership of that, when he started recording whatever he was recording, it's like he took over, like it belonged to him. Yes, it's his recordings, his device, but he took something from people.

So for me what is missing in the story of archives is the background story of the family, people, and how those societies after the culture has been taken away, the land has been taken away, those people in those societies don't relate to what is there. So my journey is to link those together, without being hostile; is to say, we understand his ignorance. I don't blame him for his ignorance. I wasn't there to check him out. But now I have power to say actually he was ignorant.

When I hear how people are speaking of him [in the recordings], when I listen to the sound, the discomfort in their voices and the confusion, they did it because of the love of art. But someone is taking away something that belongs to you without thinking of the investment for your children. But he [Tracey] has investment for his children and his children's children will have an investment to them. And for me, speaking like that I'm classified as a radical.

Maybe we need scholarships that comes from high schools, maybe we need Noel and his friends at the university to say, how do we start a scholarship that actually puts a bridge toward these two, three worlds we're living in, the US, South Africa, and the township, ILAM and the township. What is missing for us is to make a declaration that ten kids in Makhanda or in the rural Eastern Cape must learn instruments at ILAM and those instruments need to be built. And make it cooler, to go to listen to archives at ILAM. Have small audios playing on phones, buy ringtones at ILAM. These ideas need to evolve.

NOEL: What I love about all this work is the intense focus on locality in the Eastern Cape. As someone who is not from either South Africa or the US, I'm also very interested in those transatlantic moments, the lessons from South Africa. We're seeing in the current moment museums and archives scrambling to be more relevant, to respond to Black Lives Matter, making an archive contemporaneously, to document an archive now for now. What's your take on what it means to speak through an archive in South Africa? What does it mean to share this with those that don't have the grounded context you have?

LEE: What I'd like to share is the infinite possibilities of the object, how it can mediate between different times and spaces, but it's potential as a way of transforming relationships, so we move from one of inequality in terms of accessibility and knowledge production and perceptions of what knowledge is. So, we move from that to something that's more equitable.

XOLILE: OK, we were playing with one of the recordings from ILAM where there's this old man who is speaking about colonization, he's saying it in isiXhosa. He's saying, "these White people who're here in this room and the government and those who are in charge, the young people must know"—he's making a clear statement to young people—that "because we are talking about these traditions and things that are Western, it doesn't mean we are choosing them, we are making you to accept or endorse them. You must know, we have our own things as the people, our own traditions, and we want you to carry on. But we are not saying that these things are wrong. We're saying, you must know them."

In South Africa, the world is showing us about finding peace and finding ways of making money and finding ways for a green economy and an education system. We have our forms of education that have been taken away and these forms are not seen as education unless an academic does a paper on it. But people who are living day to day with these systems of knowledge, of how to recycle, making instruments out of dead trees—that's recycling. These people were doing those things way back. So I think as us in South Africa, we have to show the world that what we have is valuable, and they can learn from them to stop being destructive. But in a more creative way. We have many concepts, via music. I think ILAM is a gold, but it needs to go back to people and enrich people. I think the world can learn that from us. We can share. We can share, but only if they pay. I don't know. I might have lost myself there but I think there's so much we can give to them, but it's time for the outside world to pay now.

NOEL: Anything to add?

XOLILE: What you can add for history purposes, for archive purposes, is that I never knew Lee that much before, but we spoke. I partly remember what we spoke about but what is important now is that we're still continuing the conversation of working together and actually changing the perspective and how history, the past cannot damage the future if those willing to make a change can come together. I think at this moment right now The Black Power Station and ILAM have a lot to give to the community. Although we're both two organizations with not a lot of money to give to people, but we have a lot to share that is about making people think differently about the position that they're in. So

I think for me, for Lee, for someone who runs this beautiful mining space for African music and makes it available for people, there's a lot to learn from that place. And even from The Black Power Station, we don't have a lot of money but we know we have much energy to give to people, to give hope for the future for this town we're living in. That's my view.

LEE: Well said, X!

FIGURE E.2 Transformer for The Black Power Station complex.
July 10, 2019. *Photo by the author.*

EPILOGUE 3

Umntu ngumntu ngabantu

Masikhe simamele izandi zezinyanya,
siqhube sisebenze ukuqonda ubuntu kanye yintoni.
Masisebenzeni,
masiqubekheni,
masiqondeni ubuntu yintoni.
Sibulela kakhulu kuwe mfowethu ngethemba lika Qamatha.
Siyi mbumbha yamanyange nawe Iba ngomye wethu sibe banye.
Konke kuzokwenzeka,
makwenzeke,
izakwenzeka
kuyokwenzeka Xana uQamata evuma.

Listening Sessions and Personal Interviews (2008–2019)

The following listening sessions and interviews have been cited and used, and are listed alphabetically by surname and organized by year.

2008

Budaza, Thandeka. Interview in her house in Extension 4, Joza Township, August 13, 2008.

Butana, uSisi, and daughter, and Thembinkosi Butana. Interview in uSisi Butana's house in a township outside Port Alfred, August 30, 2008.

Butana, Thembinkosi. Interview in his flat in Fingo Village township, August 28, 2008.

Cira, Colin. Interview in his house in Vukani Township, August 13, 2008.

Ecalpar, Mngani, Zikhona, and Nombasa. Interview in Ecalpar's room in Joza Township, July 24, 2008.

Frans, Phumulelo ("Player"). Interview in his house in Extension 4, Joza Township, August 6, 2008.

Kelele, Mary. Interview in her house in Hlalani township, August 11, 2008.

Kunju, Hleze. Interview in his flat, Grahamstown, August 11, 2008.

Lwana, Silulami ("Slu"). Interview in Nyaki Tsana's house, Phumlani Township, August 17, 2008.

Madiba, Elijah. Interview, ILAM, May 21, 2008.

Madinda, Xolile ("X"). Interview, foyer of Drama Department, Rhodes University, August 26, 2008.

——, and Noize. Interview in DefKamp in Fingo Village township, July 22, 2008.

Mati, Mike. Interview in his house near Albany Road Township, July 26, 2008.

Molapisi, Mpho. Interview in his office at the Albany Museum, Grahamstown, August 28, 2008.

Mzambia. Interview in the yard of his sister's house in Joza Township, July 18, 2008.

Ncalu, Luyanda, and Silulami "Slu" Lwana. Interview in the house of Luyanda's girlfriend in an area of Joza known as Emagxmekwazini, August 17, 2008.

Nobible, Mama. Interview in the garden outside her house in Fingo Village township, August 25, 2008.

Nomcebisi. Interview at the Drama Department, Rhodes University, August 25, 2008.

Nonqane, Cecil, and Sarah (a museum assistant). Interview in Nonqane's office at the Albany Museum, Grahamstown, September 19, 2008.

Nyikilana, Zolile, Nomtwasana Nyikilana, Mr. Ngcongo, Colin Cira, and others. Interview in Nyikilana and Nomtwasana's house in Vukani Township, June 16, 2008.

Potsane, Koketso ("KK"). Interview in Cow Moon Theory Bar, Grahamstown, May 2, 2008.

Sompies, and Tera Tyota. Interview in Tera's house, Hlalani Township, August 19, 2008.

uTatomkhulu, uMakhulu Nonsans, and other oMakhulu (grandmothers). Interview in the house of uSisi Mati in Ezigodlo Village, Peddie District, September 21, 2008.

Tracey, Geoff. Interview at ILAM, February 18, 2008.

Tsana, Kondile. Interview in his home in Hlalani Township, August 6, 2008.

Tsana, Nyakonzima ("Nyaki"). Interview in my flat in Constitution Street, Grahamstown, August 23, 2008.

Tshobodi, Archbishop. Interview in his church in Joza Township, September 17, 2008.

Tyota, Tera. Interview in his house in Hlalani Township, July 20, 2008.

——, and Boniwe. Interview in Boniwe's house, Hlalani Township, September 4, 2008.

Udaba. Interview with all the band members (Sakhile Moleshe, Dineo Pule, Luyolo Lenga ["Liyo"], Sibusiso Mnyanda ["Sbo"], Pumelele Lavisa ["Pura"]) at ILAM, July 3, 2008.

Vena, Jackson. Interview in the Cory Library, Rhodes University, September 11, 2008.

Zuks. Interview in the Old Gaol Bar, Grahamstown, July 23, 2008.

uZwai. Interview in his house in Joza Township, August 10, 2008.

2017

Heshu, Masixole ("Masi"). Interview, Drama Department, Rhodes University, July 17, 2017.

Madiba, Elijah, and Akhona "Bhodl'ingqaka" Mafani. Interview in the studio at ILAM, July 19, 2017.

Madinda, Xolile ("X"). Interview in The Black Power Station, July 18, 2017.

Tsana, Nyakonzima ("Nyaki"). Interview at ILAM, July 19, 2017.

2018

Madinda, Xolile ("X"), and Andiswa ("Bliss") Rabeshu. Interview, Book'ona library, The Black Power Station, August 19, 2018.

Watkins, Lee. FaceTime interview, December 12, 2018.

2019

Makandula, Sikhumbuzo. Interview in George Street, Makhanda (with Xolile ["X"] Madinda), July 11, 2019.

APPENDIX 2
Song Translations

All songs have been transcribed into Xhosa and then translated by Nyakonzima Tsana, Xolile ("X") Madinda, and myself. Even after multiple listens, in some cases the words and lyrics may remain unclear. As X observed, "These songs can be interpreted in many ways according to the feeling and the context."[1]

"SOMAGWAZA"—AMA. TR-31 (A4): XHOSA/MPONDO.

Somagwaza, Somagwaza, ha ha ho (x2)

Somagwaza, Somagwaza, ha ha ho

Somagwaza, Somagwaza, gwazele hi ho ha (x2)[2]

Somagwaza, Somagwaza, hi ho ha

[Repeats]

Wo wo wo-yo

"MHLAHLO"—AMA. TR-13 (A1): XHOSA/NGQIKA.

Na ho yo yo vumani ho go go go ndiyahamba (x2)

You must all accept that I am going

*Lomfana opetheyo ngu Namatha
ho go go go ndiyahamba*

The boy who is in charge in Namatha,
you must all accept that I am going

ombela kamnandi Amantakwende
babenditshilo kamnandi (x2)

Amantakwende [a family's clan name] they sing nicely,
if I said it, nicely

lentwana encikane nguWalaza
ho go go go ndiyahamba

This young boy is Walaza,
you must all accept that I am going

lentwana ebaleka nguWalaza
ho go go go ndiyahamba

This boy running away is Walaza
you must all accept that I am going

he ntwana ndoyika kulamadoda
ho go go go ndiyahamba

Hey boy, I am scared to go to these men,
you must all accept that I am going

he ntwana ndoyika kulonaMatha
ho go go go ndiyahamba

Hey boy, I am scared at noMatha's place.
you must all accept that I am going

lonyaka uphelile ndihamba
ho go go go ndiyahamba

This year has finished and I am still going,
you must all accept that I am going

sabel' uyabizwa kulamadoda
ho go go go ndiyahamba

Respond, they call you, these men
you must all accept that I am going

sabel, uyabizwa kulo Walaza
ho go go go ndiyahamba

Respond, they call you at Walaza's,
you must all accept that I am going

ingom yomhlahlo ayilunganga

The mhlahlo song is not right

babenditshilo kamnandi

If I said it nicely

ingom yomhlahlo ayilunganga

The mhlahlo song is not right

babenditshilo kamnandi

If I said it nicely

lentwana ephetheyo ngu Walaza
ho go go go ndiyahamba (x2)

This boy who is in charge is Walaza,
you must all accept that I am going

kaloku bafana nandi ityala (x2)
ho go go go ndiyahamba

Boys, here is the charge
you must all accept that I am going

kaloku ndiyoyika kulamadoda
babetshilo kamnandi

I am afraid to go to these men,
they said it nicely

kaloku ndiyoyika kuloWalaza
babetshilo kamnandi

I am afraid to go to Walaza
they said it nicely

ho go go go hambani
ho go go go ndiyahamba
+ variations repeat

you must all go,
you must accept that I am going

NOTES

1. Personal communication, WhatsApp conversation, March 5, 2021.

2. "This is really just one word being played around with in different variations and tone . . . That's the power of the way they sing. It's amazing—you can't tell that they're singing one line, it's actually only Somagwaza there," according to X (Personal communication, ibid.).

NOTES

INTRODUCTION

1. www.ru.ac.za/ilam/ (accessed February 28, 2021).

2. On decolonizing knowledge, see for example: Heleta 2016, Prinsloo 2016, and Mbembe 2016, 2015.

3. Sabelo J. Ndlovu-Gatsheni, *Epistemic Freedom: Deprovincialization and Decolonization* (Abingdon and New York: Routledge, 2018), 3.

4. Pedro Mzilane and Nomalanga Mkhize, "Decolonisation as a Spatial Question: The Student Accommodation Crisis and Higher Education Transformation," *South African Review of Sociology*, 50, nos. 3–4 (2019): 106.

5. For a book-length study of "capturing sound" see Katz 2004.

6. Willemien Fronemen and Stephanus Muller, "The Ethical Incomplete," *South African Music Studies* 38, no. 1 (2019): 2.

7. Cara Stacey and Natalie Mason, "Composing, Creative Play and The Ethical Incomplete: Practice-based Approaches in Ethnomusicology," ibid., 34–35.

8. Bernie Krause, *The Great Animal Orchestra: Finding the Origins of Music in the World's Wild Places* (London: Profile, 2012), 33.

9. Salome Voegelin, *The Political Possibility of Sound: Fragments of Listening* (New York and London: Bloomsbury Academic, 2019), 59.

10. Ibid., 121.

11. Jonathan Patrick, "A Guide to Pierre Schaeffer, the Godfather of Sampling," *Fact Magazine*, February 23, 2016. www.factmag.com/2016/02/23/pierre-schaeffer-guide/ (accessed February 28, 2021).

12. James A. Steintrager and Rey Chow, eds., *Sound Objects* (Durham, NC and London: Duke University Press, 2019), 7.

13. Ibid., 8.

14. Ibid.

15. Brian Kane, "The Fluctuating Sound Object," in ibid., 66.

16. Brian Kane, *Sound Unseen: Acousmatic Sound in Theory and Practice* (Oxford and New York: Oxford University Press, 2014), 16.

17. Barbara Kirshenblatt-Gimblett, "Objects of Ethnography," in *The Poetics and Politics of Museum Display*, edited by Ivan Karp and Steven D. Levine (Washington, DC and London: Smithsonian Institution Press, 1991), 18.

18. Ibid., 30.

19. Carole Muller, "Archiving Africanness in Sacred Song," *Ethnomusicology* 46, no. 3 (2002): 410.

20. Ibid., 424.

21. Stephen Benson and Will Montgomery, eds., *Writing the Field Recording: Sound, Word, Environment* (Edinburgh: Edinburgh University Press, 2018), 5.

22. Roshanak Khesthi, *Modernity's Ear: Listening to Race and Gender in World Music* (New York and London: New York University Press, 2015), 31.

23. Deborah Kapchan, "The Splash of Icarus: Theorizing Sound Writing/Writing Sound Theory," in *Theorizing Sound Writing*, edited by Deborah Kapchan (Middletown, CT: Wesleyan University Press, 2017), 11.

24. Martin Daughtry, "Acoustic Palimpsests," in ibid., 53.

25. Joeri Bruyninckx, *Listening in the Field: Recording and the Science of Birdsong* (Cambridge, MA and London: MIT Press, 2018), 58–59.

26. Mary Caton Lingold, Darren Mueller, and Whitney Trettien, "Introduction," in *Digital Sound Studies*, edited by Mary Caton Lingold, Darren Mueller, and Whitney Trettien (Durham, NC: Duke University Press, 2018), 7.

27. Ibid.

28. John Troutman, *Indian Blues: American Indians and the Politics of Music, 1879–1934* (Norman: University of Oklahoma Press, 2009), 204.

29. Christopher Scales, *Recording Culture: Powwow Music and the Aboriginal Recording Industry* (Durham, NC: Duke University Press, 2012), 7.

30. Ibid., 2.

31. www.museumofportablesound.com/ (accessed February 28, 2021).

32. John Kannenburg, "Towards a More Sonically Inclusive Museum Practice: A New Definition of the 'Sound Object,'" *Science Museum Group Journal* 8 (2017). Component DOI: http://dx.doi.org/10.15180/170805/008 (accessed February 28, 2021, emphasis in original).

33. Carolyn Hamilton, Verne Harris, and Graeme Reid, "Introduction" in *Refiguring the Archive*, edited by Carolyn Hamilton, Verne Harris, Jane Taylor, Michele Pickover, Graeme Reid, and Razia Saleh (Dordrecht, Boston, and London: Kluwer Academic Publishers, 2002), 9.

34. Jacques Derrida, "Archive Fever: A Seminar by Jacques Derrida at Wits University, August 1998 (transcribed by Verne Harris)," in ibid., 54.

35. Ann Laura Stoler, "Colonial Archives and the Arts of Governance: On the Content in the Form," in ibid., 91.

36. Verne Harris, *Archives and Justice: A South African Perspective* (Chicago: Society of American Archivists, 2007), 31.

37. Wendy M. Duff and Verne Harris, "Stories and Names: Archival Description as Narrating Records and Constructing Meanings," *Archival Science* 2 (2002): 279.

38. Harris, *Archives and Justice*, 189 (emphasis in original).

39. Ibid., 189–90.

40. Toyin Falola, "Ritual Archives," in *The Palgrave Handbook of African Social Ethics*, edited by Nimi Waroboko and Toyin Falola (New York and London: Palgrave Macmillan, 2020), 473.

41. Ibid., 490.

42. Gabrielle Giannachi, *Archive Everything: Mapping the Everyday* (Cambridge, MA and London: The MIT Press, 2016), xvi.

43. Ibid., 95.

44. Horea Poenar, "Glitches of the Archive: On the Relation Between Memory and the Commons," *Caietele Echinox* 33 (2017): 123.

45. Ibid., 125.

46. Abigail De Kosnik, *Rogue Archives: Digital Culture and Media Fandom* (Cambridge, MA and London: MIT Press, 2016), 2.

47. Ibid., 10.

48. Ibid., 99.

49. Gavin Steingo and Jim Sykes, eds., *Remapping Sound Studies* (Durham, NC and London: Duke University Press, 2019), 7.

50. Christopher Cox, *Sonic Flux: Sound, Art and Metaphysics* (Chicago and London: University of Chicago Press, 2018), 43.

51. Ibid.

52. Ibid., 56.

53. Voegelin, *Political Possibility*, 190.

54. Ibid.

55. Viv Golding, "Collaborative Museums: Curators, Communities, Collections," in *Museums and Communities: Curators, Collections and Collaboration*, edited by Viv Golding and Wayne Modest (London and New York: Bloomsbury, 2013), 20.

56. Carolyn Landau and Janet Topp Fargion, "We're All Archivists Now: Towards a More Equitable Ethnomusicology," in *Ethnomusicology, Archives and Communities: Methodologies for an Equitable Discipline*, edited by Carolyn Landau and Janet Topp Fargion, *Ethnomusicology Forum* 21, no. 2 (2012): 125–40.

57. Terry Smith, *Thinking Contemporary Curating* (New York: Independent Curators International, 2012), 255.

58. Hans Ulrich Obrist, *Ways of Curating* (New York: Farrar, Straus and Giroux, 2014), 58.

59. Ibid. (emphasis in original).

60. Paul O'Neill, *The Culture of Curating and the Curating of Culture(s)* (Cambridge, MA and London: MIT Press, 2012), 49.

61. Ibid., 128.

62. Hans Ulrich Obrist, "Curating as Medium," in Terry Smith, *Talking Contemporary Curating*, edited by Kate Fowle and Leigh Markopoulos (New York: Independent Curators International, 2015), 126.

63. Simon Reynolds, *Retromania: Pop Culture's Addiction to Its Own Past* (London: Faber, 2011), 3.

64. Steven Lubar, *Inside the Lost Museum: Curating, Past and Present* (Cambridge, MA and London: Harvard University Press, 2017), 321.

65. www.beatingheart.bandcamp.com (accessed February 28, 2021).

66. www.youtube.com/watch?v=r_vsk-R5GdQ (accessed February 28, 2021).

67. Harry Edwards, "Dancing to Colonial Archives," *Norient.* www.norient.com/harry-edwards/dancing-colonial-archives (accessed February 28, 2021).

68. For an extensive series of pathways exploring multiple regions, case studies, and issues see Frank Gunderson, Robert C. Lancefield, and Bret Woods, eds., *The Oxford Handbook of Musical Repatriation* (Oxford and New York: Oxford University Press, 2019).

69. Robert M. Lancefield, "Musical Traces' Retraceable Paths: The Repatriation of Recorded Sound," *Journal of Folklore Research* 35, no. 1 (1988): 60.

70. Robin Gray, "Repatriation and Decolonization: Thoughts on Ownership, Access and Control," in Gunderson, Lancefield, and Woods, eds., *The Oxford Handbook of Musical Repatriation*, 723.

71. Sally Treloyn, Martin Dembal, and Rona Googninda Charles, "Cultural Precedents for the Repatriation of Legacy Song Records to Communities of Origin," *Australian Aboriginal Studies* 2 (2016): 95.

72. Ibid., 100.

73. www.sounds.bl.uk/World-and-traditional-music/Wachsmann (accessed February 28, 2021).

74. Sylvia Nannyonga-Tamusuza and Andrew Weintraub, "The Audible Future: Reimagining the Role of Sound Archives and Sound Repatriation in Uganda," *Ethnomusicology* 56, no. 2 (2012): 209.

75. Francis Bebey, *African Music: A People's Art* (Brooklyn, NY: Lawrence Hill Books, 1975), 138.

76. Ibid., 139.

77. Angela Impey, *Song Walking: Women, Music, and Environmental Justice in an African Borderland* (Chicago: University of Chicago Press, 2018), 197.

78. Chérie Rivers Ndaliko, *Necessary Noise: Music, Film, and Charitable Imperialism in the East of Congo* (Oxford and New York: Oxford University Press, 2016).

79. See, for example, Diop 1987.

80. Achille Mbembe, *On the Postcolony* (Berkeley: University of California Press, 2001), 242.

81. Carol Muller and Sathima Bea Benjamin, *Musical Echoes: South African Women Thinking in Jazz* (Durham, NC and London: Duke University Press, 2011), xviii.

82. Ibid., 116–17.

83. Louise Meintjes, *Dust of the Zulu: Ngoma Aesthetics After Apartheid* (Durham, NC and London: Duke University Press, 2017), 25.

84. Gavin Steingo, *Kwaito's Promise: Music and the Aesthetics of Freedom in South Africa* (Chicago and London: University of Chicago Press, 2016), vii.

85. Ibid., 14.

86. For a volume foregrounding the early lives, experiences, and trajectories of ethnomusicological practitioners, see Margaret Sarkisian and Ted Solis, *Living Ethnomusicology: Paths and Practices* (Champaign: University of Illinois Press, 2019).

87. See "Faces of Grahamstown: Uplifting the Mind," www.youtube.com/watch?v =VRhfXN7dnSQ (accessed February 28, 2021).

88. www.makandulas2.wixsite.com/sikhumbuzomakandula (accessed February 28, 2021).

89. Paulette Coetzee, "The White Man's Microphone: Hugh Tracey, Types of Whiteness and African Music," in *On Whiteness*, edited by Nicky Falkof and Oliver Cashman-Brown (Oxford: Inter-Disciplinary Press, 2012), 50.

ONE *Hugh Tracey Records the Sound of Africa*

1. The series currently numbers 218 long-playing records (LPs). Tracey's son, Andrew Tracey, added a further eight LPs in the years following his father's death in 1977. The catalogue to the *Sound of Africa* series includes the content of the first 210 LPs but was itself published prior to LPs 211–218, which are consequently not included (See Tracey *Catalogue* 1973A and B).

2. The vast majority of the recordings are of songs and instruments, but the series includes some examples of speech, praise poetry, and a few ambient or soundscape recordings.

3. Tracey made nineteen recording tours in total between 1948 and 1970, but most of the series was published between 1948 and 1963 and does not include material from his last two tours in 1966 and 1970.

4. The names of countries and areas are given as used by Tracey (see 1973A, 16) with contemporary names in parenthesis.

5. I return to the English spelling of countries at the time Tracey was operating while writing about this period.

6. Veit Erlmann, "Recordings of Traditional Music in South Africa," *Yearbook for Traditional Music* 20 (1988): 248.

7. Cecile Badenhorst and Charles Mather, "Tribal Recreation and Recreating Tribalism: Culture, Leisure and Social Control on South Africa's Gold Mines, 1940–1950," *Journal of Southern African Studies* 23, no. 3 (1997): 474.

8. Ibid., 475.

9. Tracey, *Catalogue* 1973A, 4.

10. Evelyn Baring, "Foreword," *African Music Society Newsletter* 1, no. 1 (June 1948): 1.

11. www.ru.ac.za/ilam/ (accessed February 28, 2021).

12. Hugh Tracey, "A Plan for African Music," *African Music* 3, no. 4 (1965): 7.

13. ILAM has reissued the original twenty-five LPs in CD format. Additions to the series mean that thirty-four albums became available, consisting of almost 450 items, and most are currently still in print. www.ru.ac.za/ilam/products/cds/musicofafricaseries (accessed February 28, 2021).

14. A full set of 218 CDs (excluding shipping) costs R21,500 (approximately $1,400). *Music of Africa* sells for R2,500 (approximately $165). www.ru.ac.za/ilam/products (accessed February 28, 2021).

15. Tracey, *Catalogue* 1973A, 9.

16. *African Music* 8, no, 1 (2007): 140.

17. Tracey, *Catalogue* 1973A, 9.

18. Hugh Tracey, "Introduction" to an untitled draft summarizing the work of ILAM (1969), 1 (unpublished).

19. Tracey, *Catalogue* 1973B, 3.

20. Unpublished and undated typescripts of Peggy Tracey's diaries, 106. This quote is from a section entitled "Lourenco Marques" and comes straight after a section titled "First Trip to Pedi, 1947." The subsection for this quote is headed "Zavala," then "At Maxixe—evening recording." In September 2008 Andrew Tracey informed me that Peggy had begun to rewrite and edit her diaries before she died, and that she had intended them for publication. The piecemeal typescripts are not typed by Peggy herself, and most are currently unorganized and unpaginated, and at times the chronology is difficult to follow.

21. Hugh Tracey, "The African Minstrel and Story-teller," lecture delivered at Cathedral Hall, Cape Town, April 24, 1934a (unpublished lecture notes).

22. Hugh Tracey, "The Significance of African Music (in Central and Southern Africa)," the Cramb Lectures, delivered at the University of Glasgow, January 16 and 17, 1967 (full typescript of unpublished lectures) (hereafter Cramb Lectures).

23. Tracey 1977 (unpublished).

24. Holiday 1986 (unpublished) is the most extensive, and the print archive also includes scattered material collected by David Bandey and Anthony Trowbridge.

25. The phrase, taken from the (unpaginated) liner notes to SWP 034, "The Very Best of Hugh Tracey," was written by Michael Baird. In collaboration with ILAM, Baird compiled and published the retrospective CD series "Historical Recordings by Hugh Tracey," www .swp-records.com (accessed February 28, 2021).

26. The name Fort Victoria was changed to Nyanda in 1982 and is now known as Masvingo.

27. Karanga is a dialect of Shona, the most populous language and ethnic group. Most of the biographical information is taken from Tracey 1977 (unpublished), Holiday 1986 (unpublished), and Trowbridge 1985.

28. Transcript of Andrew Tracey being interviewed by David Bandey, March 21, 1980, 3 (unpublished). David Bandey was the first of three authors to begin and never complete a biography of Hugh Tracey, the other two being Anthony Trowbridge and Geoffrey Holiday.

29. Tracey 1977, T21B (unpublished). Tracey is quoting from Shakespeare's *Julius Caesar*, Act 4, Scene 2, 152. The actual lines, spoken by Cassius are:

For Cassius is aweary of the world,
Hated by one he loves, braved by his brother,
Checked like a bondman; all his faults observed,
Set in a notebook, learned and conned by rote.

From Stanley Wells and Gary Taylor, eds., *The Oxford Shakespeare: The Complete Works* (Oxford: Clarendon Press, 1988), 619.

30. Tracey did transcribe some song parts while in the field, but this method was developed much more fully by Andrew Tracey. See Tracey, Andrew 1988.

31. Tracey, *Catalogue* 1973A, 8.

32. In some photographic records at ILAM, Babu Chipika and "Gumwie" are named together. It is unclear whether this is a misspelling or another person.

33. See chapter 2 for a detailed analysis of Tracey's recording methods, techniques, and sound collections.

34. Erlmann, "Recordings of Traditional Music in South Africa," 248.

35. Tracey, *Catalogue* 1973A, 3.

36. Hugh Tracey, "Report on Research into Southern Rhodesian Native Music," unpublished report sent to the president of the Carnegie Foundation, November 12, 1932.

37. Hugh Tracey, *Codification of African Music and Textbook Project: A Primer of Practical Suggestions for Field Research* (written with Gerhard Kubik and Andrew Tracey), (Roodeport, SA: International Library of African Music, 1969), 52.

38. See Kirby 2013 (1934) and 2004 (1934).

39. Tracey, *Codification*, 2.

40. Irene Frangs was an ethnomusicologist and jazz connoisseur who worked at ILAM for several years in the 1970s. During this time she edited some of Tracey's writing and publications.

41. Taken from an undated and unpaginated transcript of an interview of Tracey by Irene Frangs. The transcript at ILAM is titled "Comments on various aspects of his research work, life and codification and textbook project."

42. Ibid.

43. Portia K. Maultsby and Mellonnee V. Burnim, with contributions from Susan Oehle, "Intellectual History," in *African American Music: An Introduction*, edited by Mellonee V. Burnim and Portia K. Maultsby (New York & London: Routledge, 2006), 16.

44. The English Folk Dance Society (EFDS) was founded by Cecil Sharp in 1911 and then merged with the Folk-Song Society (FSS) in 1932 to become the English Folk Dance and Song Society (EFDSS). The Folk-Song Society was founded in 1898 and was an initiative of a number of individual folk song collectors and enthusiasts who wanted to improve the quality of collecting and publishing. www.efdss.org (accessed February 28, 2021).

45. Maud Karpeles was a founding member of the EFDS and worked as assistant to Cecil Sharp, a key figure in the collection of English songs and folklore. She remained in regular correspondence with Tracey until her death in 1976.

46. Tracey 1977, 32.

47. Ibid.

48. Hugh Tracey, letter to Mr. Edward N. Waters, assistant chief, Division of Music, Library of Congress, Washington, DC, December 29, 1944 (unpublished).

49. The first eight records were issued as AE 48-55 by Columbia in December 1933.

50. Tracey, *Catalogue* 1973A, 3.

51. International Library of African Music, Bulletin No. 1 (June 1956): 2.

52. Hugh Tracey, letter to C. K. Grierson Rickford, Esq., controller of administration, Federal Broadcasting Corporation of Rhodesia and Nyasaland, Salisbury [Southern Rhodesia], February 18, 1958, 1 (unpublished).

53. Badenhorst and Mather, "Tribal Recreation," 475.

54. Hugh Tracey, letter to Maud Karpeles, head of Radio Tapes Section, Central Office of Information, London, February 24, 1960, 1 (unpublished).

55. Tracey to Grierson Rickford, 1.

56. Hugh Tracey, "African Music Society and the International Library of African Music," report written while at UCLA, December 10, 1960, 3 (unpublished).

57. Hugh Tracey, letter to Mr. D. Crena de Iongh, 1963 (unpublished).

58. Hugh Tracey, letter to Alan Lomax, June 24, 1963 (unpublished).

59. Tracey, "Introduction," 1.

60. Tracey to Lomax.

61. Hugh Tracey, letter to John Blacking, Salisbury [Southern Rhodesia], October 5, 1954 (unpublished).

62. Tracey to Waters.

63. Hugh Tracey, letter to Volkmar Wentzel Esq., NGS [National Geographic Society], Washington, DC, September 28, 1970 (unpublished).

64. Tracey coined the phrase "self-delectative" to refer to music that was played primarily for the enjoyment of the player. See Tracey, *Catalogue* 1973A, 37–38 for the instruments he listed in this category.

65. Arthur Morris Jones, "Record Review of the Sound of Africa series of 45 12-inch records," *African Music* 2, no. 2 (1959): 96.

66. Ibid., 97.

67. Tracey to Wentzel (emphasis in original).

68. Mark Hudson, "Hugh Tracey: Pioneer Archivist," in Simon Broughton, Mark Ellingham, and Richard Trillo, eds., with Orla Duane and Vanessa Dowell, *World Music—The Rough Guide: Volume 1—Africa, Europe and the Middle East* (London: Rough Guides, 1999), 670–71.

69. Garret Felber, "Tracing Tribe: Hugh Tracey and the Cultural Politics of Retribalization," *SAMUS* 30/31 (2010): 34.

70. Hudson, "Hugh Tracey," 669 (emphasis in original).

71. David Coplan, *In Township Tonight! South Africa's Black City Music and Theatre* (Chicago and London: University of Chicago Press, 2008 [1985]), 164.

72. Hugh Tracey, "Editorial," *African Music* 2, no. 2 (1959A): 5.

73. Alan Barnard and Jonathan Spencer, eds., *Encyclopedia of Social and Cultural Anthropology* (London: Routledge, 2004 [1996]), 620. It is believed that Jacob Gruber coined the phrase "salvage ethnography." Gruber refers in particular to nineteenth-century ethnographers who were often documenting the languages of peoples being conquered and colonized by European countries or the United States. The method has been retrospectively applied to many anthropologists and ethnomusicologists, ranging from Franz Boas to Frances Densmore. See Gruber 1970.

74. Hugh Tracey, quoted in Nat Hentoff, "Recordings: Hugh Tracey, Collector of African Integrities," *New York Times,* May 29, 1966, 19. www.nytimes.com/1966/05/29/archives/recordings-hugh-tracey-collector-of-african-integrities.html (accessed February 28, 2021).

75. Gerhard Kubik, "Urban/Rural Interaction in Central African Guitar Styles of the 1960s," in *Papers Presented at the Tenth Symposium on Ethnomusicology, Music Dept.,* Rhodes University, September 30 to October 2 (ILAM, 1991), 96.

76. Ibid. (emphasis in original).

77. Basutoland was renamed the Kingdom of Lesotho in 1966 when it gained independence from Britain.

78. Hugh Tracey, *Radio Broadcast BC 1—The Union and Basutoland. Sound of Africa*

Broadcast Series 2, Pt. 1. Transmitted on South African Broadcasting Corporation on September 20, 1954 (9m, 32s ff.). The transcription is by the author.

79. Neil Lazarus, "Unsystematic Fingers at the Conditions of the Times—'Afropop' and the Paradoxes of Imperialism," in *Recasting the World—Writing after Colonialism*, edited by Jonathan White (Baltimore and London: John Hopkins University Press, 1993), 139.

80. Hugh Tracey, letter to Gilbert Rouget, Département d'Ethnomusicologie, Musée de l'homme, September 4, 1964 (unpublished).

81. Klaus Wachsmann, "The Sociology of Recording in Africa South of the Sahara," *African Music* 2, no. 2 (1959): 77.

82. Correspondence at ILAM shows that a young Kubik first wrote to Hugh Tracey in 1957 and again in 1959 when he was making preliminary plans to visit Africa.

83. Kubik, "Urban/Rural Interaction," 96–97.

84. The Companies Act, 1926 (as amended), Memorandum of Association of the International Library of African Music was signed by Tracey and lawyers on May 8, 1957 (see sections b and c).

85. Ibid., section I (a).

86. Ibid., section I (b).

87. Ibid., section I (c) (i).

88. Ibid., section I (c) (ii).

89. Ibid., section I (c) iii).

90. Ibid., section I (e).

91. Hugh Tracey, letter to John Blacking, July 7, 1954, 1–2 (unpublished).

92. Hugh Tracey, "The Development of African Music," *African Music* 3, no. 2 (1963A): 39.

93. Tracey, *Codification*, 8 ("The Objectives," Section 4.a, emphasis in original).

94. Ibid., Section 4.c (emphasis in original).

95. Ibid., Section 4.d (emphasis in original).

96. Multiple references could be given to demonstrate Tracey's belief that local African music was in danger of being vanquished, but for a clear statement see Tracey 1963A and 1967 (unpublished).

97. Tracey, *Catalogue* 1973A, 18.

98. Hugh Tracey, "The Arts in Africa—The Visual and the Aural," typescript of lecture delivered to the South African Institute of Race Relations Institute Council Meetings (RR 2/1963 R.E.O.N 2.1.63), Johannesburg, January 14–17, 1963a, 1 (unpublished).

99. Hugh Tracey, "Editorial," *African Music* 3, no. 3 (1964): 5.

100. Felber, "Tracing Tribe," 39.

101. Hugh Tracey, "Creativity in African Music," typescript of lecture delivered to the Architectural Students Symposium at the University of the Witwatersrand, August 12, 1971, 3 (unpublished).

102. John Blacking, "Venda Music: A Preliminary Report of Initial Field Research in

the Sibasa District (Not Intended for Publication)," addressed to the Research subcommittee of the ILAM, by John Blacking, musicologist MA of the ILAM, February 1957, 2 (unpublished).

103. Dave Dargie, *Xhosa Music: Its Techniques and Instruments, with a Collection of Songs* (Cape Town and Johannesburg: David Philip, 1988), 61 (emphasis in original).

104. Hugh Tracey, "The Codification of African music," unpublished draft of article written for *Race Relations*, June 19, 1968, 9.

105. Steven Feld, *Sound and Sentiment: Birds, Weeping, Poetics, and Song in Kaluli Expression* (Philadelphia: University of Pennsylvania Press, 1982), 163.

106. Kofi Agawu, *The African Imagination in Music* (New York: Oxford University Press, 2016), 25.

107. Fax sent by Andrew Tracey from ILAM to his son, Geoffrey Tracey, c/o Sally Hodges, Music Department, University of KwaZulu Natal at Durban, June 20, 1995, 3 (unpublished).

108. Tracey, Cramb Lectures, 17.

109. Tracey, "The Arts in Africa," 9.

110. Hugh Tracey, letter to Mr. Peter Gallo (Gallo [Africa] Ltd.), July 5, 1976, 2 (unpublished).

111. Robert Kauffman, letter to Hugh Tracey, New York, October 2, 1959 (unpublished).

112. Peter Mtuze, *The Essence of Xhosa Spirituality and the Nuisance of Cultural Imperialism (Hidden Presences in the Spirituality of the amaXhosa of the Eastern Cape and the Impact of Christianity on Them)* (Florida Hills, SA: Vivlia, 2003), x.

113. Hugh Tracey, "AMS—Proposed International Library of Recorded African Music, Appendix No. 1—Short Note on the Social Value of African Derived Music" (consequently, the document must predate 1954), unpaginated appendix of a proposal document for ILAM, pre-1954, 1 (unpublished).

114. Hugh Tracey, "Behind the Lyrics," *African Music* 3, no. 2 (1963B): 19.

115. Hugh Tracey, "The Wider Implications of African Music," typescript of a lecture given to Wits University Women's Goodwill Club, October 15, 1963c, 8 (unpublished).

116. Nyasaland was established as a British Protectorate in 1907 and is now known as Malawi.

117. Hugh Tracey, letter to P. H. Anderson Esq., president of the Transvaal and Orange Free State Chamber of Mines, Johannesburg, November 13, 1958, 3 (unpublished).

118. Tracey, "AMS," 1.

119. Tracey to Crena de Iongh.

120. ILAM Bulletin No. 28 (November 1958): 1.

121. Tracey, "The Significance of African Music," 19.

122. Felber, "Tracing Tribe," 41.

123. Coplan, *In Township Tonight!*, 398.

124. Max Gluckman, *Order and Rebellion in Tribal Africa* (London: Cohen & West, 1963), 215.

125. See Reader 1961, Mayer 1961, and Pauw 1963.

126. Thomas Turino, *Nationalists, Cosmopolitans, and Popular Music in Zimbabwe* (Chicago: University of Chicago Press, 2000), 41.

127. Hugh Tracey, letter to Monsieur Cousin, chairman, Union Minière du Haut Katanga, Elisabethville, Congo Belge, June 8, 1956 (unpublished).

128. Hugh Tracey, "How Far with African Music?," typescript of paper for National Union of South African Students (NUSAS), July 3, 1963b, 7 (unpublished).

129. #AllLivesMatter is widely viewed to be a criticism of the Black Lives Matter movement, and a willful misunderstanding or rejection of the issues raised by the latter.

130. Tracey, "How Far with African Music?" 8.

131. Paulette Coetzee, "Performing Whiteness, Representing Otherness: Hugh Tracey and African Music," PhD diss., Rhodes University, 2014, 1.

132. Ibid., 4.

133. Hugh Tracey, letter to Peggy Harper at the University of Ife Institute of African Studies, March 19, 1970, 3.

134. Ibid.

135. Hugh Tracey, "The International Library of African Music," *The Folklore and Folk Music Archivist* 4, no. 2 (Summer 1961): unpaginated.

136. Coetzee, "Performing Whiteness," 107.

137. Paulette Coetzee, "Hugh Tracey, African Music, and Colonial Power: Correspondence with Government Officials in the 1950s," *South African Music Studies* 36–37 (2018): 87.

138. ILAM Bulletin No. 1: 1.

139. Tracey, "The Codification of African Music," 8.

140. Hugh Tracey, letter to Shirley B. Smith, African-American Economic Associates, New York, October 23, 1958, 1–2 (unpublished).

141. Tracey, "The International Library of African Music."

142. No further information is available about the terms or conditions of the grant.

143. Hugh Tracey, letter to H. C. Finkel, Esq., director of African education, Salisbury [Southern Rhodesia], December 11, 1959, 1–2 (unpublished).

144. Ibid., 2.

145. Colonel H. W. Boardman, *Typescripts of Four Lectures and an Exam Prepared by Colonel Boardman*, sent to D. F. Botha at Anglo-American for a proposed course for native welfare officers, returned with amendments by D. F. Botha, August 29, 1958 (unpublished).

146. From an unpublished and undated typescript by Tracey entitled "Organised Research in African Music," 5.

147. Paulette Coetzee, "The White Man's Microphone: Hugh Tracey, Types of Whiteness

and African Music," in *On Whiteness*, edited by Nicky Falkof and Oliver Cashman-Brown (Oxford: Inter-Disciplinary Press, 2012), 49.

148. Ibid., 52.

149. Mcebisi Ndletyana, ed., *African Intellectuals in 19th and Early 20th Century South Africa* (Cape Town: HSRC Press, 2008), 5.

150. Hugh Tracey, "BBC HOME Service," typescript, October 12, 1965 (unpaginated and unpublished, emphasis in original).

151. Tracey, Cramb Lectures, 2.

152. Untitled and unpublished typescript by Tracey, September 3, 1968, in the Hugh Tracey Collection of Lectures and Communication at ILAM.

153. Ibid.

154. Ibid.

155. Hugh Tracey, "The Problem of the Future of Bantu Music in the Congo" [Extrait de: "Problèmes d'Afrique Centrale," *Bulletin Trimestriel de l'association des Anciens étudiants de l'institut Universitaire des Territories d'outre-Mer* 26 (Quatrième Trimestre, 1954): 7.

156. Paulette Coetzee, "Dancing with Difference: Hugh Tracey on and in (African) Music," *Safundi* 16, no. 4 (2015): 416.

TWO *Listening Behind Field Recordings*

1. From typescript by Tracey entitled "Into Mashonaland." This unpaginated and undated typescript appears to be part of Tracey, *A River Left for Me*, 1977 (unpublished).

2. Ian Brennan, *How Music Dies (or Lives): Field Recording and the Battle for Democracy in the Arts* (New York: Allworth Press, 2016), 7.

3. Brent Hayes Edwards, "The Sound of Anticolonialism," in *Audible Empire: Music, Global Politics, Critique*, edited by Ronald Radano and Tejumola Olaniyan (Durham, NC: Duke University Press, 2016), 269.

4. Mhoze Chikowero, *African Music, Power, and Being in Colonial Zimbabwe* (Bloomington: Indiana University Press, 2015), 214.

5. Hugh Tracey, letter to Reverend Arthur Morris Jones, August 3, 1965 (unpublished). The letter referred to Tracey's recent honorary doctorate awarded by the University of Cape Town on June 27, 1965.

6. Helen Myers, "Field Technology," in *Ethnomusicology: An Introduction*, edited by Helen Myers (London: Macmillan, 1992), 84.

7. Alan Merriam, *The Anthropology of Music* (Evanston, IL: Northwestern University Press, 1964).

8. Edward Evan Evans-Pritchard, "The Dance," *Africa: Journal of the International African Institute* 1, no. 4 (1928): 449 (footnote 1).

9. Ibid., 446.

10. Hugh Tracey, *African Music Transcription Library: Librarian's Handbook* (Johannesburg: Gallo [Africa] Ltd., c. 1949), 6.

11. Hugh Tracey, "The Significance of African Music (in Central and Southern Africa)," the Cramb Lectures, delivered at the University of Glasgow, January 16 and 17, 1967 (full typescript of unpublished lectures); hereafter Cramb Lectures.

12. Ibid.

13. Andrew Tracey, transcript of Andrew Tracey being interviewed by David Bandey on March 21, 1980, 3 (unpublished).

14. Professor Erich Moritz von Hornbostel (1877–1935) was an Austrian ethnomusicologist and became the first director of the Berliner Phonogramm-Archiv in 1905. Together with Curt Sachs, he is famously remembered for pioneering the Hornbostel-Sachs system of musical instrument classification.

15. Hugh Tracey, *Report on Research into Southern Rhodesian Native Music*, 3 (unpublished). Later correspondence sent by Tracey to the Carnegie Foundation suggests that the report was never received by the foundation because Harold Jowitt, the director of native development in Rhodesia, allegedly suppressed the report for its direct criticisms of the influence of missionaries on indigenous music and ways of life.

16. Ibid., 3–4.

17. Hugh Tracey, *Catalogue* 1973A, 3. In 1929 Tracey had helped make the first recordings of the indigenous music of Southern Rhodesia when he took fourteen Karanga musicians to Johannesburg to record with Columbia (London). See chapter 1 and figure 1.1.

18. Tracey, *A River Left for Me*, 25.

19. Eric Gallo began the Brunswick Gramophone House record shop in 1926, opening Gallo Recording Studios under the auspices of Gallo Africa in 1932. Gallo Africa (1926–1985) acquired the rival Gramophone Record Company (1939–1985) in 1985, becoming Gallo-GRC. In 1990 the whole company was renamed Gallo Record Company.

20. Andrew Tracey, letter to Veit Erlmann, Museum für Völkerkunde, October 14, 1988 (unpublished). Andrew Tracey is responding to some claims Erlmann had made about Hugh Tracey's recording methods.

21. Hugh Tracey, letter to the Reverend Arthur Morris Jones at Mapanza, Choma, Northern Rhodesia, March 11, 1947 (unpublished).

22. Ibid.

23. Tracey, *A River Left for Me* (unpaginated).

24. Ibid.

25. African Music Society memorandum to the South African Council for Educational, Sociological and Humanistic Research, c. 1947, 5–6.

26. Edwards, "The Sound of Anticolonialism," 270.

27. Reg Hall, "The Voice of the People— Introduction to the Series," an introduction to the twenty-CD anthology "The Voice of the People" on Topic Records. Taken from

Volume 4, *Farewell, My Own Dear Native Land: Songs of Exile & Emigration*, TSCD 654 (London: Topic, 1998), 5. Cecil Sharp (November 22, 1859–June 23, 1924) founded the English Folk Dance Society in 1911 and spearheaded the English folk music revival in the early twentieth century. He was interested in reviving English classical music by using national folk music. See Sharp 1972 and 1974.

28. Hall, "The Voice of the People," 5.

29. Hugh Tracey, "The Evolution of African Music and its Function in the Present Day," typescript of a public lecture delivered to the Institute for the Study of Man in Africa, October 1961, 20 (unpublished).

30. See Reigle 2008.

31. Tracey, *A River Left for Me*, 7.

32. Tracey, "How Far with African Music?," 3.

33. Edwards, "The Sound of Anticolonialism," 274.

34. Anthony Seeger, "Creating and Confronting Cultures: Issues of Editing and Selection in Records and Videotapes of Musical Performances," in *Music in the Dialogue of Cultures: Traditional Music and Cultural Policy*, edited by Max Peter Baumann (Wilhelmshaven: Florian Noetzel Verlag, 1991), 292.

35. Ibid., 293.

36. ILAM Bulletin No. 1 (June 1956): 2.

37. ILAM Bulletin No. 28 (November 1958): 1.

38. Hugh Tracey, letter to the director-general of the South African Broadcasting Corporation (Johannesburg), January 31, 1957, 1 (unpublished).

39. Maud Karpeles, ed., *The Collecting of Folk Music and Other Ethnomusicological Material: A Manual for Field Workers* (London: International Folk Music Council and the Royal Anthropological Institute of Great Britain and Ireland, 1958), 20.

40. See Sarno 1995 and 1993.

41. For Arom's analytical recording methods and playback techniques, see Arom 1991 and 1976. Arom made a significant collection of Aka records, originally recorded in 1978 and rereleased by Ocora (Central Africa C 560171/72 [2002]).

42. Louis Sarno, *Song from the Forest: My Life among the Ba-Benjellé Pygmies* (London: Bantam, 1993), 76.

43. Hugh Tracey, "Basutoland Recording Tour, November 19th–December 3rd, 1959," *African Music* 2, no. 2 (1959B): 69.

44. Ibid. (emphasis in original).

45. The quote is taken from an interview with Andrew Tracey by Alexa Pienaar, August 8, 2007 (emphasis in original), in "The Digitising of Historical Sound Archives at the International Library of African Music and its Effects on the Heritage and Preservation Thereof of sub-Saharan African Communities," BA honours thesis, Rhodes University, 2007, 125.

46. Hugh Tracey, letter to Alan Lomax, June 24, 1963 (unpublished).

47. Willard Rhodes was professor of music at Columbia University in New York and had at the time just been granted a Fulbright award for ethnomusicological research in Southern Rhodesia during 1958–59. Rhodes had contacted Tracey for advice on some specific regional groups and possible recording techniques.

48. Hugh Tracey, letter to Professor Willard Rhodes, September 25, 1958, 3. The unpublished letter is headed, "Passenger, Carnarvon Castle, the Docks, Cape Town, (Arriving Thursday October 9th, 1958)."

49. Ibid.

50. Hugh Tracey, "Recording African Music in the Field," *African Music* 1, no. 2 (1955): 7.

51. Taken from a transcript by David Bandey, "Record of conversation with Daniel Mabuto, known for South African registration purposes as Parry Mangubane," March 29, 1980. The interview was conducted for the purposes of writing a (never completed) biography of Tracey. Daniel Mabuto joined Tracey as a plumber in 1947, became his driver in 1952, and proved to be an invaluable field assistant.

52. "Organised Research in African Music," unpublished, undated, and unpaginated typescript by Hugh Tracey.

53. Tracey, Cramb Lectures, 2.

54. Ibid.

55. Tracey, "Recording African Music in the Field," 7.

56. Unpublished typescripts of Peggy Tracey's diaries. This is taken from the introduction to an unpaginated section, "Expedition to Moçambique, Northern and Southern Rhodesia and Nyasaland (1949)."

57. Ibid. This quote is taken from a separate and undated section, "Congo Recording." It likely refers to either the 1952 or 1957 recording tours to various regions of the Congo.

58. Hugh Tracey, letter to the director of programmes at the South African Broadcasting Corporation. The letter seems to be dated July 19, 1961, and the quote is from page 4.

59. Hugh Tracey, quoted in Nat Hentoff, "Recordings: Hugh Tracey, Collector of African Integrities," www.nytimes.com/1966/05/29/archives/recordings-hugh-tracey-collector-of-african-integrities.html (accessed February 28, 2021).

60. Tracey, "Recording African Music in the Field," 6.

61. Tracey, *Catalogue* 1973A, 11.

62. Handwritten lecture notes, "Recording in the Veld." The lecture was delivered to the Photographic Society of Southern Africa on October 10, 1968 (unpublished).

63. Tracey, "Recording African Music in the Field," 8.

64. Ibid.

65. Memorandum by Tracey entitled "International Library of African Music: Object of Recording Tour, Nov./Dec. 1959," 1 (unpublished).

66. Ibid.

67. Sound modulation refers to the process whereby the timbre of a sonic waveform

becomes increasingly complex and often liable to distortion. Tracey noted that the sound of loud drum groups, for example, tended to overmodulate in some recordings.

68. Tracey, *Catalogue* 1973A, 11.

69. Unpublished and undated handwritten lecture notes, "Recording in the Veld," 2.

70. Ibid., 2 (emphasis in original).

71. Ibid., 3.

72. Hugh Tracey, Memorandum entitled "International Library of African Music Recording Tour June–August, 1957: Preparation for Recording Sessions, 1.

73. Ibid.

74. For example, see AMA. TR-198 (A5): "Msitso wokata" (analysis), and Tracey, *Catalogue* 1973B, 452). Tracey recorded Shambini, the leader of the Chopi group Ngodo of Mavilla playing an Msitso tune, then isolated and recorded his right and left hand playing separately and in different registers.

75. Jason Hickel, *Democracy as Death: The Moral Order of Anti-Liberal Politics in South Africa* (Oakland: University of California Press, 2015), 176.

76. Ibid., 99.

77. Tracey, Cramb Lectures, 11.

78. Peggy Tracey, *The Lost Valley* (Cape Town & Pretoria: Human and Rousseau, 1975), 76.

79. Tracey, Cramb Lectures, 11.

80. Ibid.

81. Tracey, "Recording African Music in the Field," 11.

82. Ibid.

83. "Venda" is the name of an ethnic group and their language (also Tshivenda), as well as a former Bantustan in South Africa. Venda is now part of Limpopo Province. Blacking spent several years researching in Vendaland and wrote widely about the music and culture. For example, see Blacking 1967.

84. Hugh Tracey, letter to John Blacking, July 7, 1954 (unpublished).

85. John Blacking, letter to Hugh Tracey (sent from Tshakhuma, Vendaland), June 24, 1956 (unpublished).

86. John Blacking, "Venda Music: A Preliminary Report of Initial Field Research in the Sibasa District (Not Intended for Publication)," addressed to the Research subcommittee of the ILAM, by John Blacking, musicologist MA of the ILAM, February 1957, 63 (unpublished).

87. John Blacking, letter to Hugh Tracey (sent from Sibasa, Vendaland), November 27, 1956 (unpublished).

88. Blacking, "Venda Music," 2–3.

89. Ibid., 3.

90. Patricia Shehan Campbell, "How Musical We Are: John Blacking on Music, Edu-

cation, and Cultural Understanding," *Journal of Research in Music Education*, 48, no. 4 (2000): 340.

91. Blacking, "Venda Music," 2. A repeater tape is a specially designed machine that enables the close manipulation of magnetic tape, allowing relatively easy and detailed examination of recorded material.

92. Ibid.

93. Ibid., 64.

94. Hugh Tracey, "Report on the 'Report to the International Library of African Music by J. A. R. Blacking on his Vendaland Research,'" November 24, 1957, 3 (unpublished).

95. Ibid., 1.

96. Reverend Arthur Morris Jones, letter to Hugh Tracey, March 17, 1958 (unpublished).

97. Ibid. (emphasis in original).

98. Keith Howard and John Blacking, "John Blacking: An Interview Conducted and Edited by Keith Howard," *Ethnomusicology* 35, no. 1 (1991): 58.

99. "Thick description" is a term that anthropologist Clifford Geertz borrowed from the philosopher Gilbert Ryle. Geertz 1973 uses it to describe ethnography that interprets the many possible meanings of signs in a culture, rather than just the surface details.

100. For example, see Agawu 2016, 2003A, 2003B.

101. Martin Scherzinger, "Negotiating the Music-Theory/African-Music Nexus: A Political Critique of Ethnomusicological Anti-Formalism and a Strategic Analysis of the Harmonic Patterning of the Shona Mbira Song Nyamaropa," *Perspectives of New Music* 39, no. 1 (2001): 11.

102. Edwards, "The Sound of Anticolonialism," 270.

103. Andrew Tracey took over as director after his father died in 1977, and ILAM moved from Krugersdorp to Grahamstown in 1978, where it was originally affiliated with the Institute for Social and Economic Research before becoming officially attached the Rhodes University Department of Music and Musicology in 2005. Some financial support from mining companies helped establish the current purpose-designed building in 1989.

THREE *Donkey Cart Curation, Xhosa Anthems, and Township Terms*

1. Udaba, interview with all the band members (Sakhile Moleshe, Dineo Pule, Luyolo Lenga ["Liyo"], Sibusiso Mnyanda ["Sbo"], Pumelele Lavisa ["Pura"]) at ILAM, July 3, 2008. Henceforth the informal listening sessions and interviews, nearly all of which were conducted jointly with Nyakonzima "Nyaki" Tsana, will be referred to simply as interviews.

2. Anna Harris, "Eliciting Sound Memories," *The Public Historian* 37, no. 4 (2015): 15.

3. I am extremely grateful to my friend and colleague Dr. Christopher Morton at the

Pitt Rivers Museum, Oxford, who, as joint supervisor for my DPhil suggested the term "sound elicitation" for this method.

4. Harris, "Eliciting Sound Memories," 30.

5. Stephen Wade, *The Beautiful Music All Around Us: Field Recordings and the American Experience* (Urbana, Chicago, and Springfield: University of Illinois Press, 2012), xiv.

6. Jeff Peires, *The House of Phalo: A History of the Xhosa People in the Days of Their Independence* (Johannesburg: Raven, 1981), 13.

7. Nicolas Jacobus van Warmelo, "The Classification of Cultural Groups," in *The Bantu-Speaking Peoples of Southern Africa*, edited by William David Hammond-Tooke (London and Boston: Routledge and Kegan Paul, 1974), 60.

8. John Henderson Soga, *The Ama-Xosa: Life and Customs* (Lovedale, SA: Lovedale Press, 1931), 7.

9. Van Warmelo, "The Classification of Cultural Groups," 61.

10. Hugh Tracey, *Catalogue* 1973A, 15.

11. Van Warmelo, "The Classification of Cultural Groups," 62.

12. For an excellent history of Rhodes University, see Maylam 2016.

13. An inaugural Festival was held in 1974 when the 1820 Settlers National Monument was officially opened. "The Festival" was renamed The National Arts Festival (NAF) in 2002. See chapter 5.

14. Thomas Rodney H. Davenport, *Black Grahamstown: The Agony of a Community* (Johannesburg: South African Institute of Race Relations, 1980), 4.

15. "Makana" is also known as "Makhanda," and "Makhanda ka Nxele" (the Left-Handed) or "Nxele," and was a top advisor to Chief Ndlambe.

16. www.capetownetc.com/news/grahamstown-changes-to-makhanda-despite-objections (accessed February 28, 2021).

17. I mostly refer to the city as Grahamstown-Makhanda hereafter, using "Grahamstown" only when referring to the period prior to the renaming. See chapter 5 for further details.

18. Tracey was born on January 29, 1903, and died on October 23, 1977.

19. The *lesiba* is a mouth bow that is played by Basotho shepherds (see figure 1.1).

20. The *uhadi* is a large bowed Xhosa instrument that includes a calabash resonator and is played by beating the string with a stick while pinching the string to create two notes approximately a tone apart. Traditionally it would be played exclusively by women.

21. Sneezewood is native to tropical and Southern Africa and is known for its durability.

22. The word "elokishini (s.) /ezilokishini (pl.)" meaning "in the township/townships" is commonly used.

23. Isaac Schapera, *Migrant Labour and Tribal Life: A Study of the Conditions in the Bechuanaland Protectorate* (London, New York, and Cape Town: Oxford University Press, 1947), 168.

24. Broadly speaking, "colored" is used by most people to refer to people of mixed-

race origin with some sub-Saharan ancestry but who are not recognized as "Black" under South African law.

25. McConnachie's research focuses on a joint project between Smithsonian Folkways' Global Sound Network and ILAM. www.folkways.si.edu/music-partners/smithsonian (accessed September 7, 2021).

26. Boudina McConnachie, "Legal Access to Our Musical History: An Investigation into the Copyright Implications of Archived Music Recordings Held at the International Library of African Music (ILAM) in South Africa," MA thesis, ethnomusicology, Rhodes University, 2008, 86.

27. The song is AMA.TR-59 (B-5) (Xhosa/Ngqika). See Tracey, *Catalogue* 1973B, 110.

28. McConnachie, "Legal Access," 92.

29. Laurent Aubert, *The Music of the Other: New Challenges for Ethnomusicology in a Global Age*, translated by Carla Ribeiro (Aldershot, UK and Burlington, VT: Ashgate, 2007), 23.

30. Deirdre Hansen, "The Music of the Xhosa-Speaking People," Vols. 1 and 2, PhD diss., Faculty of Arts, University of the Witwatersrand, 1981, 617 (emphasis in original).

31. Dave Dargie, *Xhosa Music: Its Techniques and Instruments, with a Collection of Songs* (Cape Town and Johannesburg: David Philip, 1988), 8.

32. Hansen, "The Music of the Xhosa-Speaking People," 37. The recording referred to is AMA. TR-33 (A-1)—*Ihobe liyataka* ("Dove, don't run away, don't hop about") [Xhosa/Mpondo], recorded by Tracey in Caba Location, Tabankulu District, Cape Province. See Tracey, *Catalogue* 1973B, 63.

33. The *umrhubhe* is a mouth-resonated friction bow that is played by bowing the string. Skilled players can whistle independent melodies as they also resonate the bow. The instrument would normally be played by young girls.

34. Hansen, "The Music of the Xhosa-Speaking People," 719–20 (emphasis in original). Hansen is referring to Kirby 1934, in which he classified and described a wide variety of instruments from South Africa.

35. Dargie, *Xhosa Music*, 49 (emphasis in original).

36. Andrew Tracey, fax sent to Myrna Capp, November 29, 1995 (unpublished).

37. Martin Miller, "Singing and Dancing in Holy Spirit: An Understanding of the Xhosa Zionist Healing Service," MA thesis, clinical psychology, Rhodes University, 1984, 4.

38. Manton Hirst, "The Healer's Art: Cape Nguni Diviners in the Townships of Grahamstown," Vols. 1 and 2, PhD diss., Rhodes University, 1990, 10.

39. Ibid., 5.

40. David Coplan, *In Township Tonight! South Africa's Black City Music and Theatre* (Chicago and London: University of Chicago Press, 2008 [1985]), 11.

41. "Ras" Mpho is Tswana and was originally from near Mafikeng, which is now more commonly known as Mahikeng, and was previously known as Mafeking. Mpho was the

only trained museum anthropologist I encountered in Grahamstown and his insights were invaluable.

42. The Albany Museum consists of a number of different buildings and is an affiliated research institute of Rhodes University. www.am.org.za (accessed February 28, 2021).

43. Mpho Molapisi, interview in his office at the Albany Museum, Grahamstown, August 28, 2008.

44. See, for example, Lingold, Mueller, and Trettien, eds. 2018.

45. Tera Tyota and Boniwe, interview at Boniwe's house, Hlalani Township, September 4, 2008; Tera Tyota, interview in his house in Hlalani Township, July 20, 2008.

46. Alexa Pienaar, "The Digitising of Historical Sound Archives at the International Library of African Music," BA honours thesis, Rhodes University, 2007, 71.

47. Sebastian Jamieson is a wonderful musician who has worked as a sound engineer in the studios at ILAM and currently works in IT at a local private school.

48. "Phumlani" translates as "rest here."

49. From recordings made at the street forum, June 24, 2008. Translated from isiXhosa and summarized by Nyaki, X, and the author.

50. Ibid.

51. The group listening session at Ethembeni took place on June 30, 2008. "Ethembeni" means "in a place of hope" in isiXhosa.

52. Zolile Nyikilana, Nomtwasana Nyikilana, Mr. Ngcongo, Colin Cira, and others, interview in Zolile and Nomtwasana's house in Vukani Township, June 16, 2008. "Vukani" means "Wake up!" (pl.).

53. For a short montage (4m 41s) of video clips of this sound elicitation, mostly filmed by Nyaki using my smartphone, see www.youtube.com/watch?v=_RFno1fa7XQ (accessed September 12, 2021).

54. AMA. TR-13 (A-1): Xhosa/Ngqika, see Tracey, *Catalogue* 1973B, 24.

55. AMA. TR-28 (A-1): Xhosa/Gcaleka. Recorded in Willowvale District, Cape Province (ibid., 52), and AMA. TR-60 (B-10): Xhosa/Ngqika, recorded at Zizane, Ngede Location, Kentani District in Transkei (ibid., 114).

56. Tracey, *Catalogue* 1973B, 52.

57. Ibid., 114.

58. See appendix 2 for full song texts and translations.

59. Thandeka Budaza, interview in her house in Extension 4, Joza Township, August 13, 2008.

60. *Umqombothi* is the traditional Xhosa home-brewed beer central to most family ceremonies, made from maize, maize malt, sorghum malt, yeast, and water. It is usually low in alcohol content and has a distinctively sour aroma and taste. See McAllister 2006.

61. *Umthayi* ceremonies are family ceremonies, often hosted to give thanks to the ancestors.

62. Colin Cira, interview in his house in Vukani Township, August 13, 2008 (translated from isiXhosa by Nyaki and the author).

63. Sompies and Tera Tyota, interview in Tera's house, Hlalani Township, August 19, 2008 (translated from isiXhosa by Nyaki and the author).

64. Cira, interview.

65. uTatomkhulu, uMakhulu Nonsans, and other oMakhulu (grandmothers), interview in the house of uSisi Mati in Ezigodlo Village, Peddie District, September 21, 2008. See https://youtu.be/_RFno1fa7XQ (2m 52s ff).

66. Kondile Tsana, interview in his home in Hlalani Township, August 6, 2008.

67. Mike Mati, interview in his house near Albany Road Township, July 26, 2008.

68. Port Elizabeth (now Gqeberha) is a coastal city approximately 130 km southwest of Makhanda. There are large townships around Port Elizabeth, and Mary explained how her family perform most of their "traditional work" there, contrasting this with the lack of "traditional work" in the townships around Grahamstown-Makhanda.

69. Mary Kelele, interview in her house in Hlalani Township, August 11, 2008.

70. Archbishop Tshobodi, interview in his church in Joza Township, September 17, 2008 (translated from isiXhosa by Nyaki and the author). Traditionally, men would enter the home's kraal (cattle enclosure and ancestral meeting place). However, women were supposed to avoid this area where the ancestors were buried, in order to protect their fertility.

71. Ibid.

72. Budaza, interview.

73. Ibid.

74. Ecalpar, Mngani, Zikhona, and Nombasa, interview in Ecalpar's room in Joza Township, July 24, 2008.

75. Ibid.

76. Chief Ndlambe of the amaRharhabe (a Xhosa subgroup) was an important military leader in the Frontier Wars between amaXhosa and European settlers in the Eastern Cape (1779–1879). Makhanda was one of his most important advisors.

77. Jackson Vena, interview in the Cory Library, Rhodes University, September 11, 2008.

78. Albert Kropf, *A Kafir-English* Dictionary, Second Edition (Lovedale, SA: Lovedale Mission Press, 1915). Please note that the K-word has long been considered a term offensive to Black South African people.

79. Noel Mostert, *Frontiers: The Epic of South Africa's Creation and the Tragedy of the Xhosa People* (New York: Alfred A. Knopf, 1992), 270.

80. Julie Wells, *The Return of Makhanda: Exploring the Legend* (Scottsville, SA: University of Kwazulu-Natal Press, 2012), 248.

81. Personal communication, December 2007. For an excellent analysis of the solidarity-building nature of "anthems" in the African diaspora, see Redmond 2014.

82. AMA. TR-31 (A-4). See Tracey, *Catalogue* 1973B, 58.

83. Tracey, *Catalogue* 1973A, 14-15.

84. Tracey, *Catalogue* 1973B, 58.

85. See appendix 2 for song text and translations.

86. The *umgidi* (pl.: *imigidi*) initiation ceremony marks the point at which young boys (*amakwenkwe*) leave the family home and go to live in the bush for a period, in order to learn the responsibilities of adult life. This period of seclusion takes place in June or November and is likely to last for a few weeks, although previously it could have lasted six months or more. The boys are circumcised and then return to the family home as adult males (*amadoda*). Much singing and celebration accompanies this process and *Somagwaza* is traditionally one of the most important songs for men to sing.

87. Tessa Dowling, Anele Gobodwana, and Somikazi Deyi, "When Culturally Significant Songs are Decontextualised: The Initiation Song Somagwaza," *South African Journal of Folklore Studies* 28, no. 2 (2018): 1–19.

88. Peter Mtuze, *Introduction to Xhosa Culture—Celebrating Ten Years of Freedom* (Eastern Cape, SA: Lovedale, 2004), 60.

89. Ibid.

90. Fundile Majola, "A Man Who is Not a Man," *Mail & Guardian*, March 1, 2012. www.thoughtleader.co.za/readerblog/2012/03/01/a-man-who-is-not-a-man (accessed February 28, 2021).

91. Andile Mhlalo, "What is Manhood? The Significance of Traditional Circumcision in the Xhosa Initiation Ritual," MPhil thesis, Department of Sociology and Social Anthropology, University of Stellenbosch, 2009, 125.

92. Sitting on the Indian Ocean approximately 160 km northeast of Grahamstown-Makhanda, East London is a city on the southeast coast of South Africa in the Buffalo City Metropolitan Municipality of the Eastern Cape Province.

93. Luvuyo Ntombana, "An Investigation into the Role of Xhosa Male Initiation in Moral Regeneration," DPhil diss., Faculty of the Arts, Nelson Mandela Metropolitan University, 2011, 25.

94. Casiwa Nombembe, *Music-Making of the Xhosa Diasporic Community: A Focus on the Umguyo Tradition in Zimbabwe*, MA thesis, School of Music, University of the Witwatersrand, 2014, 42-43. Please note that "ukwaluka" would normally be referred to as "ulwaluko" in the Eastern Cape.

95. Ibid., 79.

96. An American edition of the volume was published with an introduction and some English lyrics by Pete Seeger in 1960. See Pete Seeger, ed., *Choral Folksongs of the Bantu* (New York: G. Schirmer, 1960). www.folkways.si.edu/the-song-swappers-and-pete-seeger /bantu-choral-folk-songs/world/music/album/smithsonian (accessed February 28, 2021).

97. Omotayo Jolaosho, "Cross-circulations and Transnational Solidarity: Historicizing the US Anti-Apartheid Movement Through Song," *Safundi: The Journal of South African and American Studies* 13, nos. 3–4 (2012): 323.

98. Thembinkosi Butana, interview in his flat in Fingo Village Township, August 28, 2008.

99. Xolile ("X") Madinda and Noize, interview in DefKamp in Fingo Village Township, July 22, 2008.

100. uTatomkhulu, uMakhulu Nonsans, and other *oMakhulu* (grandmothers), interview.

101. uZwai, interview in his house in Joza Township, August 10, 2008. uZwai is a blues and jazz musician who preferred to reinterpret the music in the recordings on his electric guitar rather than offering much by way of verbal explanation.

102. Vena, interview.

103. Cecil Nonqane and Sarah (a museum assistant), interview in Nonqane's office at the Albany Museum, Grahamstown, September 19, 2008.

104. Vena, interview.

105. Sompies and Tyota, interview.

106. Mama Nobible, interview in the garden outside her house in Fingo Village Township, August 25, 2008. Mama Nobible's full name is Mama Nozamile Jamela. The names of many Xhosa women begin with "No-" and she came to be known as Mama Nobible because she was a regular churchgoer.

107. uSisi Butana (and daughter), and Thembinkosi Butana, interview in uSisi's house in a township outside Port Alfred, August 30, 2008.

108. Personal communication, conversation with Nyaki, September 11, 2008.

109. Mzambia, interview in the yard of his sister's house in Joza Township, July 18, 2008.

110. ILAM outreach concert, March 7, 2008.

111. Liyo of Udaba told me that the band originally started sampling the *umrhubhe* because they could not find anyone who could play it. At the time of fieldwork Liyo and Pura of the band were learning to play *umrhubhe* (conversation with Liyo at ILAM, May 24, 2008).

112. AIMP XLIV/Gallo Records VDE-879 (1996). The group is well known for its performance of *umngqokolo* overtone singing, has performed internationally, and has been researched extensively by Dave Dargie. His own archive of CDs, DVDs, and other publications is held at ILAM. www.ru.ac.za/ilam/products/cds/davedargiecollection (accessed February 28, 2021).

113. The Vibrafarians perform many different styles of music, including reggae infused with local styles.

114. Phumulelo ("Player") Frans, interview in his house in Extension 4, Joza Township, August 6, 2008.

115. Hleze Kunju, interview in his flat, Grahamstown, August 11, 2008.

116. Sompies and Tyota, interview.

117. Nomcebisi, interview, Drama Department, Rhodes University, August 25, 2008.

118. Ibid.

119. Luyanda Ncalu and Silulami "Slu" Lwana, interview in the house of Luyanda's girlfriend in an area of Joza known as Emagxmekwazini, August 17, 2008.

120. Silulami "Slu" Lwana, interview in Nyaki Tsana's house, Phumlani Township, August 17, 2008. *Amagqirha* is plural, *igqirha* singular. See Hirst 1990 for a study of the *amagqhira* in the Grahamstown townships.

121. Ncalu and Lwana, interview. Comparative listening sessions in the rural areas in Peddie District close to where Tracey also recorded revealed that in those regions, "Somagwaza" was only used by *amagqhira* while a song called "uPoho-Poho" was used in initiations, not "Somagwaza."

122. Ibid.

123. Ibid.

124. Ibid.

125. Others disagreed that an *igwijo* is a song that fits with any ceremony. For example, when checking the manuscript with me, X stressed, "We must say that *igwijo* can't be a song that you can sing anywhere" (personal communication, March 13, 2021).

126. Tyota, interview.

127. Personal communication (conversation with Nyaki, August 24, 2008).

128. Frans ("Player"), interview.

129. Ibid.

130. Budaza, interview.

131. Ibid.

132. Nelson Mandela, *Long Walk to Freedom* (London: Abacus, 2002 [1994]), 32. "Ndiy-indoda" means "I am a man."

133. Vena, interview.

134. Budaza, interview.

135. Cecil Nonqane and Sarah, interview.

136. Ngani 1959.

137. Cecil Nonqane and Sarah, interview.

138. Ibid.

139. Ibid.

140. John Henderson Soga, *The Ama-Xosa: Life and Customs* (Lovedale, SA: Lovedale Press, 1931), 248. J. H. Soga (1860–1941) was the son of Tiyo Soga (1829–1871), who was the first Black South African to be ordained.

141. Virginia van der Vliet, "Growing up in a Traditional Society," in *The Bantu-Speaking Peoples of Southern Africa*, edited by William Hammond-Tooke (London and Boston: Routledge and Kegan Paul, 1974), 229.

142. "Abakweta" refers to boys in the "bush" initiation schools who are becoming men.

143. Soga, *The Ama-Xosa*, 258 (emphasis in original).

144. Ibid., 172.

145. Koketso ("KK") Potsane, interview in Cow Moon Theory bar, Grahamstown, May 2, 2008.

146. Nyakonzima ("Nyaki) Tsana, interview in my flat in Constitution Street, Grahamstown, August 23, 2008. Nyaki is referring back to our interview with Zolile Nyikilana, Nomtwasana Nyikilana, Mr. Ngcongo, Colin Cira, and others. This was one of the first listening sessions we shared in homes. Names in Xhosa are often prefaced with a lowercase "u" when respectfully drawing attention to the person, and Nyaki is remembering Colin's arrival in his aunt and uncle's house as a key moment when the recordings and listening sessions started to come alive for people. (Nyikilana interview.)

147. The ceremony took place on September 9, 2008, and was named *Umbulelo* ("give thanks"). It was a day filled with family songs, speeches, drinking, and laughter.

148. Hlalani means "stay" (plural).

149. Personal communication (conversation with Nyaki, July 22, 2008).

150. Comment by Nyaki during Zuks, interview in the Old Gaol Bar, Grahamstown, July 23, 2008.

151. Nyakonzima ("Nyaki") Tsana, interview at ILAM, July 19, 2017.

152. Ibid.

153. "African Electronic Music" Zoom class hosted between ILAM and UVA, April 1, 2019. See www.youtube.com/watch?v=GYQUzeshTKU (accessed February 28, 2021). The scene X is recalling can be seen at www.youtube.com/watch?v=_RFno1fa7XQ& (2m 30s), accessed February 28, 2021.

154. Luis Gimenez Amoros, *Tracing the* Mbira *Sound Archive in Zimbabwe* (New York & London: Routledge, 2018), 120.

155. Toyin Falola, "Ritual Archives," in *The Palgrave Handbook of African Social Ethics*, edited by Nimi Waroboko and Toyin Falola (New York and London: Palgrave Macmillan, 2020), 473.

FOUR *Art and Community Activism Around the Archive*

1. Lee Watkins, FaceTime interview, December 12, 2018.

2. Thram was director of ILAM from 2006–2016, a senior lecturer in ethnomusicology at Rhodes University from 1999–2005, and is now professor emerita at Rhodes.

3. Watkins, interview.

4. Lee Watkins, "Director's Report following ILAM Board Advisory Meeting," May 31, 2019, held in ILAM paper archives.

5. Ibid.

6. Jennifer Lynn Stoever, *The Sonic Color Line: Race and the Cultural Politics of Listening* (New York: New York University Press, 2016), 12.

7. Danielle Paquette, "Beyoncé Released a Video Celebrating 'African Tradition.' Then Came the Backlash," *Washington Post*, July 9, 2020. www.washingtonpost.com/world /africa/beyonce-black-is-king-africa-backlash/2020/07/08/cfaa2dd2-c079-11ea-864a-0dd 31b9d6917_story.html (accessed February 28, 2021).

8. David Garcia, *Listening for Africa: Freedom, Modernity and the Logic of Black Music's African Origins* (Durham, NC and London: Duke University Press, 2017), 19.

9. Louise Meintjes's *Sound of Africa!* (2003) shows how studio productions of Zulu *mbaqanga* music are also heavily influenced by non-Zulu sensibilities, egos, and consuming economies of fantasy and imagination.

10. Josh Kun, *Audiotopia: Music, Race and America* (Berkeley and Los Angeles: UCLA Press, 2005), 26.

11. Ibid., 2.

12. www.ru.ac.za/ilam/ilam/messagefromdirector/ (accessed February 28, 2021).

13. Lee Watkins, talk at the African Urbanism Humanities Lab, University of Virginia, September 30, 2016.

14. Watkins was seconded as director in 2016 before officially being appointed in 2018.

15. Decolonizing Music Studies colloquium held at Nelson Mandela University in Port Elizabeth, "[re] Directions: Ukutshintshwa Kwendlela: Knowledge, Praxes and the African-Purposed Curriculum," August 16, 2018. "Ukutshintshwa Kwendlela" translates as "changing direction/path," and Watkins spoke alongside a music industry professional and other music and educational experts. www.crishet.mandela.ac.za/Events/August-2018 /Decolonising-Music-Studies-Parameters-Directions (accessed September 9, 2021).

16. Including Sakhuluntu Cultural Group in Joza township (Grahamstown-Makhanda), www.facebook.com/sakhuluntu.cultural.group (accessed February 28, 2021); Intlantsi Creative Development Project in Hamburg, www.artpsychotherapy.co.za/registered -art-therapists-in-sa/merran-roy/ (accessed February 28, 2021); and the Ntinga Ntaba kaNdoda Development Centre in Keiskammahoek, www.facebook.com/groups/ntinga/ (accessed February 28, 2021).

17. See Thram 2019.

18. Watkins, talk at African Urbanism Humanities Lab.

19. Watkins, interview.

20. Ibid.

21. Ibid.

22. Watkins, talk at African Urbanism Humanities Lab. This question is addressed in Frank Gunderson, Robert C. Lancefield, and Bret Woods, eds., *The Oxford Handbook of Musical Repatriation* (Oxford and New York: Oxford University Press, 2019), which is the first major volume on musical repatriation.

23. Ibid.

24. Rose Boswell and Francis B. Nyamnjoh, eds., *Postcolonial African Anthropologies* (Cape Town: HSRC Press, 2016).

25. Watkins, interview.

26. Ibid.

27. Ibid.

28. Ibid.

29. Savo Helta, "Decolonisation of Higher Education: Dismantling Epistemic Violence and Eurocentrism in South Africa," *Transformation in Higher Education* 1, no. 1 (2016): 4.

30. Estelle Prinsloo, "The Role of the Humanities in Decolonising the Academy," *Arts and Humanities in Higher Education* 15, no. 1 (2016): 165.

31. Watkins, interview.

32. Francis Bebey, *African Music: A People's Art* (Brooklyn, NY: Lawrence Hill Books, 1975), 139.

33. Watkins, interview.

34. Funded with a R250,000 grant (approximately $2,700 at 2021 conversion rates) from the National Heritage Council, the Ntinga Ntaba kaNdoda development center in Rabula village near Keiskammahoek is a community collective that is developing its own heritage routes and tour guides, solutions for sustainable farming and economies, and designing education models that integrate the self-empowering potential of heritage, early childhood development, and youth leadership.

35. www.thousandcurrents.org/ntinga-ntaba-kandoda-african-centered-self-deter mined-people-powered (accessed February 28, 2021).

36. Godfrey Vulindlela Mona and Russell Kaschula, "South African National Recon-ciliation Discourse and isiXhosa Written Poetry: 1994–2004," *South African Journal of African Languages*, 38, no. 1 (2018): 118.

37. Jara's credentials for organizing locally empowered collective cultural initiatives while building institutional links with universities are impeccable. Chairperson of Oxfam South Africa Board, instrumental in the founding of the Treatment Action Campaign, an advocate for gay and lesbian rights, founder and editor of *Amandla*—an activist socialist magazine seeking to build a new nondogmatic politics that addresses the crisis of transi-tion in South Africa—Jara is also a research associate at the University of Cape Town's Centre for Law and Society.

38. Watkins, interview.

39. Watkins, talk at African Urbanism Humanities Lab.

40. www.amahlathi.gov.za/tourism/activities/ (accessed February 28, 2021).

41. *Imbongi* (pl. *iimbongi*) means "praise poet," and the art form is known as *izibongo*.

42. Lee Watkins, "The Relationship Between Research, Intangible Cultural Heritage and Social and Economic Development: A Possible Solution to the Intractable Problem

of Rural Poverty in the Eastern Cape" (PowerPoint presentation). Watkins presented this at the South African Cultural Observatory conference at Turbine Hall in Johannesburg on May 24, 2017. www.southafricanculturalobservatory.org.za/download/219 (accessed February 28, 2021).

43. Ibid. Watkins consults very closely with local experts such as Thabisa Dinga, who is intimately aware of all of the ceremonies and celebrations and "traditional work" regularly taking place throughout dozens of villages in the area. She accompanies Watkins and students to events such as weddings and ceremonies, confirming *amaqgirha*, keeping her own notes, translating into and out of isiXhosa and other South African languages, consummately mediating between local communities, Ntinga, and the regular groups of students working with ILAM.

44. www.reason.kzoo.edu/csjl/ (accessed February 28, 2021).

45. www.emb7d1.wixsite.com/africanurbanism (accessed February 28, 2021).

46. Presentation and performance at University of Virginia Global Grounds with Mazibuko Jara and Bongiwe "Mthwakazi" Lusizi, October 15, 2018. Thank you to Carlin Smith for her documentation of the evening.

47. Ibid. Mthwakazi is an Atlantic Fellow for Racial Equity, a program run between Columbia University in New York and Nelson Mandela University in South Africa. See www.racialequity.atlanticfellows.org/fellow/bongiwe-lusizi (accessed September 9, 2021).

48. Watkins, talk at African Urbanism Humanities Lab.

49. The first president of Ciskei after its independence in 1980, he was declared president for life in 1983. Ruthlessly authoritarian, Sebe was especially hostile to trade unions.

50. Watkins, talk at African Urbanism Humanities Lab.

51. Jason McCoy, "Memory, Trauma, and the Politics of Repatriating Bikindi's Music," in Gunderson, Lancefield, and Woods, eds., 433.

52. Watkins, talk at African Urbanism Humanities Lab.

53. www.amavaheritage.co.za/about (accessed February 28, 2021).

54. Tim Leibbrant, "A Mash-Up of Deferred Reconciliation: Thando Mama's 'Of Nationhood/Desolation' (a review)," *Arthrob*, August 25, 2017. https://artthrob.co.za/2015/08/27/a -mash-up-of-deferred-reconciliation-thando-mamas-of-nationhooddesolation/ (accessed September 9, 2021).

55. www.thandomama.com/exhibitions and www.thandomama.com/portraits (accessed February 28, 2021).

56. www.ru.ac.za/artsofafrica/latestnews/mfaexhibitionforgettingntabakandoda bythandomama.html (accessed February 28, 2021).

57. https://makandulas2.wixsite.com/sikhumbuzomakandula (accessed February 28, 2021).

58. https://makandulas2.wixsite.com/sikhumbuzomakandula/project01?lightbox =dataItem-j19e0xj61 (accessed February 28, 2021).

59. Nancy Dantas, "Looking After Freedom?" *Buala*, June 8, 2017. www.buala.org/en /ill-visit/looking-after-freedom (accessed February 28, 2021).

60. Ibid.

61. Rachel Baasch, "Bodies, Buildings, and Borders: Navigating the Divided Nation through Contemporary South African and Palestinian Art Practice," *African Arts*, 51, no. 2 (2018): 40.

62. Leibbrant, "A Mash-Up of Deferred Reconciliation."

63. See Sheldon Pearce, "How Black Panther Composer Ludwig Göransson Found the Sound of Wakanda," *Pitchfork,* February 7, 2018. www.pitchfork.com/thepitch/how -black-panther-composer-ludwig-goransson-found-the-sound-of-wakanda-interview/; and also www.youtube.com/watch?v=fcO5klPyfX4 for an introduction to Göransson's composition process (both accessed February 28, 2021).

64. www.swp-records.com/about (accessed February 28, 2021).

65. www.beatingheart.bandcamp.com (accessed February 28, 2021).

66. www.thegreatkaroo.com/news/africas_musical_heritage (accessed February 28, 2021).

67. www.facebook.com/sakhuluntu.cultural.group (accessed February 28, 2021).

68. For example, see Diane Thram's work with Singing Wells, www.npr.org /2015/06/28/417462792/in-a-kenyan-village-a-65-year-old-recording-comes-home (accessed February 28, 2021); Jocelyn and Zack Moon's work with *matepe* musicians in Zimbabwe, www.yelloweaver.com (accessed February 28, 2021); and the *Generations of Jazz* exhibition at the Red Location Museum in New Brighton, Port Elizabeth, www.ru.ac .za/ilam/publications/generationsofjazz/ (all accessed February 28, 2021).

69. Elijah Madiba, "Repatriating Xhosa Music Recordings Archived at the International Library of African Music (ILAM) and Reviving Interest in Traditional Xhosa Music among the Youth in Grahamstown," MA thesis, ethnomusicology, Rhodes University, 2017.

70. Elijah Madiba, interview at ILAM, May 21, 2008.

71. "African Electronic Music" Zoom class hosted between ILAM and UVA, April 1, 2019. See www.youtube.com/watch?v=GYQUzeshTKU (accessed February 28, 2021).

72. Madiba, "Repatriating Xhosa Music," 1.

73. Gomolemo "Pinkie" Mojaki, "Releasing the Pause Button on Hugh Tracey's Revitalisation of a Selection of the Bangwaketse Music Held at the International Library of African Music," Masters thesis, ethnomusicology, Rhodes University, 2015.

74. Madiba, "Repatriating Xhosa Music," 17.

75. Ibid., 51.

76. Ibid., 14.

77. Elijah Madiba and Akhona "Bhodl'ingqaka" Mafani, interview in the studio at ILAM, July 19, 2017.

78. Approximately 130 km northeast of Makhanda, King William's Town has been officially renamed Qonce.

79. Approximately 225 km north of Makhanda and further inland from the Indian Ocean than Qonce. Queenstown is now officially Komani.

80. Peddie (or "iNgqushwa" in Xhosa) is approximately 70 km east of Makhanda.

81. Madiba, "Repatriating Xhosa Music," 58.

82. AMA. TR-63 (B-2). "Mama ndaswelindawo ngendaba" (Mama I lack accommodation on account of the news), an *Mtshotsho* dance "for boys and girls with *Ikinki* mouth resonated musical bow," recorded in 1957, in Old Idutywa District, Transkei, Eastern Cape (see Tracey, *Catalogue* 1973B, 120).

83. Madiba, "Repatriating Xhosa Music," 73.

84. Ibid., 73–74.

85. Ibid., 74.

86. Ibid.

87. Masithembe Sazana, "'The Rise of isiNtu poetry," *Grahamstown Music Magazine* 1 (October 15, 2017): 9. www.issuu.com/michellemay78/docs/gmm_final_og (accessed February 28, 2021).

88. Mamela Gowa, "Grahamstown Poet's Career Takes Off," *Daily Dispatch*, April 26, 2013, www.pressreader.com/south-africa/daily-dispatch/20130426/281517928614956 (accessed February 28, 2021).

89. Madiba, "Repatriating Xhosa Music," 89.

90. AMA. TR-26 (A-2). Tracey documents this as "Preliminary to a Christian wedding" (see *Catalogue* 1973B, 49).

91. Madiba and Mafani, interview, July 19, 2017.

92. Since 2003 FruityLoops has been known as FL Studio, though most artists in Makhanda retain the former name.

93. Madiba and Mafani, interview, July 19, 2017.

94. Madiba, "Repatriating Xhosa Music," 113.

95. Ibid., 110.

96. AMA. TR-13 (A-5). This is one of five songs that form part of an impromptu sketch with singing and responses called "Sanusi" (The Diviner) performed in King William's Town in 1957 by Nkenkese Mgwejo. The song is sung by a woman also playing the *uhadi* bow (see Tracey, *Catalogue* 1973B, 24–25).

97. AMA. TR-63 (B-8). This is an *Mhala* (-hala means to raise a war cry, to invite, call, or summon) dance for young men with *uhadi* performed by Nodinile, a Gcaleka woman at Cizele location, and recorded in 1957 at Old Idutywa District, Transkei, Eastern Cape, 1957 (see Tracey, *Catalogue* 1973B, 121).

98. AMA. TR-63 (B-2). An *Mtshotsho* dance song for boys and girls recorded in 1957

in Old Idutywa District, Transkei, Eastern Cape, and sung by a Gcaleka girl playing an *umrhubhe* mouth bow and whistling (see Tracey, *Catalogue* 1973B, 120).

99. "Imin'Esisdenge" means something like "unexpected day, the day you did not expect, or the day of reckoning." See www.youtube.com/watch?v=l_hwIj8af6Q (accessed September 9, 2021).

100. Mzwamadoda Makalima, "Mafani's Memorable Poetry Gig," *Grocott's Mail*, February 6, 2018. www.grocotts.co.za/2018/02/06/mafanis-memorable-poetry-gig (accessed February 28, 2021). See www.youtube.com/watch?v=Ik_zU754D8M for a short introduction to the young poet and his work (accessed February 28, 2021).

101. www.facebook.com/events/1752611981449266 (accessed February 28, 2021).

102. AMA. TR-13 (A-2). A party song for young people with clapping, by five young Ngqika women and girls, recorded in Released Area 32, King William's Town District, Cape Province, 1957. Note that Tracey's title "Wdoyika" should be "Ndoyika" (Tracey, *Catalogue* 1973B, 24).

103. Madiba, "Repatriating Xhosa Music," 84.

104. David Macgregor, "Sky the Limit for Teen Talent," *DispatchLive*, January 20, 2017. www.dispatchlive.co.za/news/2017-01-20-sky-the-limit-for-teen-talent/ (accessed February 28, 2021). Xolile Madinda advised me that "iintonga" can be also be a metaphor for "songs."

105. See www.youtube.com/watch?v=Ik_zU754D8M, where Bhod'lingqaka and other artists are at work in the studio.

106. Macgregor, "Sky the Limit for Teen Talent."

107. Madiba and Mafani, interview.

108. Ibid.

109. www.youtube.com/watch?v=l5XooPZH_40 (accessed February 28, 2021).

110. The competition is aimed at youth between the ages of 13 and 19.

111. Madiba and Mafani, interview.

112. Macgregor, "Sky the Limit for Teen Talent."

113. AMA. TR-13 (A-1): Xhosa/Ngqika. "Mhlahlo" (recorded at Area 32, King William's Town in 1957). See Tracey, *Catalogue* 1973B, 24.

114. Madiba, "Repatriating Xhosa Music," 86.

115. Ibid. Translation by Madiba and Mafani.

116. From "The Praise Singer—Akhona 'Bhod'lingqaka' Mafani," www.youtube.com/watch?v=Ik_zU754D8M (accessed February 28, 2021).

117. Madiba and Mafani, interview.

118. Terence Trouillot, "Titus Kaphar on Putting Black Figures Back into Art History and His Solution for the Problem of Confederate Monuments," *Artnet*, March 27, 2019. https://news.artnet.com/art-world/titus-kaphar-erasure-art-history-1497391(accessed February 28, 2021).

119. www.vmfa.museum/about/rumors-of-war/ (accessed February 28, 2021). At the time of going to press, these Confederare statues had recently been removed. See www.apnews.com/article/robert-e-lee-statue-virginia-removed-92955a351d9fda6319f379ddc28df8a0 (accessed September 13, 2021).

120. Brenda Schmahmann, "Monumental Mediations: Performative Interventions to Public Commemorative Art in South Africa," *de arte*, 53, no. 2-3 (2018): 157.

121. Ibid., 153.

122. www.facebook.com/pages/category/Community-Organization/Isikhumbuzo-Applied-History-Unit-1854760814778335 (accessed February 28, 2021).

123. "Ubom!" means "Life!"

124. From "Like Mother, Like Son," *The Journalist*, April 7, 2015. www.thejournalist.org.za/art/like-mother-like-son (accessed February 28, 2021). See www.youtube.com/watch?v=nIRwVaCaHrE (accessed February 28, 2021).

125. The 1820 Settlers Monument was built in 1974, designed to honor the contribution of the 4,000 British settlers who arrived in the Eastern Cape. The Grahamstown Foundation, housed at the monument, has been leading a commission with public participation to change the name to honor current-day South Africa. See www.foundation.org.za (accessed February 28, 2021). Further information is included in chapter 5.

126. The Old Gaol, built in 1824, is the second-oldest building in Grahamstown-Makhanda. It has since been variously repurposed to host a backpackers' hostel, cafés, craft workshops, performances, and municipal offices. I spent my first-ever night in Grahamstown in the Old Gaol hostel, and will always be grateful for meeting the wonderful Mhleli Ngubo, Oz Kate, and Brian Peltason and many others in its vibrant bar.

127. Masixole Heshu, interview, Drama Department, Rhodes University, July 17, 2017.

128. Jeff Peires, *The House of Phalo: A History of the Xhosa People in the Days of Their Independence* (Johannesburg: Raven, 1981), 30.

129. Ibid., 174.

130. Landeg Vail, and Leroy White, *Power and the Praise Poem: Southern African Voices in History* (Charlottesville, University of Virginia Press, 1991), xi.

131. Heshu, interview.

132. Performed at TBPS on September 24, 2018. www.facebook.com/events/327878911108802 (accessed February 28, 2021).

133. Thandolwethu Gulwa, "Xhosa Chronicles: Sondelani Sizwe sa kwaXhosa!" *Cue Media*, July 7, 2018. www.cuemedia.co.za/2018/07/07/xhosa-chronicles-sondelani-sizwe-sa-kwaxhosa/ (accessed August 5, 2020).

134. Nonsindiso Qwabe, "Xhosa Play Speaks to Painful Past," *Daily Dispatch*, July 6, 2018. www.pressreader.com/south-africa/daily-dispatch/20180706/281603831220458 (accessed February 28, 2021).

135. Athi Mogezeleli Joja, "Nxele, Ndlambe, Umhlaba: Grounding with Sikhumbuzo

Makandula," in *Ubuzwe*, edited by Sikhumbuzo Makandula (Grahamstown, SA: Sikhumbuzo Makandula, 2016), 6.

136. Sikhumbuzo Makandula and Eria Nsubuga Sane, "Eria Nsubuga Sane and Sikhumbuzo Makandula in Conversational Partnership," *African Arts* 50, no. 20 (2017): 78.

137. Ibid.

138. www.makandulas2.wixsite.com/sikhumbuzomakandula/project04?lightbox=data Item-j5h7f17l (accessed February 28, 2021).

139. Makandula and Sane, "Eria Nsubuga Sane and Sikhumbuzo Makandula," 79–80.

140. Joja, "Nxele, Ndlambe, Umhlaba," 10.

141. Ibid., 9. See www.makandulas2.wixsite.com/sikhumbuzomakandula/project04 / (accessed September 13, 2021).

142. Images can be viewed at www.makandulas2.wixsite.com/sikhumbuzomakandula /project02?lightbox=dataItem-j19dk42m4 (accessed September 9, 2021).

143. www.archetypeonlinemagazine.wordpress.com/2014/07/31/blind-spot/ (accessed February 28, 2021).

144. www.mohaumodisakengstudio.com/work (accessed February 28, 2021).

145. Sikhumbuzo Makandula, "Bantu-staan!" unpublished colloquium paper (unpaginated), 2015. See www.academia.edu/35080550/BantuStaan_pdf (accessed September 13, 2021).

146. See www.infectingthecity.com/2019/artwork/zizimase (accessed September 9, 2021). "Zizimase" means "honor them."

147. The work *Ingoma ka Tiyo Soga* (The Songs of Tiyo Soga) investigates the violence of missionary work in South Africa, and was performed at the Institute for Creative Arts in Cape Town (October 2018), and the National Arts Festival in 2019. Tiyo Soga (1829–1871) was born in the Eastern Cape and was a pioneering African intellectual. He was the first Black South African to be ordained in a Christian church. Please visit www.ica.uct.ac.za /ica/theicapodcast (episode six) for an interview with Makandula, hosted by the Institute for Creative Arts (accessed February 28, 2021).

148. Sku's full name is Sikhumbuzo (Remembrance) Sizwe (The Nation) Makandula.

149. Sikhumbuzo Makandula, interview in X's house on George Street, Makhanda (with Xolile Madinda), July 11, 2019.

150. Ibid.

151. From www.ica.uct.ac.za/ica/theicapodcast (episode six) (accessed February 28, 2021).

152. Makandula, interview in X's house.

1. Xolile Madinda, personal communication, August 14, 2018.

2. Xolile Madinda, interview, foyer of Drama Department, Rhodes University, August 26, 2008.

3. Ibid.

4. Jennifer Lynn Stoever, *The Sonic Color Line: Race and the Cultural Politics of Listening* (New York: New York University Press), 2016.

5. Masixole Zinzo Patrick Heshu, "Makhanda: Reflections of Past, Present and Future," *Journal of Indigenous and Shamanic Studies* 1, no. 1 (2020): 25. Please note "surveillance, camera" is the original punctuation.

6. Russell Kaschula, "African Languages Have the Power to Transform Universities," *The Conversation,* May 18, 2015. www.theconversation.com/african-languages-have-the -power-to-transform-universities-40901 (accessed February 28, 2021). The first PhD at Rhodes University written entirely in isiXhosa was submitted in 2017 by musician Dr. Hleze Kunju. See Theto Mahlakoana, "PhD Written in isiXhosa Hailed as Milestone," *Independent Online,* April 23, 2017. www.iol.co.za/news/phd-written-in-isixhosa-hailed -as-milestone-8779991 (accessed February 28, 2021). Hleze Kunju contributes to the sound elicitation in chapter 3.

7. "Mfecane" means "the crushing" in isiZulu, and these wars took place internally in South Africa as King Shaka's kingdom grew in power during a time of drought and social unrest.

8. Personal communication, March 6, 2020.

9. www.fingovillage.blogspot.com includes some oral histories of the township and related issues (accessed February 28, 2021).

10. Poppy Fry, "Siyamfenguza: The Creation of Fingo-ness in South Africa's Eastern Cape, 1800-1835," *Journal of Southern African Studies* 36, no. 1 (2012): 32.

11. Ibid., 25.

12. Jesmond Blumenfeld and Michael Nuttall, "Grahamstown's Fingo Village: From Poverty to Paradise?" *Reality* 4, no. 3 (1972): 16. www.disa.ukzn.ac.za/rejul727 (accessed February 28, 2021).

13. Personal communication while checking details in this chapter with me, email March 6, 2020.

14. www.youtube.com/watch?time_continue=4&v=vUKSX61qTno (accessed February 28, 2021).

15. Alistair Maxegwana died on May 26, 2018. www.facebook.com/aroundhiphop /posts/2085549498436166 (accessed February 28, 2021).

16. www.thinkfest.wordpress.com/2014/08/04/my-journey-started-with-a-book-xolile -madinda-on-hip-hop-art-and-steve-biko (accessed February 28, 2021).

17. Steve Biko, *I Write What I Like* (Northlands, SA: Picador Africa, 2004 [1978]), 52.

18. Ian M. Macqueen, *Black Consciousness and Progressive Movements Under Apartheid.* (Pietermaritzburg, SA: University of Kwazulu-Natal Press, 2018), 5.

19. Nyameko Barney Pityana, Mamphela Ramphele, Malusi Mpulwama, and Lindy Wilson, "Introduction," in *Bounds of Possibility: The Legacy of Steve Biko and Black Consciousness,* edited by Nyameko Barney Pityana, Mamphela Ramphele, Malusi Mpulwama, and Lindy Wilson (Cape Town: David Philip, 1991), 9.

20. www.thinkfest.wordpress.com/2014/08/04/my-journey-started-with-a-book-xolile -madinda-on-hip-hop-art-and-steve-biko (accessed February 28, 2021).

21. Ibid.

22. www.facebook.com/FingoFestival (accessed February 28, 2021).

23. www.sa-venues.com/events/easterncape/grahamstown-national-arts-festival (accessed February 28, 2021).

24. With the outbreak of Covid-19, like most other festivals throughout the world the NAF was delivered entirely online in 2020.

25. www.nationalartsfestival.co.za/about (accessed February 28, 2021).

26. Ibid.

27. Bryan Schmidt, "Fault Lines, Racial and Aesthetic: The National Arts Festival at Grahamstown," *Theatre Research International* 43, no. 3 (2019): 318.

28. www.nationalartsfestival.co.za/news/2020-featured-artist (accessed February 28, 2021).

29. www.facebook.com/unmutedance/ (accessed February 28, 2021).

30. https://www.nationalartsfestival.co.za/news/the-gruffalo-struts-on-to-joburg -stage/ (accessed February 28, 2021).

31. Nyaki featured as one of the core writers and performers of this excellent and well-received show.

32. Schmidt, "Fault Lines," 318–19.

33. Brett Pyper, "Towards a Deeper Collaborative Curatorial Practice: On the Challenges of Presenting Indigenous Performance at the National Arts Festival in Grahamstown," *de arte,* 51, no. 2 (2016): 36.

34. Ibid., 34.

35. Khulumani is a membership-based organization "of more than 100,000 victims and survivors of Apartheid-related gross human rights violations in South Africa," gaining "national and international recognition as the foremost stakeholder in South Africa's on-going campaign for transformational justice—to hold government and our society as a whole to meet its promises of truth, justice, redress and reconciliation." www.khulumani .net/about-us/ (accessed February 28, 2021).

36. At the time of going to press in 2021, R40,000 was approximately $2,700.

37. Zaza Hlalethwa, "What Happens After the Fest?" *Mail & Guardian,* July 13, 2018. www.mg.co.za/article/2018-07-13-00-what-happens-after-the-fest (accessed February 28, 2021).

38. www.sa-venues.com/events/easterncape/grahamstown-national-arts-festival/ (accessed February 28, 2021).

39. Hlalethwa, "What Happens After the Fest?"

40. www.youtube.com/watch?v=Iy1iyYkiaj4 (accessed February 28, 2021).

41. www.youtube.com/watch?v=xD1Q1MkbOjQ (accessed February 28, 2021).

42. www.sofisaphillips.co.za/waainek-wind-power-gyd (accessed August 5, 2020).

43. www.youtube.com/watch?v=eCB1KwAC1dM (accessed February 28, 2021).

44. www.thinkfest.wordpress.com/2014/08/04/my-journey-started-with-a-book -xolile-madinda-on-hip-hop-art-and-steve-biko (accessed February 28, 2021).

45. www.facebook.com/watch/?v=1911080269120766 (accessed February 28, 2021).

46. www.lunakill.bandcamp.com/releases (accessed February 28, 2021).

47. Personal communication, outside The Black Power Station, Waainek, Makhanda, July 18, 2017.

48. www.thepowerstation.co.za/ (Statement of Significance PDF, 9).

49. www.facebook.com/tonylankester/posts/10156907223646841 (accessed February 28, 2021).

50. Xolile Madinda, interview in The Black Power Station, July 18, 2017.

51. www.warehouse21.org (accessed February 28, 2021).

52. Madinda, interview.

53. https://www.facebook.com/tonylankester/posts/10156907223646841 (accessed February 28, 2021).

54. Madinda, interview. The album was released in 2016.

55. Eusebius Mckaiser, "The Makhanda Disaster Cannot be Ignored," *Mail & Guardian,* February 6, 2020. www.mg.co.za/analysis/2020-02-06-the-makhanda-disaster-cannot -be-ignored/ (accessed February 28, 2021).

56. www.scifest.org.za/grahamstown-foundation/ (accessed February 28, 2021).

57. www.foundation.org.za/index.php?pid=23 (accessed August 5, 2020). At the time of going to press, this link was no longer active, but the Grahamstown Foundation was actively engaged in a "process to identify a new name for the building we call home—the 1820 Settlers Monument." See www.foundation.org.za (accessed February 28, 2020).

58. Mpho Ngoepe, "Archives Without Archives: A Window of Opportunity to Build Inclusive Archive [*sic*] in South Africa," *Journal of the South African Society of Archivists* 52 (2019): 151.

59. Ibid., 163.

60. Schmidt, "Fault Lines," 327.

61. www.youtube.com/watch?v=JCGGFSQPvSY (accessed September 9, 2021).

62. www.news24.com/SouthAfrica/News/Grahamstown-named-for-butcher-20050526 (accessed February 28, 2021).

63. Sue Maclennan, "Campaign Cries Foul Over Name Change," *Grocott's Mail,* June 29, 2018. www.grocotts.co.za/2018/06/29/campaign-cries-foul-over-name-change/ (accessed February 28, 2021).

64. www.keepgrahamstown.co.za/background-to-debate (accessed February 28, 2021).

65. Adrienne Carlisle and Zizonke May, "Grahamstown Lobby Loses Court Battle Over Makhanda," *Herald Live,* December 12, 2019. www.heraldlive.co.za/news/2019-12-12-grahamstown-lobby-loses-court-battle-over-makhanda/ (accessed February 28, 2021).

66. Originating in the Black townships around Johannesburg in the 1950s–'60s, *pantsula* is a rapid-stepping dance style embracing a wide culture that today blends aspects from tap dance, hip hop, jazz, physical comedy, and much more.

67. www.facebook.com/wamkelwa.nkone (accessed February 28, 2021). Uitenhage, now renamed Kariega, is a town in the Nelson Mandela Metropolitan Municipality approximately 35 km inland from Port Elizabeth (Gqeberha).

68. Julie Wells, *The Return of Makhanda: Exploring the Legend* (Scottsville, SA: University of Kwazulu-Natal Press, 2012), 16.

69. Tim Stapleton, "Review of *The Return of Makhanda: Exploring the Legend*, by Julie Wells," *Historia* 60, no. 1 (2015): 184.

70. Personal communication (FaceTime), December 17, 2018.

71. Jeff Opland and Patrick McCallister, "The Xhosa Imbongi as Trickster," in *Journal of African Cultural Studies* 22, no. 2 (2010): 159.

72. Jeff Opland, *Xhosa Oral Poetry: Aspects of a Black South African Tradition* (New York: Cambridge University Press, 1983), 67 (emphasis in original).

73. Personal communication (FaceTime), December 17, 2018.

74. Ibid.

75. Landeg Vail and Leroy White, *Power and the Praise Poem: Southern African Voices in History*, (Charlottesville: University of Virginia Press, 1991), 56.

76. Ibid., 57 (emphasis in original).

77. Personal communication, March 7, 2021.

78. Michail Exarchos (a.k.a. Stereo Mike), "Sample Magic: (Conjuring) Phonographic Ghosts and Meta-illusions in Contemporary Hip-Hop Production," *Popular Music* 38, no. 1 (2019): 33-53.

79. Diane Thram, "Music Archives and Repatriation," in *The Oxford Handbook of Musical Repatriation*, edited by Frank Gunderson, Robert C. Lancefield, and Bret Woods (Oxford and New York: Oxford University Press, 2019), 56.

80. Xolile Madinda and Andiswa ("Bliss") Rabeshu, interview, Book'ona, The Black Power Station, August 19, 2018.

81. 9th Wonder's work is well told in the film *The Hip Hop Fellow*, see www.thehiphop fellow.com/ (accessed February 28, 2021). 9th Wonder was a Music Arts Board resident at UVA in 2017. See www.arts.virginia.edu/uva-music-arts-board-presents-9th-wonder -residency/ (accessed September 13, 2021).

82. Judith A. Peraino, "I'll Be Your Mixtape: Lou Reed, Andy Warhol and the Queer Intimacies of Cassettes," *The Journal of Musicology* 36, no. 4 (2019): 407.

83. Joanna Demers, "Cassette Tape Revival as Creative Anachronism," *Twentieth-Century Music* 14, no.1 (2017): 111.

84. www.aroundhiphop.co.za (accessed August 5, 2020).

85. www.youtube.com/watch?v=XfXLgI4Ni-g (accessed February 28, 2021).

86. Video shoot for "Premonition," outside The Black Power Station, evening of August 9, 2018.

87. Lindsey Shavers, personal communication shared with our "African Electronic Music" class at the University of Virginia, May 29, 2019.

88. Kholisa B. Gogela, "Perceptions of Ulwaluko in a Liberal Democratic State: Is Multiculturalism Beneficial to AmaXhosa Women in the Eastern Cape Province of South Africa?" PhD diss., Rhodes University, 2017, 16.

89. For example, see The Black Power Station YouTube channel, www.youtube.com /channel/UCnVVoWKe6PBJAyQt8T20vmA/featured, and Blah ze Blah YouTube Channel, www.youtube.com/user/blaqilluminous (both accessed February 28, 2021).

90. www.youtube.com/watch?v=XfXLgI4Ni-g (accessed February 28, 2021).

91. www.youtube.com/watch?v=CaIFKVOv7lI (accessed February 28, 2021).

92. Toyin Falola, "Ritual Archives," in *The Palgrave Handbook of African Social Ethics*, edited by Nimi Waroboko and Toyin Falola (New York and London: Palgrave Macmillan, 2020), 473.

93. Ibid.

94. Ibid., 483.

95. Personal communication (Skype) with Xolile Madinda and Oz, April 4, 2019.

96. Stoever, *The Sonic Color Line*, 1.

97. Ibid., 19.

98. Alan Jenkins, "The Global Significance of Black Panther," *The Hollywood Reporter*, February 23, 2018. www.hollywoodreporter.com/heat-vision/black-panther-global-signif icance-1087878 (accessed February 28, 2021).

99. Xolile Madinda, personal communication (WhatsApp call), December 6, 2018.

100. Xolile Madinda, personal communication (WhatsApp call), December 16, 2018.

101. Ibid.

102. Ibid.

103. www.music.virginia.edu/xolile-madinda-residency (accessed February 28, 2021).

104. Madinda, personal communication, December 16, 2018.

105. Richard Bullock, "It's Hard to be a Man: A Month with Three Initiates During the Xhosa Circumcision Ritual," *Africa Geographic*, May 29, 2015. www.magazine.africageo graphic.com/weekly/issue-48/xhosa-circumcision-ritual-south-africa-its-hard-to-be-a -man/ (accessed February 28, 2021).

106. www.aljazeera.com/program/people-power/2013/1/3/ndiyindoda-i-am-a-man (accessed September 9, 2021).

107. www.inxeba.com (accessed February 28, 2021).

108. Bullock, "It's Hard to be a Man."

109. Ibid.

110. Lizabé Lambrechts, "Performing the Aporias of the Archive: Towards a Future for South African Music Archives," *Historia* 6, no. 1 (2016): 150.

111. Lizabé Lambrechts, "Ethnography and the Archive: Power and Politics in Five South African Music Archives," PhD diss., University of Stellenbosch, 2012, 220.

112. Lambrechts, "Performing the Aporias of the Archive," 151.

113. Carol Muller, "Jazzing the Bushmen: Khoisan Migrations into South African Jazz," in *Out of Bounds—Ethnography, History, Music: Essays in Honour of Kay Kaufman Shelemay*, edited by Ingrid Monson, Carol J. Oja, and Richard K. Wolf (Cambridge, MA and London: Harvard University Press, 2017), 203.

114. Ibid., 209.

115. Madinda, personal communication, March 6, 2021.

CONCLUSION *Curating Sound Stories*

1. Denis Etheredge, "Tribute to Dr. Hugh Tracey," delivered at the memorial service held at Saronde Farm, Krugersdorp, October 26, 1977, 2.

2. Landeg Vail and Leroy White, *Power and the Praise Poem: Southern African Voices in History* (Charlottesville: University of Virginia Press, 1991), 45.

3. Mhoze Chikowero, *African Music, Power, and Being in Colonial Zimbabwe* (Bloomington: Indiana University Press, 2015), 137.

4. Ibid., 142.

5. Paulette Coetzee, "Dancing with Difference: Hugh Tracey on and in (African) Music," *Safundi* 16, no. 4 (2015): 416.

6. Toyin Falola, "Ritual Archives," in *The Palgrave Handbook of African Social Ethics*, edited by Nimi Waroboko and Toyin Falola (New York and London: Palgrave Macmillan, 2020), 73.

7. Ibid., 74.

8. Grant Olwage, ed., *Composing Apartheid: Music for and Against Apartheid* (Johannesburg: Wits University Press, 2008), 39–40.

9. Chikowero, "African Music, Power, and Being in Colonial Zimbabwe," 132.

10. Ibid., 139.

11. Ibid., 141.

12. Ibid.

13. Ibid., 142.

14. Roshanak Khesthi, *Modernity's Ear: Listening to Race and Gender in World Music* (New York and London: New York University Press, 2015), 133.

15. Frank Gunderson and Bret Woods, "Pathways Toward Open Dialogues about Sonic Heritage," in *The Oxford Handbook of Musical Repatriation*, edited by Frank Gunderson, Robert C. Lancefield, and Bret Woods (Oxford and New York: Oxford University Press, 2019), lii.

16. Ngũgĩ wa Thiong'o, *Decolonising the Mind: The Politics of Language in African Literature* (Woodbridge, Suffolk, and Rochester, NY: James Currey, 2005 [1986]), 16.

17. www.theblackpowerstation.art (accessed February 21, 2021).

18. Russell Rickford, "Toppling Statues as a Decolonial Ethic," *Africa Is a Country*, July 28, 2020. www.africasacountry.com/2020/07/toppling-statues-as-a-decolonial-ethic (accessed February 28, 2021).

19. Verity Platt, "Why People are Toppling Monuments to Racism," *Scientific American*, July 3, 2020. www.scientificamerican.com/article/why-people-are-toppling-monuments -to-racism/ (accessed February 28, 2021).

20. I am extremely grateful to one of my anonymous manuscript reviewers for this invaluable insight.

21. Viv Golding, "Collaborative Museum: Curators, Communities, Collections," in *Museums and Communities: Curators, Collections and Collaboration*, edited by Viv Golding and Wayne Modest (London and New York, Bloomsbury, 2013), 20.

22. The course was called "Arts Activism: Liberated Spaces and Creative Economies at The Black Power Station," (January 4–15, 2021), and was co-taught by Nomalanga Mkhize, Xolile "X" Madinda, Basile Koechlin, Jessica Copeland, and the author, along with a range of invited guest speakers and artists. www.Januaryterm.virginia.edu/arts-activism-liber ated-spaces-and-creative-economies-black-power-station (accessed February 28, 2021).

23. James Clifford, *Returns: Becoming Indigenous in the Twenty-first Century* (Cambridge, MA and London: Harvard University Press, 2013), 6.

24. Ibid., 224.

25. Ibid., 213.

26. Gunderson and Woods, "Pathways Toward Open Dialogues about Sonic Heritage," xxix.

27. Liner notes to the compact disc *Black Mirror: Reflections in Global Music (1918–1955)*, [DTD-010], unpaginated.

28. Coetzee 2012.

29. Danielle Brown, "An Open Letter on Racism in Music Studies: Especially Eth-

nomusicology and Music Studies," *My People Tell Stories* Blog, June 12, 2020. www.my
peopletellstories.com/blog/open-letter (accessed February 28, 2020).

30. Samuel Araujo, "From Neutrality to Praxis: The Shifting Politics of Ethnomusicology in the Contemporary World," *Musicological Annual* 44, no. 1 (2008): 13.

31. Ibid., 15.

32. Rose Boswell, "Introduction: Continuities and Contradictions in Postcolonial African Anthropologies," in *Postcolonial African Anthropologies*, edited by Rose Boswell and Francis B. Nyamnjoh (Cape Town: HSRC Press, 2016), 3.

33. Ibid., 6.

34. Francis B. Nyamnjoh, "Conclusion: Incompleteness and Conviviality. Towards and Anthropology of Intimacies," in ibid., 206.

35. Jean Comaroff and John Comaroff, *Theory From the South: Or, How Euro-America is Evolving Toward Africa* (Boulder and London: Paradigm Publishers, 2012), 64.

36. Toop 2010.

37. Nicole Furlonge, *Race Sounds: The Art of Listening in African American Literature* (Iowa City: University of Iowa Press, 2018), 7.

38. Dylan Robinson, *Hungry Listening: Resonant Theory for Indigenous Sound Studies* (Minneapolis and London: University of Minnesota Press, 2020), 25.

39. Ibid., 11–12.

40. Ibid., 25.

41. Ibid.

42. Ibid., 239.

43. Ibid., 246.

44. Ibid.

45. Sabelo J. Ndlovu-Gatsheni, *Epistemic Freedom: Deprovincialization and Decolonization* (Abingdon and New York: Routledge, 2018), 229.

46. Ibid., 236.

47. Brian Kamanzi, "#FeesMustFall: Decolonising Education," Aljazeera.com, November 3, 2016. www.aljazeera.com/indepth/opinion/2016/10/feesmustfall-decolonising
-education-161031093938509.html (accessed February 28, 2021).

48. Savo Heleta, "Decolonisation of Higher Education: Dismantling Epistemic Violence and Eurocentrism in South Africa," *Transformation in Higher Education* 1, no. 1 (2016): 3.

49. Harry Garuba, "What is an African Curriculum?" *Mail & Guardian*, April 17, 2015. www.mg.co.za/article/2015-04-17-what-is-an-african-curriculum/ (accessed February 28, 2021).

50. Comaroff and Comaroff, *Theory From the South*, 12.

51. Duncan Omanga is program officer for both the African Peacebuilding Network and Next Generation Social Sciences in Africa. The former "operates to strengthen tertiary education in Africa," and the latter supports the "integration of African knowledge into

global policy communities." www.ssrc.org/programs/view/apn/ (accessed February 28, 2021). www.ssrc.org/programs/view/nextgenafrica/ (accessed February 28, 2021).

52. Duncan Omanga, "Decolonization, Decoloniality, and the Future of African Studies: A Conversation with Dr. Sabelo Ndlovu-Gatsheni," *Social Science Research Council*, January 14, 2020. www.items.ssrc.org/from-our-programs/decolonization-decoloniality -and-the-future-of-african-studies-a-conversation-with-dr-sabelo-ndlovu-gatsheni/ (accessed February 28, 2021).

53. Xolile Madinda, personal communication while planning for a collaborative class at UVA, April 12, 2020.

54. https://thebridgepai.org/calendar/telemetry-with-x/ (accessed February 28, 2021).

55. https://thebridgepai.org/calendar/music-matters-xhosa-collaborations-and -makhanda-at-dawn/ (accessed February 28, 2021).

56. A short video of some of the exchanges can be viewed here: www.youtube.com /watch?v=GYQUzeshTKU (accessed February 28, 2021).

57. Ryan Maguire, or R.P.M., is a composer and beatmaker from the US who visited The Black Power Station in July 2019. Tragically, late in 2020 Ryan died suddenly and he is sorely missed and dearly loved. A ceremony was held in his honor at TBPS, welcoming him as an ancestor. www.ryanmaguiremusic.com/ (accessed February 28, 2021).

58. "African Electronic Music," Zoom class hosted between ILAM and UVA, April 1, 2019. The quote is taken from video recordings of the exchange.

59. Ibid.

60. The original website template is at www.bps.aslearningdesign.net/. The domain has since been transferred back to South Africa and the permanent address is now www .theblackpowerstation.art/ (both accessed February 28, 2021).

61. Charlene Rhinehart, "This Black-Owned Cafe is Redefining the Culture for People in Richmond, Virginia," *Black Enterprise*, January 1, 2020. www.blackenterprise.com/this -black-owned-cafe-is-redefining-the-culture-for-people-in-richmond-virginia/(accessed February 28, 2021).

62. The event took place on February 27, 2020. See www.facebook.com/reneewj/posts /10221246135721574 and www.youtube.com/watch?v=WKvDg1xnMqU (both accessed February 28, 2021).

63. Press release in author's possession, "UVA Student and Richmond Native Lindsey Shavers to Showcase South African and American Hip Hop Artists and Historians at RVA'S Urban Hang Suite," February 23, 2020.

64. www.nationalartsfestival.co.za/show/we-exist-we-live-amongst-you/ for The Black Power Station's dedicated page in vNAF 2020 (accessed February 28, 2021).

65. An African incense commonly used by Xhosa and Zulu traditional healers, also known as Helichrysum.

66. Xolile Madinda, personal communication, August 1, 2020.

67. A trailer for *Lost Conversations* is at www.youtube.com/watch?v=KjV7A_AvfKM, and the first full-length episode can be viewed at www.youtube.com/watch?v=gwL -uiXPMek&t=2s (both accessed February 28, 2021).

68. Madinda, personal communication, August 1, 2020.

69. www.pittrivers-sound.blogspot.com/2014/05/curating-sound-galleries-at-pitt -rivers.html (accessed February 28, 2021).

70. Phoebe Crisman, "From Industry to Culture: Leftovers, Time and Material Transformation in Four Contemporary Museums," *The Journal of Architecture* 12, no.4 (2007): 406.

BIBLIOGRAPHY

Agawu, Kofi. *The African Imagination in Music.* New York: Oxford University Press, 2016.

———. *Representing African Music: Postcolonial Notes, Queries, Positions.* New York and London: Routledge, 2003A.

———. "Contesting Difference: A Critique of Africanist Ethnomusicology," in *The Cultural Study of Music: An Introduction,* edited by Martin Clayton, Trevor Herbert, and Richard Middleton, 227–37. New York and London: Routledge, 2003B.

Araujo, Samuel. "From Neutrality to Praxis: The Shifting Politics of Ethnomusicology in the Contemporary World." *Musicological Annual* 44, no. 1 (2008): 13–30.

Arom, Simha. *African Polyphony and Polyrhythm: Musical Structure and* Methodology. Cambridge: Cambridge University Press, 1991.

———. "The Use of Play-back Techniques in the Study of Oral Polyphonies." *Ethnomusicology* 20, no. 3 (1976): 483–519.

Aubert, Laurent. *The Music of the Other: New Challenges for Ethnomusicology in a Global Age,* translated by Carla Ribeiro. Aldershot, UK and Burlington, VT: Ashgate, 2007.

Baasch, Rachel. "Bodies, Buildings, and Borders: Navigating the Divided Nation through Contemporary South African and Palestinian Art Practice." *African Arts,* 51, no. 2 (2018): 32–43.

Badenhorst, Cecile, and Charles Mather. "Tribal Recreation and Recreating Tribalism: Culture, Leisure and Social Control on South Africa's Gold Mines, 1940–1950." *Journal of Southern African Studies* 23, no. 3 (2007): 473–89.

Baring, Evelyn. "Foreword," *African Music Society Newsletter* 1, no. 1, June 1948.

Barnard, Alan, and Jonathan Spencer, eds. *Encyclopedia of Social and Cultural Anthropology.* London: Routledge, 2004 (1996).

Bebey, Francis. *African Music: A People's Art.* Brooklyn, NY: Lawrence Hill Books, 1975.

Benson, Stephen, and Will Montgomery, eds. *Writing the Field Recording: Sound, Word, Environment.* Edinburgh: University of Edinburgh Press, 2018.

Biko, Steve. *I Write What I Like.* Northlands, SA: Picador Africa, 2004 (1978).

Blacking, John. *Venda Children's Songs: A Study in Ethnomusicological Analysis*. Johannesburg: Wits University Press, 1967.

Blumenfeld, Jesmond, and Michael Nuttall. "Grahamstown's Fingo Village: From Poverty to Paradise?" *Reality* 4, no. 3 (1972): 15–19.

Boswell, Rose. "Introduction: Continuities and Contradictions in Postcolonial African Anthropologies," in *Postcolonial African Anthropologies*, edited by Rose Boswell and Francis B. Nyamnjoh, 1–12. Cape Town: HSRC Press, 2016.

Brennan, Ian. *How Music Dies (or Lives): Field Recording and the Battle for Democracy in the Arts*. New York: Allworth Press, 2016.

Brown, Danielle. "An Open Letter on Racism in Music Studies: Especially Ethnomusicology and Music Studies." *My People Tell Stories Blog*, June 12, 2020. www.mypeopletell stories.com/blog/open-letter (accessed February 28, 2021).

Bruyninckx, Joeri. *Listening in the Field: Recording and the Science of Birdsong*. Cambridge, MA and London: The MIT Press, 2018.

Bullock, Richard. "It's Hard to be a Man: A Month with Three Initiates During the Xhosa Circumcision Ritual." *Africa Geographic*, May 29, 2015. www.magazine.africageo graphic.com/weekly/issue-48/xhosa-circumcision-ritual-south-africa-its-hard-to-be-a-man/ (accessed February 28, 2021).

Campbell, Patricia Shehan. "How Musical We Are: John Blacking on Music, Education, and Cultural Understanding." *Journal of Research in Music Education,* 48, no. 4 (2000): 336–59.

Carlisle, Adrienne, and Zizonke May. "Grahamstown Lobby Loses Court Battle Over Makhanda." *Herald Live*, December 12, 2019. www.heraldlive.co.za/news/2019-12-12 -grahamstown-lobby-loses-court-battle-over-makhanda/ (accessed February 28, 2021).

Chikowero, Mhoze. *African Music, Power, and Being in Colonial Zimbabwe*. Bloomington: Indiana University Press, 2015.

Clifford, James. *Returns: Becoming Indigenous in the Twenty-first Century*. Cambridge, MA and London: Harvard University Press, 2013.

Coetzee, Paulette. "Dancing with Difference: Hugh Tracey on and in (African) Music." *Safundi* 16, no. 4 (2015): 396–418.

———. "Hugh Tracey, African Music, and Colonial Power: Correspondence with Government Officials in the 1950s." *South African Music Studies* 36–37 (2018): 83–109.

———. "Performing Whiteness; Representing Otherness: Hugh Tracey and African Music." PhD diss., Rhodes University, 2014.

———. "The White Man's Microphone: Hugh Tracey, Types of Whiteness and African Music," in *On Whiteness*, edited by Nicky Falkof and Oliver Cashman-Brown, 49–58. Oxford: Inter-Disciplinary Press, 2012.

Comaroff, Jean, and John Comaroff. *Theory from the South: Or, How Euro-America is Evolving Toward Africa*. Boulder and London: Paradigm Publishers, 2012.

Coplan, David. *In Township Tonight! South Africa's Black City Music and Theatre*. Chicago and London: University of Chicago Press, 2008 (1985).

Cox, Christopher. *Sonic Flux: Sound, Art and Metaphysics*. Chicago and London: University of Chicago Press, 2018.

Crisman, Phoebe. "From Industry to Culture: Leftovers, Time and Material Transformation in Four Contemporary Museums." *The Journal of Architecture* 12, no. 4 (2007): 405–21.

Dantas, Nancy. "Looking After Freedom?" *Buala*, June 8, 2017. www.buala.org/en/ill-visit /looking-after-freedom (accessed February 28, 2021).

Dargie, Dave. *Xhosa Music: Its Techniques and Instruments, with a Collection of Songs*. Cape Town and Johannesburg: David Philip, 1988.

Daughtry, Martin. "Acoustic Palimpsests," in *Theorizing Sound Writing*, edited by Deborah Kapchan, 65–85. Middletown, CT.: Wesleyan University Press, 2017.

Davenport, Thomas Rodney H. *Black Grahamstown: The Agony of a Community*. Johannesburg: South African Institute of Race Relations, 1980.

De Kosnik, Abigail. *Rogue Archives: Digital Culture and Media Fandom*. Cambridge, MA and London: The MIT Press, 2016.

Demers, Joanna. "Cassette Tape Revival as Creative Anachronism." *Twentieth-Century Music* 14, no. 1 (2017): 109–17.

Derrida, Jacques. "Archive Fever: A Seminar by Jacques Derrida at Wits University, August 1998 (transcribed by Verne Harris)," in *Refiguring the Archive*, edited by Carolyn Hamilton, Verne Harris, Jane Taylor, Michele Pickover, Graeme Reid, and Razia Saleh, 38–54 (even pages only). Dordrecht, Boston, and London: Kluwer Academic Publishers, 2002.

Diop, Cheikh Anta. *Precolonial Black Africa: A Comparative Study of the Political and Social Systems of Europe and Black Africa, from Antiquity to the Formation of Modern States*. Chicago: Lawrence Hill Books, 1987.

Dowling, Tessa, Anele Gobodwana, and Somikazi Deyi. "When Culturally Significant Songs are Decontextualised: The Initiation Song Somagwaza." *South African Journal of Folklore Studies* 28, no. 2 (2018): 1–19.

Duff, Wendy M., and Verne Harris. "Stories and Names: Archival Description as Narrating Records and Constructing Meanings," *Archival Science* 2 (2002): 263–85.

Edwards, Brent Hayes. "The Sound of Anticolonialism," in *Audible Empire: Music, Global Politics, Critique*, edited by Ronald Radano and Tejumola Olaniyan, 269–91. Durham, NC: Duke University Press, 2016.

Edwards, Harry. "Dancing to Colonial Archives." *Norient*, 2020. www./norient.com /harry-edwards/dancing-colonial-archives (accessed September 9, 2021).

Erlmann, Veit. "Recordings of Traditional Music in South Africa." *Yearbook for Traditional Music* 20 (1988): 247–51.

Evans-Pritchard, Edward Evan. "The Dance." *Africa: Journal of the International African Institute* 1, no. 4 (1928): 446–62.

Exarchos, Michail (a.k.a. Stereo Mike). "Sample Magic: (Conjuring) Phonographic Ghosts and Meta-illusions in Contemporary Hip-Hop Production," *Popular Music* 38, no. 1 (2019): 33–53.

Falola, Toyin. "Ritual Archives," in *The Palgrave Handbook of African Social Ethics*, edited by Nimi Waroboko and Toyin Falola, 473–98. New York and London: Palgrave Macmillan, 2020.

Felber, Garret. "Tracing Tribe: Hugh Tracey and the Cultural Politics of Retribalisation." *South African Music Studies* 30/31 (2010): 31–43.

Feld, Steven. *Sound and Sentiment: Birds, Weeping, Poetics, and Song in Kaluli Expression.* Philadelphia: University of Pennsylvania Press, 1982.

Fronemen, Willemien, and Stephanus Muller. "The Ethical Incomplete." *South African Music Studies* 38, no. 1 (2019): 1–5.

Fry, Poppy. "Siyamfenguza: The Creation of Fingo-ness in South Africa's Eastern Cape, 1800–1835." *Journal of Southern African Studies* 36, no. 1 (2012): 25–40.

Furlonge, Nicole. *Race Sounds: The Art of Listening in African American Literature.* Iowa City: University of Iowa Press, 2018.

Garcia, David. *Listening for Africa: Freedom, Modernity and the Logic of Black Music's African Origins.* Durham, NC and London: Duke University Press, 2017.

Garuba, Harry. "What is an African Curriculum?" *Mail & Guardian*, April 17, 2015. www.mg.co.za/article/2015-04-17-what-is-an-african-curriculum/ (accessed February 28, 2021).

Geertz, Clifford. *The Interpretation of Cultures.* New York: Basic Books, 1973.

Giannachi, Gabrielle. *Archive Everything: Mapping the Everyday.* Cambridge, MA and London: MIT Press, 2016.

Gimenez Amoros, Luis. *Tracing the* Mbira *Sound Archive in Zimbabwe.* New York and London: Routledge, 2018.

Gluckman, Max. *Order and Rebellion in Tribal Africa.* London: Cohen and West, 1963.

Gogela, Kholisa B. "Perceptions of Ulwaluko in a Liberal Democratic State: Is Multiculturalism Beneficial to AmaXhosa Women in the Eastern Cape Province of South Africa?" PhD diss., Rhodes University, 2017.

Golding, Viv. "Collaborative Museums: Curators, Communities, Collections," in *Museums and Communities: Curators, Collections and Collaboration*, edited by Viv Golding and Wayne Modest, 13–31. London and New York, Bloomsbury, 2013.

Gowa, Mamela. "Grahamstown Poet's Career Takes Off." *Daily Dispatch*, April 26, 2013. www.pressreader.com/south-africa/daily-dispatch/20130426/281517928614956 (accessed February 28, 2021).

Gray, Robin. "Repatriation and Decolonization: Thoughts on Ownership, Access and Control," in *The Oxford Handbook of Musical Repatriation*, edited by Frank Gunderson, Robert C. Lancefield, and Bret Woods, 723–37. Oxford and New York: Oxford University Press, 2019.

Gruber, Jacob. "Ethnographic Salvage and the Shaping of Anthropology." *American Anthropologist* 72, no. 6 (1970): 1289–99.

Gulwa, Thandolwethu. "Xhosa Chronicles: Sondelani Sizwe sa kwaXhosa!" *Cue Media*, July 7, 2018. www.cuemedia.co.za/2018/07/07/xhosa-chronicles-sondelani-sizwe-sa -kwaxhosa/ (accessed August 5, 2020).

Gunderson, Frank, and Bret Woods. "Pathways Toward Open Dialogues about Sonic Heritage," in *The Oxford Handbook of Musical Repatriation*, edited by Frank Gunderson, Robert C. Lancefield, and Bret Woods, xliii–lvi. Oxford and New York: Oxford University Press, 2019.

Gunderson, Frank, Robert C. Lancefield, and Bret Woods, eds. *The Oxford Handbook of Musical Repatriation*. Oxford and New York: Oxford University Press, 2019.

Hall, Reg. "The Voice of the People—Introduction to the Series." An introduction to the 20-CD anthology "The Voice of the People," Topic Records. Taken from Volume 4, *Farewell, My Own Dear Native Land: Songs of Exile & Emigration*, TSCD 654. London: Topic, 1998.

Hamilton, Carolyn, Verne Harris, and Graeme Reid. "Introduction," in *Refiguring the Archive*, edited by Carolyn Hamilton, Verne Harris, Jane Taylor, Michele Pickover, Graeme Reid, and Razia Saleh, 6–18. Dordrecht, Boston, and London: Kluwer Academic Publishers, 2002.

Hansen, Deirdre. "The Music of the Xhosa-Speaking People," Vols. 1 and 2. PhD diss., University of the Witwatersrand, 1981.

Harris, Anna. "Eliciting Sound Memories." *The Public Historian* 37, no. 4 (2015): 14–31.

Harris, Verne. *Archives and Justice: A South African Perspective*. Chicago: Society of American Archivists, 2007.

Heleta, Savo. "Decolonisation of Higher Education: Dismantling Epistemic Violence and Eurocentrism in South Africa." *Transformation in Higher Education* 1, no. 1 (2016): 1–8.

Hentoff, Nat. "Recordings: Hugh Tracey, Collector of African Integrities." *New York Times*, May 29, 1966. www.nytimes.com/1966/05/29/archives/recordings-hugh-tracey -collector-of-african-integrities.html (accessed February 28, 2021).

Heshu, Masixole Zinzo Patrick. "Makhanda: Reflections of Past, Present and Future." *Journal of Indigenous and Shamanic Studies* 1, no. 1 (2020): 24–27.

Hickel, Jason. *Democracy as Death: The Moral Order of Anti-Liberal Politics in South Africa*. Oakland: University of California Press, 2015.

Hirst, Manton. "The Healer's Art: Cape Nguni Diviners in the Townships of Grahamstown," Vols. 1 and 2. PhD diss., Rhodes University, 1990.

Hlalethwa, Zaza. "What Happens After the Fest?" *Mail & Guardian*, July 13, 2018. www

.mg.co.za/article/2018-07-13-00-what-happens-after-the-fest (accessed February 28, 2021).

Howard, Keith, and John Blacking. "John Blacking: An Interview Conducted and Edited by Keith Howard." *Ethnomusicology* 35, no. 1 (1991): 55–76.

Hudson, Mark. "Hugh Tracey: Pioneer Archivist," in *World Music — The Rough Guide: Volume 1 — Africa, Europe and the Middle East,* edited by Simon Broughton, Mark Ellingham, and Richard Trillo, with Orla Duane and Vanessa Dowell, 669–71. London: Rough Guides, 1999.

International Library of African Music (ILAM). Bulletin No. 1, June 1956.

———. Bulletin No. 18, November 1957.

———. Bulletin No. 28, November 1958.

Impey, Angela. *Song Walking: Women, Music, and Environmental Justice in an African Borderland.* Chicago: University of Chicago Press, 2018.

Jenkins, Alan. "The Global Significance of Black Panther." *Hollywood Reporter,* February 23, 2018. www.hollywoodreporter.com/heat-vision/black-panther-global-significance-1087878 (accessed February 28, 2021).

Joja, Athi Mogezeleli. "Nxele, Ndlambe, Umhlaba: Grounding with Sikhumbuzo Makandula," in *Ubuzwe,* edited by Sikhumbuzko Makandula, 5–11. Grahamstown: Sikhumbuzo Makandula, 2016.

Jolaosho, Omotayo. "Cross-circulations and Transnational Solidarity: Historicizing the US Anti-Apartheid Movement Through Song." *Safundi: The Journal of South African and American Studies* 13, nos. 3–4 (2012): 317–37.

Jones, Arthur Morris. "Record Review of the Sound of Africa Series of 45 12-inch Records." *African Music* 2, no. 2 (1959): 96–97.

Kamanzi, Brian. "#FeesMustFall: Decolonising Education." Aljazeera.com, November 3, 2016. www.aljazeera.com/indepth/opinion/2016/10/feesmustfall-decolonising-education-161031093938509.html (accessed February 28, 2021).

Kane, Brian. "The Fluctuating Sound Object," in *Sound Objects,* edited by James A. Steintrager and Rey Chow, 53–70. Durham and London: Duke University Press, 2019.

———. *Sound Unseen: Acousmatic Sound in Theory and Practice.* Oxford and New York: Oxford University Press, 2014.

Kannenburg, John. "Towards a More Sonically Inclusive Museum Practice: A New Definition of the 'Sound Object.'" *Science Museum Group Journal* 8 (2017). DOI: www.dx.doi.org/10.15180/170805 (accessed February 28, 2021).

Kapchan, Deborah. "The Splash of Icarus: Theorizing Sound Writing/Writing Sound Theory," in *Theorizing Sound Writing,* edited by Deborah Kapchan, 1–23. Middletown, CT: Wesleyan University Press, 2017.

Karpeles, Maud, ed. *The Collecting of Folk Music and Other Ethnomusicological Material:*

A Manual for Field Workers. London: International Folk Music Council and the Royal Anthropological Institute of Great Britain and Ireland, 1958.

Kaschula, Russell. "African Languages Have the Power to Transform Universities." *The Conversation*, May 18, 2015. www.theconversation.com/african-languages-have-the -power-to-transform-universities-40901 (accessed February 28, 2021).

Katz, Mark. *Capturing Sound: How Technology Has Changed Music*. Berkeley: University of California Press, 2004.

Khesthi, Roshanak. *Modernity's Ear: Listening to Race and Gender in World Music*. New York and London: New York University Press, 2015.

Kirby, Percival. "The Effect of Western Civilization on Bantu Music," in *Western Civilization and the Natives of South Africa*, edited by Isaac Schapera, 131–40. London: George Routledge and Sons, 2004 (1934).

———. *Musical Instruments of the Indigenous People of South Africa*, Third Edition. Johannesburg: Wits University Press, 2013 (1934).

Kirshenblatt-Gimblett, Barbara. "Objects of Ethnography," in *The Poetics and Politics of Museum Display*, edited by Ivan Karp and Steven D. Levine, 17–78. Washington and London: Smithsonian Institution Press, 1991.

Krause, Bernie. *The Great Animal Orchestra: Finding the Origins of Music in the World's Wild Places*. London: Profile, 2012.

Kropf, Albert. *A Kafir-English Dictionary*, Second Edition. Lovedale, SA: Lovedale Mission Press, 1915.

Kubik, Gerhard. "Urban/Rural Interaction in Central African Guitar Styles of the 1960s," in *Papers Presented at the Tenth Symposium on Ethnomusicology, Music Dept., Rhodes University, September 30 to October 2*, 96–103. Grahamstown, SA: ILAM, 1991.

Kun, Josh. *Audiotopia: Music, Race and America*. Berkeley and Los Angeles: UCLA Press, 2005.

Lambrechts, Lizabé. "Ethnography and the Archive: Power and Politics in Five South African Music Archives." PhD diss., University of Stellenbosch, 2012.

———. "Performing the Aporias of the Archive: Towards a Future for South African Music Archives." *Historia* 6, no. 1 (2016): 132–54.

Lancefield, Robert M. "Musical Traces' Retraceable Paths: The Repatriation of Recorded Sound." *Journal of Folklore Research* 35, no. 1 (1988): 47–68.

Landau, Carolyn, and Janet Topp Fargion. "We're all Archivists Now: Towards a More Equitable Ethnomusicology." *Ethnomusicology Forum* 21, no. 2 (2012): Special Issue: "Ethnomusicology, Archives and Communities: Methodologies for an Equitable Discipline," 125–40.

Lazarus, Neil. "Unsystematic Fingers at the Conditions of the Times—'Afropop' and the Paradoxes of Imperialism," in *Recasting the World—Writing after Colonialism*, edited by Jonathan White, 137–60 . Baltimore and London: John Hopkins University Press, 1993.

Leibbrant, Tim. "A Mash-Up of Deferred Reconciliation: Thando Mama's 'Of Nationhood/ Desolation' (a review)." *Arthrob*, August 25, 2017. www.artthrob.co.za/2015/08/27/a -mash-up-of-deferred-reconciliation-thando-mamas-of-nationhooddesolation/ (accessed February 28, 2021).

Lingold, Mary Caton, Darren Mueller, and Whitney Trettien. "Introduction," in *Digital Sound Studies*, edited by Mary Caton Lingold, Darren Mueller, and Whitney Trettien, 1–25. Durham, NC: Duke University Press, 2018.

Lubar, Steven. *Inside the Lost Museum: Curating, Past and Present*. Cambridge, MA and London: Harvard University Press, 2017.

Macgregor, David. "Sky the Limit for Teen Talent." *DispatchLive*, January 20, 2017. www .dispatchlive.co.za/news/2017-01-20-sky-the-limit-for-teen-talent/ (accessed February 28, 2021).

Maclennan, Sue. "Campaign Cries Foul Over Name Change." *Grocott's Mail*, June 29, 2018. www.grocotts.co.za/2018/06/29/campaign-cries-foul-over-name-change/ (accessed February 28, 2021).

Macqueen, Ian M. *Black Consciousness and Progressive Movements Under Apartheid*. Pietermaritzburg, SA: University of Kwazulu-Natal Press, 2018.

Madiba, Elijah. "Repatriating Xhosa Music Recordings Archived at the International Library of African Music (ILAM) and Reviving Interest in Traditional Xhosa Music Among the Youth in Grahamstown," MA thesis, ethnomusicology, Rhodes University, 2017.

Mahlakoana, Theto. "PhD Written in isiXhosa Hailed as Milestone." *Independent Online*, April 23, 2017. www.iol.co.za/news/phd-written-in-isixhosa-hailed-as-mile stone-8779991 (accessed February 28, 2021).

Majola, Fundile. "A Man Who is Not a Man." *Mail & Guardian*, March 1, 2012. www.thought leader.co.za/readerblog/2012/03/01/a-man-who-is-not-a-man/ (accessed February 28, 2021).

Makalima, Mzwamadoda. "Mafani's Memorable Poetry Gig." *Grocott's Mail*, February 6, 2018. www.grocotts.co.za/2018/02/06/mafanis-memorable-poetry-gig (accessed February 28, 2021).

Makandula, Sikhumbuzo. "Bantu-staan!" Unpublished colloquium paper, 2015. www .academia.edu/35080550/BantuStaan_pdf (accessed September 13, 2021).

———. *Ubuzwe*. Grahamstown, SA: Sikhumbuzo Makandula, 2016.

———, and Eria Nsubuga Sane. "Eria Nsubuga Sane and Sikhumbuzo Makandula in Conversational Partnership." *African Arts* 50, no. 20 (2017): 68–83.

Mandela, Nelson. *Long Walk to Freedom*. London: Abacus, 2002 (1994).

Maultsby, Portia K., and Mellonnee V. Burnim with contributions from Susan Oehle.

"Intellectual History," in *African American Music: An Introduction*, edited by Mellonee V. Burnim and Portia K. Maultsby, 7–32. New York and London: Routledge, 2006.

Mayer, Philip. *Xhosa in Town II—Townsmen or Tribesmen: Conservatism and the Process of Urbanization in a South African City*. Cape Town, London, New York, and Toronto: Oxford University Press, 1961.

Maylam, Paul. *Rhodes University, 1904–2016: An Intellectual, Political and Cultural History*. Grahamstown, SA: Institute of Social and Economic Research, 2016.

Mbembe, Achille. "Decolonizing Knowledge and the Question of the Archive." Document written as spoken text for a series of public lectures given at the Wits Institute for Social and Economic Research (WISER), University of the Witwatersrand, at conversations with the Rhodes Must Fall Movement at the University of Cape Town and the Indexing the Human Project, Department of Sociology and Anthropology at the University of Stellenbosch, April 22, 2015 (unpaginated).

———. "Decolonising the University: New Directions." *Arts and Humanities in Higher Education* 15, no. 1 (2016): 29–45.

———. *On the Postcolony*. Berkeley: University of California Press, 2001.

McAllister, Patrick A. *Xhosa Beer Drinking Rituals: Power, Practice, and Performance in the South African Rural Periphery*. Durham, NC: Carolina Academic Press, 2006.

McConnachie, Boudina. "Legal Access to our Musical History: An Investigation into the Copyright Implications of Archived Music Recordings Held at the International Library of African Music (ILAM) in South Africa." MA thesis, ethnomusicology, Rhodes University, 2008.

McCoy, Jason. "Memory, Trauma, and the Politics of Repatriating Bikindi's Music," in *The Oxford Handbook of Musical Repatriation*, edited by Frank Gunderson, Robert C. Lancefield, and Bret Woods, 419–35. Oxford and New York: Oxford University Press, 2019.

Mckaiser, Eusebius. "The Makhanda Disaster Cannot be Ignored." *Mail & Guardian*, February 6, 2020. www.mg.co.za/analysis/2020-02-06-the-makhanda-disaster-cannot-be-ignored/ (accessed February 28, 2021).

Meintjes, Louise. *Dust of the Zulu: Ngoma Aesthetics After Apartheid*. Durham, NC and London: Duke University Press, 2017.

———. *Sound of Africa! Making Music Zulu in a South African Studio*. Durham, NC and London: Duke University Press, 2003.

Merriam, Alan. *The Anthropology of Music*. Evanston, IL: Northwestern University Press, 1964.

Mhlalo, Andile. "What is Manhood? The Significance of Traditional Circumcision in the Xhosa Initiation Ritual." MPhil thesis, University of Stellenbosch, sociology and social anthropology, 2009.

Miller, Martin. "Singing and Dancing in Holy Spirit: An Understanding of the Xhosa Zionist Healing Service." MA thesis, clinical psychology, Rhodes University, 1984.

Mojaki, Gomolemo "Pinkie." "Releasing the Pause Button on Hugh Tracey's Revitalisation of a Selection of the Bangwaketse Music Held at the International Library of African Music (ILAM)." MA thesis, ethnomusicology, Rhodes University, 2015.

Mona, Godfrey Vulindlela, and Russell Kaschula. "South African National Reconciliation Discourse and isiXhosa Written Poetry: 1994–2004." *South African Journal of African Languages* 38, no. 1 (2018): 115–23.

Mostert, Noel. *Frontiers: The Epic of South Africa's Creation and the Tragedy of the Xhosa People*. New York: Alfred A. Knopf, 1992.

Mtuze, Peter. *The Essence of Xhosa Spirituality and the Nuisance of Cultural Imperialism (Hidden Presences in the Spirituality of the amaXhosa of the Eastern Cape and the Impact of Christianity on Them)*. Florida Hills, SA: Vivlia, 2003.

———. *Introduction to Xhosa Culture—Celebrating Ten Years of Freedom*. Eastern Cape, SA: Lovedale, 2004.

Muller, Carol. "Archiving Africanness in Sacred Song." *Ethnomusicology* 46, no. 3 (2002): 409–43.

———. "Jazzing the Bushmen: Khoisan Migrations into South African Jazz," in *Out of Bounds—Ethnography, History, Music: Essays in Honour of Kay Kaufman Shelemay*, edited by Ingrid Monson, Carol J. Oja, and Richard K. Wolf, 185–209. Cambridge, MA and London: Harvard University Press, 2017.

———. "Why Jazz? South Africa 2019." *Daedalus: Journal of the American Academy of Arts and Sciences* 148, no. 2 (2019): 115–27.

———, and Sathima Bea Benjamin. *Musical Echoes: South African Women Thinking in Jazz*. Durham, NC and London: Duke University Press, 2011.

Myers, Helen. "Field Technology," in *Ethnomusicology: An Introduction*, edited by Helen Myers, 50–87. London: Macmillan, 1992.

Mzilane, Pedro, and Nomalanga Mkhize. "Decolonisation as a Spatial Question: The Student Accommodation Crisis and Higher Education Transformation." *South African Review of Sociology* 50, nos. 3–4 (2019): 104–15. DOI: 10.1080/21528586.2020.1733649 (accessed February 28, 2021).

Nannyonga-Tamusuza, Sylvia, and Andrew Weintraub. "The Audible Future: Reimagining the Role of Sound Archives and Sound Repatriation in Uganda." *Ethnomusicology* 56, no. 2 (2012): 206–33.

Ndaliko, Chérie Rivers. *Necessary Noise: Music, Film, and Charitable Imperialism in the East of Congo*. Oxford and New York: Oxford University Press, 2016.

Ndletyana, Mcebisi, ed. *African Intellectuals in 19th and Early 20th Century South Africa*. Cape Town: HSRC Press, 2008.

Ndlovu-Gatsheni, Sabelo J. *Epistemic Freedom: Deprovincialization and Decolonization*. Abingdon and New York: Routledge, 2018.

Ngani, Marcus. *Umkhonto kaTshiwo*. Fort Hare, SA: Lovedale Press, 1959.

Ngoepe, Mpho. "Archives Without Archives: A Window of Opportunity to Build Inclusive Archive [sic] in South Africa." *Journal of the South African Society of Archivists* 52 (2019): 149–66.

Nombembe, Casiwa. "Music-making of the Xhosa Diasporic Community: A Focus on the Umguyo Tradition in Zimbabwe." MA thesis, University of the Witwatersrand, School of Music, 2014.

Ntombana, Luvuyo. "An Investigation into the Role of Xhosa Male Initiation in Moral Regeneration." DPhil diss., Nelson Mandela Metropolitan University, Faculty of the Arts, 2011.

Nyamnjoh, Francis B. "Conclusion: Incompleteness and Conviviality. Towards an Anthropology of Intimacies," in *Postcolonial African Anthropologies*, edited by Rose Boswell and Francis B. Nyamnjoh, 195–215. Cape Town: HSRC Press, 2016.

Obrist, Hans Ulrich. "Curating as Medium," in Terry Smith, *Talking Contemporary Curating*, edited by Kate Fowle and Leigh Markopoulos, 114–38. New York: Independent Curators International, 2015.

———. *Ways of Curating*. New York: Farrar, Straus and Giroux, 2014.

Olwage, Grant, ed. *Composing Apartheid: Music for and Against Apartheid*. Johannesburg: Wits University Press, 2008.

Omanga, Duncan. "Decolonization, Decoloniality, and the Future of African Studies: A Conversation with Dr. Sabelo Ndlovu-Gatsheni." *Social Science Research Council*, January 14, 2020. www.items.ssrc.org/from-our-programs/decolonization-decoloniality -and-the-future-of-african-studies-a-conversation-with-dr-sabelo-ndlovu-gatsheni/ (accessed February 28, 2021).

O'Neill, Paul. *The Culture of Curating and the Curating of Culture(s)*. Cambridge, MA and London: The MIT Press, 2012.

Opland, Jeff. *Xhosa Oral Poetry: Aspects of a Black South African Tradition*. New York: Cambridge University Press, 1983.

———, and Patrick McCallister. "The Xhosa Imbongi as Trickster." *Journal of African Cultural Studies* 22, no. 2 (2010): 157–67.

Paquette, Danielle. "Beyoncé Released a Video Celebrating 'African Tradition.' Then Came the Backlash." *Washington Post*, July 9, 2020. www.washingtonpost.com/world /africa/beyonce-black-is-king-africa-backlash/2020/07/08/cfaa2dd2-c079-11ea-864a -odd31b9d6917_story.html (accessed February 28, 2021).

Patrick, Jonathan. "A Guide to Pierre Schaeffer, the Godfather of Sampling." *Fact Magazine*, February 23, 2016. www.factmag.com/2016/02/23/pierre-schaeffer-guide/ (accessed February 28, 2021).

Pauw, Berthold A. *Xhosa in Town III—The Second Generation: A Study of the Family Among Urbanized Bantu in East London*. Cape Town: Oxford University Press (on behalf of the Institute of Social and Economic Research, Rhodes University), 1963.

Pearce, Sheldon. "How Black Panther Composer Ludwig Göransson Found the Sound of Wakanda." *Pitchfork*, February 7, 2018. www.pitchfork.com/thepitch/how-black -panther-composer-ludwig-goransson-found-the-sound-of-wakanda-interview/ (accessed February 28, 2021).

Peires, Jeff. *The House of Phalo: A History of the Xhosa People in the Days of Their Independence*. Johannesburg: Raven, 1981.

Peraino, Judith A. "I'll Be Your Mixtape: Lou Reed, Andy Warhol and the Queer Intimacies of Cassettes." *Journal of Musicology* 36, no. 4 (2019): 401–36.

Pienaar, Alexa. "The Digitising of Historical Sound Archives at the International Library of African Music and its Effects on the Heritage and Preservation Thereof of sub-Saharan African Communities." BA honours thesis, Rhodes University, 2007.

Pityana, Nyameko Barney, Mamphela Ramphele, Malusi Mpulwama, and Lindy Wilson. "Introduction," in *Bounds of Possibility: The Legacy of Steve Biko and Black Consciousness*, edited by Nyameko Barney Pityana, Mamphela Ramphele, Malusi Mpulwama, and Lindy Wilson, 1–12. Cape Town: David Philip, 1991.

Platt, Verity. "Why People are Toppling Monuments to Racism." *Scientific American*, July 3, 2020. www.scientificamerican.com/article/why-people-are-toppling-monuments -to-racism/ (accessed February 28, 2021).

Poenar, Horea. "Glitches of the Archive: On the Relation Between Memory and the Commons." *Caietele Echinox* 33 (2017): 115–31.

Prinsloo, Estelle. "The Role of the Humanities in Decolonising the Academy." *Arts and Humanities in Higher Education* 15, no. 1 (2016): 164–68.

Pyper, Brett. "Towards a Deeper Collaborative Curatorial Practice: On the Challenges of Presenting Indigenous Performance at the National Arts Festival in Grahamstown." *de arte*, 51, no. 2 (2016): 32–43.

Qwabe, Nonsindiso. "Xhosa Play Speaks to Painful Past." *Daily Dispatch*, July 6, 2018. www.pressreader.com/south-africa/daily-dispatch/20180706/281603831220458 (accessed February 28, 2021).

Reader, D. H. *Xhosa in Town I — The Black Man's Portion: History, Demography and Living Conditions in the Native Locations of East London Cape Province*. Cape Town: Oxford University Press (on behalf of the Institute of Social and Economic Research, Rhodes University), 1961.

Redmond, Shana L. *Anthem: Social Movements and the Sound of Solidarity in the African Diaspora*. New York and London: New York University Press, 2014.

Reigle, Robert. "Humanistic Motivations in Ethnomusicological Recordings," in *Recorded Music: Philosophical and Critical Reflections*, edited by Mine Doğantan-Dack, 189–210. London: Middlesex University Press, 2008.

Reynolds, Simon. *Retromania: Pop Culture's Addiction to Its Own Past*. London: Faber, 2011.

Rhinehart, Charlene. "This Black-Owned Cafe is Redefining the Culture for People in

Richmond, Virginia." *Black Enterprise*, January 1, 2020. www.blackenterprise.com
/this-black-owned-cafe-is-redefining-the-culture-for-people-in-richmond-virginia/
(accessed February 28, 2021).

Rickford, Russell. "Toppling Statues as a Decolonial Ethic." *Africa is a Country*, July 28,
2020. www.africasacountry.com/2020/07/toppling-statues-as-a-decolonial-ethic (accessed February 28, 2021).

Robinson, Dylan. *Hungry Listening: Resonant Theory for Indigenous Sound Studies*. Minneapolis and London: University of Minnesota Press, 2020.

Sarkisian, Margaret, and Ted Solis, eds. *Living Ethnomusicology: Paths and Practices*.
Champaign: University of Illinois Press, 2019.

Sarno, Louis. *Bayaka: The Extraordinary Music of the Babenzélé Pygmies*. New York:
Ellipsis Arts, 1995.

———. *Song From the Forest: My Life among the Ba-Benjellé Pygmies*. London: Bantam,
1993.

Sazana, Masithembe. "The Rise of isiNtu Poetry." *Grahamstown Music Magazine* 1 (October 15, 2017): 9. www.issuu.com/michellemay78/docs/gmm_final_og (accessed
February 28, 2021).

Scales, Christopher. *Recording Culture: Powwow Music and the Aboriginal Recording
Industry*. Durham, NC: Duke University Press, 2012.

Schapera, Isaac. *Migrant Labour and Tribal Life: A Study of the Conditions in the Bechuanaland Protectorate*. London, New York, and Cape Town: Oxford University Press, 1947.

Scherzinger, Martin. "Negotiating the Music-Theory/African-Music Nexus: A Political
Critique of Ethnomusicological Anti-Formalism and a Strategic Analysis of the Harmonic Patterning of the Shona Mbira Song Nyamaropa." *Perspectives of New Music*
39, no. 1 (2001): 5–117.

Schmahmann, Brenda. "Monumental Mediations: Performative Interventions to Public
Commemorative Art in South Africa." *de arte* 53, nos. 2–3 (2018): 142–59.

Schmidt, Bryan. "Fault Lines, Racial and Aesthetic: The National Arts Festival at Grahamstown." *Theatre Research International* 43, no. 3 (2019): 318–37.

Seeger, Anthony. "Creating and Confronting Cultures: Issues of Editing and Selection in
Records and Videotapes of Musical Performances," in *Music in the Dialogue of Cul-
tures: Traditional Music and Cultural Policy*, edited by Max Peter Baumann, 290–301.
Wilhelmshaven, DE: Florian Noetzel Verlag, 1991.

Seeger, Pete, ed. *Choral Folksongs of the Bantu*. New York: G. Schirmer, 1960.

Sharp, Cecil. *Cecil Sharp's Collection of English Folk Songs*, edited by Maud Karpeles.
London and New York: Oxford University Press, 1974.

———. *English Folk Song: Some Conclusions*, Fourth Edition, edited by Maud Karpeles,
with an appreciation of Cecil Sharp by Ralph Vaughan Williams. East Wakefield,
Yorkshire, UK: EP Publishing, 1972.

Smith, Terry. *Talking Contemporary Curating*, edited by Kate Fowle and Leigh Markopoulos. New York: Independent Curators International, 2015.

———. *Thinking Contemporary Curating*. New York: Independent Curators International, 2012.

Soga, John Henderson. *The Ama-Xosa: Life and Customs*. Lovedale, SA: Lovedale Press, 1931.

Stacey, Cara, and Natalie Mason. "Composing, Creative Play and the Ethical Incomplete: Practice-based Approaches in Ethnomusicology." *South African Music Studies* 38, no. 1 (2019): 19–40.

Stapleton, Tim. "Review of *The Return of Makhanda: Exploring the Legend* by Julie Wells, *Historia* 60, no. 1 (2015): 182–85.

Steingo, Gavin. *Kwaito's Promise: Music and the Aesthetics of Freedom in South Africa*. Chicago and London: University of Chicago Press, 2016.

———, and Jim Sykes, eds. *Remapping Sound Studies*. Durham, NC and London: Duke University Press, 2019.

Steintrager, James A., and Rey Chow, eds. *Sound Objects*. Durham, NC and London: Duke University Press, 2019.

Stoever, Jennifer Lynn. *The Sonic Color Line: Race and the Cultural Politics of Listening*. New York: New York University Press, 2016.

Stoler, Ann Laura. "Colonial Archives and the Arts of Governance: On the Content in the Form," in *Refiguring the Archive*, edited by Carolyn Hamilton, Verne Harris, Jane Taylor, Michele Pickover, Graeme Reid, and Razia Saleh, 83–100. Dordrecht, Boston, and London: Kluwer Academic Publishers, 2002.

Thram, Diane. "Music Archives and Repatriation: Digital Return of Hugh Tracey's 'Chemirocha' Recordings in Kenya," in *The Oxford Handbook of Musical Repatriation*, edited by Frank Gunderson, Robert C. Lancefield, and Bret Woods, 37–62. Oxford and New York: Oxford University Press, 2019.

Toop, David. *Sinister Resonance: The Mediumship of the Listener*. London: Continuum, 2010.

Tracey, Andrew. "Transcription of African Music," in *Papers Presented at the Sixth Symposium of Ethnomusicology*, Music Department, Rhodes University, October 1–3, 43–52. Grahamstown, SA: ILAM, 1988.

Tracey, Hugh. *African Music Transcription Library: Librarian's Handbook*. Johannesburg: Gallo (Africa) Ltd., c. 1949.

———. "Basutoland Recording Tour, November 19th–December 3rd, 1959." *African Music* 2, no. 2 (1959B): 69–77.

———. "Behind the Lyrics." *African Music* 3, no. 2 (1963B): 17–22.

———. *Catalogue—The Sound of Africa Series*: 210 long-playing records of music and songs from Central, Eastern, and Southern Africa, Volume 1. Roodeport, SA: International Library of African Music, 1973A.

———. *Catalogue—The Sound of Africa Series*: 210 long-playing records of music and songs from Central, Eastern, and Southern Africa, Volume 2. Roodeport, SA: International Library of African Music, 1973B.

———. *Codification of African Music and Textbook Project: A Primer of Practical Suggestions for Field Research*. Written with Gerhard Kubik and Andrew Tracey. Roodeport, SA: International Library of African Music, 1969.

———. "The Development of African Music." *African Music* 3, no. 2 (1963A): 36–40.

———. "Editorial." *African Music* 2, no. 2 (1959A): 5.

———. "Editorial." *African Music* 3, no. 3 (1964): 5.

——— "The International Library of African Music." *The Folklore and Folk Music Archivist* 4, no. 2 (Summer 1961), unpaginated.

———. "A Plan for African Music." *African Music* 3, no. 4 (1965): 6–13.

———. "The Problem of the Future of Bantu Music in the Congo." Extrait de: "Problèmes d'Afrique Centrale," *Bulletin Trimestriel de l'Association des Anciens Etudiants de l'Institut Universitaire des Territoires d'Outre-Mer* 26 (Quatrième Trimestre, 1954).

———. "Recording African Music in the Field." *African Music* 1, no. 2 (1955): 6–11.

———. *Songs from the Kraals of Southern Rhodesia*. Salisbury: Rhodesian Print and Publishing Co., 1934A.

Tracey, Peggy. *The Lost Valley*. Cape Town and Pretoria: Human and Rousseau, 1975.

Treloyn, Sally, Martin Dembal, and Rona Googninda Charles. "Cultural Precedents for the Repatriation of Legacy Song Records to Communities of Origin." *Australian Aboriginal Studies* 2 (2016): 94–103.

Trouillot, Terence. "Titus Kaphar on Putting Black Figures Back into Art History and His Solution for the Problem of Confederate Monuments." *Artnet*, March 27, 2019. https://news.artnet.com/art-world/titus-kaphar-erasure-art-history-1497391 (accessed February 28, 2021).

Troutman, John. *Indian Blues: American Indians and the Politics of Music, 1879–1934*. Norman: University of Oklahoma Press, 2009.

Trowbridge, Anthony. "Profile: Hugh Travers Tracey." *African Insight* 15, no. 1 (1985): 4–9.

Turino, Thomas. *Nationalists, Cosmopolitans, and Popular Music in Zimbabwe*. Chicago: University of Chicago Press, 2000.

Vail, Landeg, and Leroy White. *Power and the Praise Poem: Southern African Voices in History*. Charlottesville: University of Virginia Press, 1991.

Van der Vliet, Virginia. "Growing up in a Traditional Society," in *The Bantu-Speaking Peoples of Southern Africa*, edited by William David Hammond-Tooke, 211–45. London and Boston: Routledge and Kegan Paul, 1974.

Van Warmelo, Nicolas Jacobus. "The Classification of Cultural Groups," in *The Bantu-Speaking Peoples of Southern Africa*, edited by William David Hammond-Tooke, 56–84. London and Boston: Routledge and Kegan Paul, 1974.

Voegelin, Salome. *The Political Possibility of Sound: Fragments of Listening*. New York and London: Bloomsbury Academic, 2019.

Wa Thiong'o, Ngũgĩ. *Decolonising the Mind: The Politics of Language in African Literature*. Woodbridge, UK and Rochester, NY: James Currey, 2005 (1986).

Wachsmann, Klaus. "The Sociology of Recording in Africa South of the Sahara." *African Music* 2, no. 2 (1959): 77–79.

Wade, Stephen. *The Beautiful Music All Around Us: Field Recordings and the American Experience*. Urbana, Chicago, and Springfield: University of Illinois Press, 2012.

Watkins, Lee. "The Relationship Between Research, Intangible Cultural Heritage and Social and Economic Development: A Possible Solution to the Intractable Problem of Rural Poverty in the Eastern Cape." PowerPoint presentation, www.southafrican culturalobservatory.org.za/download/219 (accessed February 28, 2021).

Wells, Julie. *The Return of Makhanda: Exploring the Legend*. Scottsville, SA: University of Kwazulu-Natal Press, 2012.

Wells, Stanley, and Gary Taylor, eds. *The Oxford Shakespeare: The Complete Works*. Oxford: Clarendon Press, 1988.

The Hugh Tracey Collection of Lectures and Communication

UNPUBLISHED DOCUMENTS IN THE INTERNATIONAL LIBRARY
OF AFRICAN MUSIC ARCHIVE

Bandey, David. "Record of conversation with Daniel Mabuto, known for South African registration purposes as Parry Mangubane," March 29, 1980.

Blacking, John. "Venda Music: A Preliminary Report of Initial Field Research in the Sibasa District (Not Intended for Publication)," addressed to the Research subcommittee of the ILAM, by John Blacking, musicologist MA of the ILAM, February 1957.

Boardman, Colonel H. W. *Typescripts of Four Lectures and an Exam Prepared by Colonel Boardman*. Sent to D. F. Botha at Anglo-American for a proposed course for native welfare officers. Returned with amendments by D. F. Botha, August 29, 1958.

Etheredge, Denis. "Tribute to Dr. Hugh Tracey," delivered at the memorial service held at Saronde Farm, Krugersdorp, October 26, 1977.

Frangs, Irene. "Comments on various aspects of his research work, life and codification and textbook project", undated and unpaginated transcript of an interview of Tracey by Irene Frangs.

Holiday, Geoffrey. *The Last River*. Typescript of a biography of Hugh Tracey. Catalogue number HOL 1986 (also numbered 920TRA and 804540), 1986.

Tracey, Andrew. Fax sent by Andrew Tracey from ILAM to his son, Geoffrey Tracey, c/o Sally Hodges, Music Department, University of KwaZulu Natal at Durban, June 20, 1995, 3.

————. Fax sent by Andrew Tracey to Myrna Capp, November 29, 1995.

————. Transcript of Andrew Tracey being interviewed by David Bandey, March 21, 1980.

Tracey, Hugh. "The African Minstrel and Story-teller." Lecture delivered at Cathedral Hall, Cape Town, April 24. Lecture notes, 1934a.

————. "African Music Society and the International Library of African Music." Report written while at the University of California, Los Angeles, December 10, 1960.

————. "AMS—Proposed International Library of Recorded African Music, Appendix No. 1—Short Note on the Social Value of African Derived Music" [consequently, the document must predate 1954]. Unpaginated appendix of a proposal document for ILAM, pre-1954.

————. "The Arts in Africa—The Visual and the Aural." Typescript of a lecture delivered to the South African Institute of Race Relations. Institute Council Meetings (RR 2/1963 R.E.O.N 2.1.63), Johannesburg, January 14–17, 1963a.

————. "BBC HOME Service." Unpaginated typescript, October 12, 1965.

————. "The Codification of African Music." Draft of an article written for *Race Relations*, June 19, 1968.

————. "Creativity in African Music." Typescript of a lecture delivered to the Architectural Students Symposium at the University of the Witwatersrand, August 12, 1971.

————. "The Evolution of African Music and its Function in the Present Day." Typescript of a public lecture delivered to the Institute for the Study of Man in Africa, under the auspices of ISMA, October 1961.

————. "How Far with African Music?" Typescript of a paper for the National Union of South African Students (NUSAS), July 3, 1963b.

————. "Introduction," to an untitled draft summarizing the work of ILAM, 1969.

————. Memorandum entitled "International Library of African Music: Object of Recording Tour, Nov./Dec. 1959."

————. Memorandum entitled "International Library of African Music Recording Tour June–August, 1957: Preparation for Recording Sessions."

————. "Organised Research in African Music." Unpublished and undated typescript.

————. "Recording in the Veld." Handwritten notes for a lecture delivered to the Photographic Society of Southern Africa on October 10, 1968 (unpublished).

————. "Report on the 'Report to the International Library of African Music by J. A. R. Blacking on his Vendaland Research.'" November 24, 1957.

————. "Report on Research into Southern Rhodesian Native Music." Report sent to the president of the Carnegie Foundation, November 12, 1932.

————. *A River Left for Me*. Typescript of an incomplete autobiography, 1977.

————. "The Significance of African Music (in Central and Southern Africa)." The Cramb Lectures, delivered at the University of Glasgow, January 16-17, 1967. Full typescript of lectures.

———. "The Wider Implications of African Music." Typescript of a lecture given to Wits University Women's Goodwill Club, October 15, 1963c.

Tracey, Peggy. Unpublished, undated, and unpaginated typescripts of diaries.

LETTERS FROM AND TO HUGH TRACEY, AND OTHER CORRESPONDENCE (UNPUBLISHED)

Blacking, John. Letter to Hugh Tracey, sent from Sibasa, Vendaland, November 27, 1956.

———. Letter to Hugh Tracey, sent from Tshakhuma, Vendaland, June 24, 1956.

Jones, Reverend Arthur Morris. Letter to Hugh Tracey, March 17, 1958.

Kauffman, Robert. Letter to Hugh Tracey, sent from New York, October 2, 1959.

Tracey, Andrew. Letter to Veit Erlmann, Museum für Völkerkunde, October 14, 1988.

Tracey Hugh. Letter to Peter Gallo (Gallo [Africa] Ltd.), July 5, 1976.

———. Letter to Volkmar Wentzel Esq., NGS [National Geographic Society], Washington, DC, September 28, 1970.

———. Letter to Peggy Harper at the University of Ife Institute of African Studies, March 19, 1970.

———. Letter to Reverend Arthur Morris Jones, August 3, 1965.

———. Letter to Gilbert Rouget, Département d'Ethnomusicologie, Musée de l'homme, September 4, 1964.

———. Letter to Mr. D. Crena de Iongh, July 9, 1963.

———. Letter to Alan Lomax, June 24, 1963.

———. Letter to the director of programmes at the South African Broadcasting Corporation; this letter seems to be dated July 19, 1961.

———. Letter to Maud Karpeles, head of Radio Tapes Section, Central Office of Information, London, February 24, 1960.

———. Letter to H. C. Finkel, Esq., director of African education, Salisbury [Southern Rhodesia], December 11, 1959.

———. Letter to P. H. Anderson Esq., president of the Transvaal and Orange Free State Chamber of Mines, Johannesburg, November 13, 1958.

———. Letter to C. K. Grierson Rickford, Esq., controller of administration, Federal Broadcasting Corporation of Rhodesia and Nyasaland, Salisbury [Southern Rhodesia], February 18, 1958.

———. Letter to Professor Willard Rhodes, September 25, 1958.

———. Letter to Shirley B. Smith, African-American Economic Associates, New York, October 23, 1958.

———. Letter to the director-general of the South African Broadcasting Corporation [Johannesburg], January 31, 1957.

———. Letter to Monsieur Cousin, chairman, Union Minière du Haut Katanga, Elisabethville, Congo Belge, June 8, 1956.

———. Letter to John Blacking, Salisbury [Southern Rhodesia], October 5, 1954.

———. Letter to John Blacking, July 7, 1954.

———. Letter to the Reverend Arthur Morris Jones at Mapanza, Choma, Northern Rhodesia, March 11, 1947.

———. Letter to Mr. Edward N. Waters, assistant chief, Division of Music, Library of Congress, Washington, DC, December 29, 1944.

Radio Broadcasts

Tracey, Hugh. *Radio Broadcast BC 1—The Union and Basutoland. Sound of Africa Broadcast Series 2, Pt. 1.* Transmitted on South African Broadcasting Corporation on September 20, 1954.

Companion Websites

The Black Power Station | www.theblackpowerstation.art
The International Library of African Music | www.ru.ac.za/ilam
Sound Fragments | www.soundfragments.com

INDEX

Page numbers in *italics* indicate figures,
and page numbers with "n" indicates an endnote.

MUSIC / CULTURE

A series from Wesleyan University Press
Edited by Deborah Wong, Sherrie Tucker, and Jeremy Wallach
Originating editors: George Lipsitz, Susan McClary, and Robert Walser

The Music/Culture series has consistently reshaped and redirected music scholarship. Founded in 1993 by George Lipsitz, Susan McClary, and Robert Walser, the series features outstanding critical work on music. Unconstrained by disciplinary divides, the series addresses music and power through a range of times, places, and approaches. Music/Culture strives to integrate a variety of approaches to the study of music, linking analysis of musical significance to larger issues of power—what is permitted and forbidden, who is included and excluded, who speaks and who gets silenced. From ethnographic classics to cutting-edge studies, Music/Culture zeroes in on how musicians articulate social needs, conflicts, coalitions, and hope. Books in the series investigate the cultural work of music in urgent and sometimes experimental ways, from the radical fringe to the quotidian. Music/Culture asks deep and broad questions about music through the framework of the most restless and rigorous critical theory.

Marié Abe
Resonances of Chindon-ya:
Sounding Space and Sociality
in Contemporary Japan

Frances Aparicio
Listening to Salsa: Gender, Latin Popular
Music, and Puerto Rican Cultures

Paul Austerlitz
Jazz Consciousness: Music, Race,
and Humanity

Christina Baade and Kristin McGee
Beyoncé in the World: Making Meaning
with Queen Bey in Troubled Times

Emma Baulch
Genre Publics: Popular Music, Technologies,
and Class in Indonesia

Harris M. Berger
Metal, Rock, and Jazz: Perception
and the Phenomenology
of Musical Experience

Rebecca S. Miller
*Carriacou String Band Serenade:
Performing Identity in the
Eastern Caribbean*

Tony Mitchell, editor
*Global Noise: Rap and Hip-Hop
Outside the USA*

Christopher Moore and
Philip Purvis, editors
Music & Camp

Rachel Mundy
*Animal Musicalities: Birds, Beasts,
and Evolutionary Listening*

Keith Negus
*Popular Music in Theory:
An Introduction*

Johnny Otis
*Upside Your Head: Rhythm and Blues
on Central Avenue*

Jeff Packman
*Living from Music in Salvador:
Professional Musicians and the
Capital of Afro-Brazil*

Kip Pegley
*Coming to You Wherever You Are:
MuchMusic, MTV, and Youth Identities*

Jonathan Pieslak
*Radicalism and Music: An Introduction
to the Music Cultures of al-Qa'ida, Racist
Skinheads, Christian-Affiliated Radicals,
and Eco-Animal Rights Militants*

Matthew Rahaim
*Musicking Bodies: Gesture and Voice
in Hindustani Music*

Matthew Rahaim
*Ways of Voice: Vocal Striving and Ethical
Contestation in North India and Beyond*

John Richardson
*Singing Archaeology:
Philip Glass's Akhnaten*

Tricia Rose
*Black Noise: Rap Music and Black Culture
in Contemporary America*

David Rothenberg and
Marta Ulvaeus, editors
*The Book of Music and Nature:
An Anthology of Sounds, Words, Thoughts*

Nichole Rustin-Paschal
*The Kind of Man I Am: Jazzmasculinity
and the World of Charles Mingus Jr.*

Marta Elena Savigliano
*Angora Matta: Fatal Acts
of North-South Translation*

Joseph G. Schloss
*Making Beats: The Art
of Sample-Based Hip-Hop*

Barry Shank
*Dissonant Identities: The Rock 'n' Roll
Scene in Austin, Texas*

Jonathan Holt Shannon
*Among the Jasmine Trees: Music and
Modernity in Contemporary Syria*

Daniel B. Sharp
*Between Nostalgia and Apocalypse:
Popular Music and the Staging of Brazil*

Helena Simonett
*Banda: Mexican Musical Life across
Borders*

ABOUT THE AUTHOR

Noel Lobley is Assistant Professor in the Department of Music at the University of Virginia. He is a sound curator, ethnomusicologist, and artist. At the core of his creative practice, he is committed to developing new and ethical ways to exhibit sound. His installations have been presented across South Africa, Europe, and the US in spaces ranging from art galleries and festivals to rainforests, schools, and streets. In addition to his careers as a curator and academic, he also has worked as a DJ, in radio, and in the music industry for twenty years.